The Branding of Right-Wing Activism

THE BRANDING OF RIGHT-WING ACTIVISM

The News Media and the Tea Party

Khadijah Costley White

OXFORD
UNIVERSITY PRESS

OXFORD
UNIVERSITY PRESS

Oxford University Press is a department of the University of Oxford.
It furthers the University's objective of excellence in research, scholarship,
and education by publishing worldwide. Oxford is a registered trade mark of
Oxford University Press in the UK and certain other countries.

Published in the United States of America by Oxford University Press
198 Madison Avenue, New York, NY 10016, United States of America.

Library of Congress Cataloging-in-Publication Data

Names: Costley White, Khadijah, author.
Title: The branding of right-wing activism : the news media and the Tea Party /
Khadijah Costley White.
Description: New York, NY : Oxford University Press, 2018. | Includes
bibliographical references and index.
Identifiers: LCCN 2017061042 (print) | LCCN 2018015356 (ebook) |
ISBN 9780190879334 (Updf) | ISBN 9780190879341 (Epub) | ISBN 9780190879310
(hardcover : alk. paper) | ISBN 9780190879327 (paperback : alk. paper)
Subjects: LCSH: Tea Party movement-Press coverage. | Press and
Politics-United States. | Conservatism in the press-United States. |
Mass media-Political aspects-United States. | United States-Politics
and government-2009-2017. | BISAC: LANGUAGE ARTS & DISCIPLINES /
Journalism. | SOCIAL SCIENCE / Media Studies. | POLITICAL SCIENCE /
Political Ideologies / Conservatism & Liberalism.
Classification: LCC JK2391.T43 (ebook) | LCC JK2391.T43 C67 2018 (print) |
DDC 320.520973-dc23
LC record available at https://lccn.loc.gov/2017061042

1 3 5 7 9 8 6 4 2
Paperback printed by Webcom, Inc., Canada
Hardback printed by Bridgeport National Bindery, Inc.,
United States of America

CONTENTS

HEADPHONE CULTURE: A PREFACE

On May 26, 2016, Donald Trump—alleged billionaire, real estate mogul, former reality TV star and Fox News contributor—cinched the final numbers necessary to become the Republican Party nominee for president. In response it seemed that, finally, the news media woke to the part they had played in his success. In a *New York Times* column titled "My Shared Shame: The Media Helped Make Trump," Nicholas Kristof made the case that the news media had given Trump $1.9 billion "in free publicity"—190 times more than Trump had spent in advertising—and had failed to fact-check Trump or look thoroughly enough at his policy proposals. "On the whole," Kristof concluded, "we in the media empowered a demagogue and failed the country. We were lap dogs, not watchdogs."[1]

Media scholar Victor Pickard wrote in *The Huffington Post* that because Trump was good for news ratings and ad sales, the news media had "popularized Trump and, in doing so, turned our political process into a reality TV spectacle."[2] Seemingly clueless to this reflexive move in news, a later *New York Times* headline declared a "Battle of the Network Stars: Trump vs. Clinton," saying that the Republican and Democratic conventions would be "rebooting two series we've been watching for decades."[3]

President Barack Obama gave a statement soon after Trump's primary win, pushing back at the sensationalism surrounding the presidential campaigns and declaring, "This is not entertainment. This is not a reality show. This is a contest for the presidency of the United States."[4] He was wrong; Trump's victory was each of those things, reflecting patterns in political branding and news coverage that well preceded the 2016 campaign.

I would later write in an online essay that "Trump is the natural consequence of the Tea Party, an anti-establishment brand that—through the sheer force of its hostility—now controls the media and political elite that first started it." Like the Tea Party, the Trump political brand drew on racial resentment, religiosity, and angry emotions to connect with media audiences and voters.[5] Famed white supremacist David Duke issued a national endorsement for Trump, declaring him to be a candidate "riding a wave of anti-establishment feeling that I've been nurturing for years."[6] A *New York Times* headline chimed in: "Is Trump Winning? Among Whites and Men, for Sure."[7]

Trump's brand as a presidential candidate did more than appeal to fans and voters; it made money off its political publicity, too. The day after Trump's daughter Ivanka wore a dress from her own fashion line during a speech at the 2016 Republican National Convention, New York news outlets reported on all the items she wore selling out in stores. They even provided further instructions on how to buy more Ivanka products.[8] Soon after Donald Trump was elected president, the White House website posted a page promoting the jewelry line of his wife, Melania.[9] Trump made it clear that he saw himself and his politics as key to a valuable brand. On Twitter, he referred to himself as a "ratings machine" and boasted that news of performing at his upcoming inauguration had boosted one music artist's sales.[10] "Some people just don't understand the 'Movement,'" he wrote. The Trump triumph and the political skyrocketing of his brand took me back not only to the Tea Party, but to a single moment on a family vacation the very same year that the conservative activist phenomenon was born.

* * *

During a holiday weekend a few years ago, several relatives and friends sat around after an afternoon meal in our small cabin. My fourteen-year-old brother lay stretched out on the couch with my computer, watching a film with headphones on. Everyone else was holding different conversations— my mom and sister, my boyfriend and me, my grandmother and a family friend, each pair engaging in their own boisterous discussions. My brother, still wearing headphones, occasionally took his eyes off the computer screen to comment on a topic in the room that caught his attention. Then, just as quickly, he would return to his movie. At one point my grandmother directed a question at him, repeating it several times while he continued staring seemingly oblivious at the computer. We all laughed as she dryly remarked, "Oh, you can hear everything you want with those headphones on, but now you can't hear me?"

Today's media environment is much like this scene of a teenager with headphones in a room full of clamoring adults. In the digital era, the incessant availability of information through a variety of devices, platforms, mediums, and formats seems like the noise of many voices in a crowded room. My brother, like many media consumers, chose to tune out of the numerous discussions that surrounded him. But he also chose when to *tune in*, like countless others who regularly engage the discourse that constructs the ever-expanding, digitally enhanced public sphere. He used the headphones to focus attention on his selected media *and* took them off to respond to the topics and discussions that interested him and to share the information he gathered with the rest of the family. "Headphones" here stand in for the dialogic and dualistic identity of all citizens, including journalists, as media consumers and producers in a digital media environment. In today's expanded media system, Facebook, Twitter, political blogs, YouTube, and other social media provide people with the opportunity to screen out, consume, engage with, distribute, and produce a variety of political news and information all at the same time. It is a news and information culture that emphasizes circulation over professional norms and is frequently directed (or misdirected) by users who have the ability to speak back, fact-check, and amass their own news audiences. Moreover, it emphasizes marketing practices, profits, and success as key to understanding, appreciating, and evaluating contemporary politics. As a result, the news media have become more like their users and engage in branding practices that I call "raising the volume."

The Tea Party that rose soon after the inauguration of President Barack Obama in 2009 was created by a news media raising the volume in a headphone culture: the Tea Party was a story produced by conservative leaders, reified by media echo chambers, shaped by competing nonprofessional media narratives, and intentionally promoted, lent significance, and given meaning by the national news media on the right, left, and center. "Headphone culture" refers to a set of factors that have made old, familiar journalism categories and debates increasingly outdated and irrelevant. These factors include the consolidation and fragmentation of news media; advances in digital technology, including the growth and accessibility of mobile media; the popularity of user-generated content, social media, and alternative media; the rise of mediated politics, such as political branding; and the prevalence of neoliberalism as an ideology.

In this environment, journalists are pressed to raise the volume when they address their audiences and professional peers, presenting their content in a way that pushes people either to take off their headphones and relay the journalists' messages, or to keep their headphones on and choose their messages to the exclusion of all others. News outlets and journalists today literally *raise the volume* by yelling their reports, increasing the quantity of ads (visually, numerically, and sonically), and producing more content across multiple platforms.[11] Whether it is a reporter ranting about the Tea Party or an outlet passing on a deliberately deceptive video about an Obama official, journalists raising the volume often violate traditional news norms, ethics, and practices to get their messages to readers, listeners, or viewers and drown out their ubiquitous competition. It's a state of affairs of which anyone familiar with fake news stories and the Russian meddling in the 2016 American presidential election is now well aware.

The Tea Party's national rise both reflects larger ideological and rhetorical shifts in news and exemplifies headphone culture as a unique branding environment in which the news media engage their topics through the language of marketing, promotion, consumption, differentiation, and competition. In the process, a journalistic emphasis on facts, policy, investigation, and serving the public interest falls at the wayside, prioritizing the coverage of viral spectacles that sell over reporting on issues and policies that promote the public good.

This project specifically defines "raising the volume" as a set of branding practices by which members of the news media effectively created and sustained the Tea Party. The news media did not just *cover* the Tea Party in a way that fueled its publicity and growth—alongside conservative activists and political strategists, numerous news reporters, anchors, and commentators in outlets across the political spectrum actively began the Tea Party and branded it, functioning as its brand strategists, purveyors, and promoters. That is, the rise of the Tea Party in news narratives provides a specific account of how the news media moves beyond serving as a mere instrument when it comes to political branding practices. The discursive and categorical distinctions between the press, publicists, activists, politicians, and celebrities are increasingly muddled. Tea Party news stories reveal how the news media discuss and portray the meaning and role of journalism in the contemporary moment.

The Tea Party coverage shows that news outlets respond to, provoke, and target one another in an effort to stand out in today's media landscape. Similar to the observations of Joe Cappella and Kathleen Hall Jamieson[12] in their study of Reagan-era conservative media, this book shows that partisan news outlets covering the Tea Party got people to tune in to their conversations by working with producers in other platforms to produce ideologically or topically coherent news stories that dominated the public sphere. Still, it is clear in this analysis that these outlets did not just produce pieces that targeted their individual audiences; they also aimed their reports at one another. They echoed one another; launched rhetorical attacks at one another; responded to the same themes, ideas, and claims about the Tea Party; and contributed new insights, angles, and information with each new piece or segment. Each news outlet contributed to the Tea Party story, shaped its importance, and perpetuated its circulation. They were not just an echo chamber—they were a feedback loop, each creating the Tea Party brand through storytelling, circulation, and promotion. While media conversations with the audience and one another are not new, the immediacy of today's communication and the widespread access to video and Internet equipment produces a feedback loop that is much more rapid, fluid, and interactive.

In this landscape, this book tracks the ways that news reporters cause scenes; participate and organize political events; and use race, gender, and class to draw attention to their coverage with sensational, hyperbolic, and even inaccurate information. The use of marketing tactics and narratives helped the Tea Party advance as a political brand and national story. Pundits create debates, manufacture controversy, and rush to distribute messages before there is enough time to analyze, validate, and contextualize them. Columnists recast the same story in conflicting ways that fit it into prevailing cultural and political stereotypes and norms. Reporters call for protests, promote personal political causes, and emphasize emotional and personal connections to the stories they cover. Perhaps most important, news organizations and professionals are swayed and manipulated by their own attempts to raise the volume in the contemporary media environment, and are frequently misled and goaded by other media groups shouting more loudly and quickly. In an age where everyone has the opportunity to tune out, tune in, and speak back, Tea Party news coverage ultimately shows how, in raising the volume, the distinctions between citizens, journalists, activists, and consumers are made increasingly tenuous, inadequate, and obsolete. In the process, the potential for democracy and social change is left unrealized.

ACKNOWLEDGMENTS

As a kid moving between a city home in a Black neighborhood and a sub-urban Christian school in a predominantly white town, I grew up fascinated about how stories and ideas about the world help make such a starkly divided society seem like a natural state of affairs. Journalists tell these stories that both create and challenge these unequal worlds we make. Politicians, at their best, try to change them. So I start with thanking them for their work and those always willing to make it better.

This project was started while I was a student at the Annenberg School for Communication at the University of Pennsylvania. There Michael Delli Carpini, Elihu Katz, Kathleen Hall Jamieson, and other brilliant scholars gave me consistent support, insight, and advice as the project developed. Kathleen encouraged me to intern at the White House, where the idea for this book first occurred. Special thanks go to John Jackson Jr. for his guidance then and now. His patience, generosity, and thoughtfulness will continue to guide my work and me for many years to come. During my time at Penn, I have also been nurtured and learned from the wealth of expertise brought by visiting scholars and professors outside of my depart-ment: Deborah Thomas, Radhika Parameswaran, Mark Anthony Neal, Melissa Harris Perry, and Don Mitchell have all extended themselves beyond the confines of a single course.

The staff at the Annenberg School for Communication are incredible. They prepared homemade dinners, offered to read chapters, and hoarded newspaper articles for me. These include Dr. Debra Williams, Kyle Cassidy, Waldo Aguirre, Sharon Black, Emily Plowman, Lizz Cooper, Donna Edwards, Yogi Sukwa, Deb Porter, Rose Halligan, Joe Diorio, and so many more. Mrs. Beverly Henry, especially, made it her mission to support rising scholars of color and we are all in her debt.

As for my colleagues, my mentors, my friends, my partners in crime: there are too many to count. At Annenberg: Aymar Jean Christian, Cabral Bigman, Jasmine Salters, Jasmine Cobb, Dan Berger, C. Riley Snorton, Mary

Bock, Adrienne Shaw, Robin Stevens, and Jeff Gottfried have advised me, taught me, laughed with me, and shared with me. Cabral read early drafts of the work and Aymar helped me think through key ideas. Thank you. My historian comrades and sister-friends, Maryan Soliman and Richara Heyward, brought me brilliance, joy, and adventure. I met colleagues who helped give light, camaraderie, and knowledge along the way: Al Martin, Dayna Chatman, Sarah Jackson, Kristen Warner, Andre Brock, Andre Carrington, Catherine Steele, Racquel Gates, Kishonna Gray-Denson, Sarah Florini, Brandy Monk-Payton, and Madison Moore. Fredrika Thelandersson gave needed editorial assistance at the end. Thanks, too, to members of a certain clandestine feminist enclave who helped me with navigating politics, work, personal life, and everything in between.

At Rutgers, I have been blessed with an abundance of excellent colleagues who have given help in many different ways: Bernadette Gailliard, Rebecca Reynolds, Todd Wolfson, Jack Bratich, Brittney Cooper, Melissa Aroncyzk, Lauren Feldman, David Greenberg, Chenjerai Kumanyika, Susan Keith, Deepa Kumar, Regina Marchi, Amy Jordan, John Pavlik, and Jeff Lane. Administrators Harty Mokros, Karen Novick, and Jorge Schement have helped with the hurdles. Senior colleagues provided mentorship and advice that shaped (and reshaped) this book: thanks go to Ralina Joseph, Sarah Banet-Weiser, Amy Jordan, Jonathan Gray, Lisa Henderson, Robin Means Coleman, Roopali Mukherjee, Herman Gray, and Susan Douglas. Special thanks to Bambi Haggins and Allison Dorsey for all your support, advice, and example. Pablo Boczkowski did me the great favor of introducing me to my editor at Oxford University Press, Angela Chnapko. From beginning to end, Angela was a joy to work with in this process—she believed in the project and was always helpful and available. I am in your debt. Additionally, Cathy Hannabach and Sarah Grey helped edit and prepare early drafts. Cathy, especially, helped me with seeing the light at the end of the tunnel.

Friends and mentors from my days in news, politics, and journalism no doubt shaped my ideas about media and society that have landed in this book: Lewis Erskine, David Brançaccio, Karine Jean-Pierre, Candace White, Reniqua Allen, Marty Spanninger, Ty West, Maria Hinojosa, Sarah Burns, Ken Burns, David McMahon, and many more. Heather Booth, I especially appreciate your love and support.

My grandmother Lorraine Baumgardner Costley was an artist who did not have much schooling, but her genius knew no bounds. My brilliant mom, Donna White, finished college with me in her arms. I am grateful that she helped carry me across this finish line, too. My sister Khaleah White battled illness throughout the time this book was written, but still took time to shop, cook, and check on me. My youngest two siblings, Khaneisha and Khalil

White, reminded me to never take myself too seriously throughout the process.

And the rest of the village that holds me up—Cassandra Campbell, Clarice Peterson, Mama Donna Costley, Guy Costley, Deborah Johnson, Katrina Morison, Andria Matthews, Brandis Belt, Rachel Thomas, Deborah Johnson, Lashann Baumgardner, Steven Baumgardner, Coven Baumgardner, Ashley Freeman, the Reeves family, and endless lists of uncles, aunties, cousins, and colleagues with whom I bonded and received love and support along the way—you've not only kept me going, you've helped me realize this goal. I had a baby in the year before this book was completed. Women in my community brought food and checked on me as I fervently wrote—thanks to Jessie Pepper, Allyson Murphy, Devyani Guha, Lana Curzon, Rhea Mokund-Beck, Susan Bergin, and others. Seth, too, *mailed* me a cake. At the very end, friends stepped in to read chapters when I just couldn't read anymore—Alexia Bucciarelli, Justin Crosby, Leslie Varghese, Chen Reis, and Tamika Songster. Thank you.

My grandfather David Costley and my uncle Reginald Burl passed away before this was completed. I am so grateful I had them here to see me start this journey, and so sad they are gone.

My baby boy, Akin, celebrated his first birthday a mere week before this book was finished. He gave me a reason to take breaks, enjoy the sunshine, and smile. My husband, partner, and best friend, Anthony Olarerin, helped make this all possible. He gave me clean laundry, delicious meals, big hugs, unending encouragement, assistance, and a constant faith in my ability to finish. I needed space and time to write, think, and heal—you made sure I had it. I love you.

The Branding of Right-Wing Activism

CHAPTER 1

Welcome to the Party

On a February morning only a few weeks after President Barack Obama's historic inauguration, a business reporter from the financial cable news network CNBC went on what several major newspapers referred to as a "rant." Clutching his news microphone on the Chicago Mercantile Exchange trading floor, Rick Santelli railed against federal stimulus spending in the midst of a debilitating economic recession:

> How about this, president and new administration...have people vote on the Internet...to see if we really want to subsidize the losers' mortgages or...reward people who want to carry the water instead of just drink the water!
>
> We're thinking of having a Chicago Tea Party in July. All of you capitalists who want to show up to Lake Michigan, I'm going to start organizing!

Back in the studio, an anchor expressed surprise at the traders loudly cheering Santelli on in the background and joked, "This is like mob rule here, I'm getting scared!" In response, Santelli motioned to the all-white and all-male group of financial traders around him and responded, "This is America! President Obama, are you listening?"[1]

In a single move, a journalist on the job claimed the mantle of "revolutionary leader" and became known as the catalyst of the Tea Party movement. The news of Santelli's remarks spread quickly. The next day, *The New York Times* reported on his call for a Tea Party in Chicago.[2] A *Wall Street Journal* guest columnist wrote that Santelli's "rant heard 'round the world" had given the Tea Party its "moniker" and motivated others to start organizing their own Tea Party rallies.[3] *The New York Times, USA Today*, and *The Wall Street Journal* referenced Santelli's tirade as the impetus for the nationwide Tea Parties and tax protests that occurred on

April 15, 2009, marking his onscreen outburst to be the beginning of the Tea Party.[4] Regardless of the attribution—as inspiration or founder—reporters and activists alike have credited Santelli with starting the Tea Party movement.

Santelli's tirade was a major departure from traditional news values such as objectivity and nonpartisanship, yet it was widely described in the press as a success and not a journalistic failure. CNBC immediately posted the footage of its reporter's tirade on its website; with almost 2 million views, it became CNBC's most popular video clip ever and quickly elicited an official White House response.[5] A *New York Times* writer noted that while this type of outburst would have been seen as unacceptable for journalists in the past, it now presented an opportunity for the network to "maximize publicity and Web traffic."[6] The *Chicago Tribune* argued that the "self-described rant" had raised Santelli's profile and increased his value to the network. Sociologist Clarence Lo explained it as a way to "test market" the concept of the Tea Party to conservative constituents and trigger a political mobilization of networks that advanced the Tea Party brand.[7]

In his outburst, Santelli framed the Tea Party as a phenomenon that rebelled against the leadership of President Barack Obama, aimed to restore the ideals of capitalism, and represented a specific group of mostly white and male Americans. It was a spectacular feat that recast an eighteenth-century anticolonial tax protest as a twenty-first-century opposition movement targeting a democratically elected African American president. In a later interview with *Politico*, Santelli described the Tea Party as "steeped in American culture" and reflective of a pivotal moment in American democracy.[8] Through Santelli's tirade, the Tea Party was formed as a white, anti-Obama (and, implicitly, anti-Black and people of color), pro-business, and conservative protest. In one move, Santelli had helped establish the Tea Party brand. Politicians, strategists, journalists, media pundits (including those in left-leaning and "objective" news outlets), and activists on the ground continued the work in moving the Tea Party forward.

Moreover, Santelli's seminal Tea Party speech took place within a journalistic landscape altered by the expansion and increased accessibility of information and news through digital technologies (such as online political reporting and amateur web journalism). Both the press and subsequent books attributed the rise of the Tea Party to new media technology. Indeed, a *Wall Street Journal* guest columnist and conservative blogger argued that the Tea Party was "appearing on its own" through social media, echoing a larger media framing of the Tea Party as a digitally decentralized social movement that allowed it to be easily constructed by and within the news media.⁹ As a "leaderless movement" with no clearly identifiable leaders, the making of the Tea Party was constructed by and through the press. As a result, the digital age provided a crucial and critical context for news media's engagement and co-construction of the Tea Party, as did the recent prominence and emergence of branding in the last twenty years.¹⁰

Examining news media stories about the Tea Party is also an assessment of modern journalism: the practice of collecting, interpreting, and distributing information about current events to the public. While there is clear overlap in these two terms, "news media" and "journalism" convey distinct meanings that become even more apparent throughout the Tea Party news stories. My approach to news texts draws on the notion of journalism as an "interpretive community united through its shared discourse and collective interpretations of key events."¹¹ In studying the texts that journalists produce for the public, this book tracks how journalists evaluate, challenge, describe, and perform their own work and the political world.

The "news media" (abbreviated frequently throughout this book as "the media") refers to the converging ideological tendencies of the topics, routines, discourse, and rhetoric among a vast array of news providers, formats, and platforms. Jack Lule encourages an understanding of news as myth, "a societal story that expresses prevailing ideals, ideologies, values and beliefs."¹² Greco Larson affirms this notion of news, arguing that news functions as a value system and a moral narrative with characters, structures, and legitimizing tendencies that advance certain ideas, while T. E. Cook adds that the news is "an outcome of interaction between journalists and other political actors."¹³ Looking at the news coverage of the Tea Party teaches us both about the ideological frames of the news media as an interactive and fluid conglomerate that reflects public life and beliefs, while also providing insight into the routines, practices, and values of the journalists and professionals that assemble the news narratives themselves.

Thus, the Santelli moment illustrates the way that members in the news media actively constructed, framed, propelled, and instigated the Tea Party's ascent to public consciousness in a brand culture. Much early coverage of the Tea Party focused on how it was largely organized through its circulation on conservative sites, covered and mobilized through established media outlets, and led by people who simultaneously functioned as politicians, news hosts, fundraisers, and Tea Party leaders, like Santelli. Fox News, especially, was actively involved in not just promoting the Tea Party but organizing its own Tea Party events and provoking media coverage in other news outlets. This level of news media engagement in a social movement was virtually unprecedented, as was the level to which outlets and reporters targeted their coverage not just at their audience but also at one another. Alongside activists and political strategists outside the media, journalists and reporters co-produced the Tea Party brand because they were themselves implicated within it. In examining the Tea Party news narratives, the active role of the news media in the production of the Tea Party as a brand becomes clear.

While there were clear examples of collaboration and cross-platform pollination throughout the conservative media, I am not suggesting here that there was a mutual and cohesively organized political effort among *all* networks and publications to create and promote the Tea Party. The branding occurred on three different levels—from activists and politicians who used the media to promote the Tea Party; between activists, journalists, and media pundits who worked together to promote the Tea Party; and among news reporters and journalists who did not explicitly promote and support the Tea Party, but covered it and conveyed it as a brand by emphasizing its symbolic value and certain attributes as key to its political importance. Even if conservative outlets and reporters were the only ones to intentionally, explicitly, and strategically promote the Tea Party brand, the other networks and outlets followed their lead (and, in some instances, their explicit provocation) in arguing the importance and newsworthiness of the Tea Party and constructing a coherent identity for its brand.

At a time when a majority of Americans had never heard of the Tea Party and only small and moderately sized crowds were turning out to its rallies, the news media featured the Tea Party as a key character in stories about immigration, the economy, health care, patriotism, domestic terrorism, political ethics, racism, elections, and sexism. It was a dynamic conservative brand that drew attention and bolstered support for conservatives during a "crisis of neoliberalism" that nearly collapsed the economy under Republican leadership and policies.[14] Depending on the story and its source, the Tea Party played different roles—it was variously cast as a major political power changing the course of Republican politics and American democracy, a social movement, a series of antiestablishment protests, an assortment of groups manufactured by invisible corporate backers, an uprising in response to an economic recession and wasteful government spending, a mobilization of conservatives driven by anti-Black sentiment, and an entirely fabricated media spectacle.

In all of these stories, journalists mobilized race, gender, and class narratives to describe the Tea Party's symbolic significance in the press and American society at large. Moreover, they frequently described it as a brand, highlighting its profits, marketability, brand leaders, and audience appeal. The Tea Party became a brand through news media coverage; in defining it as a brand, the Tea Party was a story, message, and cognitive shortcut that built a lasting relationship with citizen-consumers through strong emotional connections, self-expression, consumption, and differentiation.[15] The interconnected and meta-media nature of news coverage allowed for the production of a coherent media identity related to the Tea Party that did not depend upon a single organization or movement leader.

Challenging dominant accounts, I argue then that the Tea Party was less social movement and more mass-mediated brand—a construct fashioned, facilitated, managed, assisted, organized, and maintained by the national press. This book describes how the "news media" (itself a complex cultural discursive construction that is unpacked throughout this book) produced and constructed the Tea Party movement, in large part as a heuristic through which it defined and negotiated the tensions between identity, politics, and ideology at a particular historical moment. Moreover, as most studies of social movements focus on left-wing activism, this book helps provide important insight into how the media covers right-wing movements.

In some ways, this book is and is not about the Tea Party. It investigates what the mass-mediated construction of the Tea Party tells us about the current media and cultural moment, specifically the role of journalism in a digital age, and contemporary American notions of identity, democracy, and citizenship. I analyze the tropes in the news coverage of the Tea Party and draw on a cultural reading of these texts to better understand its development. The news stories show that the Tea Party's perceived influence and power relied on the symbolic and cognitive impact of its label, not on its resulting mobilization, grass-roots protests, or leadership. The making of the Tea Party in news demonstrates how branding has become a key mobilizing discourse and practice in political reporting, transforming the way we understand social movements, civic engagement, activism, and journalism in this moment.

By using the term "brand," this book claims that the Tea Party is a convergent creation within media that functioned more as a cultural signifier aimed at mobilizing the votes, dollars, and attention of a citizen-consumer audience than a particular movement with concrete goals, policies, or aims. As constructed through the narrative tropes and themes emphasized by the press, the key Tea Party brand qualities were constitutionalism, militarism, religiosity, anti-Obama, anger, working- and middle-class, white and female-led. Of all these, the Tea Party brand's race, gender, and class attributes were key in attracting and generating news coverage.

According to Naomi Klein, a brand is an identity, an essence, or "corporate consciousness"—not about the products but what the "brands mean to the culture and to people's lives."[16] This book investigates the ways that the media helped build this consciousness and meaning for the Tea Party, emphasizing specific qualities that related to its marketability, success, and identity. As Maurice Manring notes,

> The relationship between the product and the package, however, goes beyond mere functionality: to a great extent the package creates the product's personality and in turn enables the consumer to establish a relationship with a stranger: the distant producer of a mass product.[17]

Because of the decentralized nature of the Tea Party and the various tactics deployed by its many producers and leaders on the ground, this journalistic production was especially fundamental to the making of the Tea Party brand. The cross-promotional and interactive function of *all* news media allowed the Tea Party brand to be promoted across all outlets, not just Fox News or other conservative media. While the Tea Party brand had politicos, strategists, and organizers on the ground, the Tea Party reached most Americans as a news story, one grand mastered through the gatekeepers and reporters of the press.

The old newspaper adage says that "stories sell papers," and the Tea Party was indeed a story that sold, drawing news coverage like many other political spectacles and sensational events. What *is* new about it is the way technology and a branding culture allowed the news media to produce, perpetuate, and participate in what they depicted as a populist revolt. The Tea Party was a social movement frequently instigated, propelled, and integrated into the news media that reported on it—what makes it a brand is its function as an emotionally laden symbol that mobilized people through its reporting, rather than mobilizing its reporting based on people. Without the active intervention and participation of the press, the Tea Party as it exists (and existed) would never have come to be.

The Tea Party was, of course, not the first American right-wing or populist movement to gain traction in media, but as a brand it differed from previous iterations in important ways. While journalists, pundits, and politicians referred to the Tea Party as populism, the nineteenth-century progressive "prairie populism" in the US first rose in opposition to big business. Instead, the Tea Party largely advocated on the behalf of businesses and corporations.[18] Later versions of pro-business conservative movements that some deemed as populist, such as the Ku Klux Klan and John Birch Society, were centrally and hierarchically organized with thousands of chapters and millions of members and sympathizers—unlike the Tea Party, which was comparatively small and leaderless.[19] The conservative activism organized via radio by Father Charles Coughlin during the Great Depression was hampered by federal oversight and focused on the views of a single charismatic leader, characteristic of the populist movement.[20] Typically, social movements are organized by political outsiders and are marginalized by mainstream media.[21] Instead, professional reporters were involved in the creation and development of the Tea Party in a way that provoked coverage across all platforms and outlets regardless of partisan ideology.

This book makes the case that journalists and reporters covering the Tea Party did three things. First, they used branding discourse to tell stories that drew attention to specific attributes, qualities, and sentiments; second, they engaged actively in branding and promoting the Tea Party in their news stories; third, by focusing on branding and identity in news, they revealed how race, gender, class, and journalism are portrayed and understood within the modern press. Members of the news media were more than just conduits for the Tea Party message and publicity (though they were that, too). They also shaped the Tea Party narrative, explored its meaning and significance, defended it, and provided it with leadership.

The media did not just cover the Tea Party in a way that fueled its promotion and growth—news reporters actively branded the Tea Party and functioned as its brand strategists, monitors, and promoters. That is, the rise of the Tea Party in news narratives tracks the extent to which the news media has moved beyond functioning in simply an instrumental way when it comes to political branding practices and shows that the discursive distinctions between the press, publicists, activists, politicians, and celebrities are becoming more symbolic than concrete. In the process, the Tea Party news stories show how the news media discuss and depict the meaning and role of race, gender, class, and journalism in the contemporary moment.

BRANDING THE TEA PARTY

The changes in technology and media that produced the Tea Party are part of an ever-expanding twenty-first-century brand culture. The term "brand culture" refers to the contemporary context in which commerce, political action, and identity construction overlap within a competitive capitalist landscape.[22] Notably, this emphasis on brands has been marked by a societal shift to private-sector partnership and market-oriented imperatives in previously idealized public spaces, like schools, universities, museums, and parks.[23] Historically considered the "fourth estate" for its value in serving the public, journalism has also been altered by an "image economy" in which "attention is monetized and notoriety, or fame, is capital"; journalistic labor has become increasingly more market-oriented and less driven by societal ideals.[24] In concurrently promoting themselves through reporting on the Tea Party, reporters, pundits, and journalists became the co-producers, consumers, and creators of the Tea Party brand. The rise of the Tea Party thus was indicative of the impact of brand culture on journalism today, a snapshot of what is possible in a moment of political branding and journalism.

Specifically, the branding of the Tea Party through news discourse occurred in six ways: (1) describing it as a brand; (2) conveying shifting identities; (3) relaying brand attributes; (4) providing it with a platform; (5) serving as brand manager, activist, and promoter; and (6) producing meta-journalism that centered the press within the Tea Party narrative. In the more conservative press such as Fox News, the promotion of and profit from the Tea Party was extremely explicit. For example, Fox News host Glenn Beck recruited his viewers to attend the first Tea Party rallies on websites where he also earned money from online ventures.[25] Other outlets offered editorial and reporting space to Tea Party representatives and spokespersons as a subtler form of brand promotion, or explicitly reviewed the promotion of the Tea Party among other platforms.

When CNN broadcast the "Tea Party State of the Union" address in 2011 and became the first television network to ever air a third party's rebuttal to the president's annual speech, MSNBC anchor Rachel Maddow called it "a remarkable act of journalistic intervention to elevate, in effect, a group with which they are co-sponsoring a presidential debate to...the level of the major parties in this country."[26] In the process of generating and reifying the Tea Party brand, journalists also engaged in media criticism and self-expression. In complex ways, Tea Party news content frequently functioned as an extension of a news outlet's or reporter's brand, making the presentation of stories and narratives consistent with that outlet or reporter's core values and ideals. The news preoccupation with the profit, celebrity, and spectacle of the Tea Party cemented the Tea Party brand and its influence in American politics.

While some form of branding has always been present in journalism, the Tea Party news stories suggest that these particular approaches are much more amplified in the digital, headphone culture era. Over the last few decades, branding has intensified as a dialectic in journalism in response to deregulation, the commercial success of news, conglomeration, increased competition, and shifts in political marketing. During the 1980s, the Federal Communications Commission (FCC) rolled back requirements for impartiality and balanced news reporting and instead emphasized a free-market approach to news regulation. About the same time, conservative leaders, foundations, and think tanks began forming crucial coalitions with media networks that helped fuel, promote, and disseminate right-wing viewpoints for a mass audience.[27] As cable news and internet news sources have gained wider audiences, the news media have also increased their niche targeting and marketing to specific demographic groups based on taste, ideology, income, and consumer tastes—sometimes even transforming the content of the same stories to suit particular audiences.[28] In reaching for a more "upscale audience," the news media changed its discourse to more consumer-oriented framing.[29]

In particular, I contend that the Tea Party was a product of a digital economy in which consumers and producers play interchangeable roles, and consumers become marketing tools and salespeople through "talking up" a brand.[30] Indeed, the Tea Party was instigated, mobilized, concretized, and facilitated primarily through its mediated representations and coverage within news, and members of the press functioned as both its consumers and producers. Journalists understood the Tea Party as a story that would sell, criticizing the disproportionate coverage of the Tea Party in news stories that aimed for "clicks" online even as they continued to report on it. In effect, consumers and users create their own social worlds around a brand that help, in turn, develop and strengthen it. Moreover, Denzil Meyers[31] writes of brands,

> Rather than being an object of exchange, [a brand] can be viewed as the sum total of relationships among stakeholders, or the medium through which stakeholders interact and exchange with each other. This dynamic is true for all stakeholders, not just for the stakeholder class we call "consumers."

Despite small crowds and disparate on-the-ground organization, journalists, reporters, pundits, and strategists in the news media engaged in what Celia Lury calls "contemporary brand management" by (1) "providing and managing a context in which the productivity of consumers is likely to produce desirable experiences of, or relations to, the brand, that in turn reproduce and strengthen the standing of a desirable brand image" and (2) "contributing to brand equity: the communicative sociality of consumer activity—attention and affect—accumulated under the propertied symbol of the brand."[32]

Examining branding in the media means looking not only at the way stories describe money or profit but also at the communication "of emotion or affect, intensity, and qualities,"[33] all of which were central to Tea

Party news coverage. The news stories about the Tea Party overwhelmingly focused on the meaning, style, sentiments, emotion, reception, and financial success of the Tea Party and frequently described it as a brand. As such, this book analyzes branding in Tea Party news stories as a specific frame that emphasizes the commercial, consumerist, and capitalist logics that guide and structure narratives.

The use of the term "branding" rather than "framing" in this narrative analysis aims for more precise language in understanding the rise of the Tea Party in twenty-first-century news stories. The term "framing" more generally functions as a metaphor for literal frames, such as windows, that allow some parts of a scene to be viewed while excluding others.[34] In analyzing frames in media narratives, scholars look at how news stories are written to convey clear ideologies, definitions, agents, associations, and beliefs about an event, person, or topic.[35] Framing theory generally presumes that the media are separate from the phenomena they cover and only shape public perception of those phenomena. But as a subset of framing in media discourse, *branding* specifically refers to the way the media deploys and engages in marketing aspects of storytelling that "focus on particular attributes that might be flattering or derogatory and, thus, advantageous or disadvantageous to message sponsors in persuasive communication."[36]

Along these lines, I employ the term "brand" to refer to market-oriented frames in storytelling that not only describe a news item's attributes but also engage in and monitor its success in mobilizing profit, support, and influence. Through branding the Tea Party, the media (at various levels) were focused not only on reporting on the Tea Party, but on forming institutional and political alliances around its brand. "Branding" also refers to a frame that positions a media audience as consumers and participants in a consumerist cycle or dialectic. For this reason, Celia Lury refers to brands as "dynamic frames" that "organiz[e] the two-way exchange of communication between the inner and outer environments of the market in time and space, informing how consumers relate to producers and how producers relate to consumers."[37] This idea is supported by other scholars, like Kenneth Cosgrove who argues that "a frame can be a single shot or deal with a single issue but it rarely takes on equity and essence as does a brand."[38] In a brand culture—or what Melissa Aronczyk and Devon Powers refer to as a "promotional culture"—media consumers (and, I would add, media producers) "become promotional intermediaries themselves, working in the service of the brand yet without the financial remuneration that its owners enjoy."[39]

Instead of selling a product with a simple use, brands have become the affective and experiential relationship between products and their consumers. Aronczyk concludes that "the concept of the brand has escaped its corporate origins."[40] While brands historically were created to distinguish similar merchandise and signal quality for manufactured products, over time brands have developed their own value independent of the products they sell. According to Lury, specifically, a brand functions as a personality for products that represents core values and a pleasurable emotional and familial connection that meets a consumer's social, psychological, and emotional needs, desires, and satisfaction.[41] More important, brands are a product of a "mediated economy," an object that "emerges at the convergence of media and computing" and a "more 'nomadic' [form] of sociality...constructed in response to the flexibility demanded by a transitory and complex environment."[42]

Newsmakers consistently depicted the Tea Party as a brand by focusing on its representations, appeal, motivations, influence, and circulation—in other words, emphasizing its persona more than its policies. Indeed, reporters represented the Tea Party as a signifier with a set of values and emotions that appealed to particular voting constituencies; they served as its spokespersons, helped mobilize its constituents, tracked its profitability, and fluidly moved between identifying it as a protest, a social movement, a campaign, and a political party. As Sarah Banet-Weiser explains, "Brands are actually a story told to the consumer. When that story is successful, it surpasses simple identification with just a tangible product; it becomes a story that is familiar, intimate, personal, a story with a unique history."[43] Holt adds that "a brand emerges as various 'authors' tell stories that involve the brand."[44] Through storytelling, brand advocates endow the brand with specific associations, origins, quality levels, experiences, benefits, and performance.[45] Chapter 2 shows that, more than just being a story that sold newspapers, the Tea Party was a label begun, propelled, organized, and facilitated by the news media that reported on it. The second chapter discusses the news media start, construction, and promotion of the Tea Party as a political brand.

Moreover, visual racial cues in implicitly racial political messages are key to their branding and storytelling effectiveness; gender and class, too, function as highly legible attributes that help bolster and define a brand. In short, race and racial meaning have a long history of conveying themselves via nonverbal, metaphorical, and tacit communication. As Arviddson notes, "The source of brand value is to create a social world through productive communication."[46] In particular, as Shalini Shankar points out, branding maps racial notions of citizenship and belonging onto constructions of the ideal consumer.[47] But then, conversely, these essentialist, capitalist, and commoditizing tendencies of a brand culture in which certain racial groups are seen as worthwhile and valuable (or not) can also shape mediated messages about politics and public service. Chapter 3 of this book more closely examines how news coverage of race, gender, and class not only constructed the Tea Party brand but also relayed the ways the media define, articulate, and problematize these identities in a contemporary brand culture.

My approach in this book stresses branding as a discursive practice in mediated storytelling that produces, facilitates, and circulates a brand, with (or without) intent, collaboration, and strategy between brand managers and producers. As Lury explains, "Branding posits a different logic of value from that of the classic marketing approach . . . *consumers value products according to the position they occupy in the flow of media culture.*"[48] The branding of the Tea Party in the news media was both explicit and implicit, affecting both the content and style of the news coverage.

Our contemporary headphone culture makes media particularly conducive and vulnerable to the news promotion and co-creation of a brand. The term "headphone culture" denotes the current news media landscape as a convergence of various trends that facilitated the Tea Party's rapid development and exposure, including the growth of "spreadable media," user-generated information sharing and production as participatory media, fragmented and identity-based media audiences, the neoliberal turn of American politics and ideology, and the expansion of mediated politics and political branding.[49] According to Andrew Chadwick, the Internet and other new communication technologies have created more adaptive and interdependent hybrid political and media institutions. Operating from what he calls an "ontology of hybridity," Chadwick argues that studying media technologies, norms, behaviors, actors, repertoires, genres, and organizational forms in the social world requires a move away from binary categories and a focus on interactive exchanges.[50]

It is this "hybrid mediality"[51] to which I gesture with headphone culture. The Tea Party news coverage shows that in a headphone culture, news stories rely on highly legible frames such as race, gender, and class; news media consumers and producers are frequently interchangeable; unverified information can be easily (and swiftly) distributed and publicized by established news organizations; and the line between hard and soft news is further eroded. Further, officials are able to evade journalistic interrogation and convey their messages directly to the public. As a result, news outlets and reporters increase their interpretive and editorializing function in storytelling, interact with one another through cross-media coverage, and center themselves as actors in the media they create—primarily to the benefit of those who support (rather than challenge) existing power structures and ideologies. These news narratives provide insight into the function and discursive approaches of the press in an era transformed by digital technology, as discussed more fully in chapter 4.

This book lays out the way in which novelty; dehistoricization; decontextualization; emphases on race, gender, and class signifiers; and other long-standing news practices all contributed to branding a movement in a brand culture. While many of the journalistic processes that help brand the Tea Party are not new, they have changed in significance and importance in a constantly mediated world. What is novel here is the way that a largely manufactured movement can now represent itself as grass roots so easily within the contemporary news environment, doing so with the assistance of an interdependent, frequently ideologically driven, and market-focused news media. By walking through the case study of the Tea Party's rise, the flows, functions, aims, and impact of modern media and politics becomes clearer.

In a headphone culture, news reporters raise the volume not only to reach their outlet's regular audience but to also get that audience and their competitors to share their news stories with others. As journalists raise the volume, opinion and commentary set the agenda for hard-news reporting. News reporters maximize their roles as political insiders, increase their focus on celebrity, and emphasize consumptive politics as key to democratic engagement.

APPROACHES

Initially, this project began as an investigation of the cultural significance of the Tea Party's spectacular political presence in the Obama-era news landscape. The data, however, reveal the Tea Party as not just part of a political environment altered by the election of the first African American president, but also shaped by the expansion of neoliberal values and practices that emphasize deregulation, privatization, and corporate rule within journalism and politics. This book thus ultimately became a larger analysis of how the media depicted, actively promoted, and constructed the Tea Party as a political brand. In this way, this book explains the Tea Party as a product of a particular technological, economic, cultural, and political moment. Brand culture, in particular, comes into effect under neoliberalism as the ways consumer identities manifest as cultural practice, activism, and interaction and exchange (see chapter 2). As a result, it aims to answer one key question: What does the Tea Party's branding in news discourse tell us about journalism and politics in contemporary society? Implicitly, I also address other related questions, such as how American journalists write about politics and what recurring ideologies they produce in their narratives. I use the Tea Party's meteoric rise in national news as a case study to explain the key themes, characters, and features of national news and political storytelling in a digital age. Essential to this analysis of the Tea Party as a mass-mediated construction is the way it indexes the contemporary intersections and overlaps of contemporary media technology, journalism, and politics (particularly identity politics).

This study is one of the few multiplatform narrative analyses of social movement news coverage in the digital age. In a similar vein, it is one of the first qualitative examinations of the early life cycle of a single national political story as produced by both partisan and nonpartisan online, cable, broadcast, and print news outlets. While journalism studies scholars frequently argue that the content and discourse of news texts are important objects for empirical study, S. Elizabeth Bird points out that few scholars privilege interpretive textual analysis of news content, despite the value of such examinations.[52] This is not to say that there are no studies of news text or discourse; there is an abundant literature on this topic. Rather, most of these studies of news media or journalism also include additional methods such as audience surveys, interviews, and ethnographies. Mass media "effects" research often prioritizes the study of audience reception or industry production and pairs it with cultural textual analysis. For example, in social movement studies, scholars frequently focus on the impact of specific news frames upon the development or support of a social movement (or vice versa) within the media audience.[53]

This book moves away from such approaches. My project aims to capture the journey itself, tightening the analytical lens on the Tea Party tale as a case in political media coverage and interrogating its meanings as a cultural and historical artifact of twenty-first-century American society and politics. This book identifies the news media as not just a conduit through which political messages are conveyed to an awaiting audience, but a site in which political struggles, identities, activism, and rhetoric actually play out between media actors. As such, this study stands at the intersections of various fields and disciplines, including American studies, communications, cultural studies, journalism, media anthropology, political science, sociology, gender studies, Black studies, and whiteness studies.

The remaining pages of this book detail the Tea Party's prescriptive significance in news coverage to better understand the political, cultural, and journalistic terrain of the terms in office of the first African American president of the United States and this moment in digital media. At the same time, I am aware that my analysis of the Tea Party chronicles constitutes its own narrative, in which I am lending my critical voice to a still-unfolding story.

LET THE PARTY BEGIN

Even before the first box of tea landed in Boston Harbor in 1773, the American colonies were the site of ongoing tax-related skirmishes that emblematized larger political battles over belonging, citizenship, democracy, and power. Since then, the 1773 Boston Tea Party has become a popular symbol of American resistance, revolution, and patriotism that subtly conveys the potentially violent threat of a dissatisfied populace. As I elaborate in chapter 3, while "tea parties" were connected to the feminine notion of women's gatherings and social events, this radical Boston Tea Party came to overshadow this meaning and placed "tea parties" in the political realm. Though subsequent "tea party" protests have occurred for much of American history, the press-initiated resurgence of the concept to describe the April 15, 2009, "Tax Day" protests imbued it with newfound meaning, fueled by a digital age and by debates over journalism, politics, and identity.

The contemporary Tea Party's literal and symbolic roots lie in an event that occurred on the cold, dark waters of Boston Harbor in 1773, as part of an ongoing political crisis over British import taxation that had erupted in numerous American coastal cities.[54] That December, a group of tax protestors departed from a particularly contentious town meeting, dressed up as Mohawk Indians, and proceeded to the nearby docks. They boarded a British import ship and spent the next few hours throwing 342 chests of tea into the Atlantic Ocean. This action eventually became known as the "Boston Tea Party" and the "catalyst for revolution."[55] The dissidents' call for "no taxation without representation" emerged as a founding tenet of the United States of America. The Boston Tea Party came to mark the daring rise of what would become one of the most powerful nations in the world.

The current use of the term "Tea Party" evokes distant imaginings of American revolution, patriotism, and belonging—it produces, at its core, a question of *who* and *what* makes the nation. Antagonisms over eighteenth-century import taxation were, in part, fueled by fears that British soldiers were inciting slave rebellions and stripping American colonists of their liberties—early white Americans expressed concern that the British were disrupting the existing social order and disenfranchising *them* under colonial rule. A Boston lawyer protesting the Boston Port Bill wrote:

"I speak it with grief, I speak it with anguish—Britons are our oppressors...*we are slaves.*"[56] The donning of Indian costumes during the late-night vandalism showed the Tea Party at its roots to be a spectacle about both race and politics; or, rather, race as a metaphor for political marginality. Whites in the eighteenth century understood that, as Cheryl Harris argues, their whiteness functioned as a form of property that allowed them to move through society with more access and privileges than those marked by nativeness or blackness, who were deemed disposable, savage, and inferior.[57] By using race as a clarion call, protestors argued that white disenfranchisement, in effect, undermined the very nature of American society and violated the racial contract upon which it relied.[58]

Two centuries later, an attendee at a 2010 Tea Party rally described President Obama's health care bill as "just another way to enslave the American public" and demanded that the president "prove he's an American citizen."[59] Glenn Beck mentioned slavery at least two hundred times the year President Obama was inaugurated and argued that the president was "moving us all quickly into slavery."[60] Conversely, on MSNBC, an anchor called tea partiers "a bunch of greedy, water-carrying corporate-slave hypocrites defending the rich against the poor."[61]

In 2010, Kentucky senatorial candidate Rand Paul declared in his Republican primary victory speech, "I have a message from the Tea Party. A message that is loud and clear and does not mince words: we've come to take our government back."[62] In the news coverage of the tea partiers, this "us versus them" rhetoric functioned as a way of distinguishing often racialized "others" from the "real America" that the tea partiers were purported to represent, while also alluding to the violence upon which a highly stratified America was built and maintained. While patriotism and democratic participation figure prominently within the American recollection of the original Tea Party, its less frequently acknowledged racial spectacle, deviance, and rebellion also map onto its current incarnations in news reports in some ways. Through this racial appropriation, Tea Party supporters and activists have drawn on the rhetorical power of racial oppression as a trope that both exposes and reifies the racial order.

According to historian and columnist Jill Lepore, the captivating tale of the Boston Tea Party functions primarily as an American myth. In her book, *The Whites of Their Eyes*, Leopore describes how the Boston Tea Party was originally a minor historical event that grew in importance through nostalgia, historical fundamentalism, revisionism, and presentism. For fifty years after the colonists dumped tea into wintry waters, the event was referred to as "the destruction of the tea"—not the "Tea Party"—and received no special commemoration.[63] As the heroes of the American

Revolution began to die, the changing political landscape brought the newly named Boston Tea Party to the forefront:

> Calling the dumping of the tea a "tea party" made it sound like a political party: in the 1770s, parties were anathema, but in the 1830s, parties ran politics....By parading Hewes through the streets of the city, Boston's Whigs... claimed the so-called Tea Party as their own.[64]

As historian Alfred F. Young notes, the Tea Party was an event that was "'lost,' and then 'found' and given a new name."[65] Countless other political groups in America would subsequently lay claim to the rehistoricized legacy of the Boston Tea Party.

Since its initial rebranding, Americans have frequently used the Boston Tea Party in American political and protest rhetoric. Right-wing and left-wing activists in the 1960s and 1970s drew on Boston Tea Party rhetoric variously to defend civil disobedience, advocate for the equal rights of women and gays (who felt they were being taxed without representation), and object to property taxes.[66] Groups ranging from the Boy Scouts to medical practitioners have ceremonially dumped tea into Boston Harbor. A 1973 "Boston Tea Party" demonstration of mostly white mothers protested the use of tax funds to racially integrate public schools, drawing a clear link between racism and objections pertaining to taxes (and tax spending).[67] As further explained in chapter 4, these tax protests often fixated on excluding and marginalizing racialized others who were seen as not "belonging" to the American public. Thus, the Tea Party as a myth lends itself well to political branding through the history, emotion, and values that its label conveys. Indeed, we might call the Boston Tea Party one of the oldest political brands.

A MODERN TEA PARTY—ASTROTURF OR GRASS ROOTS?

While the Boston Tea Party has long had a strong influence on American activism, there is no record that any of its subsequent reprisals has been as frequently covered, received as much prolonged national attention, or accumulated as much political power as the one that emerged into the national news public sphere in early 2009. Although the first nationwide Tea Party–based tax protests started during the last few months of George W. Bush's presidency, they didn't receive attention in the national press as a populist social movement (and specifically a white social movement) against the federal government until after President Obama was inaugurated.

Early news references to the Tea Party during the last months of the 2008 campaign relayed key aspects of what would later become the Tea Party brand.

The Wall Street Journal fulfilled its well-established role as the conservative media "vanguard" in introducing the Tea Party into contemporary political rhetoric and national news, covering Tea Party activists before their wider recognition in the press.[68] The first mentions of the "Tea Party" appeared in The Wall Street Journal during the very end of the 2008 presidential campaign and at the close of George W. Bush's second term. In August and September 2008, Wall Street Journal editorials invoked the "tea party" in diatribes that strongly criticized high tax rates and the "tax and spend status quo" represented by Barack Obama and Joe Biden.[69]

Through these articles, The Wall Street Journal integrated the historical symbolism of the Tea Party into a specious modern narrative. The original Boston tea partiers did not protest taxation, but aimed to eradicate an imperial tax system that denied colonists access to political participation and power—eighteenth-century revolutionaries wanted taxation *with* representation. Arguably, this (mis)appropriation of the Boston Tea Party is critical to its contemporary reincarnation. As the first twenty-first-century mention of the Tea Party in relation to contemporary politics, these editorials laid the foundation for the plot and characters that came to define the Tea Party news narrative and brand. The Wall Street Journal introduced Sarah Palin, the Obama administration, religion, patriotism, taxes, activists, and revolutionary symbolism as key to the political landscape that would unfold in subsequent reports about the modern Tea Party.

In January 2009, The Wall Street Journal again published another article describing coordinated citizen protests of local property-tax increases in different locations around the country.[70] This was the first article to cover a tax protest that was also a Boston Tea Party reenactment—indeed, this was the first Tea Party–related protest covered by the national press in this century. However, this initial Tea Party mobilization went by without much acknowledgment in the national press or conservative leadership. For the rest of the nation, and according to all later news reports, the Tea Party did not begin until a month after President Obama had officially begun his first term, during the spectacular media moment with Santelli on CNBC. The Wall Street Journal's initial reports on tea parties as general tax protests at the end of the Bush presidency, on the other hand, have been neglected in subsequent narratives of the Tea Party movement.[71]

Numerous citizens, fundraising groups, institutions, and established conservative think tanks adopted the Tea Party label, in some cases renaming already existing organizations, making clear the perceived power and influence of its brand. This made it difficult to identify a central leadership or organizing group (or even surmise the Tea Party's origins). The dispersed and decentralized nature of the Tea Party allowed the press to shape its story and required journalists to connect seemingly unrelated events into one coherent narrative about the "movement." Self-appointed Tea Party spokespersons were granted authority through press interviews and features, rather than through any official or organizational process. Thus, news pundits and journalists helped construct the Tea Party as a unified group, producing specific frames that transformed a loosely connected set of protests into a major political power based on reimaginings of eighteenth-century revolt, nationhood, and independence. The Tea Party brand's rhetorical force helped fuel its narrative rise in twenty-first-century American news and politics.

The Tea Party's authenticity as a movement—and the question of whom it really represented—was a source of constant debate in news coverage. If inauthentic, the Tea Party movement was just politics as usual, a carefully crafted political or corporate strategy. If it was not a grass-roots citizen movement, the Tea Party was a form of subterfuge, an expansive political co-optation and an attack on democracy itself by the wealthy and powerful. If grass-roots activists were driving it, the Tea Party represented one of the most influential and concerted efforts of conservative voters on the ground. The debate over whether the Tea Party was a movement reflects the centrality of performativity and spectacle in political reporting, and the anonymity of digital organizing. Was the Tea Party *real*? Who was the Tea Party? What were its goals? With such ambiguous origins, the Tea Party's meaning, significance, and power were hashed out across pages and airwaves. While Tea Party scholars have divergent takes on what the Tea Party represents, they all share a focus on the media as integral to its development and significance.

According to Skocpol and Williamson, the media was critical to the development of the Tea Party by shaping public opinion, orchestrating and promoting events, and increasing awareness about the movement.[72] Still, they contend that the Tea Party was not an Astroturf (fake grass-roots) movement, noting that approximately a thousand Tea Party groups formed between fall 2009 and spring 2010.[73] They paint the Tea Party as a complex movement in which "grassroots activists, roving billionaire advocates, and right-wing media purveyors" were working to collectively produce "new variants of long-standing conservative claims about government, social programs, and hot-button social issues."[74] In a similar vein, scholars have argued that the Tea Party was a brand phenomenon produced by consumer-activists on the ground who gave it an identity and political influence.[75]

On the other hand, Anthony DiMaggio argues that the twenty-first-century Tea Party was a rhetorical construction manufactured by national political figures using the media and cloaked in the language of protest movements. He finds that the Tea Party was primarily a media phenomenon, brought into being through the way pundits, commentators, and reporters assembled its narratives. According to DiMaggio, the mass media gave the Tea Party positive coverage, unlike other historical and progressive social movements, and falsely portrayed it as a bottom-up organization, despite its top-down leadership and mobilization. For him, the media coverage of the Tea Party showed that "the majority of those writing in the media cannot distinguish between real and artificial movements."[76] This is particularly true in a digital age, in which social movement mobilization and labor appear substantially different from traditional forms of activism.[77] While social media allows protestors to better "preach to the converted," they still require mass media to lend visibility and legitimacy to their movement.[78]

The tension here reflects a larger question of authenticity in a society increasingly defined by the constant blending of virtual and material worlds and a culture produced via branding. The interrogation and construction of the Tea Party's identity as a social movement was symptomatic of the inherent ambiguity of a political brand culture. The question that pervaded the Tea Party was not just paranoia about who controlled this movement but also who controlled all of American politics and, by extension, society. In this way, the Tea Party news coverage shows that movements are no longer "Astroturf" or "grass roots" but a blending of branding, media, politics, and activism that depends heavily upon the constantly interchangeable roles people play as both consumer and producer.

Was the Tea Party a "real" movement? Well, the answer to this frequently asked question depends on the definition of a movement. In the sense that the Tea Party mobilized average people around the country with a common sense of politics and values, the answer would be a resounding yes. Numerous articles and books written by scholars and journalists alike have described the meetings, rallies, and events organized by laypeople who identified with the Tea Party brand.[79]

On the other hand, as this book shows, the Tea Party was exceedingly unique in the extent to which it was mobilized by and within existing media and political institutions. The beginning of the Tea Party movement is attributed to a CNBC financial reporter; many of its initial rallies were mobilized through already existing conservative political fundraising organizations; large amounts of its resources and direction came from billionaire funders; and it gained supporters through the on-air event organizing of Fox News hosts and anchors. The Tea Party was a populist brand started, proliferated, and amplified by media and political personalities. In that way, while it was still a veritable political movement with "boots on the ground," it was far from the grass-roots uprising it was often painted to be. It was, as *Philadelphia Daily News* writer and book author Will Bunch describes, "an unabashedly for-profit venture, a right-wing movement®."[80]

Ultimately, the news branding and coverage of the Tea Party exemplified what theorist Guy Debord calls the "society of the spectacle," in which "all that was once directly lived has become mere representation."[81] As a news spectacle, the Tea Party's "realness" did not rely on its actual physical presence—that is, the number of activists or voters who participated. Rather, the performance of activism—and the mass mediation of this performance—made the Tea Party real. Critiques of the Tea Party as "Astroturf" and debates about whether it was organized by lay citizens or skilled political strategists failed to diminish its pervasive portrayal as an energetic uprising of conservatives. The meaning of the Tea Party lay not only in its authenticity as a grass-roots or populist movement, but in its importance as a construct that gained meaning from the mediums that conveyed it to the public that, in turn, understood it as real. As Debord writes:

> The spectacle cannot be set in abstract opposition to concrete social activity, for the dichotomy between reality and image will survive on either side of any such distinction. Thus, the spectacle, though it turns reality on its head, is itself a product of real activity.[82]

In this way, mediated representations of the Tea Party *as a brand* are arguably as significant as the people and brick-and-mortar organizations that helped drive it. More precisely, the media's representation of the Tea Party brand was inextricably bound to its development as an unfolding movement, making the media analysis of the Tea Party news coverage crucial to understanding its formation, success (or failure), and significance.

WHY LOOK AT NEWS NARRATIVES?

Essential to the power of journalism is that it presents itself as an objective reporting of truth and, thus, functions as a medium that defines reality. In cultural studies, scholars who examine news narratives see them as more than an assemblage of reported facts: they are coherently scripted stories that place a specific set of events within a well-defined explanatory frame. Scholars who study news language argue that narratives tell us about our culture; affect public opinions and attitudes, particularly about race; and (re)construct people's conceptions of reality.[83] Zelizer writes that journalism can be understood as a form of culture that "impart[s] value preferences and mediat[es] meanings about how the world does and should work."[84] By examining Tea Party news narratives as both a performance and a representation of different forms of citizenship and belonging, this book aims to better understand the current configuration of American political, social, and journalistic norms.

The main objective of the news is to produce and circulate discourse that depicts what is happening, why it's important, who's involved, and, perhaps most important, how the audience may be implicated. As media scholar Todd Gitlin explains, journalism composes reality, and such compositions enter "into our own deliberations—and more, our understandings of who we are and what we [are] about."[85] The final "factual" product depends upon subjective choices regarding which material complements an existing understanding of social life.[86]

The television age expanded the role of the news media as a primary intermediary between politicians and voters.[87] In the last few decades, politicians have become increasingly reliant on public relations strategies and techniques in their self-promotion and campaigning. While the news media continue their key function in mediating between parties and publics, they have also assumed the roles previously handled by political parties in the "premodern campaign era"—that is, they conduct outreach to voters, facilitate face-to-face interaction with social movements and actors, and "generally provid[e] all the machinery linking voters and candidates."[88] As a result, "campaigning for office and governing are increasingly tailored to the needs and interests of the mass media"[89] and the news media has been transformed into "the major instrument of political communication," largely through marketing practices that target voters like businesses target consumers.[90] The emphasis on branding in politics in recent years is reflected in the way politicians apply consumer logics to political decision-making, often appealing to the "ideal voter," who is seen as "a well-paid consumer whose disposable income goes largely toward product purchases."[91]

The news media's increased influence in politics, and their push to entertain and attract highly fragmented mass audiences, has led to the "permanent convergence of branded entertainment and the formal political system."[92] Consequently, journalism in the last few decades has become "overcome with the charms of celebrity, commercial success and national reach."[93] Elihu Katz notes that, in the modern era, the Habermasian public sphere has transformed into a "political and economic establishment that has armed itself with image makers and spin doctors who dazzle and charm in the name of the legitimacy and prerogatives of their clients."[94]

Neoliberalism—an economic approach that "maximize[s] the role of markets and profit-making and minimize[s] the role of nonmarket institutions" such as the state—is another major factor in the corporatization and depoliticization of American journalism.[95] David Harvey explains neoliberalism as:

> [a] theory of political economic practices which proposes that human well-being can best be advanced by the maximization of entrepreneurial freedoms within an institutional framework characterized by private property rights, individual liberty, free markets, and free trade.[96]

While the neoliberal turn in global economics and politics began during a severe recession in the early 1970s, the scope of commercialization in the twenty-first century is significantly greater and more extensive than in any other historical moment.[97] In more recent years, the neoliberal shift in technology means companies and government have invested more in information management than infrastructure. This has produced media tools that allow people to further individuate their personal content and consumption, and the news media have adapted accordingly.

Neoliberal changes in the economic sector have meant the privatization of previously public resources like schools, land, military, and social services and an increased concentration of wealth among a few ruling elites. Sociopolitically, neoliberalism has bolstered conservative and individualist attitudes and undermined the collective gains of twentieth-century social movements (such as worker protections, civil rights, gender equality, entitlement programs, environmental safety, and so on). Under these commercial pressures, the traditional notion of journalism as a vehicle for maintaining an informed citizenry and serving the public interest is destined to fail— McChesney and Nichols argue that journalism stands in need of government intervention for its survival precisely at a moment in which neoliberalism and austerity measures demand social disinvestment.[98] However, deregulation of news and lax federal oversight have only contributed to these privatized shifts and lack of public service goals.

In the news media, this increased emphasis on privatization and niche markets has led to a type of political journalism focused more on pleasing consumers than informing them.[99] With technology that allows for users to more effectively convey their media preferences, news content has adapted to these predilections. Deindustrialization and automation within Western economies throughout the twentieth century led to precarious work environments, especially for media professionals in a constantly evolving and fragmenting media system.[100] As McChesney and Nichols explain, news media consolidation and staff shrinkage have increased corporate influence on journalism in the form of often unverified and undisclosed public relations materials, an amplified focus on sensationalism and entertainment, and decreased attention to workers and the poor. At the same time, communication between politicians and voters transitioned into less personal interactions and a much heavier reliance on broadcasting mediated images to voters. This led to an increase in political branding and marketing tactics, facilitated by the ease of interactive technologies like email, Twitter, and other social media in which consumers also produce (and circulate) content. In media and politics, these economic shifts and the expansion of the digital landscape have led to a cultural emphasis on producing brands over products.[101] One study of news coverage found that people received more information about political candidates from paid political ads than from news coverage, while news instead focused significantly more on campaign strategy and polling data than on policy.[102]

The rise of branding in political communication has meant a switch in news media's focus from substantive political issues and policies to an emphasis on image, personality, and emotions, especially when reporting on social movements like the Tea Party. Sarah Banet-Weiser argues that the neoliberal emphasis on branding in political communication has changed the essential nature of social change and political movements, so that "profitability, not ethical or collective ideals, forms the moral framework, and consumerism is an efficient route to social change, best achieved through 'free' market force."[103] This media-centric political landscape has only been exacerbated by the introduction of social and digital media, particularly in regard to social movements.[104] Simon Cottle calls the "extent to which protests and demonstrations today have become reflexively conditioned by their pursuit of media attention," and the importance of this coverage, "unprecedented."[105] As such, Banet-Weiser concludes that "we need to rethink those practices that historically have been considered 'progressive' or even 'anticapitalist.'" The Tea Party news narratives clearly show how media coverage of activism and militancy takes shape in a neoliberal framework.

While the news coverage did frequently cover Tea Party policy stances more often than is typical of media reporting on social movements, it was largely described in opposition to certain issues rather than advocating for a particular platform. In part, that was because there was no widespread agreement among tea partiers in regards to key policies.[106] But, I contend that it was also because the Tea Party was conveyed as a brand in opposition to Obama and mentioned in the context of policies that helped support that identity. It was depicted as anti-welfare, anti-immigrant, anti-Obama, anti-tax, anti-government spending, anti-tax increases (when no new federal taxes had been proposed), anti-stimulus (though not anti-business), anti-financial regulation, anti-government control, anti-bureaucracy, anti-socialist, anti-abortion, anti-bailout, and anti-busing. This is why early in the news coverage, *The Wall Street Journal* called the Tea Party's stance on issues "mysterious" and an MSNBC anchor admitted it was "still unclear what teabaggers stand for."[107] It was, as Busby and Cronshaw note, a movement and brand "defined by what it opposed."[108]

Throughout this book, I argue that the coverage of Tea Party policy platform lacked substance and specificity—it was not as though the Tea Party was presented as lacking a policy agenda, instead it was presented as supporting *every* policy for which right-wing American movements have ever advocated. The news coverage of Tea Party policy preferences reflected little ideological coherence and functioned more as a multiple signifier for its brand. The lack of policy specificity was about mooring up affective ties to the Tea Party brand while also avoiding fundamental ruptures in its political mobilization.

This book looks specifically at Tea Party news stories as integral to its brand and "the setting around which individuals weave their own stories."[109] Political strategists increasingly rely on the news media to "sell" their political brands. James Karrh explains that there has been a rise in using the news media for "brand placement," which occurs when brand marketers work with the "creative professionals involved with the programs (such as producers, directors, writers, actors, or set designers) [and] strategically use brands to create particular impressions on the audience."[110] A survey of news stations found that up to 78 percent frequently use externally supplied public relations video (referred to as video news reports, or VNRs) in their own news reports, often airing this material as news without any edits.[111] In terms of costs, using the news media to convey promotional brand messages to a target audience is generally viewed as a less expensive alternative to paid advertising; it also boosts the trustworthiness of a brand.[112]

In particular, the Tea Party news stories highlight how the news media mobilize a political brand identity, buttressing long-standing arguments about the importance of press activism and partisanship in political branding. While most branding literature emphasizes the important function of the news media in publicizing and endorsing promotional material, there are few case studies that examine specifically how news stories track, engage, and participate in the development of political brands. Much of the research on political branding has looked at the news media as a tool by which political strategists can reach voters, rather than discussing the active and explicit way the news media engage in these practices themselves. Though scholars argue that we have entered a new era in contemporary mediated politics through branding and marketing, the role of the media is often downplayed as ancillary in modern political messaging.[113] As this book reveals, however, news outlets do more than passively mediate and reiterate political messaging passed on by strategists—they also intentionally, actively, and explicitly analyze, manage, and participate in the establishment of a political brand. The Tea Party coverage shows not just the strength and interdependence of the conservative media, but the ways in which other media adopt, reiterate, and reify their notions of the political phenomena.

This analysis highlights the specific ways that the press played much more than an instrumental role in relaying the Tea Party brand and shows that distinctions between campaigners, political strategists, and news media professionals are becoming increasingly anachronistic and irrelevant. Ultimately, the Tea Party news coverage shows the impact of brand culture on journalism today:

- a fixation on consumer politics that portrays and depicts citizens as shareholders;
- focusing on profit or money-generating "social movements";
- framing the government as a corporation (with its own economic indicators, not too dissimilar from tracking stocks and bond performances of public corporations); and
- collapsing distinctions between information and opinion-based journalism (and any substantial differences in the influence thereof).

METHODOLOGY

Theoretical Approaches and Rationale

This book functions as a case study: a close examination of early twenty-first-century American culture and politics through its media discourse. As a method, case studies are useful for holistic and in-depth investigations, particularly because they use multiple sources of data and produce findings with real-world anchoring.[114] As Alexander George and Andrew Bennett argue, the "detailed examination of an aspect of a historical episode to develop or test historical explanations that may be generalizable to other events" is beneficial for conceptual validity, deriving new hypotheses, exploring causal mechanisms, and addressing causal complexity—such examinations are "generally strong precisely where statistical methods and formal models are weak."[115]

This book embraces two distinct approaches: (1) discourse analysis and (2) semiotics. Neither prescribes a specific method for research—rather, each provides the theoretical guidelines for a research approach. Discourse is defined broadly as any social text (or set of texts) that can be analyzed that "brings an object into being" through "practices of their production, dissemination, and reception."[116] Scholars who undertake discourse analysis embrace a social constructivist approach to understanding the world.

> In other words, social reality is produced and made real through discourse, and social interactions cannot be fully understood without reference to the discourses that give them meaning.... As discourse analysts, then, our task is to explore the relationship between discourse and reality.[117]

David Machin and Sarah Niblock add that discourse is useful in thinking about branding, "about the kinds of values and identities that are transmitted in news, and what kinds of social relations these favour."[118] Semiotics research adds an additional and necessary component to discourse analysis—it allows for the interpretive understandings and meaning-making that surround certain signs (such as icons, indexes, and symbols).[119] In regard to news discourse specifically, I analyze reports according to various elements highlighted in Teun Van Dijk's proposed structure of a news schemata: background, evaluation, history, expectations, situation, main events, and conclusion.[120]

As a part of this close examination of discourse, I narratively and rhetorically analyze Tea Party news texts. I borrow here from Noha Mellor, who describes narrative analysis of the news as

> the analysis of the news texts as social products produced in specific social and cultural contexts. Narrative here refers to the element of storytelling offered in the news texts and through which people represent themselves and their worlds to themselves and to others.... Thus news becomes a social construction, and repeated telling of familiar stories with familiar themes, actors, and moral lessons, reflecting journalists' view of their world. Such an analysis helps show how the text, as a semiotic code, serves to encourage the readers to act upon the information in the text in particular way.[121]

A close examination of the political institutions and leaders described in Tea Party narratives lends a better understanding of the news media environment and its cultural and epistemological commitments.

Sample

For many people, newsmakers included, it seemed like the Tea Party phenomenon came from nowhere. Out of thousands, likely hundreds of thousands, of political organizations around the country, one particular group of people carrying homemade signs suddenly captivated national attention and debate. I focus my analysis on the first two years of Tea Party news coverage to isolate and understand the enigmatic qualities that propelled the Tea Party's initial emergence into mass media and the political public sphere.

What is the news media? As it is generally deployed, "the media" represent multiple platforms and venues. The term "media" functions as an abstraction that reminds people that what they know is based primarily on what they have been told via information conveyed through an external conduit. The term does not necessarily describe any particular outlet, program, or media platform, but, rather, all of them. For most politicos, "the media" stand in for the way that issues affecting the public are portrayed and conveyed to mass audiences. It includes, of course, more than just professional news outlets. Political institutions and actors depicted in satires, such as "fake news"[122] programs like *The Daily Show* or sketch comedies like *Saturday Night Live*, entertain audiences while conveying important political information. The news media is at the center of these circulations, often providing information and commentary for citizen bloggers and talk-show hosts alike. More generally, the phrase "mainstream media" has come to signal highly profitable and agenda-setting media institutions (in other words, media outlets that have major political, social, and even economic influence and reach).[123]

The news media are different, however, than other segments of the media because they not only report on "what's happening" but also lay authoritative claim to their telling of "the real." National news outlets convey the story of the country, construct its national identity, collectivize its struggles, and highlight its most important moments. I look at four specific media genres that played a major role in constructing and disseminating the Tea Party's news narratives: cable news, broadcast news, print newspapers, and political news blogs.

Geoffrey Baym notes that the "once-authoritative nightly news has been fractured"—yet many scholars continue to study news in traditional ways.[124] Circulation and viewership have fallen in platforms across the board; conclusions drawn only from newspapers or broadcast news programming tell a decreasingly significant and comprehensive story.[125] Since breaking news reports are generated, circulated, and affected by multiple platforms today, a broader analysis of these three genres better elucidates the Tea Party's construction within the changing news landscape and identifies key differences in its reporting. The Tea Party, in particular, was in large part produced by what Cappella and Jamieson call the "echo chamber": the "mass-audience, ideologically coherent, conservative opinion media outlets" that "play both offense and defense in service of conservatives' objectives."[126] In taking note of the "transformed world" of media partisanship Cappella and Jamieson look at radio, print, and cable news programming.[127] I follow their lead in this multi-platform and multi-partisan analysis of news outlets.

I look at content from four mass media platforms from December 1, 2008, to January 1, 2011. These parameters were established by the date of the first print news report on national tea parties (as explained earlier) available Pew data regarding Tea Party coverage, and by the Tea Party's first nationally televised response to President Obama's State of the Union address in 2011.[128] Within each platform, I picked the outlets with the largest audience. The sources were also selected to represent a range of political and ideological spectrums. For print news, I examined the three newspapers with the highest circulations: *USA Today*, *The New York Times*, and *The Wall Street Journal*. In broadcast media, I looked at programs on three cable news networks that market themselves as twenty-four-hour news stations and carry the most viewers: MSNBC, Fox News, and CNN. For comparison to cable news, I also included a non-cable broadcast news program, *ABC World News*. In terms of online sources, I looked at *Politico*, *Newsmax*, and *The Huffington Post*, political news sites with both the highest unique-visitor rankings and substantial original news content.[129] Additionally, I also extended my analysis to content that is mentioned significantly within these narratives or that helps provide further context—for example, a *Chicago Tribune* article helped clarify how the media responded to Rick Santelli's "rant" and is included in that discussion. Through narrative and textual analysis, I examined news reports produced during ten peak periods in the Tea Party news coverage.

Each of these top-performing news outlets can be fairly easily placed along a political and ideological spectrum. Fox News, *The Wall Street*

Journal, and *Newsmax* are all considered right-leaning, conservative outlets. MSNBC, *The New York Times*, and *The Huffington Post* target a progressive audience. *USA Today*, *Politico*, and CNN are arguably the most neutral, compared to their more partisan counterparts. All of the newspapers publish right- and left-leaning columns.

Though I have divided these outlets according to their primary modes of distribution, they are all part of a complex media environment that blurs such boundaries more every day. *Politico* is both a blog and a print newspaper, and does more original reporting than either *Newsmax* or *The Huffington Post*. Based on content alone, its focus on breaking news means it has more in common with *The New York Times* or *USA Today* than the other two political blogs. Though all of the online news sites produce some original content and commentaries, they also take advantage of their digital platform to repost, summarize, and link to stories from print and broadcast news outlets. On cable news, Fox News, CNN, and MSNBC all run and discuss clips of news reports from the other print and online outlets. All of these media groups have an online presence that provides unique content, including multimedia and user-generated stories. The lines between print and digital media are blurry and overlap in intricate ways that defy easy categorization.

Numerous scholars studying the news media have noted trends in media convergence and intertextuality.[130] Disentangling them from one another in the Tea Party narratives is not only difficult but inherently limited. For these reasons, I not only explain how each outlet's Tea Party news narratives diverges from those of the others but also compare the key tropes and themes that surface throughout them all. Within this more generalized approach to analyzing Tea Party news narratives, I take time to highlight points of convergence and divergence.

I focus on journalism as a landscape for analyzing the Tea Party not because of the veracity of news, but because of its societal authority in reflecting and articulating reality. What is a journalist, anyway? While it's been useful to conceive of journalists as professionals or reporters, even these typologies neglect the production dynamic within journalistic spaces, such as the editorial impact of news laborers like production associates or camera operators and the somewhat questionable projection of the title "journalist" onto a person whose primary function may be to read text from a teleprompter. To avoid this quagmire, I point to news institutions as spaces that endow legitimacy, where the authority of truth-telling and the "fourth estate" is bestowed upon all actors (and content) within a news production. As a result, this book engages the early Tea Party coverage in these journalistic spaces comprehensively, with the understanding that all content produced by mainstream news aims to portray, create, and produce social reality.

CONCLUSION

In a headphone culture, the lines between activist and journalist, news and rumor, and new and old media are not only blurred but also made increasingly obsolete. In a media environment constantly filled with information, journalists act and perform as consumers, debating, discussing, engaging and performing politics in their professional work; news reporters and pundits are experts not only in producing news, but in consuming and generating it as well. Within news narratives, the Tea Party was a trope and a vehicle by which various news outlets addressed modern conflicts over race, class, gender, electoral politics, nationhood, and authority after the election of the first African American president. Radical conservatives, old-fashioned feminists, and tech-savvy senior citizens provided new and appealing archetypes that propelled the Tea Party and reestablished traditional political values as still central to an evolving nation. Members of the news media created and facilitated the Tea Party as a brand—a signifier by which they could reflect, examine, decipher, and influence American society and politics as activists, promoters, journalists, consumers, and citizens.

This book demonstrates the inextricable links among discrete discursive domains, arguing for a more holistic and empirically accurate accounting of their rhetorical moves within a brand culture. As Stuart Hall writes,

> Signifiers refer to the systems and concepts of the classification of a culture to its making meaning practices. And those things gain their meaning, not because of what they contain in their essence, but in the shifting relations of difference, which they establish with other concepts and ideas in a signifying field.[131]

Through an intense interrogation of the contexts, stories, and discourse of Tea Party news narratives, this book shows that old divisions between politics, journalism, and personal subjectivities have dissolved, shifting American culture, ideology, news, and identity in unprecedented and important ways.

CHAPTER 2

The Tea Party as Brand

The story of the Tea Party is one of political transition, a narrative that describes how a set of national protests developed into a renewed brand of American conservatism. Unlike with media coverage of other social and political movements, reporters constructed the Tea Party as a brand through diverse political narratives. In its early stages, the Tea Party was described as a type of event (a demonstration or rally) and a burgeoning grass-roots movement. As coverage continued, the Tea Party was also portrayed as a mainstream political party seeking leadership, governance, and institutional status, and a party that challenged traditional Republican and Democratic two-party leadership.

Throughout these early characterizations, journalists conveyed the Tea Party as a successful brand of politics that combined a particular set of social and fiscal values and appealed to a specific subset of Americans. News coverage helped construct the Tea Party as a new conservative identity that reshaped allegiances; represented a particular racial and class demographic; and generated profit, publicity, and political power. In short, news coverage about the Tea Party both tracked and co-constructed the Tea Party brand for a wider media audience. In return, they generated a profit and attracted an audience for themselves while cultivating the Tea Party as a political constituency.

This chapter discusses how the "Tea Party as a Brand" news stories functioned on three levels: first, explicitly reporting on the Tea Party as a lucrative brand; second, emphasizing and, consequently, developing key attributes of the Tea Party brand; and, third, allowing reporters and news pundits to intentionally engage the Tea Party to manage and represent its brand within and across media outlets. The initial sections explain the ways that our contemporary political brand culture provided the requisite environment for the Tea Party's unique development and growth and show that news media outlets understood and described the Tea Party as a political brand. Next, the chapter identifies the ways that professional news journalists, pundits, and commentators actively involved themselves in developing and maintaining the Tea Party brand, including their performances as brand spokespersons and strategists. The final sections describe the two primary brand identities highlighted by the press: the Tea Party as a "social movement" and the Tea Party as a "third political party." The chapter concludes by reviewing some of the implications of the news media's role in constructing the Tea Party brand. Moreover, as most literature that studies the press coverage of social movements focus on left-wing groups and activism, this chapter also provides insight into the news coverage of a right-wing movement.

BACKGROUND

Political Branding through News

On January 25, 2011, nearly three million CNN viewers witnessed an unprecedented live event that reflected a major shift in the ideological underpinnings of contemporary American news culture and electoral politics.[1] After the applause and fanfare of President Barack Obama's second annual State of the Union address and the traditional Republican Party rejoinder, another politician appeared on television screens. Describing the Tea Party as "a dynamic force for good in our national conversation," Minnesota congresswoman Michele Bachmann delivered an official Tea Party rebuttal that promoted limited government, deregulation, and spending cuts. Never before had a national television news station broadcast a third political party's response to a State of the Union address.

The airing of Bachmann's landmark State of the Union response speech exemplifies the mainstream news media's production and promotion of the Tea Party as a function of numerous cultural shifts, including the complementary growth of new media technology, political branding, brand journalism, and the 2008 historic election of the first African American president of the United States. President Barack Obama's primary defeat of Hillary Clinton and victory over the first Republican ticket with a female vice-presidential candidate revitalized a public dialogue on the progress and obstacles that confront professional women. Moreover, his election provoked questions about the contemporary function of race and racism in American culture. By integrating race and gender identities into their production of the Tea Party brand, as I analyze in chapter 3, the news media created a trope by which they could continue the national conversation on feminist progress and the "post-racial" landscape.

Though Bachmann's speech was made available to every media outlet via both a webcast and a pool camera, only CNN chose to air it entirely live on TV.[2] This broadcast was viewed as a ratings-driven decision. Other news outlets, including ABC, CBS, and NBC, instead streamed the speech live on their websites.[3] Bachmann's speech was recorded and distributed by Tea Party HD, a group that explained itself as a web-based network made up of "journalists, producers, shooters and editors...empowered to seek out and produce the unreported news that the main stream media can't tell."[4] That the Tea Party Express, a political action committee (PAC), had collaborated with Tea Party HD to promote Bachmann's speech was itself an example of political branding and brand journalism. As a fundraising group, the PAC previously known as "Our Country Deserves Better" had rebranded itself as "Tea Party Express," raising millions of dollars to support selected conservative political candidates and recruit politicians like Michele Bachmann and Sarah Palin as spokespersons at Tea Party Express events, rallies, and tours.As part of the Tea Party Express promotional campaign, Bachmann's State of the Union rebuttal reflected the targeted use of branding by media makers to connect with voters as a form of political news. Moreover, CNN's broadcast of what Scott Rasmussen and Douglas Schoen call "insurgent media" reflects the news outlet's decision to collaborate, partner with, and benefit from the making of the Tea Party brand.[5]

MSNBC anchor Rachel Maddow openly questioned the ethics of CNN's choice to air the Tea Party response on its primary platform, calling it "a remarkable act of journalistic intervention to elevate, in effect, a group with which they are co-sponsoring a presidential debate to...the level of the major parties in this country."[6] Here, Maddow echoed a larger concern that the news media covering the Tea Party was too invested, financially and politically, in the success of the newly emerged group. The public journalistic clash over the airing of the Tea Party State of the Union speech was a powerful moment—one that captured the complexity, strength, and significance of both the Tea Party brand and its relationship to the news media environment that constructed, framed, and propelled its ascent to public consciousness.

The Tea Party was more than just a news story for the media to report on—it was a *lucrative* news story. In a rare candid moment that highlighted the financial incentive in reporting on the Tea Party, *Washington Post* columnist Dana Milbank in 2011 called for a one-month press moratorium in covering Tea Party leader and former vice-presidential candidate Sarah Palin:

> Palin is a huge source of cheap Web clicks, television ratings and media buzz. If any of us refused to partake of her Facebook candy or declined to use her as blog bait, we would be sending millions of Web surfers, readers, viewers and listeners to our less scrupulous competitors.
>
> The media obsession with Palin began naturally and innocently enough, when the Alaska governor emerged as an electrifying presence on the Republican presidential ticket more than two years ago. But then something unhealthy happened: Though Palin was no longer a candidate, or even a public official, we in the press discovered that the mere mention of her name could vault our stories onto the most-viewed list.... So much so that this former vice presidential candidate gets far more coverage than the actual vice president.[7]

As Milbank explained in a CNN interview, the number of comments and views an article receives functions as a "gauge of how much interest is in that sort of thing" and "drives traffic and ratings."[8] In a similar way, polling data—both informal polls on media websites or formal public opinion studies collected by researchers—can drive news coverage of a topic.[9] Still, although polls showed that most Americans knew very little about the Tea Party and few people attended their political demonstrations, reporters and pundits across media outlets (led by Fox News) heavily covered the Tea Party. On MSNBC, analyst Richard Wolffe argued that reporting on the Tea Party "helped [Fox News] ratings," describing it as "first and foremost a commercial enterprise."[10] And, in *Politico*, Tea Party organizer Eric Odom described the intense Tea Party news coverage on Fox News as a "wise business decision," declaring that "you find out what people want and you give it to them [and] people want news related to the tea parties."[11] As a profitable news narrative, the Tea Party was a political brand that both drew an audience for the news media and allowed them to help mobilize a social movement.

News media reporters and commentators reporting on the Tea Party co-produced its brand by producing stories that examined Tea Party fundraising, identity, values, and branding challenges. In a classic marketing model, a brand's value is measured by seven factors:

1. leadership: ability to influence the market,
2. stability: ability to maintain a consumer franchise,

3. market: vulnerability of market demand to changes in tastes or technology,
4. international scope: cross-national/cultural potential,
5. trend: long-term appeal to consumers,
6. support: strength of communications, and
7. protection: security of the brand owners' legal or property rights.[12]

Much of the Tea Party press coverage paid close attention to these specific key brand value factors, emphasizing the brand's importance as a political asset instead of its usefulness to the public, relevance to the general electorate's desires, or rhetorical veracity. Again, these reports went beyond simply providing facts and information about the Tea Party's origins, goals, policies, leadership, and activities; rather, the news media raised the volume by emphasizing the Tea Party persona and brand, solidifying, bolstering, and publicizing its identity through news narratives. At the same time, they also used the Tea Party brand to establish their own brand identities and ideological underpinnings. By dedicating airtime and profuse writing on the meaning, significance, and symbolism of the Tea Party, the journalists not only discussed the Tea Party brand but also became its cocreators. As the news stories helped create, shield, and publicize the Tea Party brand, the media inherently became characters in their own descriptions of the Tea Party's rise.

POLITICAL BRANDING AND THE NEWS MEDIA

The defining attribute of a brand is its emphasis on developing distinctive "sentimental," or affective, connections with consumers rather than simply providing them with information about a product's quality, function, or use.[13] For example, "human personality traits associated with Harley-Davidson might be described as macho, American, patriotism, and freedom."[14] In other words, branding is about both "creating relationships with customers that cultivate an emotional preference for your brand" through particular affective characteristics *and* differentiating a product from its competitor (for example, ranchers who use literal brands to mark their cattle).[15] While the term "brand" became used primarily in marketing and sales research for selling and labeling products throughout the twentieth century, in recent decades campaigns and parties have turned to political branding to successfully cultivate brand identities using the news media.[16] Branding engages citizens as consumers—it frames citizenship through consumption, producing rhetoric that focuses on affluence and choice, instead of "hard" political issues like rules, regulation, finances, and oversight.

Branding tactics have become popular in contemporary political contests because the increased legislative and ideological similarity between Democrats and Republicans has produced a growing need to distinguish between the two factions. As political parties have constructed more moderate and universally appealing policy agendas, they have become more like one another and require more effort to set themselves apart.[17] In the United States, political parties heavily rely on financial support from corporations and the super wealthy, which has spurred corporate-friendly messaging and regulation by both political parties.[18] Moreover, the desire to target and attract "floating" or undecided voters has also transformed each party to tend towards "non-ideological 'catch-all' parties."[19] In this landscape of conformist and converging politics, political actors depend heavily on the news media to develop brand identities and maintain voter loyalty.

The contemporary branding model is part of an era of widespread communication technologies, an increasingly self-interested press, and political campaigns that are capital intensive, rely on fewer volunteers, and engage in much less face-to-face communication with voters.[20] As Robert McChesney explains, while branding, corporate influence, and commercialism have existed throughout the United States's political history, "there is an enormous difference between the degree and nature... in what is emerging today [at] the dawn of the twenty-first century."[21] Margaret Scammell argues that in today's "consumerized paradigm of political communication," there is a distinct shift from the older model of a permanent campaign to the more recent model of a "brand concept."[22] While elected leaders in the permanent campaign model prioritized the constant courting of public opinion and approval when making policy decisions (i.e., "horse-race" politics), elected leaders in the branding model target specific groups of voters and deemphasize substantive, issue-based decision-making.[23]

In other words, political branding (also called political marketing) is the process by which political actors apply consumerism's operational logics to electoral engagement and use intangible values and cultural authority to shape voters' tastes and desires, create emotional connections, generate profit, and yield voter allegiance. By cultivating a brand identity, political parties and actors can standardize their messaging, influence citizen preferences for policies and leaders, attract donors, and enhance political power—all through symbolic and cognitive shortcuts that make a brand's meaning readily accessible to a citizen-consumer. Eleanora Pasotti writes that a citizen-consumer can use a political brand to express his or her identity as a form of political participation. For example,

> The self-expressive need to be hip and environmentally conscious can be satisfied by owning a hybrid vehicle or by voting for a Green Party candidate, while the self-expressive need to be part of the establishment can be satisfied by driving a Lexus or voting for a member of the business elite.[24]

Branding, then, is more than mere commodification (turning social and cultural experiences into objects to be bought and sold). Political branding aims to satisfy the emotional needs of citizens more than their functional ones and "transforms the consumption experience" rather than the consumption outcome.[25] For example, while President Barack Obama bolstered his brand among Latinos by appointing the first Latina to the Supreme Court, he simultaneously oversaw an intensification of Bush-era immigration measures and deported immigrants at a faster rate than any other US president.[26] Similarly, while President Bill Clinton was popularly branded as the "first Black president," his administration was responsible for unprecedented cuts to welfare programs, harsher crime sentencing, and regulations that led to an explosion in the growth of mass incarceration and poverty, disproportionately harming African American communities.

Since the use of value-based words—terms of persuasion that "trigger a value judgment" and aim to arouse emotions, such as *bravery, comfort, barbarian,* or *dictator*[27]—phrases, and symbols to emotionally connect with a public is vital to the production of a brand, the media plays a crucial role in a brand's success and development. As Natalia Yannopoulou, Epaminondas Koronis, and Richard Elliott put it, "The media constitutes a third party, which influences the trusted relationship between consumers and brands."[28] Through this process, the media creates vital "brand awareness," which is a consumer's recognition of a brand based on specific associations.[29] The stories that foster a brand's emotional connection to consumer-citizens are primarily conveyed through media narratives.[30] Indeed, "the process of branding impacts the way we understand who we are, how we organize the world, [and] what stories we tell ourselves about ourselves."[31]

Thus, like traditional business marketing, political branding occurs through "the proliferation of emotional messages across various media through the use of sound bites, and talking points, and repetition/saturation strategies within each medium."[32] Politicians cultivate brand identities that generate group feelings of belonging and transcend traditional political divisions. For example, Pasotti's study of political branding among city mayors found that they eschewed party politics in favor of generating support around a carefully constructed personality.[33] These mayors built a collective sense of identity for the city and its residents through annual celebrations and public spectacles that created loyalty toward their political brand, while deploying neoliberal and pro-business policies that often undermined these same constituencies—in other words, affect over policy. This emotional connection to a branded object, concept, or person is called "sentimental utility."[34] According to Schneider, sentimental utility results from "a feeling of solidarity with a group of like-minded voters in the sense of a community *of* values or a feeling of identification."[35]

Research has shown that news media exposure and media representatives strongly shape political brand perception. One study showed that in a diverse media environment, a person's preference for news is a better indicator of political knowledge than even their education.[36] News reports gather and summarize the political information that citizens (who tend to have low involvement in party politics) need in making voting decisions.[37] Moreover, not only does the news media contribute to what people know about politics, they shape what people *believe* to be true about politics and politicians. Information communicated by the news media has been shown to significantly impact the trust people place in a brand's reputation, the loyalty they have to that brand, and the decisions they make about it.[38] Media outlets have become "direct participants in the creation of partisan information and not mere conduits of it," but they are still primarily seen as only vehicles by which politicos convey political messages to the public.[39]

The placement of public relations material in news broadcasts has been shown to increase the recognition of branded content through the perceived trustworthiness of the news source.[40] Brand placement in the news media has more persuasive impact than similarly constructed advertisements, and brands that are paired with media characters are particularly effective at connecting to an audience. For example, video news releases (VNRs), or what *TV Guide* once called "fake news," are promotional content used in a news story that are often narrated, edited, and aired by a television news station without explicitly identifying it as paid or marketed content. These types of unlabeled promotional content embedded in news run rampant throughout news content. In 2001, Mark D. Harmon and Candace White found that fifteen VNRs alone aired at least 4,245 times on news programs across the country.[41]

Other forms of implicit news media advertising have been called "sponsored content" or "native advertising," occasionally causing controversy once uncovered (as in an incident involving a Church of Scientology ad featured ambiguously on the website of *The Atlantic* in 2013).[42] By reporting, repeating, sharing, or repackaging carefully stitched political messaging (such as press releases, social media announcements, and speeches), the news media function as a highly trusted and credible mass media platform for promoting political brands, while also helping to co-produce and reposition that brand in the public spotlight. As Republican presidential hopeful Donald Trump frankly explained about his campaign to news anchor Chuck Todd in a 2016 *Meet the Press* interview, "Hey look, I'm 50 million dollars under budget ... I've spent very little, because I haven't had to—because people like you put me on all the time, what do I take the commercial for?"[43]

Like political strategists and candidates, news outlets also became more reliant on branding techniques in messaging and audience outreach for themselves. Scholars David Machin and Sarah Niblock describe in detail the way branding and marketing reshaped the substance and format of news.[44] Publishers have redesigned newspaper layouts to attract advertisers and target niche consumers, while reducing reporting staff and relying more heavily on materials produced by publicists for news content. On radio, newscasters tailor and redistribute the same news stories to reach specific consumers, adapting the content to fit that audience's particular lifestyles, beliefs, and opinions. In this way, the news media has adopted branding as a

> process of associating the right kinds of discourses with the appropriate set of consumer process preferences. This allows consumers to recognize themselves in the product, or to align themselves with the values connoted by the product.[45]

In this way, news is considered a product by media outlets, rather than a public service or a form of governmental oversight. Media makers treat news like a commodity or product that requires a brand to sell goods, make sentimental connections to audiences, and generate preferences for their specific content. In other words, media corporations brand news outlets—and, particularly in cable and print news, these brands correspond with ideological and political differences to reach progressive or conservative audiences. As conservative pollsters Rasmussen and Schoen put it, the goal of the contemporary news media is to "generate compelling programming from the passions that roil American politics."[46]

Fueled by conservative media and activism, Tea Party supporters conveyed the Tea Party brand to the press. But, in differentiating themselves from one another by promoting, celebrating, debating, or criticizing the Tea Party, news media outlets also facilitated and co-created the Tea Party brand. Not only has the news media learned to use branding techniques to shape its content, in the process they also (often unintentionally) develop, draw attention to, and provide affective meaning to key political brands like the Tea Party.

Through brand journalism, media organizations frame a brand's stories with the use of its own correspondents, production teams, editors, and publications.[47] This type of reporting is not limited to positive framings of the brand—it can also involve placing a brand in news stories as part of an importantevent, incident, or topic for consumers as a way of providing exclusive insider access (for example, stories about professional football on NFL. com).[48] By participating as brand journalists, the news media helped create the Tea Party as a brand through narratives that emphasized emotion, differentiation, profitability, brand attributes, strategy, and promotion.

In helping the Tea Party rise in national attention, the news media actively mobilized and constructed the Tea Party brand by explicitly discussing its brand strategy, describing its values, serving as a platform for Tea Party messaging and brand promotion, attributing human emotional characteristics to the Tea Party brand, identifying and serving as its spokespersons, and participating in brand placement through advertising, appearances, and news coverage. According to Theda Skocpol and Vanessa Williamson, the conservative media was one of the "main forces" that orchestrated the Tea Party.[49] A number of traits distinctive to the Tea Party brand become clear through the news stories. While overt Tea Party branding tactics were most apparent among the conservative media, media outlets across the political spectrum also manifested the Tea Party brand. Ultimately, the Tea Party news stories capture the roles the news media play in contemporary political brand culture.

NEWS PROFESSIONALS BRANDING THE TEA PARTY

A journalist on the job started the modern Tea Party and contributed to the early development of its brand. In eliciting cheers from the traders who surrounded him, CNBC business reporter Rick Santelli's 2009 impromptu tirade transformed him into a Tea Party leader even as he was doing professional journalistic work. His live on-air news report from the Chicago Board of Trade, delivered as a diatribe against President Obama's newly minted administration, earned shocked responses from news reporters Becky Quick and Wilbur Ross who were talking to him from the studio:

QUICK: Wow. You get people fired up.

SANTELLI: We're thinking of having a Chicago Tea Party in July. All you capitalists that want to show up to Lake Michigan, I'm going to start organizing.

QUICK: What are you dumping in this time?

SANTELLI: We're going to be dumping in some derivative securities. What do you think about that?

WILBUR ROSS, in studio: Mayor Daley is marshaling the police right now.

. . .

ROSS: Rick, I congratulate you on your new incarnation as a revolutionary leader.

SANTELLI: Somebody needs one. I'll tell you what, if you read our Founding Fathers, people like Benjamin Franklin and Jefferson, what we're doing in this country now is making them roll over in their graves.[50]

Santelli's combination of Founding Father historicism, anti-Obama sentiment, explicit anger, and passionate conservatism provided the foundational attributes of the Tea Party brand. His speech quickly found a wide audience among those paying attention to conservative news, fueled by numerous postings on conservative blogs and its record-breaking popularity on the CNBC website.

In a lengthy press conference the following day, White House press secretary Robert Gibbs drew even more attention to Santelli's "rant heard 'round the world" by disputing the reporter's assertions and extending an invitation to join him for a cup of "decaf" coffee—as opposed, of course, to tea.[51] Conservative activists who later became Tea Party organizers and leaders referenced Santelli's speech, and its swift circulation and publicity, as inspiration for their subsequent participation.[52] Within hours of Santelli's outburst, dozens of Tea Party websites and Santelli fan clubs had formed.[53] When the Tax Day Tea Party protests began in April, Santelli admitted that he was "pretty proud" of the nationwide events.[54] For many others, including Republican strategists and former White House staffer Karl Rove, Santelli was the "father" of the Tea Party.[55] In one illustrative case, scholars of the major conservative think tank and advocacy group FreedomWorks posted a photo of Rick Santelli on its website, asking, "Are you with Rick? We are."[56]

In addition to Santelli, Fox News was also discussed as a key player in the production of the Tea Party brand, its advocacy, support of, and collaboration with the Tea Party was repeatedly mentioned across news outlets. Through various reports, events, segments, activism, on-air panels, advising, and media provocation, Fox News explicitly branded the Tea Party. A *New York Times* story included a Jon Stewart quote that described Fox News as the Tea Party's "media arm."[57] In *Politico*, a reporter noted that

Fox News was hosting a "virtual tea party" on its website and described show hosts directing viewers to Tea Party rallies, concluding:

> Nobody's covering the tea parties quite like Fox—and that's prompting critics and cable news competitors to say that the network is blurring the line between journalism and advocacy.
>
> "Fox appears to be promoting these events at the same time it is presenting them in a way that looks like reporting," said Stephen Burgard, director of Northeastern University's School of Journalism. Burgard called the practice "pseudo-journalism."[58]

In a later story, *Politico* also described an incident in which a Fox News producer "rallied a crowd to cheer" during a Tea Party protest. Fox later blamed this action on a "young, relatively inexperienced associate producer" and claimed to discipline her.[59] Still, as Trost and Rosenthal found, Fox News "spared no effort in helping organize and publicize Tea Party events."[60]

In another widely discussed example, Fox News host Sean Hannity was advertised as a headliner for a Tea Party event that charged admission, and he planned to broadcast his show there. When Fox News executives cancelled what *The Huffington Post* referred to as Hannity's "starring role appearance in a tea party rally," they explained that the news company had never agreed to "allow Cincinnati tea party organizers to use Sean Hannity's television program to profit from broadcasting his show."[61] *The New York Times* wrote that this incident showed that Fox News leadership was sensitive to concerns over the network's "perceived closeness to the antigovernment Tea Party movement."[62] News reports on the Tea Party also frequently mentioned the participation of Fox News hosts and paid commentators, such as Neil Cavuto and Sarah Palin, as speakers, leaders, and supporters of the Tea Party.

More than simply promoting the Tea Party on its network, Fox News also helped manage the Tea Party brand's publicity in the news. In one of the most striking and unprecedented instances, Fox targeted its "media war" enemies in a newspaper. In response to the perceived lack of attention given to a Tea Party event organized by former Fox News anchor Glenn Beck, Fox News took out a full-page ad in *The Washington Post* accusing ABC, CBS, MSNBC, and CNN of "miss[ing] the story." "We cover all the news," the ad claimed (Figure 2.1).

The Huffington Post and *Politico* reported on the ad as evidence of Fox News's close relationship with the Tea Party and argued that the networks had, in fact, covered the event. CNN reporters responded to the charge on air and showed clips proving that they were at the Tea Party rally:

Figure 2.1. Fox News ad in *The Washington Post* on September 18, 2009.

We usually like to stay out of the way when certain cable channels take cheap shots, but, tonight, we're standing up to a flat-out lie being told about CNN by the FOX News Channel....I was watching on Saturday, our team was all over that story. We had four reporters there. There were two live trucks and more than a dozen staffers. Heck, we even sent the CNN Express.

Saturday's march was a major news event. CNN covers major news events. It's what we do. It's why we're here. So to think that we'd "miss something that big," well, that's just ridiculous. Let me also add, the FOX ad sends a false message that we at CNN are not listening to a whole lot of people out there, that their views somehow don't matter to us, and that their events don't merit our attention. And that's also just not true.[63]

In this case, Fox News used advertising space in a separate news outlet to launch accusations against another news competitor, ultimately provoking additional coverage of Tea Party protests and generating wide consensus among news groups that the Tea Party was "major" news. More than that, by deeming it inherently newsworthy, it was also bolstering the value of the Tea Party brand and producing the publicity that Fox aimed to elicit. This level of active news media engagement in a social movement is unprecedented, as was the level to which outlets and reporters targeted their reports not just at their audience but also at each other. While Fox intentionally branded the Tea Party, other outlets contributed to the affective and symbolic cultivation of its brand identity in reporting that emphasized its spectacular attributes and context over more substantive goals.

In other outlets, the coverage of the Tea Party more implicitly branded the Tea Party, by providing editorial space and news reports that concretized its brand identity (as discussed more in chapter 4). In the news coverage of the Tea Party, the management and protection of the Tea Party brand functioned as both a topic and practice.

Concern about counter-branding from other news media outlets, especially those with a more liberal ideological positioning such as MSNBC, was a major part of the news coverage related to the Tea Party. As discussed more in the next chapter, Fox News anchor Bill O'Reilly, in particular, accused other news organizations of mounting accusations of Tea Party racism as an effort to counter-brand the Tea Party and "keep people from joining up."[64] One anchor said that the president of the NAACP was "on a mission to brand the Tea Party as racist."[65] Reporters also described (and expressed) anxieties that the Tea Party brand—with its emotional connections and far-right conservative values—could alienate more moderately right-leaning voters and sponsors. Through counter-branding, defined as "circulating organized narratives to counter the master story by appropriating and reversing it," reporters who disagreed with the Tea Party were able to use the working-class aspect of the Tea Party brand to paint them as racists and buffoons.[66] Counter-branding was a key component in the way news outlets helped establish the Tea Party brand, moving beyond the identity conveyed by supporters and activists.

Across all of the outlets, media professionals not only offered the Tea Party legitimacy through regular coverage but also functioned as sources and spokespersons that publicized it. On cable news, show hosts frequently interviewed journalists as political experts and insiders. These guests not only reported on current political events but also used them to explain the political and media landscape, their feelings about it, and its symbolic meaning (thus, articulating and clarifying the Tea Party brand). Mark Williams, a conservative radio host and chairman of the Tea Party Express (the most powerful and profitable Tea Party PAC), was interviewed as a Tea Party spokesperson in multiple media outlets, including CNN, Fox News, and MSNBC. Fox News host and Tea Party Express spokesperson Sarah Palin functioned as a major brand promoter and publicist in news stories about national bus tours, endorsements of Tea Party candidates, and fundraising. Dana Loesch, a St. Louis radio host, was also interviewed on Fox News as a Tea Party leader. On political blogs, media experts, personalities, and reporters were frequent contributors or sources. Articles in *The Huffington Post*, for example, quoted a CNN reporter and other Fox News hosts acting as Tea Party promoters; one article asked, "Guys, what happened to we're-just-covering-the-events?"[67] The bulk of another *Huffington Post* piece featured the entire transcript of an interview with Tea Party Federation leader Mark Skoda, positively portraying the group's values and ideas.[68] In this way, easy access to media venues amplified the Tea Party brand and regularly blurred the boundaries separating political analyst, party strategist, reporter, and journalist.

Significantly, Matt Guardino and Dean Snyder's study of Tea Party news coverage in cable news was overall favorable to the populist phenomena, "despite the Tea Party's radically conservative economic ideology."[69] Specifically, they argue that the movement's appeal to a key advertising demographic—older, white, middle class, and more affluent viewers—fueled its coverage on CNN. According to them, CNN covered the Tea Party favorably because of the "logic of advertising" and "a media policy regime which privileges profits and consumerism over public service and democratic citizenship."[70] Arguably, such influences appealed to other networks and news sources as well.

Through their reports, news outlets also selected key Tea Party brand spokespersons to convey Tea Party messaging points, as is typical of decentralized social movements.[71] Classic social movements that receive news coverage have been typically led by people who function as formal leaders in established organizations that often have a hierarchical bureaucratic structure.[72] Since no single entity claimed credit for organizing the Tea Party protests, news pundits and reporters were able to argue that the Tea Party was a "leaderless," "grass-roots," or "bottom-up" movement of normal Americans. In *The Wall Street Journal*, a guest columnist explained:

> The tea-party protest movement is organizing itself, on its own behalf. Some existing organizations, like Newt Gingrich's American Solutions and FreedomWorks, have gotten involved. But they're involved as followers and facilitators, not leaders. The leaders are appearing on their own, and reaching out to others through blogs, Facebook, chat boards and alternative media.[73]

Although the Tea Party was described as leaderless, reporters credited various politicians and organizers as leaders and consulted them as sources. For example, former congressman Dick Armey was identified as both the chairman of FreedomWorks and a major financial Tea Party sponsor, fundraiser, organizer, and strategist. He was given a platform to promote Tea Party messaging in various television news interviews, and even a *New York Times* op-ed. As a result, the Tea Party movement's goals and aims were largely articulated by the news media and by whomever an outlet selected as a spokesperson. While studies show that in leftist social movements, journalists often select deviant or bizarre members to represent them on the national stage,[74] the media chose a more conventional establishment figure in Armey and others.

For social movements, media coverage is particularly vital for raising a movement's public profile; validating its importance; and showing activists how others view the movement, understand its causes, and evaluate their actions, beliefs, and behaviors.[75] Though it is generally difficult for social movements to access media visibility and coverage,[76] usually only succeeding when there are reports of violence and disruption, the Tea Party received regular news coverage that far outpaced the number of participants at events and (based on the content of the reporting) required little to no spectacle on behalf of those present to draw attention. Instead, due to its overwhelming support among established and well-known politicians and media outlets, such as Fox News, it was able to gain regular publicity, access, and support for its events throughout the media: television, print, and online news. More than that, the media, and conservative media in particular, were also able to shape, articulate, and cultivate the Tea Party brand.

Essential to understanding the media's role in branding the Tea Party is recognizing branding as a framing process. As discussed in chapter 1, framing is a way of selecting certain key aspects of an issue, event, or actor for storytelling in a way that communicates clear ideologies, beliefs, and associations.[77] As a specific market-oriented subset of framing, branding emphasizes commercial, consumerist, and neoliberal logics in storytelling. That is, the news media branded the Tea Party not by merely reporting on it or framing it in media narratives, but by overwhelmingly depicting it through a particular set of narratives that emphasized branding, profit, image management, and evaluative marketing approaches (like polling data) as key to Tea Party storytelling.

As it was deemed a "leaderless" movement, the news media had a major role in advancing the recognition, messaging, and growth of the Tea Party brand through news narratives. As described more in chapter 4, news outlets and reporters frequently reported on one another as Tea Party promoters, sponsors, supporters, and even strategists, and debated these roles within their coverage. In the Tea Party news coverage, reporters repeatedly drew attention to specific Tea Party values and qualities. These recurring themes articulated the meaning of Tea Party identity through polls, interviews, and coverage of Tea Party rallies and signs. Through stories that emphasized anger, constitutionalist fervor, and antigovernment, anti-media, and anti-Obama sentiment and linked the Tea Party's power to its financial value and ability to raise money, the Tea Party brand was born.[78] Throughout news reports, media outlets clearly described and conveyed the Tea Party as a political brand, and reporters explicitly referred to the Tea Party as a brand. On Fox News, an anchor complained about the actions of some tea partiers and said, "Every time a Tea Party person threatens to overthrow the government or other nonsense, the brand gets hammered."[79] In *The New York Times*, a candidate was mentioned as being known for his own "brand" of Tea Party politics.[80] *The Huffington Post* described the "Tea Party brand of right-of-the-GOP conservatism" and discussed "the ability of some smart politicians to brand themselves as 'Tea Party' candidates."[81]

Some members of the news media reported specifically on the Tea Party as a massive branding and marketing scheme. A *Wall Street Journal* editorial contended that the Tea Party movement in Pennsylvania was just the repackaging of an already-existing conservative initiative called "Operation Clean Sweep":

The Keystone State's tea party movement actually began several years ago...when our state legislature rammed through a pay hike for its members and the state's judiciary....Editorial pages and radio show hosts denounced the pay hike while voters took to the streets of their capital city with placards and bullhorns and giant inflatable pigs. The movement became broadly known as Operation Clean Sweep.

Over the past year, Operation Clean Sweep rebranded itself into a tea party movement. But it's still the same people.[82]

Other news organizations similarly described the rise of Tea Party PACs as taking advantage of the financial profits generated by the Tea Party brand. An MSNBC anchor reported that one Republican PAC had added "Tea Party" to its name and "stole[n] the brand name to make money."[83] A report in USA Today specifically noted the expansion of the Tea Party's branding effort:

A dozen political action committees bearing the Tea Party name have been created since July 2009, filings with the Federal Election Commission show. Another 24 fundraising committees have been established with the IRS. Those groups, known as 527s for the section of the tax code under which they operate, can raise unlimited amounts of money for their political activity. Political action committees can collect no more than $5,000 a year from an individual.[84]

The Tea Party Express, a particularly powerful PAC, was frequently mentioned in terms of the money and influence it accrued by using the Tea Party label. The USA Today article also discussed the Tea Party Express as a clear example of the Tea Party's profitability, marketing, and branding:

The Tea Party-affiliated PAC raising the most—$4.4 million so far in this election cycle—is not led by political upstarts. Its top officials are veterans of GOP politics, including Sal Russo, a Sacramento-based consultant who was an aide to Ronald Reagan when he was California governor. The group was organized in 2008, as Our Country Deserves Better PAC to oppose Obama's presidential campaign before launching national "Tea Party Express" bus tours and adding TeaPartyExpress.org to its name.

Russo is the PAC's chief strategist and nearly $1.5 million—or about a third of the PAC's spending through the end of April—was paid to Russo's firm, Russo Marsh, and an affiliated company, according to campaign filings compiled by CQ MoneyLine.[85]

Politico also noted that the Tea Party Express had "made a conscious decision to adopt tea party branding for its PAC" to give itself a "boost" in the midterm elections.[86] A *USA Today* article reported on Tea Party groups in Florida filing lawsuits against one another over the right to use the name.[87]

The news stories additionally described the Tea Party as a brand through narratives about its profitability. Reports described the Tea Party as a money-making scheme and a way of attracting donations from social and fiscal conservatives. ABC reported concerns that a Tea Party convention had been "set up for profit."[88] In *The Huffington Post*, a blogger wrote that "big bucks are pouring into the tea party movement," including online sales of Tea Party merchandise and "500 dollar-a-plate" fundraisers.[89] When the Tea Party failed to reach its financial goals, a *Politico* reporter published an article titled "Tea Party's Growing Money Problem."[90] *USA Today* quoted "fake news" comedian Stephen Colbert on joking about Tea Party event marketing:

> [Sarah Palin] was in Nashville giving a rousing speech to a for-profit...national Tea Party convention. A little-known fact, folks. The Boston Tea Party also turned a profit. Hence their slogan: "No taxation without representation. But there is a two-drink minimum."[91]

To rebut these ideas, Sarah Palin wrote an op-ed column in *USA Today* denying that the Tea Party was "a commercial endeavor."[92]

News coverage from progressive outlets particularly reinforced this profit-driven brand narrative by describing the Tea Party as a manufactured rhetorical enterprise backed by the wealthy and powerful. A *New York Times* article reported that two billionaire brothers had organized a "secret network" of "ultrawealthy" donors and business people to provide money to "[help] Tea Party groups set up."[93] On MSNBC, an anchor argued that "corporate sponsors" had been offering "5,000 dollars in prizes for the best promotion of Tea Bagging Day."[94] A blogger at *The Huffington Post* said the Tea Party would not criticize Wall Street during the economic recession because it was "manipulated by right-wing organizations funded by corporate America" and its members were "ignorant dupes being led by the nose by their corporate overlords."[95] An earlier piece on *The Huffington Post* suggested that the Tea Party was a profitable political invention, and encouraged readers "to take a look behind the [Tea Party's] curtain— where Dick Armey is laughing and counting his cash."[96]

Additionally, news stories described Tea Party branding as a political tool in electoral contests. *The New York Times* detailed the Northern Illinois Patriots as a "Tea Party group," and *Politico* reported on a candidate with "few ties to the tea party movement" running with the Tea Party name. In Florida, a Democrat tried to weaken a Republican challenger by sending out mailings to "conservative voters labeling [one candidate] as 'the Tea Party candidate' and [his opponent] as a 'raging liberal' by comparison."[97]

Through news coverage that explicitly described the Tea Party as a brand, the media made clear their use of branding as a key framing discourse in Tea Party reporting. Though the media understood the Tea Party was a brand, they continued to talk about it as a social movement and political party, circulating and proliferating attention on these brand identities that helped legitimize the attention and influence they gave the Tea Party.

TEA PARTY BRAND IDENTITY

Similar to previous American white populist movements, Tea Party news stories frequently focused on anger as a key theme. As with traditional marketing, this emphasis on anger as an important Tea Party trait attached human characteristics to the diffuse group and helped establish the Tea Party brand's emotional connection with citizens.[98] A *Wall Street Journal* guest columnist called the Tea Party a "post-partisan expression of outrage."[99] In other outlets, the Tea Party was "mad," "angry," and full of "rage."[100] Other reporters described Tea Party activists as "mad-as-hellers" who were expressing "moral outrage," and the collective group as the "mad-as-hell party."[101] Anger was described as the Tea Party's "motivation" and source of "energy," an energy that was "contagious" (suggesting that its growth was inevitable).[102] Significantly, the targets of Tea Party fury were mentioned far less frequently than the anger itself—in the new stories anger functioned more as a branding mechanism than an explanatory detail. One news story even mentioned a Nevada Tea Party group that had named itself as "Anger is Brewing."[103] The attention given to anger as a key character in Tea Party news stories prioritized the group's affective qualities over its strategic goals and actions.

One key recipient of Tea Party ire that was mentioned in the press was President Obama. The Tea Party brand was decidedly portrayed as "anti-Obama," as evidenced in Santelli's seminal tirade. President Obama was mentioned so often as a target of the Tea Party's anger that one MSNBC guest referred to the Tea Party as "Obama derangement syndrome."[104] A *Huffington Post* blogger argued that the movement was clearly "anti-Obama" after "judging from the crowds and the signs they waved."[105] The *Huffington Post* also illustrated this anti-Obama sentiment with a slideshow that featured Tea Party signs reading: "Obama's Plan: White Slavery," "The American Taxpayers are the Jews for Obama's Ovens," and "No Taxes.

Obama Loves Taxes. Bankrupt USA. Loves Baby Killing." One particularly offensive sign included a drawing of Obama bowing in front of a man dressed in stereotypical Middle Eastern clothing, and read "Obama was NOT bowing. He was sucking Saudi Jewels."[106]

A *Wall Street Journal* columnist explained the political function of anger and its disconnection from President Obama:

> But whatever our politics, we don't want people to be free from anger alto-gether. We want them to be moved by injustice to act, and to do so with a vigor tinged every now and then with righteous wrath. Which is why President Obama's enthusiasts have been so distressed at his seeming inability to rage. Ever since BP started glopping up the Gulf of Mexico with crude, they've been begging him to drop his cool demeanor, to exhibit some anger.[107]

This quote in particular highlights the branding process in the media and the accentuation of emotional and affective Tea Party qualities in news stories. As President Obama's personal political brand conveyed him as calm and collected, it seemed fitting that the brand of his Tea Party adversaries was premised upon anger and strong emotions.

Former president Ronald Reagan was also a recurring figure mentioned in Tea Party news texts, a gesture to 1980s Republican populism. In many ways, Reagan was deployed as a brand in this coverage. This is not surprising since, as Kenneth Cosgrove notes, "the brand built around Reagan has transformed how conservatives sell themselves to the public, largely due to his humble small-town origins, media savviness, and keen oratorical skills that played well to populist sensibilities."[108] America's last major economic recession occurred during his tenure, and Reagan's response of anti-taxation policy and austerity, bolstered by white populism, also offered a clear historical comparison to Obama's response to the 2008 Great Recession. *Newsmax* wrote that there are "many parallels between the modern tea party movement and forces that brought Reagan to power" and that tea partiers are "on the verge of triggering another 'Reagan revolution.'"[109] One *Wall Street Journal* article compared the presidencies of Ronald Reagan and Barack Obama to contextualize the Tea Party.[110] In this and similar stories, Reagan represented the age of successful white conservatism—an aspirational model for tea partiers, and an exemplar for the Republican Party.

Journalists consistently used language that described the Tea Party as new, reinforcing novelty as a central Tea Party brand characteristic that conveyed authenticity. They frequently cast protestors as "first-time" activists, depicted Tea Party candidates as "inexperienced" in politics, and described the Tea Party as trendy and "fashionable." A guest on Fox News referred to the Tea Party as the "Republican renaissance."[111] One *Wall Street Journal* guest columnist wrote: "What's most striking about the tea-party movement is that most of the organizers haven't ever organized, or even participated, in a protest rally before."[112] Similarly, Senator John Cornyn referred to Tea Party activists as "relative newcomers to the political process."[113] A *Huffington Post* blogger wrote that the Tea Party was "a new group of the dispossessed [which has] taken to the streets."[114] In a *USA Today* article, a conservative consultant dismissed the comparatively small numbers of Tea Party turnout by arguing that "the strength of the Tea Party movement is the emergence of people not known for street action."[115] *The Huffington Post* also quoted Sarah Palin, who said the Tea Party was a "fresh, young and fragile" movement that was "the future of American politics."[116]

In cable news, a CNN guest and *Politico* columnist explained that a lack of qualifications was actually a Tea Party selling point in the current political landscape:

> I think inexperience [of Tea Party candidates] is clearly an advantage, so they're saying change and don't worry whether they can balance the books, they're going to get in the way of Obama's agenda. That's what they've been selling.[117]

Many stories contrasted the Tea Party with the political "establishment," which situated the Tea Party as an entirely new political actor responding to historical political divisions. Frequently, the Tea Party was also described as a source of "energy" for conservative politicians that could reinvigorate the Republican base and be a major "force" in the upcoming midterm elections.[118] While Tea Party leaders and supporters writing or functioning as commentators, pundits, and experts in the press introduced this frame, it was also taken up and maintained by news reporters throughout the media.

Unconventional rhetorical displays and dress were also highlighted to imply Tea Party extremism. *The New York Times* wrote that "some people wore their teabags hanging from umbrellas or eyeglasses. Others simply tossed them on the White House lawn."[119] MSNBC anchor Keith Olbermann played on the double entendre of "teabag" as a sexual reference.[120] Typical of social movement coverage, this media attention to image and spectacle displaced a focus on group organizing, a clear policy agenda, and goals in telling the story of the Tea Party.

Of course, newness, rage, and a focus on spectacle was not unusual in media coverage of activism; moreover, they were also important to the Tea Party's portrayal as a populist and grass-roots movement. Activist movements such as the "New Right" in the 1980s, "New Conservatism" of the 1950s, or the "New Negro" movement of the Harlem Renaissance embed novelty into their identity in order to project the sense of bringing new citizens into political formation. Media coverage of new movements typically focuses on the appearance, behavior, mental abilities, or perceived violence of protestors rather than the cause or issues.[121]

In particular, the media fixation on anger and outrage among tea partiers helped fuel the notion that it was a populist movement that pitted ordinary people against elites. As Ritchie Savage argues, the media characterized the Tea Party as populist primarily because of its "anti-elitist rhetoric and psychological/emotional states ranging from paranoia to simple anger and outrage."[122] In doing so, they were able to discursively redirect anger away from the corporations and business leaders at the center of the economic crisis. This focus on anger also generated collective "emotional identification" that "underpins the Tea Party brand."[123] Moreover, the media emphasis on the spectacle of Tea Party events, tactics, signs, and protests fits the typical news coverage of activism and helped reify its brand identity as a social movement.

In establishing a clear Tea Party brand identity, the news media repeatedly and almost universally attributed a select set of additional characteristics to the Tea Party, thereby presenting it with a coherent image. Reporters asserted that tea partiers opposed taxes, as reiterated by the spokespersons and activists at rallies and events as anti-taxation. Journalists also reported that tea partiers had a "distrust of government." For example, one poll cited by *Newsmax* said that "94 percent of the tea party movement" believes that the federal government "poses an immediate threat to the rights and freedoms of ordinary citizens."[124] In reporting on the Tea Party slogan "Burn the books," a *Huffington Post* writer emphasized the movement's anti-intellectual character.[125] A devout commitment to religion and the Constitution was also key to the Tea Party brand. *The New York Times* described the Tea Party as hungry for "high-minded constitutional talk"; a tea partier on Fox News saw the Tea Party as a way of stopping the president and his allies from "destroy[ing] the Constitution."[126]

Another Tea Party brand quality commonly mentioned by journalists was an aversion to the "mainstream media"—which tea partiers defined as any media source that critiqued (or potentially critiqued) the Tea Party and other conservatives. For example, a *Politico* story noted that tea partiers "were boisterous in their denunciations of...the hated mainstream media they believe unfairly linked them to the harassment [of health care bill supporters]."[127] Instead of discussing the components of the healthcare bill and the policies that tea partiers highlighted as objectionable, the story focused on the ire and frustration that tea partiers expressed about the bill being signed into law. Again, this emphasis on emotional and affective qualities over more substantive analysis highlights the formation of the Tea Party brand through news. Not only did the media clearly describe the Tea Party as a brand but it also conveyed its brand identity through repeated mentions and regular emphasis of specific qualities and characteristics.

To be clear, emphasis on affective or emotional qualities is not unique to Tea Party news. Lance Bennett argues that in recent years, political news has become increasingly similar to reality television. This "reality journalism," as he puts it, tends to favor dramatic and pop culture narratives that minimize facts and accentuate feelings and "emotionalized experience."[128] A study by Mervi Katriina Pantti and Karin Wahl-Jorgensen suggests that the emotionality of news content has increased in recent decades, possibly with the introduction of digital modes of journalism. According to Wahl-Jorgensen, affect is the sensory component of feeling while emotion is a form expressed through discourse—in effect, emotion is articulated by the affect imbued within news narratives.[129] The Tea Party news coverage demonstrates the extent to which emotional news storytelling can help bring a political brand to bear, particularly as a major social movement with no clear or coherent leader, goals, or impetus.

TEA PARTY NEWS BRANDING: INTERPRETING EVENTS

Reporters also highlighted other Tea Party brand attributes through their coverage and interpretation of Tea Party signs and rhetoric. While a preoccupation with symbolism and iconography was not unusual in news reporting, the process of deciphering the signs of a "leaderless" movement gave news reporters and pundits the primary responsibility to define and articulate the Tea Party brand. In its earliest media descriptions, the press largely used the term "tea party" to refer to a specific event or rally in which conservatives met at a location to protest taxes (as opposed to a type of activist or political party). Media pundits and reporters treated Tea Party events as messaging platforms that relayed Tea Party brand characteristics. Events were especially important because the Tea Party was described as leaderless, which meant most reporters had to rely on what Kevin Michael DeLuca and Jennifer Peeples call "image events," spectacular events that aim to provoke massive publicity, to explain the phenomenon's meaning, motivation, and objective.[130] Arie Soesilo and Philo Wasburn explain that political events like protests and demonstrations function either "as a symbolic representation of political reality, or as a symbolic construct reflecting and serving political, economic, and ideological interests."[131] One *Newsmax* blogger referenced both of these definitions, writing that "the tea party effort is both symbolic and a catalyst."[132] In reporting on and broadcasting Tea Party events, news journalists gauged the meaning, qualities, and power of the Tea Party brand.

Journalists used Tea Party events such as conventions and rallies as a way of assessing the brand's political influence, success, and goals. In one story about the first Tea Party convention, a *New York Times* reporter wrote: "As they opened their inaugural national convention here, Tea Party advocates from across the country declared that they would turn the grass-roots anger that burst onto the streets a year ago into real political power." Another *New York Times* reporter covering the first Tea Party rallies wrote that "it was hard to determine from the moderate turnout just how effective the parties would be."[133]

While online interactions and digital organizing obfuscated the identities of the factions driving the Tea Party, the homemade signs carried by tea partiers helped verify its authenticity. The signs were held by "real" people and written in their own handwriting. The signs gave the Tea Party a genuineness that was hard to locate in anonymous websites, blogs, and online discussion boards that are ubiquitous in a digital age. To borrow from Walter Benjamin, the signs had an "aura" that made them even more important in news reports that described the Tea Party as a movement.[134] The signs that Tea Party activists carried at rallies and demonstrations were frequently cited in news stories to explain Tea Party sentiments, goals, and beliefs—key components of a political brand. Often handwritten on poster board, these signs allowed journalists to interpret the goals and beliefs of Tea Party activists. Print reporters, especially, cited the text of the signs verbatim. For example, in *The New York Times*:

> In Pensacola, Fla., about 500 protesters lined a busy street, some waving "Don't Tread on Me" flags and carrying signs reading "Got Pork?" and "D.C.: District of Corruption."
>
> In Austin...American flags abounded, along with hand-painted placards that bore messages like "Abolish the I.R.S.," "Less Government More Free Enterprise," "We Miss Reagan" and "Honk if You Are Upset About Your Tax Dollars Being Spent on Illegal Aliens."[135]

In *The Wall Street Journal*:

> At a tea party I attended...speakers railed against the administration's stimulus package and defended deregulation and free markets. "Your Mortgage is Not My Problem," read one placard.[136]

USA Today also described the signs in detail:

> Yellow flags bearing the slogan "Don't tread on me" were flying high. "Impeach Obama" posters and T-shirts were spotted. One poster depicted the president as a vampire about to sink bloody fangs into the neck of a prostrate Statue of Liberty. "I fought in Vietnam to stop communism, and now I have one in the White House," another sign read.[137]

These events not only gained publicity but also conveyed the messages by which the news media would articulate the Tea Party brand.

News organizations particularly tracked Tea Party signs for inflammatory or racist rhetoric, which often overlapped with anti-Obama sentiment, and interpreted it as a central aspect of Tea Party identity. A *Huffington Post* blogger argued that the movement was clearly "anti-Obama" after "judging from the crowds and the signs they waved."[138] A Tea Party group coordinator chastised CNN news anchor Campbell Brown specifically for the news media's tendency to read the signs as Tea Party ideology:

> BROWN: The people carrying those signs of the president of the United States as an African witch doctor, is that how you define the movement or is that the fringe element in this movement?
>
> WIERZBICKI: That is not representative at all of what this movement is about. And that's what my point of contention is.
>
> By showing that as indicative of what the tea party movement is about is misleading.[139]

Reporters, pundits, and commentators deciphering the significance of event signs continued to be a major part of the Tea Party narrative, as was the idea posed by news sources that these signs posed a threat to the Tea Party's larger messaging. A *Newsmax* blogger noted that "tea party organizers" were distancing themselves from "potentially controversial views" by hiring security and renting private venues to keep out "extremists" with "racist signs."[140]

Tea Party leaders and brand representatives were also identified through their appearances at Tea Party events and perceived influence in drawing or mobilizing crowds. Sarah Palin, the former Alaska governor and Republican vice-presidential candidate, was the person most often mentioned in Tea Party reporting. Ron Paul, a Republican Senate candidate, was also considered a Tea Party leader. One *Newsmax* blogger drew on poll data to argue that Ron Paul and Sarah Palin each represented the values of the Tea Party's key constituencies:

Tea partyers are almost evenly divided between those who favor former Alaska Republican Gov. Sarah Palin and those who support Rep. Ron Paul, R-Tex., according to a new *Politico*/TargetPoint poll. . . . Palin best reflects the 43 percent who say the government is too big and should do more to promote traditional values. Meanwhile Paul most represents the 42 percent who say government is too big but shouldn't try to promote any particular set of values—the libertarian philosophy.[141]

Other frequently mentioned "Tea Party candidates" include Nevada Republican Senate candidate Sharron Angle and Delaware Senate candidate Christine O'Donnell. It was frequently the case that politicians themselves did not identity as Tea Party candidates, but rather were identified as such by the reporter or news anchor covering the story.

TEA PARTY BRAND IDENTITIES: MOVEMENT OR POLITICAL PARTY?

While political branding aims to make people feel like they belong to a community based on shared values, it often accomplishes this sense of unity by allowing multiple items to fit under the same label.[142] For example, in more traditional marketing, a soap company like Dove is able to use its brand associations of "pure," "clean," "moisturizing," and "fresh-smelling" to sell a range of distinct items like deodorant, shampoo, conditioner, aftershave, and lotion all under the same label. Differentiation constructs a brand as unique through an emphasis on specific attributes and associations that separate it from other competitors, and helps to attract a target audience.[143] In this way, although selling similar products, a company like Dove portrays itself as different from competing brands like Olay and Nivea. Moreover, Dove branders try to get consumers to buy these products by emphasizing Dove's brand recognition and reputation. In media and politics, brand names and attributes also help citizen-consumers distinguish similar political products from one another based on packaging and image.[144] Similarly, the media created the Tea Party brand as a symbol representing multiple "products" with a shared label; they (figuratively) packaged the Tea Party as a protest event, social movement, and political party. The news media collectively reported on the Tea Party as a brand with two key shifting identities for voters to consume: a social movement and political party. In helping create the Tea Party, they also produced a political brand that would attract consumers to their news.

Journalists' alternating identification of the Tea Party as a social movement and a political party both differentiated and politically strengthened its brand. Through helping to brand the Tea Party as a social movement, the news media invoked civil rights imagery and legitimized traditional conservative values and goals. Through helping to brand the Tea Party as a political party, the news media concretized it as an identity that united social and fiscal conservatives and differentiated official Republican Party members from other GOPers.

TEA PARTY AS A SOCIAL MOVEMENT

While news coverage of activism and social movements is fairly common, the framing of the Tea Party as social movement was a brand identity distinct from traditional news coverage. First, the Tea Party was initially portrayed in news largely among opinion spaces (discussed further in chapter 4), which allowed political leaders and celebrities to construct the Tea Party as a social movement through race, class, and gender tropes that concretized it as a particular brand without necessitating any of the evidence, reporting, and detail that more hard news spaces typically provide in social movement coverage. In this sense, the Tea Party *became* a social movement through the arguments and narratives of opinion spaces that wove a story of the Tea Party as brand activism and, subsequently, attracted brand supporters.

The emphasis on branding discourse in discussing the Tea Party meant that the media did not have to rely on centralized organization and charismatic leaders with formal organizing ties to attract media attention.[145] This led to a de-emphasis of some of the more important and substantive features that typically occur in social movement news coverage, such as noting crowd size at events or proposed solutions to a specific social problem, and less demonization and delegitimization.[146] Moreover, the involvement of conservative reporters from various news organizations, most notably Fox News, provided a space to legitimize and interpret Tea Party events as indicative of a larger social movement despite its lack of centralized and grass-roots leadership, stated goals, and its media-galvanized mobilization.

Reports naming the Tea Party as a social movement reflected the long-standing symbolic, dynamic, and interdependent relationship between the media and activism. In journalism studies, social movements are seen as

> carriers of extant ideas and meanings that grow automatically out of structural arrangements, unanticipated events, or existing ideologies.... Movement actors are viewed as signifying agents actively engaged in the production and maintenance of meaning for constituents, antagonists, and bystanders or observers.[147]

News narratives use social movements as a way of discussing larger societal issues, problems, and debates, and often legitimize and bolster prevailing ideas about power. While key actors in social movement news reporting are typically real activists and politicians, they are also used to represent larger trends, cultural rifts, and schools of thought. Social movements "embody and exploit the fact that the dominant ideology enfolds contradictory values: liberty versus equality, democracy versus hierarchy, public rights versus property rights."[148] In this way, reporters who characterized the Tea Party as a social and political movement conveyed the actions, beliefs, and values of the Tea Party brand (and its supporters), and also the political structures that it engaged.

According to Jackie Smith et al., "social movement organizations are by definition outsiders to political institutions and processes,"[149] and yet the Tea Party was promoted, articulated, and galvanized through political elites who also frequented as news media contributors, writers, and staffers. By opening up its opinion spaces to Tea Party politicians and conservative leaders that conveyed the Tea Party brand characteristics and identities, the news media were a platform that emphasized the Tea Party as social movement brand while operating in contradiction to typical social movement coverage.

As a result, the portrayal of the Tea Party in the media differed from other social movements. Most social movements are ignored by the media—those that do receive coverage tend to stand out in terms of size of demonstration, existing media attention, and advanced coordination with news outlets.[150] While, as Jackie Smith et al. argue, social movements are generally reliant on "external or indirect mechanisms to help convey their messages to influential actors," the Tea Party branding by reporters and journalists meant that it did not require a formal structure for this outreach or mobilization.[151] Unlike typical activist rallies or protests, accounts of the Tea Party from public officials[152] (especially police) also did not dominate Tea Party reporting; instead they focused on views from pundits, political consultants, Tea Party attendees, Tea Party signs, and Tea Party leaders in media and politics.

The Tea Party also did not suffer from the delegitimization typical of the protest paradigm in news.[153] The press typically treats social movements as nuisances and demonizes them; the news media also tend to focus on protest events as a threat and reports on negative consequences (such as traffic congestion, costs of policing, or violence). Matt Guardino and Dean Snyder found that the Tea Party was legitimized substantially within news coverage through discussion of various policy issues and received favorable coverage overall.[154] David Weaver and Joshua Scacco argue that this is because conservative social movements tend to support the status quo.[155] Studies have found that the less a movement poses a threat to the status quo, the less harsh its news coverage.[156] Guardino and Snyder also note that the treatment of the Tea Party depended upon the ideological bend of the broadcast network. Overall, this attention to negative outcomes or nuisance aspects of Tea Party rallies rarely occurred in most news covering the Tea Party, even during the numerous protests and demonstrations in which tea partiers brandished guns.[157]

In the case of the Tea Party, images, reports of rallies, and assembled supporters at events helped the news media construct the Tea Party brand as a movement. Todd Gitlin points out that in the age of large-scale mass communication that can transmit visual representations to vast media audiences, the "image tends to *become* 'the movement' for wider publics and institutions."[158] Indeed, the Tea Party functioned more as a political brand in its coverage than as a social movement. In social science literature, social movements are understood as passing through distinct maturation phases—moving "from informal groups or networks to complex voluntary organizations able to lobby corporations, unions, and legislative bodies."[159] Social movement coverage typically features statements from rival political actors, mentions attendee numbers at events, and focuses on specific policy issues that actors oppose or embrace.[160] Tea Party news coverage, however, generally did not give space to opposing political views on relevant topics, rarely mentioned crowd numbers, and seldom discussed particular issues (outside of an anti-Obama agenda) or proposed solutions supported by tea partiers. Instead, this coverage focused primarily on positively (or, at least, not negatively) describing emotionally evocative Tea Party theatrics and rhetoric at events organized largely by Tea Party PACs and framed it as a social movement, without mention of concrete goals or positions (possibly because, as Charles Postel states, there were no universal goals or ideals across Tea Party groups, which were composed mostly by a tenuous alliance between white evangelicals and libertarians).[161] Weaver and Scacco argue that cable news networks MSNBC and Fox neglected to mention issues in covering the Tea Party in order to attract a larger audience and attract more viewers.[162]

In part, the Tea Party's ideological and formative similarities to earlier right-wing movements and groups helped fuel its identity as a social movement. The John Birch Society (JBS) was movement formed by business leaders, mirroring the Tea Party backing from billionaire Koch brothers Charles and David Koch. It was also similar to movements such as the Ku Klux Klan of the 1920s and even McCarthyism by embracing what Christopher Parker and Matt Barreto call a "preservatist" tendency to protect the dominance of white, male, Christian, and native-born Americans.[163]

As a result, tea partiers were frequently shown articulating nativist, racist, and anti-immigrant stances. Like the rise of the American New Right in the 1970s, the Tea Party linked itself to neoliberalism by advocating an anti-statist ideology and return to free-market orthodoxy. In particular, the New Right movement was effective in tying business tycoons, evangelical Christians, and the white middle and working class in a collective cause against economic and social crises. The Tea Party also importantly brought these seemingly at odds coalition of social and fiscal conservatives together, such as pro-life Christians and limited-government libertarians.

But the Tea Party was also notably different from previous right-wing movements. The Tea Party was in large part the result of conservative media network formation that had developed since the late 1970s during the rise of the New Right, tying conservative foundations, think tanks, magazines, websites, and radio and TV programming to one another to advance conservative policies and ideas. Its rise was propelled by the now-fluid interconnections and exchanges between these platforms in the form of pundits, experts, and information. The Tea Party was also viewed as leaderless and had no clear policy agenda, centralized infrastructure, membership, or mobilizing efforts that other right-wing movements and organizations have had in the past. On MSNBC, a Bloomberg News reporter named Margaret Carlson explicitly marked the Tea Party as "differ[ent] from the Christian Right," describing it as a conglomeration of "birthers," "vaccine-deniers," "militiamen," and "secessionists."[164] Tea Partiers were also different from the Christian Right in that they focused largely on economic and not social values.[165] They were described by the media as not just a conservative movement, but a fringe one—one *Huffington Post* writer summarized its portrayal in one news article as "a collective of gang-eyed loons, awash in conspiracy theories and swastikas, and birtherism, and general nutloggery."[166]

The extent to which the Tea Party was a social movement was frequently debated in the press, but the news *emphasis* on the Tea Party as a social movement made this a key brand identity. As Douglas B. Holt notes, "A brand emerges as various 'authors' tell stories that involve the brand."[167] My argument here is that the news media promoted "social movement" as a key identity, or pushed back against it as a promotional front, while simultaneously neglecting typical social movement frames in news coverage. That is, Tea Party leaders promoted events and rallies that attracted both supporters and the news media to turnout—in turn, the news media promoted the identity of the Tea Party as a social movement, an identity already projected by Tea Party leaders. As Celia Lury explains,

The "use-value" of the brand to consumers consists in what they can make with it, what kinds of social relations they can form around it. And what consumers "just do" is what increases the exchange-value of the brand for brand managers and brand owners.[168]

In framing the Tea Party as a social movement, with little regard to its leadership, funding, organizational structure, membership, policies, and goals (or lack thereof), the news increased value and meaning of the brand. Similar to what Gitlin observed in studying social movement news coverage, the new media reporting on the Tea Party relied on depicting centralized organization and charismatic leaders. But while "social movement organizations are by definition outsiders to political institutions and processes,"[169] the insider status of the Tea Party in terms of its attachment, funding, and mobilization through powerful political and media organizations was frequently downplayed in news reports that depicted it as a social movement. Moreover, the identity of the Tea Party as a social movement was often in question within the press, reflecting the ambiguity of this label. While the Tea Party did not experience the marginalization that social movements typically experience in seeking mainstream media attention, it was able to retain this identity within the press.

The depiction of the Tea Party as a movement was the most common news trope in its coverage. In one of *The Wall Street Journal*'s first Tea Party stories, guest columnist Karl Rove argued that the "large numbers of Americans turning out for an estimated 2,000 tea parties across the country" showed that "this movement is significant."[170] Another *Wall Street Journal* guest columnist portrayed the Tea Party as "a mass movement of ordinary people who don't feel that their voices are being heard."[171] ABC described the Tea Party as a "rebel yell that signals a conservative movement rediscovering its voice."[172] In *The Huffington Post*, a blogger wrote that the Tea Party was a real movement that the left should not "write off."[173] Skocpol and Williamson found that Fox News was publicizing and celebrating tea parties, "linking its brand to protests" and covering rallies six weeks before they occurred.[174]

In part, the conflict over whether the tea party was a social movement was linked to its portrayal as populist. While reporters and commentators covering the Tea Party frequently referred to it as "populist," this label was also a contentious designation. The first group referred to as "Populists" in the United States was the late nineteenth-century People's Party, which organized farmers to protest against business elites such as bankers, encouraged an uprising of laborers against exploitative industrial conditions, and supported pro-corporate economic policies. Historian Richard Hofstadter introduced the notion of "paranoia" and "persecution" as key to populist movements, which he saw as a resistance of common people against traitorous elites.[175] Hofstadter theorized that populism was a conservative impulse that relied on xenophobia, isolationism, demagoguery, and anti-intellectualism to defend an imagined sacrosanct rural America from urban encroachment. Similarly, Cynthia Burack and R. Claire Snyder-Hall argue that right-wing populist movements since the nineteenth century have largely been racist and nativist, targeting foreigners or anyone else deemed an inferior other. As a result, the Tea Party was seen as populist because of the performance of outrage, extremism, racism, and anger within its rhetoric, rallies, and events.[176]

But, Charles Postel argues that this notion of populism as an angry mob is false. Rather, populism was originally a movement of rural education, redistributive politics, and progressive economic justice and these markers are central to its definition. Through this lens, the Tea Party's support of corporations and its funding from business and political leaders undermines and contradicts its populist label. So, too, does the Tea Party's advocacy for policies that primarily benefit corporations and its base of supporters that are wealthier than the average American. Moreover, Postel points out that tea partiers refer to themselves as conservatives, not populists.[177]

Still, the use of the label of "populist" within the news stories about the Tea Party helped maintain its image as a movement of "the people." Populism's "referential context," as Hall et al. put it, is conveyed with the term—as populists, tea partiers are people from America's heartland, a nostalgic link to a farming and rural history, and Puritan roots. The term also conveyed distinctly racialized and class notions of how the media define "the people"; for example, antiwar and civil rights protests have not been similarly identified as populist, even though they were also seen as movements of disaffected Americans targeted at elites. As populist, the Tea Party invoked historical notions of an angry and disempowered group of outraged white citizens. By deeming the Tea Party "populist," reporters and pundits in the media helped the Tea Party signify a disaffected and maltreated working and laborer class abused by business, social, and political elites. The Tea Party as populist was key to its social movement brand.[178]

As a populist social movement, the news media largely portrayed the Tea Party as a new civil rights protest group and analogous to historical and left-leaning activism. Along these lines, Jonathan Gray explains that "branding is about surrounding a product with layers of symbolism in an attempt to give it a meaning both for those new to the product and, as value added, to those already owning the product." Describing the Tea Party as a group of angry citizens engaged in civil disobedience made it a familiar American trope that easily conjured images of oppressed people fighting against an unjust society. A *Huffington Post* blogger wrote, "Now a new group of the dispossessed have taken to the streets." In *USA Today*, Sarah Palin declared that "the spark of patriotic indignation that inspired those who fought for our independence and those who marched peacefully for civil rights has ignited once again." On MSNBC, anchor Keith Olbermann quoted a Tea Party organizer who said the "tea party movement has a lot in common with the civil rights movement."[179]

In keeping with this civil rights and oppression theme, *The Huffington Post* later contended that tea partiers "see the federal government as oppressors and enemies of the people."[180] This underlying rhetorical argument implied that the federal government, led by an African American president, now oppressed white conservatives. Reporters and news columnists implicitly (and explicitly) described the predominantly white and conservative Tea Party movement as a newly marginalized faction of society. More important, the brand identity of social movements helped present the Tea Party as a group with legitimate grievances based on systemic discrimination and disenfranchisement *that had not actually occurred*. This particular narrative of the Tea Party as a national social movement against the federal government is especially remarkable because the first tea party protests in the Obama era had been described as a movement against *local* taxes prior to President Obama's election.

Other articles similarly described the Tea Party as appropriating characteristics of the civil rights movement organized by African American activists in the 1960s. *Newsmax* referred to a large Tea Party rally in Nevada as "a conservative Woodstock."[181] *Politico* wrote about the Tea Party's use of leftist symbolism, quoting an organizer of a rally that mobilized tea partiers and other conservatives to "March on Washington" on the anniversary of Martin Luther King Jr.'s historic speech at the 1963 rally:

> [The organizer] explains they were "trying to evoke the imagery of the counterrevolutionary protests of the 1960s that captured the imagination of the world." And as for the phrase "March on Washington," [Adam] Brandon says, "this is something people said in the office. If we had been alive back in the 1960s, we would have been on the freedom bus rides. It was an issue of individual liberty. We're trying to borrow some from the civil rights movement."[182]

In this way, a conservative movement, branded through whiteness, racism, a resistance to federal intervention, and an antagonistic posture toward the first African American president somehow also conceived of itself as an extension of one of the most progressive movements for racial equality in American history. While "freedom rides" were racially integrated bus trips that aimed to challenge segregation and oppose state-sanctioned violence and race-based discrimination through government enfranchisement, they get reframed here as a movement for individual liberty and choice.

Moreover, while the reporters acknowledged that Adam Brandon was also a press secretary for FreedomWorks, a conservative political advocacy group formed by former Republican House Majority Leader Dick Armey, they did little to analyze the complexity in functioning as both a political group designed to raise funds and as "grass-roots" leaders. The media generated stories that uncritically allowed the Tea Party to co-opt the civil rights movement narrative and position their rallies and events as a social movement.

In another example that seemed to subtly draw on Seattle's well-known reputation for influential leftist protest, one *Wall Street Journal* guest columnist and Tea Party supporter tried to implicityly evoke this radical history within the narrative of Tea Party origins by claiming that "the [Tea Party] protests began with bloggers in Seattle, Wash., who organized a demonstration."[183] He continued making parallels between the Tea Party and the radical left by explaining that the Tea Party was using the very same tactics and technological expertise employed by leftist activists, including those who helped elect President Obama:

> We saw a bit of this in the 2004 and 2008 presidential campaigns, with things like Howard Dean's use of Meetup, and Barack Obama's use of Facebook. But this was still social networking in support of an existing organization or campaign. The tea-party protest movement is organizing itself, on its own behalf.[184]

In other words, this op-ed framed the Tea Party as a real movement by arguing that conservatives were "catching up" with tech-savvy liberals and its ambiguity in terms of leadership and goals was emblematic of a digital landscape. Similarly, a commentator on Fox News argued that new media was key to the organization and promotion of the Tea Party, fueled by people who "talked to each other on the Internet" and "city organizers [who] created their own city-centric sites."[185] Under the cover of technology, it was much easier for the news media to create the Tea Party as social movement narrative and blame lapses in terms of typical social movement coverage on the influence of new technology. Moreover, the use of online technology to recruit and disseminate messages among Tea Party supporters made it more difficult for the news media to track its origins, funders, and goals.

Several journalists critiqued the Tea Party's branding in news as a national social movement, instead describing it as entirely counterfeit, and (secretly) strategically driven by Republican corporate powers. In part, this critique echoed earlier concerns about the Tea Party co-opting leftist and activist rhetoric to give itself the allusion of a populist uprising. *New York Times* columnist Paul Krugman, for example, referred to the Tea Party as "AstroTurf," rhetorically differentiating it from an authentic "grass-roots" movement:

> It turns out that the tea parties don't represent a spontaneous outpouring of public sentiment. They're AstroTurf (fake grass roots) events, manufactured by the usual suspects. In particular, a key role is being played by FreedomWorks, an organization run by Richard Armey, the former House majority leader, and supported by the usual group of right-wing billionaires.[186]

On CNN, a Democratic strategist said:

> This is what I refer to as—as everyone refers to as kind of Astroturfing. The only people that think these protests are real are the people that think George Bush was a good president. I mean, the fact is, you know, to be brutal about it, this is a Milli Vanilli type of movement. It sounds real, but it's not.[187]

"Astroturfing" meant that the Tea Party had the appearance of a grass-roots movement, but that it was artificial. Rather than a movement coming from concerned citizens organizing on the ground, critics argued that the Tea Party was organized by political and societal elites (like the billionaire Koch brothers) from the top down. In *The Wall Street Journal*, a columnist called the Tea Party "plastic populism" and at MSNBC a guest commentator maintained that the Tea Party was maybe "grassrootsy" but not a "party" or "a movement." Determining who was right is complicated. While numerous Tea Party groups were formed by local activists in various parts of the country as documented by Skocpol and Williamson and Barreto and Parker, a number of them pointed to media professionals like Rick Santelli, Fox News, or Tea Party Political Action Committees like the Tea Party Express as initiating, mobilizing, and organizing their participation.[188]

Numerous articles aimed to expose the major conservative powers behind the Tea Party's formation. An MSNBC anchor described "sponsors" offering money in exchange for Tea Party publicity and refuted the idea that the gatherings were organized by common folk:

> Eric Telford of Americans for Prosperity, one of the corporate sponsors of the completely spontaneous Operation Tea Bag. Again, it's completely spontaneous,

which is why Mr. Telford posted a message on Facebook yesterday offering, on behalf of his group, and the also totally uninvolved Heritage Foundation, 5,000 dollars in prizes for the best promotion of Tea Bagging Day, [including the] best testimonial, best frustration video, best letter.[189]

Other reports described tea partiers circulating fake photos of a Tea Party rally, and an organizer inflating an *ABC News* crowd estimate to make rallies seem larger than they were. Inherently, the idea that the Tea Party was run by experienced political strategists contradicted the Tea Party's claims (and various news stories) that describe it as being run by first-time activists. These vying frames were used interchangeably, allowing the Tea Party's brand identity as a social movement to proceed even when the clear leadership by media and political elites undermined its image. As the Tea Party functioned primarily as a brand, these various labels were able to be fluid and dexterous, without a need for a specific framework.

In response, conservatives pushed hard against the notion that the movement was a sham, by accusing detractors of elitism (alluding to derogatory stereotypes about the Democratic Party brand as well as a key motivator of populist fervor) and explaining the Tea Party's mass media presence as reflecting contemporary mediated political culture. A *Wall Street Journal* guest columnist and chief Republican strategist, Karl Rove, argued the Tea Party was "derided by elitists as phony," but was actually "spontaneous, decentralized, frequently amateurish, and sometimes shrill."[190] In *USA Today*, Sarah Palin wrote that those who dismiss this "grassroots uprising…don't understand the frustration everyday Americans feel."[191] Proponents explained that the Tea Party was a spontaneous product of the digital age:

> The leaders are appearing on their own, and reaching out to others through blogs, Facebook, chat boards and alternative media.
> …The protests began with bloggers in Seattle, Wash., who organized a demonstration on Feb. 16. As word of this spread, rallies in Denver and Mesa, Ariz., were quickly organized for the next day.
> …The movement grew so fast that some bloggers at the Playboy Web site— apparently unaware that we've entered the 21st century—suggested that some secret organization must be behind all of this. But, in fact, today's technology means you don't need an organization, secret or otherwise, to get organized. [192]

In other words, these authors argued that the Tea Party's ambiguous origins were emblematic of a digital landscape. A *USA Today* article echoed Reynolds's argument:

The Information Age has given people the ability to network as never before. . . . In that sense, the Tea Party movement resembles the early days of MoveOn.org, which began in 1998 as a small, tech-savvy liberal group and became a behemoth in Internet fundraising and rallying.[193]

As a grass-roots movement, the Tea Party was modern, net-savvy, and, most important, difficult to dispute, verify, or assess. In short, new media and technology made it difficult for journalists to identify whether or not the Tea Party was a "real" movement and reporters relied upon conservative political leaders to shape its narrative.

Accordingly, the mass-mediated construction of the Tea Party as a movement captured the public renegotiation of ideology, digitized identities, and social practices, and the ways these disrupt and reformulate our contemporary social order. The success of the Tea Party brand as a social movement highlighted the importance of conservatism, patriotism, whiteness, capitalism, and anti-Black racism as prevailing American ideologies, as explained further in chapter 3. It was, in short, "status quo oriented."[194] For, as Todd Gitlin observes, "The more closely the concerns and values of social movements coincide with the concerns and values of elites in politics and media, the more likely they are to become incorporated in the prevailing news frames."[195] In the digital age, the values and concerns of political and media elites seem even more difficult to distinguish from those of the movements they support (and, especially, the ones they begin). As it was made visible by government officials and established politicians, promoted and organized by news reporters, supported by wealthy political groups and donors, and substantiated as a movement by sign-wielding crowds, the Tea Party took both an outsider and insider approach to gaining media attention that conveyed and co-produced its brand.[196]

TEA PARTY AS A POLITICAL PARTY

In addition to constructing the Tea Party as a social movement, news stories also constructed the Tea Party as an autonomous political party by highlighting its focus on elections, labeling its candidates, and distinguishing it from the major parties. One key example was Michele Bachmann's televised Tea Party response to the State of the Union Address, which framed the Tea Party as a third-party challenger to the Republican Party even with a speech delivered by a Republican congresswoman. As the Tea Party was described in news narratives as "leaderless" and "nonpartisan," it was able to avoid the media portraying it as a fractious split of the Republican Party, as the Democrats experienced over the 1950s rise of its Dixiecrat contingent.[197] While the media typically pays little attention to third parties, the Tea Party as a multifaceted brand—which included its identity as a third party—allowed it to draw significant coverage. Portraying the Tea Party as a third-party threat to Republican and Democratic dominance propelled it as a major news topic and helped to differentiate Tea Party Republicans from other GOPers. It also helped center candidates who represented the Tea Party brand in reporting and voters as brand ambassadors to support it.

American political parties are generally defined as groups that primarily function to pursue and obtain political office and work hard at maintaining their own brand to maintain voter loyalty. Framing the Tea Party as a political party helped legitimize it as a key political influence and distinguish it from being an interest or advocacy group, which primarily seeks to influence legislators and decision makers. Political scientist Joseph Schlesinger explains that political parties are groups defined by their attempt to seek office and gain control of government, which includes three phases: nominations, elections, and government.[198] Building on this definition, Cohen, et al. adds that political parties move beyond office-seekers to include the informal selection of key office-seekers, like presidential candidates, attaching a familiar electoral brand to an office-seeker (thus, reducing the information that a voter needs to select a candidate), and functioning as vehicles by which the most powerful and active populations create policy (often producing laws in contradiction to what the majority voters actually want).[199] As brands, political parties generate a sense of authenticity, build community connection, foster bonds with consumer-voters, and convey a set of values that seem useful. While based on historical patterns the Tea Party would likely not succeed as a third party in usurping much power in a two-party system, being branded as such a challenger helped lend it important momentum.

As the Tea Party was a dispersed, still-developing phenomenon, journalists who drew attention to the Tea Party as pursuing and obtaining public office helped frame it as a developing third political party. Third parties have always been particularly influential in shaping American politics, and constructing the Tea Party as a developing third party likely helped to amplify its coverage. For example, third parties advocated for abolition and suffrage long before mainstream parties began to publicly debate the issues. Third parties even initiated the tradition of national party conventions.[200] One scholar, J. David Gillespie, explained that "the greatest social utility lies in what third parties contribute to our relatively free marketplace of ideas."[201] In constructing the Tea Party as a third party, the media helped establish its legitimacy and bolster the sense of its political power. This was a key identity that added value to the Tea Party brand without it having to manifest the actual operations, organization, outreach, apparatuses, function, or governance of a political party.

News texts frequently attached these standard political party characteristics to the Tea Party. An *ABC News* correspondent reported that the Tea Party focused on "the nuts and bolts of politics, like voter registration" at its first national convention.[202] *Newsmax* described a typical tea partier as someone who "holds candidate meet-and-greets to help get out the vote."[203] *Newsmax* also reported on the Tea Party Express's work as a third party, writing that the group's bus tour would stop "in key battleground states where Democrats are fending off serious challengers in the midterm elections" (Newsmax, 2010).[204] News stories repeatedly credited the Tea Party with winning elections, supporting its characterization as a third party. For example, the Tea Party was described as having its own candidates, who were often nominated or supported by Tea Party—affiliated groups. Republican politicians running in midterm elections, such as Sharron Angle, Christine O'Donnell, Michele Bachmann, and Scott Brown, were all labeled as "Tea Party candidates," even when—as members of the Republican Party and GOP candidates in electoral races—they did not claim this label. *Newsmax* reported that "in two high-profile primary elections Tuesday [June 8, 2010], establishment GOP candidates were stunned by come-from-behind winners backed by tea party activists."[205] *The New York Times* reported that "the Tea Party Express, whose political action arm spent about $350,000 to help make Scott Brown the new Republican senator from Massachusetts, released a list of seats, all Democratic, it had set its sights on in November."[206] In particular, the Tea Party Express PAC propelled the narrative of the Tea Party as an emergingthird party, which became a regular theme in the press, picked up by the media and repeated without attribution.

In some news stories, the Tea Party was not only described as having third-party characteristics, but was explicitly referred to as being or becoming a third party, separate from both Democrats and Republicans. In *The Huffington Post*, one writer explained that the Tea Party was "alienated by a two party system that doesn't meet" its needs.[207] A *USA Today* article described Republicans running "against candidates claiming the Tea Party mantle."[208] *The Wall Street Journal* wrote that the Tea Party could be considered

> [a] third party—the "I'm mad as hell" party—a ragtag collection of tea partiers furious at establishment Republicans, left-wing Democrats angry at what they consider lily-livered Democrats in Washington, and independents disgusted with everybody inside the Beltway.[209]

A Fox News host asked guests to vote in an online poll about whether "Sarah Palin will run for president on the Tea Party ticket," suggesting that the Tea Party might run its own presidential candidate as a third-party challenger. On CNN, a correspondent questioned whether the Tea Party movement would "morph into a third party."[210] In *Newsmax*, a writer argued that "the decision confronting the tea party is whether to become a third party, à la Ross Perot, or become a powerful political force, much like the NRA."[211] *The New York Times* reported that its poll showed that Tea Party supporters did "not want a third party," but that it might potentially develop.[212]

Much of the "Tea Party as third party" news narrative focused on the Tea Party as a potential threat to the Republican Party. A *Wall Street Journal* guest columnist ominously wrote that "the tea-party movement may lead to a new third party that may replace the GOP, just as the GOP replaced the fractured and hapless Whigs."[213] Another *Wall Street Journal* article argued that the conservative Tea Party had an adversarial relationship with its umbrella group, the Republican Party:

> At New York's GOP convention two weeks ago, candidates with strong support from the conservative grass-roots were almost routinely denied backing from the establishment. In response, tea-party candidates seeking federal, state and local offices are mounting large-scale petition challenges to face off against fellow Republicans.[214]

A *Newsmax* blogger also argued that Tea Praty activists were "wary of both parties."[215] Through this framing, the Tea Party was portrayed as an outside challenger to both Republicans and Democrats.

News reports suggested that the Tea Party becoming a third party would weaken the Republicans by dividing the support of conservative voters. Pundits and columnists repeatedly voiced anxiety over this possibility. On Fox News, a guest commentator said:

> As long as it stays within the Republican Party and helps them nominate good, conservative candidates and defeat Democratic candidates, it's good. But if it starts getting into its head to be a third party, it could be the Republican equivalent of Ralph Nader and hand Congress back to Obama for another term.[216]

The Huffington Post wrote that "the GOP is working to head off the danger of the Tea party movement forming a third party." In *The New York Times*, Governor Haley Barbour "argued in favor of the two-party system [and warned] against the creation of a third." In Nevada, a political candidate registered under the Tea Party of Nevada, raising concerns about leeching votes from Republican challengers.[217]

Indeed, by describing the Tea Party as a third party, reporters and columnists gave it credibility as a news topic by framing it as the historic emergence of a major third party, and characterized it as a threat to the major political parties. Additionally, their framing allowed both Republicans and Democrats to avoid potentially negative associations with Tea Party rhetoric and ideas. This allowed the Tea Party a brand identity that distinguished it not only from the other two major political parties, but from other social movements and political organizations as well. As a brand, the identity of the Tea Party as a formal political party could potentially attract viewers and supporters that other brand identities would not. And, as recent research shows that Congressional Tea Party Caucus members vote like a third political party, this branding has had an impact in material and substantive ways.[218]

CONCLUSION

In allowing news reporters to function as both activists and journalists in covering the Tea Party, the news media raised the volume on the Tea Party—they constructed it as a brand and gave it shape as a multifaceted signifier. At times, the media described it as a third party and profitable commodity. At other times they described it as a social movement, constructing activists and supporters as oppressed and marginalized. And still other times they described it as a series of events. In all of these figurations, reporters and journalists interpreted the Tea Party's meaning, power, and leadership; co-produced a spectacle for media consumption; and mobilized Tea Party leaders and activists. The Tea Party's variable brand allowed voters, activists, conservative groups, elected representatives, and ambitious politicians to unite and amplify their influence under the same label. The Tea Party was the "un-party" party, and its activists were non-revolutionary revolutionaries.

In news narratives, the Tea Party was branded by the press as a decentralized movement with no leadership and a political party with celebrity and high-profile supporters (who used their frequent media op-eds and interviews to reinforce the message that the Tea Party was "leaderless"). This framing is distinct and makes the news media's coverage of the Tea Party stand out. Historically, in news coverage of decentralized social movements, the media have typically identified certain movement participants as leaders and spokespersons to cover these stories, and focused such coverage on the marginal and most militant characters displaying "telegenic theater."[219] Instead, the news media provided space for the Tea Party's key strategists to do its own reporting, supported its events, and emphasized its importance as a legitimate, or at least powerful, political institution. This coverage likely decreased the negative and fractious effect that such celebrity and spokesperson press selection has had on other movements.[220] The feedback loop inherent to today's headphone culture gave the Tea Party its own momentum, prioritizing its symbolic significance over its concrete goals and issues.

News reports that emphasized the Tea Party's financial value as a brand appeared to shield the phenomenon from the denigration that media typically give to social movements. For example, Todd Gitlin studied the way the news media covered the 1970s leftist Students for a Democratic Society and found that the media trivialized, polarized, marginalized, and disparaged protestors, and emphasized violence at demonstrations.[221] While the media's framing of the Tea Party did at times portray the movement as a threat, overall its reporting on the Tea Party as both a political party and social movement, and descriptions of its participation in conventions, candidate nominations, fundraising, and electoral contests, presented it as part of the status quo. Negative depictions and conclusions about the Tea Party were a matter of debate among journalists, but were not the overall theme of its coverage. This is important because Gitlin and others argue that social movement activists are usually depicted as threats to the existing social structure and its ideology.[222] By being portrayed as "non-radical" activists, tea partiers were able to maintain the veneer of conventionality, even as a social movement, which helped protect it from negative coverage.

The Tea Party's various brand identities in the press also collapsed the distinctions between protest movements and political parties upon which other scholarship has touched. Gerhards and Rucht argue:

> In contrast to political parties, social movements and protest groups do not compete to occupy administrative positions in order to propose and implement solutions to problems. Therefore, protest groups, unlike parties, are not usually expected to offer solutions to the defined problems.[223]

News coverage that described the Tea Party as a brand allowed it to accrue power through the rhetoric and performance of both a political party *and* a protest group, and focused attention on its fundraising instead of specific policies or goals. However, as Tea Party candidates started running for political office, coverage honed in on their lack of policy solutions and ideas, criticism from which their branding had initially been able to shield them. Unlike typical social movement coverage, Tea Party news coverage did not provide the perspective of elected officials, and attendee numbers at Tea Party events was rarely mentioned. As such, news stories about the Tea Party constructed it as a political and cultural indicator instead of a nationwide revolution.

Tea Party branding in news stories illustrates how political power is mobilized in contemporary brand culture. As one Tea Party PAC leader explained, the Tea Party did not have to become a political party because "candidates elected with PAC support would be expected to caucus around those first principles" (i.e., lower taxes, states' rights, and constitutionalism).[224] Another *New York Times* reporter concluded that Sarah Palin's ability to raise and dispense funding had transformed her into a new political ideal:

> Whether she ever runs for anything else, Ms. Palin has already achieved a status that has become an end in itself: access to an electronic bully pulpit, a staff to guide her, an enormous income and none of the bother or accountability of having to govern or campaign for office.[225]

The news coverage affixed the Tea Party with specific identities that allowed it to convey a brand that relied on little substance. The media engaged in the political branding of the Tea Party by relying on frames that targeted messages to citizen-consumers, bolstered their images, generated affective connections, and downplayed (or even obfuscated) policy agenda and decisions.

Tea Party news narratives poignantly reflect a major shift in how citizens today express their criticism of government—through the language of investors and shareholders, rather than society and community building. Tea Party branding in news stories also gestures to the meaning of political participation in the age of the citizen-consumer, a "new consumer world of empowerment, self-actualization, and personal values." As formal parties increasingly articulate their principles and policies through capitalist language, citizens have also changed the way they interacted with government. In media interviews, a number of Tea Party activists and spokespersons defined their values and explained their positions using rhetoric and metaphors based on money and spending. In part this was due to the rise of neoliberalism as an ideology that reveres privatization and promotes the notion that public institutions like government are best run as corporations. But it also reflected an orientation based on branding and consumption, shaping the relationship between citizens and their representatives to be one between consumers, products, and brands.

As branding experts explain, the postmodern rise of political branding yields only short-term benefits—in the long term, "political brand equity has shallow roots and is easily buffeted. This is a striking difference from commercial branding where much of the effort is directed at retaining the loyalty of existing customers."[226] As politics have become more dependent upon constructing the citizen as a consumer, citizen-consumers' value is dependent upon the money they spend and the ways they contribute to the economy. As Scammell notes, "Individuals' greater control as consumers exacerbated their sense of loss of control as citizens," concluding that "branding is yet another step on the road to *Politics Lost*."[227] In the rise of the Tea Party, "hard" political issues like policy were less important than the performance of the Tea Party brand. The media covering the Tea Party were more concerned with image, spectacle, and speculation in their reporting and portrayal of it as a social movement, giving less attention to any social problems activists sought to address or ideas proposed, showing how easily it is to manipulate political news in a brand culture.

In its coverage of, participation in, and publicity for the Tea Party, the news media raised the volume in a headphone culture, demonstrating the ways their role in politics has been transformed in a media-centric, digitally altered, consumer-oriented political culture. If branded celebrity, money, and publicity are key drivers in contemporary news coverage, then the goals and focus of individual reporters and news organizations will continue to diverge from the civic and informational needs of the larger public. News branding constructs politics through consumption and engages citizens as consumers—it frames citizenship through consumption, producing rhetoric that focuses on affluence and choice. In reporting on the Tea Party as a money-making brand supported by key politicians and strategists, the news media emphasized profits over substance and served primarily as a vehicle for its publicity. Through their reporting, the media made it easy for an unidentifiable, untraceable, and media-initiated political phenomenon to gain national recognition and influence. In actively starting, promoting, and participating in Tea Party events, news reporters reconfigured the boundaries of journalism and activism in a digital age.

CHAPTER 3

Rebranding Political Conservatism through Race, Gender, and Class

Reporters covering the Tea Party frequently questioned whether the hostility aimed at President Obama and the federal government was about more than taxation. A *Huffington Post* blogger observed that "taxes [under President Obama] are at their lowest levels in 60 years."[1] Conservative *Wall Street Journal* columnist Ben Stein expressed skepticism about the Tea Party's anti-tax sentiment:

> These tea parties strike me as off-base.... First, I don't quite get the taxation uproar. As far as I know, no new taxes of any size have been enacted. The only new tax I can spot immediately in front of us is the "cap and trade" levy on carbon emissions....And even that, based on a questionable idea, doesn't seem imminent.[2]

One *Huffington Post* blogger added that "some people think that the Tea party seriously opposes taxes and big government. But, come on, does anyone really think it's a violation of the Constitution to raise taxes?"[3]

Taxes functioned more symbolically than materially in Tea Party discourse. According to Theda Skocpol and Vanessa Williamson, most Tea Party supporters "fall into income categories that have enjoyed tax cuts under President Obama, not tax increases."[4] Their anxieties about taxes, they argue, were actually based on "generational and class fears about who gets what and who pays."[5] Moreover, historian Jill Lepore notes, "In an age of universal suffrage, the citizenry could hardly be said to lack representation. Something more was going on, something not about taxation or representation."[6] Although taxation was the openly stated reason that tea parties formed, media stories also emphasized race, gender, and class as key attributes of Tea Party mobilization and identity as a key underpinning to this rhetoric. More than that, stories about race and racism drove at least three of the top ten surges in Tea Party news coverage in its first two years; identity politics were a key way to get people and newsmakers to tune in to stories about the Tea Party in a headphone culture.

Within the news media, the reporting and commentary on the "Taxed Enough Already (TEA)" Party as an "anti-tax" movement foregrounded racialized arguments about citizenship, identity, and worthiness. Rick Santelli's rhetoric in his landmark CNBC "rant" plainly linked taxes and ideologies about the value of certain citizens:

> How about this, President and new administration—Why don't you put up a web site to have people vote on the Internet as a referendum to see if we really want to subsidize the losers' mortgages, or would we like to, at least, buy cars and buy houses in foreclosure and give them to people who might have a chance to actually prosper down the road, and reward people that could carry the water, instead of drink the water....This is America!! [referring to traders behind him][7]

As Santelli identifies his immediate surrounding audience of white, male financial traders as "America," he made a clear distinction between them and the "losers" who "drink" rather than "carry"—differentiating those who make money from those who spend money. Drinking literally involves draining—the rhetorical implication being that these "drinkers" are not America but, instead, are a drain on America and on wealthy, white men.

Who were these "losers" in the subprime mortgage crisis to which Santelli refers? According to Jacob Rugh and Douglass Massey, the mortgage crisis was the result of a "highly racialized process" that disproportionately targeted Hispanics and Blacks.[8] Accordingly, those most likely to benefit from subsequent mortgage assistance and protection programs were people of color. Santelli's call for a Tea Party protest movement was implicitly predicated upon an "us vs. them"[9] rhetoric criticizing non-white "losers" and distinguishing them from the white people who counted as the "real America."

The news coverage of the Tea Party as a brand also highlighted race, gender, and class. According to Naomi Klein, at the height of branding was the notion that "corporations should produce brands, not products....Nike isn't running a shoe company, it is about the idea of transcendence through sports, Starbucks isn't a coffee shop chain, it's about the idea of community."[10] Similarly, in the wake of a presidential campaign that fixated on race and gender, the news media helped produce the Tea Party as the idea of the American white working (and middle) class. As the news coverage of the Tea Party showed, the topic of taxes invokes discussions of national citizenship and belonging, and the historic exclusion of African Americans, women, and poor and working-class people in governing the nation. One *Huffington Post* reporter noted, "The Tea party brand of right-of-the-GOP conservatism is particularly unsympathetic to the African-American, the poor and the immigrant"— in other words, the Tea Party excluded historically marginalized groups.[11]

Debates on taxation, tax policy, and federal spending have often pivoted on who is assumed to benefit from federal revenues—and frequently rely on ethnocentrism, racial resentment, and racist attitudes towards the "undeserving poor."[12] As Thomas and Mary Edsall explain of politics since the 1960s, "The rise of the presidential wing of the Republican Party over the past generation has been driven by the overlapping issues of race and taxes."[13] In particular, Edsall and Edsall note that the use of race and taxes in political discourse was key to the "initial Republican mobilization in the 1970s of the white fundamentalist Christian community."[14]

Media and political rhetoric pitted taxpayers and tax recipients against each other, and domestic policies related to welfare, drug use, housing regulation, and a host of other issues reflected the idea of Blacks as racial beneficiaries and whites as economically burdened. Of course, the focus on Black welfare recipients was grossly disproportionate to their actual impact on the federal budget—most welfare recipients in the United States are white Americans and social safety net programs providing cash assistance to needy Americans (including children, senior citizens, and people with disabilities) only make up 9 percent of the federal budget.[15] Still, couched political discourse about tax spending that maligned Black people and welfare recipients as lazy and undeserving, and even criminal, was widespread and effective.[16]

The GOP's implicit use of race to discuss taxes was made explicit in an infamous 1981 quote from a Ronald Reagan White House aide named Lee Atwater:

> You start out in 1954 by saying, "Nigger, nigger, nigger." By 1968 you can't say "nigger"—that hurts you, backfires. So you say stuff like, uh, forced busing, states' rights, and all that stuff, and you're getting so abstract. Now, you're talking about cutting taxes, and all these things you're talking about are totally economic things and a byproduct of them is, blacks get hurt worse than whites...."We want to cut this," is much more abstract than even the busing thing, uh, and a hell of a lot more abstract than "Nigger, nigger."[17]

Referred to as the "Southern Strategy," the use of economic and financial policy debates to reference and exploit racial divisions became a well-recognized conservative approach. This rhetorical turn has allowed political discussion of taxes to easily mobilize around racial resentment and bias. For the Tea Party, such messaging was particularly effective, as noted by a *Huffington Post* blogger who wrote that the Tea Party "use[d] the Southern Strategy to rally white support" and referred to Fox News contributor Sarah Palin as "a Southern strategist."[18]

Tea Party news coverage unmistakably referenced a binary that divides the "we" that the Tea Party defends from the "they" that serve as the source of Tea Party ire and contention. On CNN, one tea partier put it simply: "We have got to take the country back by taking back the way they take our money from us."[19]

In examining the deployment of race and gender in Tea Party news coverage, this chapter shows how the Tea Party's brand identity was rhetorically constructed through tropes of race, gender, and class. As news narratives depicted the Tea Party as a largely white, working- and middle-class phenomenon, they also mobilized branding discourses of race, gender, class, consumption, belonging, and social ideology.[20] When some in the conservative media argued that media accusations and coverage of Tea Party racism represented a counter-branding effort that aimed to undermine and diminish the Tea Brand, Tea Party women were held up as brand leaders in response. Thus, this chapter discusses what these news stories tell us about modern conceptions of race, gender, and class identities in media and politics. In raising the volume of racialized, gendered, and classed Tea Party spectacles, journalists and pundits targeted each other and helped establish the Tea Party brand.

Brands are not just labels or identifiers; they are identities rooted in social relationships.[21] Race, gender, and class, in particular, help anthropomorphize a brand and increase its emotional appeal to consumers.[22] When brands mirror a consumer's image of himself or herself, its appeal is stronger. For marketers, these social categories represent consumer and subculture group memberships, and marketers assume that group members share beliefs, experiences, norms, and consumptive behavior.[23] Race, gender, and class identities thus lend themselves to the formation of brand communities in which users feel a strong attachment to a brand (such as the Tea Party) and one another. Branding creates a product image in the consumer psyche through specific associations and characteristics, and the media establish brand familiarity by conveying these attributes to a mass audience.[24] Tea Party news coverage shows that race, gender, and class were essential to its influence and the enduring significance of its narrative.

In drawing on race, gender, and class as key tropes, news reporters and pundits across both conservative and liberal media outlets created stories that (1) paradoxically described collective social action as a form of self-expression and individualism; (2) produced a Tea Party brand commodity that garnered both financial profits and social recognition through heightened media attention and support among various newsmakers; and (3) validated existing social and economic inequalities through emotional and symbolic frames that de-emphasized the importance of racism, sexism, and classism. In producing these narratives, journalists created a meaningful consumer-citizen experience for themselves and their audiences, raising the volume through Tea Party branding practices such as promotion, storytelling, and publicity.[25] Reporters who framed and helped brand the Tea Party told a story about how race, gender, and class are understood and deployed in contemporary media and politics.

The first section of this chapter describes how media coverage of the 2008 presidential campaign served as a backdrop and foundation for the Tea Party's rise in early 2009. Race, gender, and class in Tea Party news stories signaled that the 2008 candidates' gender and racial diversity, and the subsequent election of a Black president, reflected a deeper shift in the ways race, gender, and class are reported in the public sphere. The following sections address this point by examining media coverage of race, gender, and class as attributes of the Tea Party brand and discuss the larger implications of these discursive configurations of race, gender, and class in contemporary media and politics. Finally, I close with a discussion of how the media portrayal of these identities intersected in complex ways that propelled the Tea Party news narrative and concretized its brand.

THE HOPE AND CHANGE BRAND: SETTING THE STAGE

The Tea Party story relied heavily on the news media's commodification of race, gender, and class identities that occurred during the 2008 campaign. The 2008 presidential race marked a substantial change in heightening media focus on the racial and gender identities of political candidates as indicative of a new age. Significantly, the candidates *looked* different from those of previous presidential runs. On the Republican side, Sarah Palin, the first woman vice-presidential GOP nominee represented a new fusion of traditional and conservative values. For the Democrats, this change was captured by Hillary Clinton's primary contest with Barack Obama. The excitement generated by the potential election of the first female or Black president drew regular press attention, and Obama's campaign slogan of "Yes We Can" encouraged voters to revise American history through the corporeal transformation of national leadership. Media emphasis on racial and gender newness helped propel a campaign built on "change" and "hope," and set the stage for the Tea Party brand.

In cultivating his own brand, Obama brought media attention to race and gender as signs of progress. After a loss to Clinton in the New Hampshire primary, Obama gave a highly acclaimed speech that conveyed his electoral campaign as the beginning of a new era. His rhetoric carefully wove his campaign into the tapestry of American racial unity and social advancement:

> It was a creed written into the founding documents that declared the destiny of a nation. Yes we can. It was whispered by slaves and abolitionists as they blazed a trail toward freedom through the darkest of nights. Yes we can. It was sung by immigrants as they struck out from distant shores and pioneers who pushed westward against an unforgiving wilderness. Yes we can.
>
> It was the call of workers who organized; women who reached for the ballot; a President who chose the moon as our new frontier; and a King who took us to the mountaintop and pointed the way to the Promised Land. Yes we can to justice and equality. Yes we can to opportunity and prosperity. Yes we can heal this nation.
>
> ...We will remember that there is something happening in America; that we are not as divided as our politics suggests; that we are one people; we are one nation; and together, we will begin the next great chapter in America's story with three words that will ring from coast to coast; from sea to shining sea—Yes. We. Can.[26]

Indeed, the frame of renewal through identity helped propel Obama to ultimately defeat Clinton in the Democratic primary.

While Clinton did not similarly frame her campaign as a part of the longer arc of history for all Americans (perhaps to her detriment), she did believe that her presidency would signal major progress for American women. In one interview, Clinton said, "Too many people have fought too hard to see a woman continue in this race, this history-making race, and I want everybody to understand that."[27] According to Clinton, "Being the first woman president" would be a "huge change" for the country, and in her campaign concession speech she concluded that women were still unable to "shatter that highest, hardest glass ceiling."[28]

Both candidates understood the racial appeals of their political brands. Clinton made it clear that she expected support from white voters and, thus, had a broader base than her opponent. Obama, she claimed at one point, was slipping among "working, hard working, white Americans."[29]

Clinton's campaign staff made more waves by saying that Obama's South Carolina victory had branded him the "Black candidate," suggesting that his popularity among Black southern Democrats reflected the way he used his blackness as a way of marketing himself to prospective voters.[30] A *Boston Globe* article title summed up the primary contest in five words: "Black man vs. white woman."[31] Few were surprised when, during a CNN debate, each candidate was asked to address critics who thought that "either one is not authentically black enough, or the other is not satisfactorily feminine."[32]

Both Clinton and Obama produced brands, in which gender and racial identity figured prominently. Klein describes Obama's brand as carefully cultivated around his race, as well as his youth. But beyond creating a brand that was "hip, young, and exciting," Klein argues that Obama "won office by capitalizing on our profound nostalgia for those kinds of social movements [that become powerful and make demands of elites]."[33] But these characteristics were rooted firmly in the personal and symbolic— while Clinton was said to be "breaking the glass ceiling" for women and Obama was advancing racial progress, little attention was paid to systemic racial or gender discrimination and oppression. The anti-capitalist history of the women's liberation movement from which Clinton claimed to successfully emerge was also omitted. Though the frames of race and gender made for dynamic and easy-to-circulate reporting on the Clinton and Obama brands, they also reflected a persistent lack of depth in journalistic reporting in a brand culture that could fill a larger responsibility of engaging and informing the public on social issues. As Klein further notes, "The surest way to sell magazines and newspapers in these difficult times is to have an Obama on the cover."[34] Obama and Clinton produced political brands that newscasters, reporters, and outlets could capitalize on, setting the stage for newsmakers to embrace and help produce a conservative brand like the Tea Party that also relied on attributes of race, gender, and class (as well as religious conservatism, anger, and militancy). Such a practice could help sell and circulate news content.

Although either Clinton's gender or Obama's race would have made for a historical presidency, their differences in age and political experience helped only one fully embody newness in the media coverage. According to Charlton McIlwain and Stephen Caliendo,

The heightened attention to race drawn out in news stories about election contests involving racial minority candidates is in large part due to the sense of racial novelty and the journalistic presumption that *what is new is news*, so that journalists consider the racial dynamics of certain election contests newsworthy. [35]

News coverage of the Democratic primary competition pit newness, embodied by a young African American man with little government experience, against oldness, embodied by a white, politically savvy, former First Lady who was just short of senior citizen status. For example, *New York Times* reporter Mark Halperin wrote:

> Your typical reporter has a thinly disguised preference that Barack Obama be the nominee. The narrative of him beating her is better than her beating him, in part because she's a Clinton and in part because he's a young African American.... There's no one rooting for her to come back.[36]

Obama's newness and his campaign promise of "change" were embodied in his age, political (in)experience, racial identity, and age of his supporters. In comparison, the older Clinton seemed out of date and old-fashioned.

Simon Jackman and Lynn Vavreck's study of Democratic primary voters found that race and age overlapped in complex ways and boosted Obama's candidacy and support among young white voters as a signifier of white political progress in regard to racial attitudes toward Blacks. They observed that Obama's racial identity helped to "powerfully structure preferences over who should be the party's nominee" and that Clinton's younger voters were much more likely to switch to Obama than her older supporters.[37] As a *Newsmax* blogger summed it up, President Obama "got more young whites to compensate for defections among older whites."[38] This difference in Obama support among old versus young white voters was important. As a news frame it represented a split between two potential versions of America and the victor depended on the outcome of Obama's candidacy: one America led by the country's future and the other led by its past.

In Obama's brand narrative, young voters' support for his candidacy would reflect a triumph over America's racist past, while his loss would potentially reaffirm American white supremacy—and the "old" America. In this way, the Obama campaign and reporters used branding rhetoric to emphasize that by electing him, American whites could embrace progress and a new America. This explains why Ray Block Jr. found that "Obama's race mattered more to White voters than to Blacks" and that "Whites, not African Americans, were most liable to base their backing on Barack's 'Blackness.'" [39] Newness through race and age overlapped in complex ways and boosted Obama's candidacy as a signifier of white progress on race. (Furthermore, the decades of public service and white maleness of his vice-presidential candidate, Joe Biden, helped bolster any perceived weaknesses in regard to race and experience in national politics.)

The presence of a major female Republican candidate also transformed how the news media described the 2008 campaign. Alaskan governor Sarah Palin became the first woman to run on the party's presidential ticket. Just as Clinton's presidential run signaled progress for women in American society, Palin claimed that the success of the McCain/Palin ballot would "shatter that glass ceiling once and for all."[40] A woman who had embraced feminized gender roles in her professional and personal life as a former beauty contestant, wife, and mother of five children, Palin publicly identified herself as a feminist even as high-profile Democratic women like Michelle Obama veered away from the term.[41] As a preamble to the Tea Party, and the leadership role she would eventually assume within its ranks, Sarah Palin claimed progressive labels in a way that modernized her brand while ignoring the radical and substantive policies and goals of leftist organizing.

Palin was also the youngest person and only woman to ever be elected Alaska's governor and as such represented a repackaging of American conservatism retrofitted to accommodate right-leaning female voters and appeal to the young. Her symbolic function was essential to her brand, which one scholar described as "an average hockey mom whose approach to how the nation should be governed combines kitchen-table economics and the rugged self-reliance ascribed to the Alaskan frontier."[42] Being a woman was incredibly important to her brand as a political pioneer, as Palin noted in the speech announcing her nomination:

> It's fitting that this trust has been given to me 88 years almost to the day after the women of America first gained the right to vote....It was rightly noted in Denver this week that Hillary left 18 million cracks in the highest, hardest glass ceiling in America. It turns out the women of America aren't finished yet.[43]

Palin represented something new in a media landscape formatted for a remade political era, as exemplified by the race and gender identities of its leaders. In addition to frequent parodies of her on *Saturday Night Live*, Palin's subsequent book deals, reality TV show on TLC, job as a Fox News contributor and host, and other media coverage helped publicize and concretize her brand. As a modern conservative woman who defied traditional gender norms with regard to occupation, age, and engagement in the public sphere, Palin provided her running mate John McCain with a much-needed freshness.

In turn, news coverage of McCain, the Republican presidential nominee, branded him a relic. In the matchup against Obama, the candidates' ages, experience, and technological expertise placed them on opposite sides of the new-versus-old divide. Questions about McCain's age and health were frequent topics of news stories, as were references to Obama's youth. In one example, in the final days of the campaign, McCain told a *New York Times* reporter that he had little familiarity with computers.[44] Democratic strategists were able to transform this ill-advised admission into the perception that McCain lacked meaningful engagement with average American citizens' reality and the needs of an advanced society. McCain's campaign responded to criticisms about his age by painting Obama as a "young man with very little experience."[45] In the end, inexperience won and "old" lost. The political stage was set as a modern and unfamiliar terrain—and only something perceived as new could make clear the reconfigured parameters of the contemporary American political landscape.

Journalists also reflexively discussed their own coverage of these atypically diverse candidates. American race and gender were not just campaign topics—they *were* the campaign—and reporters paid attention to candidates' media depictions circulating in the public sphere. Reporters often accused one another of racial or gender bias in campaign reporting, and debated perceived violations of acceptable political discourse. For example, *The Nation* reporter Ari Berman pointed to multiple instances of the press furthering rumors that racialized Obama, including references to him as Muslim, terrorist, and drug user in outlets such as *The Washington Post* and NBC's *Meet the Press*.[46] In another instance, numerous outlets accused MSNBC news anchor Chris Matthews of sexism when he reported on Hillary Clinton with a series of denigrating, gendered comments. He accused Clinton of trying to play "the Betty and Veronica number" in terms of policy (a reference to teenage girl comic-book characters), described her as the "queen bee" in a "matchmaking" and "pimping operation," remarked that her husband, Bill Clinton, kept her on a "short leash," and suggested the reason she was "a front-runner [in the Democratic presidential campaign] was because her husband messed around."[47] In *Jezebel*, Dodai Stewart asked of Matthews, "Can we agree that no matter what your political allegiances, this is not the way you speak of a woman?"[48] Later, Matthews responded to the criticism, saying:

> Some people I respect, politically concerned people like you who watch this show so faithfully...think I've been disrespectful to Hillary Clinton not as a candidate but as a woman....I will try to be clearer, smarter, more obviously in support of the right of women, all people, to full equality of respect and ambition.[49]

For Matthews, it was tough to be a reporter that spoke "almost always without a script, and almost always on tricky subjects of gender and race."[50]

The media paid close attention to what was being said about the candidates' identities and "displayed a renewed interest in talking about race."[51] As reflected in political branding as a process that emphasizes individual traits, journalists and reporters often treated each political candidate as a symbolic stand-in for America's progress on various fronts. While John McCain was branded as an older, archetypal politician, Barack Obama represented how far Black and white Americans had come from their own racial past. Sarah Palin and Hillary Clinton, similarly, demonstrated the success of (white) women. No matter the outcome of the 2008 election, journalists were prepared for a new American era, symbolically represented in the bodies of the nation's elected leaders. On November 4, 2008, Barack Obama was elected president, America was altered, and the media sought to identify the new boundaries of the American political sphere.

From the start of Obama's first term as president, reporters heralded his symbolic win as nationally, socially, and politically transformative and indicative of a new political age that overcame race and racism in modern society. In the *Chicago Sun-Times*, Dave McKinney and Abdon M. Pallasch wrote, "Instead of cringing at war rioters and club-wielding National Guardsmen, America cast aside centuries of racial prejudice and elected its first black President."[52] Similarly, *The Washington Post* reported: "With the election of its first black president, [the country] can now begin to erase one of the stains on that reputation, one that repeatedly shamed us in front of other countries."[53] In an MSNBC segment, *Huffington Post* editorial director Howard Fineman remarked that "Barack Obama as a public figure is about making history. He said in 2008, we are the change we've been waiting for. The fact of his very election as an African-American made history."[54] The day after his election, the front-page headline of *The Guardian* declared that President Obama's win signaled a "magical new spell that will open new American era."[55] Only a few weeks before his historic victory, he had already won "Marketer of the Year" from the Association of National Advertisers, affirming his success as both a candidate and a masterful political brand.[56] He had, according to Klein, helped rebrand America itself.

The 2008 presidential campaign and election changed how reporters talk openly about identity politics, identity as part of a political brand, how their own identities affect their views of society, their roles as reporters, and even the style and meaning of news. Through explicit news rhetoric that gave heightened attention to the dynamics of race, racism, gender, and sexism in American politics, reporters created an anticipatory frame that constructed Obama as a symbol of racial progress. Simultaneously, they also set the stage for a racist and conservative rival to play out a larger racial melodrama and forge a new political brand.

IN THE WAKE OF OBAMA: THE RISE OF THE TEA PARTY BRAND AS "NEW"

Only one month after President Obama's inauguration, Rick Santelli's rant on CNBC marked the beginning of the Tea Party as a new, anti-Obama social movement, predominantly defined by the social group status and signifiers of its supporters and spokespersons. In this period, journalists and Tea Party members presented the Tea Party as a "new" political story—not just because it was an emergent social phenomenon, but because its race- and gender-laden identity was easily linked to a new political era marked by the success of highly visible candidates branded through their race, gender, and class identities. Debates about the Tea Party's newness (or oldness) cloaked larger concerns about American racial and gender progress. The Tea Party's "newness" extended beyond the novelty of its media spectacle—the news media's portrayal of the Tea Party as new was integral to its overall characterization, symbolism, and political significance. As a result, news reporters covering the Tea Party focused not on the lack of originality in Tea Party values, philosophies, and beliefs, but rather on the way the Tea Party brand relied on race, gender, and class as key attributes.

With the Obama-era mediascape primed for explicit discussions about identity and politics, reporters articulated the Tea Party's significance through these lenses. Reporters used Tea Party stories as an opportunity to extend the campaign debates and discuss whether the Tea Party represented old or new versions of America. News narratives consistently used language that described the Tea Party as new. In stories about the Tea Party, protestors were frequently cast as "first-time" activists, Tea Party candidates were depicted as "inexperienced" and new to politics, and the Tea Party was described as trendy and "fashionable." One *Wall Street Journal* guest columnist wrote: "What's most striking about the tea-party movement is that most of the organizers haven't ever organized, or even participated, in a protest rally before."[57] Similarly, Senator John Cornyn referred to Tea Party activists as "relative newcomers to the political process."[58] A *Huffington Post* blogger referred to the Tea Party as "a new group of the dispossessed [who] have taken to the streets."[59] The *Huffington Post* quoted Sarah Palin, who said the Tea Party was a "fresh, young and fragile" movement and "the future of American politics."[60] A guest on Fox News referred to the Tea Party as the "Republican renaissance."[61] Similarly, other stories portrayed the Tea Party as opposing the political "establishment," which situated the Tea Party as an entirely new political actor responding to historical political divisions.

Emphasizing the importance of this "new vs. old" binary, other journalists and commentators challenged this media conception of the Tea Party as a new brand of conservatism and argued that the Tea Party was, in fact, "old." *New York Times* columnist Paul Krugman wrote, "One way to get a good sense of the current state of the G.O.P., and also to see how little has really changed, is to look at the 'tea parties.'"[62] In a blog post describing a typical "tea-partyer" as elderly, a *Newsmax* blogger likened the Tea Party to a "soft-spoken" senior citizen.[63] Various news sources corroborated the characterization of tea partiers as older and part of an old-fashioned generation, with polls that showed tea partiers were more likely to be "Republican, white, male, married and older than 45."[64] *New York Times* columnist Gail Collins described tea partiers as old people who wanted to be young again, writing, "I think they just want to go back to the country that existed when they were 28 and looked really good in tight-fitting jeans."[65] These debates over whether the Tea Party was old or new functioned as a larger discussion of Tea Party branding within the media—in this new mediascape, reporters and pundits aimed to separate the Tea Party's reality from the narratives they were producing about the Tea Party that contributed to its public image.

In part, journalists emphasized the Tea Party's newness by frequently discussing the centrality of new media and technology in the Tea Party's rise. According to a *Wall Street Journal* guest columnist, the Tea Party was a product of a new media age, a reflection of changing technology that allowed citizens to unite without centralized organization or leadership:

> As I write this, various Web sites tracking tea parties are predicting anywhere between 300 and 500 protests at cities around the world. A Google Map tracking planned events, maintained at the FreedomWorks.org Web site, shows the United States covered by red circles, with new events being added every day.[66]

The representation of "new technology" as advanced, progressive, superior, dispersed, and a challenge to preexisting media forms was embodied in the form of the Tea Party rallies—a new movement for a new century. "They want to start this new movement," Fox News reporter Chris Wallace explained to anchor Bill O'Reilly:

It would glaze your eyes over in the kind of detail about the Internet and Twitter and Facebook and social networking and taking a leaf out of the Obama campaign. I mean this is the very practical nuts and bolts stuff about how you organize a political movement.[67]

The Tea Party's use of new technology to organize its rallies and publicize its message associated it with newness and, like technology, positioned it as potentially threatening to existing structures of power, in contrast to the news media's excoriation of John McCain's technological deficiency. Through this technological framing, the Tea Party was cast as a new and improved version of American conservative politics. As I show later in this chapter, Tea Party leader Sarah Palin harnessed this notion of a more technologically savvy Republican brand through her own use of social media messaging and outreach.

Even the news media's common reference to the Tea Party as a form of "populism" reinforced newness as part of Tea Party brand identity. Populism is "about a crisis of representation in which people are weaned off their old identities and embrace a new 'popular' one....There is no populist leadership unless there is a successful constitution of new identities and of a representative link with those identities."[68] The clearest difference in the news coverage of the Tea Party versus previous versions of conservative Republican populism in American politics was how media explicitly interrogated the significance of race in relation to Tea Party activism and appeal. For example, the national media covered and even mobilized supporters for the 1980s Reagan revolution—an earlier white populist movement.[69] During the 1980s, both the Democratic and Republican parties experienced major ideological and demographic shifts in the aftermath of the women's liberation and modern civil rights movements. As discussed earlier, political and media rhetoric included coded references to people of color in discussions about drugs, welfare, school integration, and crime.[70] However, in the twenty-first century, reporting on the Tea Party explicitly and openly discussed the role of race and racial resentment in mobilizing conservative opposition.

As discussed throughout this chapter, news reporters and pundits portrayed the Tea Party as an updated brand of traditional Republican conservatism for a political era marked by Black leadership, made novel through its high-profile women supporters and construed as authentic through its reliance on working-class class identity. Journalists often framed the Tea Party as a "new" political player able to match Obama's "new" form of president, each relying on narrative emphases on race, gender, and class to convey newness. Whether arguing for or against the construction of the Tea Party's newness, the news media's characterization produced a useful dichotomy that reified the Tea Party brand— modern Tea Party versus archaic conservatism. Symbolically, the news media's construction of the Tea Party as a new type of movement strengthened its brand and came with larger cultural resonance—in describing the Tea Party's newness, the media used the Tea Party to interrogate and highlight the fundamental transformation that America's political landscape was presumed to have undergone in the wake of President Obama's 2008 election.

SECTION 1—ON CLASS

No Class Populism

In Tea Party news coverage, class functioned as a central component of the Tea Party brand. Through both explicit and implicit labeling, the news media depicted tea partiers' class position in slippery ways, variously portraying them as working-class, middle-class, and wealthy people. Journalists and pundits just as easily described the Tea Party as a rebellious group of the economically downtrodden *and* as a coalition of affluent citizens who favored anti-poor policies. These narratives lent legitimacy to the Tea Party story by drawing on the "authenticity" conveyed by a working-class identity, the disarming normalcy of the middle class, and the societal esteem given to the wealthy and powerful. The variability of Tea Party class identity in news stories helped situate the Tea Party as a socially important group early on, despite its relatively small size and low influence among American voters. Ultimately, the Tea Party's various class identities within news reports gave it a narrative fungibility that both expanded its media characterization and amplified the potential reach of its political brand.

Media scholars explain that American news media often downplay class by attaching vague or nonspecific class labels to the people they cover. In news stories, "signs of cultural capital or lack thereof function as markers of social class, even when explicit references are not verbalized."[71] In the public imagination and in news stories, African Americans are often portrayed as the "poor," but not as the "working poor" or the "working class."[72] Herbert Gans writes that the news recognizes four class strata—the poor, the lower middle class, the middle class, and the rich.[73] According to Gans, the news media have historically avoided using "the term 'working class'" and instead used the term "middle class" to describe both working- and middle-class people in order to rhetorically bring "blue-collar workers into the middle class."[74] Journalists avoid mentioning class and thus perpetuate the notion that "the vast majority of citizens belong to the middle class."[75] Stories about working-class people are often absent in media representations except in "periods of class struggle."[76]

In reality, more than 62 percent of employed Americans are working class—a group of people with little discretion or control over their work. 32 percent of employed Americans are middle class—people who do not own the means of production but have autonomy in their work. News stories tend to be more favorable toward the capitalist class—the wealthiest and most powerful 2 percent of the population.[77]

While Americans generally avoid specificity around class status, it is a powerful brand identity and construct to which people attach strong beliefs and values.[78] In marketing, class categories are understood as denoting subcultures and brand communities—groups defined by shared beliefs, values, social practices, and consumptive habits rather than their collective experiences of marginalization, discrimination, employment, or systemic oppression.[79] In branding, drawing on class tropes does not necessitate critiquing social inequality; instead, marketers use class to represent familiar images, portray class hierarchies and desirable lifestyle preferences and choices, and evoke contentment and nostalgia that affirm the status quo.[80] As an ideological and branding platform, news media discourse tends to naturalize the social and historical order when representing class categories.[81] In the wake of the 2008 economic recession, described as the impetus for the Tea Party's rise, journalists used class differences to explain Tea Party activism and characterize its brand.

Across all news networks and outlets, reporters and pundits frequently used implicit references to link particular class identities to the Tea Party. Instead of describing tea partiers through specific class categories, news stories often referred to them as "average folks," "ordinary," "plain," or part of "middle America"—code words that signaled white, working-class status while obfuscating class and race divisions.[82] A *Wall Street Journal* guest columnist quoted a satirical blogger named Ioawahawk who suggested that Republican intellectuals were "being overrun by the unsightly hordes of Wal-Mart *untermenschen* typified by the loathsome 'Tea Party' rabble."[83] On CNN, Tea Party organizer Dick Armey described tea partiers as "real working men and women in America."[84] One Fox News anchor reporting on the first Tax Day rallies said that they were "average folks. They're not rich folks."[85] In *USA Today*, Sarah Palin referred to the tea partiers as farmers, small business owners, teachers, soldiers, and civil servants, conflating middle-class and working-class signifiers.[86]

Tea Party news narratives often combined the "working class" with the "middle class" to form one consolidated category. For example, tea partiers were described as "middle class, working class" people and as "doctors and real housewives and real farmers," collapsing variations in income and education between all of these occupations.[87] The Tea Party's middle-class identity was also used to connect it to other class groups, such as the "poor and middle class" and the "rich or the middle class."[88] For the most part, though, references to Tea Party class identity depended on innuendo and wordplay.

Reporters generally based their class descriptions on anecdotal interviews and interpretations of visual cues on display at Tea Party rallies. In particular, reporters used the racial makeup of tea partiers and descriptions of their outlandish clothing, appearance, behavior, and homemade signs to identify their social status. In early Tea Party news coverage, tea partiers were often depicted as working-class people. At one of the first Tax Day rallies, a Fox Business News anchor reporting on the event said that he "didn't find many in the Grey Poupon crowd here. [He] didn't find many of the top 1 percent or 2 percenters."[89] A *Huffington Post* writer attending another Tea Party event wrote:

> I didn't see any seemingly *rich* dudes in NY, Chicago, DC and elsewhere parking their Benz's and raising any protest signs at these rallies. The crowds, though small, were filled with the same types who've been used and abused before: low and middle-income taxpayers.[90]

Similarly, a *New York Times* columnist described tea partiers as working-class people who would not fit in at an event hosted by the intellectual and wealthy Republican elite.

> Whither the conservative establishment in today's bilious political landscape? Certainly the typical Tea Party denizen, with his "I Wanna Party Like It's 1773" T-shirt and "You Lie!" trucker hat, would seem out of place on the Frums' well-tended grounds, nibbling chicken skewers and mini-B.L.T.'s. In the presence of Ms. Hirsi Ali, at least, there was a sense of shared purpose.[91]

Trucker hats, Wal-Mart, and the Nazi term for inferior people (*untermenschen*) were symbols that bestowed upon the Tea Party a working-class status. In discussing a large rally a few months later, a Fox News host said, "Overwhelmingly the crowd was white middle class, working class....But it seems the message, the anti-Obama message is being heard by white working class people."[92] This quote highlights the way news reports mobilized class and interchangeably described the Tea Party as both middle class and working class. In branding the Tea Party, news stories tended to use working-class identity to explain away objectionable (i.e., racist or eccentric) behavior, and use a middle-class label to allow tea partiers to generally stand in for rational, upstanding, and relatable Americans.

The use of class as a marker of civility continued in other media reports. In *Newsmax*, a detailed profile of a rally participant named Bill Warner described him as a savvy former businessman and distinguished him from lower-class Tea Party "wackadoos":

> Bill Warner is hardly a naive man. He ran his own engineering firm for three decades, and sold the assets just before the economy tanked. He built his dream home on a majestic hill abutting a national park, back when the housing market was steady. While some neighbors have since been foreclosed upon, Warner is resurfacing his flagstone deck.
>
> ...Warner packed up his motorhome and drove with his wife, Pat, to Searchlight, Nev., to join thousands of others at a tea party rally dubbed the Woodstock of conservatism.
>
> There were, as his friend put it, some "wackadoos" among the masses: The Barrel Man wearing only a barrel and a hat, the guy dressed like Jesus.
>
> There were also plenty of people just like Warner, who held a coffee mug instead of a sign.[93]

On ABC, a reporter drew a contrast between a middle-class tea partier and another tea partier wearing unusual apparel and criticizing the government, subtly excluding people who dress strangely and use extremist rhetoric from middle-class status:

> REPORTER: The first ever national Tea Party convention brought in delegates as diverse as the Dams, who came in from Indiana in a car....
>
> ATTENDEE (TEA PARTY CONVENTION): We're really normal people. Very middle class.
>
> REPORTER: ...to William Temple, who came in a kilt.
>
> WILLIAM TEMPLE (ATTENDEE): The government, now for the last 50 years, has been moving away from the Constitution and to governing as a tyranny.[94]

Regardless of the news outlet or platform, reporters and commentators frequently blamed inappropriate and offensive antics at Tea Party events on its low-class variants, while the Tea Party's virtue was established through its middle-class respectability. News reporters also used the working-class characterization of tea partiers to construct them as oppressed people and consequently legitimize their hostile behavior and extremist rhetoric. A *Wall Street Journal* guest columnist (and paid Fox News contributor) argued that Tea Party anger was rooted in the struggles of white working-class men:

> That is a key shift in this recession—white men, notably working-class white men, being hit hard and concerned that their needs are not a priority in Washington. A top White House official told me recently that working-class white men are going through today the kind of economic pain, and the social breakdown that comes with it, that black men went through in the recession of the late 1970s and early 1980s.

> This all makes for populist anger, embodied in the tea party movement, at politicians who are not focused on the jobs agenda.[95]

Through syllogism, this writer blames irresponsible politicians and a failing economy for the overt and misdirected anger of white male tea partiers, whom he paints as a marginalized and disenfranchised group acting out of fear. For him, the anti-Obama venom of "opposition to health-care reform from the tea party is not based on racism but self-interest." Through this rhetoric, white impoverished men become poor Black men, neatly allowing whites to lay symbolic claim to centuries of systemic marginalization and subjugation—and, in this reversal of history, the president, a Black man, becomes refitted as a white oppressor. The Tea Party movement is justified as the unpolished expression of white working-class men's legitimate concerns. Through the language of class, journalists not only altered the perception of Tea Party activists but also explained their motivation.

Later Tea Party news stories began to depict tea partiers as affluent, but continued to use class identities to distinguish between tea partiers. Right before the second annual Tax Day protests in April 2010, *The New York Times* published polling data that described tea partiers as "wealthier and more well-educated than the general public" and mostly "Republican, white, male, married and older than 45."[96] Once *The New York Times* poll showed that tea partiers were (on average) wealthier than most people, some journalists deepened their criticism of the movement's racism and working-class persona. Whereas before the poll, an MSNBC guest had called the tea partiers a "bunch of teabagging rednecks" and an anchor said they represented the way that "poor and middle-class voters" were easily manipulated, the Tea Party was now described as a "prosperous looking revolution" made up of "elite, well-off intellectuals" who were "out of step with the real America" and "led by people who are in the upper tax brackets."[97]

Without the defense of class oppression, the Tea Party's racialized anger toward the Black commander-in-chief was hard to justify and their anti-poor sentiment hard to explain. According to *Huffington Post* editor-in-chief Arianna Huffington, *The New York Times* poll showed that the Tea Party had an "anti-poor, anti-black sentiment" and triggered a "debate about whether [tea partiers] are fueled by rage, racism, or class divisions."[98] As a result, various reporters, columnists, and pundits alternately described tea partiers as affluent people *and* as members of the working and middle classes, depending on the political message they wanted to convey.

Instead of describing them as working-class white men, reporters began to describe tea partiers as small-business owners or "stay-at-home moms."[99] In *Newsmax*, one blogger wrote, "Those who think of tea party members as a bunch of country bumpkins will have to think again."[100] An exchange between two Fox News anchors illustrates how the upward shift in the Tea Party's perceived class status helped some reporters legitimize its supporters in subsequent stories.

CHRIS WALLACE: I was going to say, it's 24 percent according to polls. But also, if you look at the [*New York Times*] poll, they're better educated than most Americans.

BILL O'REILLY: They make more money.

WALLACE: They're wealthier than most Americans.

O'REILLY: Right, right. They don't—they're not rubes. And that's my next question on this.

WALLACE: They're not rubes, they're not yahoos and they're not Timothy McVeigh. They are—it's like a meeting of the Rotary Club.
O'REILLY: Yes—

WALLACE: They are small businessmen and women.

O'REILLY: —they're regular folks. They're regular folks.

WALLACE: Who are professionals in California. You know, they are thoughtful Americans.[101]

In essence, news reporters here helped promote and defend the Tea Party brand using a class-based argument about Tea Party attributes and qualities. Bill O'Reilly, the same Fox News anchor who had disparaged the Tea Party's racist, sign-toting, "militant folks" in earlier reports, used this new class information to brand tea partiers as "thoughtful Americans."[102] Moreover, he bolstered his argument by drawing from *The New York Times*—the very media source he described in another broadcast as his media "enemy"—emphasizing the importance of circulation of news texts and information across outlets in raising the volume around the Tea Party.

As new texts constructed the Tea Party as both middle class and working class, it simultaneously normalized it as a political group and rationalized any spectacles of overt racism, extremism, violence, or lack of knowledge among its activists.

Populism as Class Identity in the Tea Party Brand

By far, the news media most frequently used the term "populism" to allude to the Tea Party as a working- and middle-class group, which emphasized these class markers as key Tea Party brand characteristics.[103] Francisco Panizza specifically defines populism as "an anti-status quo discourse that simplifies the political space by symbolically dividing society between 'the people' (as the 'underdogs') and its 'other'...that is deemed to oppress or exploit the people."[104] According to Michael Kazin, American populism is a process by which citizens "protest social and economic inequalities without calling the entire system into question." In this regard, populist protest ignores class barriers and instead maintains the idea that most Americans "are moral, hardworking people."[105]

However, populism as a political identity is historically rooted in the nineteenth-century People's Party, a political group "radical in [its] animus...toward capitalism and [the] ownership class." It "adopted a platform with the principle that all wealth belongs to the workers and farmers who produced it" across racial groups and demanded the nationalization of socially beneficial infrastructure, such as the railroads and telephones.[106] Originally, populism targeted the rich and explicitly demanded more taxes and the expansion of government-funded public infrastructure to protect the poor against industrial interests.[107] Populist Party leaders advocated *for* a "redistribution of wealth."[108] In short, populists were concerned that "industrial-capitalist" money was corrupting society, and they wanted *bigger* government to ameliorate it.[109] This notion of populism was the complete opposite of Tea Party rhetoric. Still, tea partiers and reporters adopted populism's connotation of white working-class resistance to bolster the Tea Party brand.

News coverage that described Tea Party activism as "populism" evoked images of tea partiers as the disenfranchised working class while relying upon the inherent class ambiguity of the term "populist." Even as the Tea Party policy agenda targeted the poor, news descriptions of Tea Party " protestors" deployed the familiar Robin Hood archetype: an impoverished social rebel and classic underdog resisting the greed of the rich and powerful. In language that drew on the class critique in traditional populist sentiment, the media transformed tea partiers into a modern-day People's Party. News stories used populism to depict the Tea Party as ordinary people mobilizing against the structural forces that led to the recession. A *New York Times* columnist explained that the Tea Party was "the latest iteration of [America's] populist tendency," and a CNN anchor called it "the voice of the people."[110] Along these lines, tea partiers were painted as a small but powerful group of people resisting unjust and greedy rulers.

News reporters similarly described the tea partiers as financially devastated citizens rising up in response to the economic crisis. In *USA Today*, a guest columnist wrote:

> The Tea Party movement comprises protesters politically awakened by the recession. Many Tea Partiers voice their protest by describing lives freshly toppled by a layoff, a foreclosure, a bankruptcy, a catastrophic illness, a depleted retirement account.[111]

Other news stories also describe economically downtrodden people suffering in an economy ruined by the wealthy and powerful. A *Huffington Post* blogger wrote:

> The financial crisis has made clear to millions of Americans that we now live in a billionaire bailout society where economic elites can gamble, lose, get bailed out and then refill their coffers with our money in preparation for the next round, while millions of the rest of us are thrown out of our jobs and homes. Frankly, we'd be stupid not to join a populist revolt against that kind system. For the moment the Tea Party represents much of this anger.[112]

Newsmakers used populist imagery to minimize the contradiction of the Tea Party's anti-populist, pro-business, and anti-tax agenda. In *The Huffington Post*, a reporter argued that it was ironic for a wealthy Tea Party candidate to claim a populist mantle:

> [Ron] Johnson, who currently enjoys an eight point lead in the polls, is a millionaire businessman who has never held office....Like all Tea Party candidates, he believes he is running a populist campaign—no matter that he has personally poured 4.4 million dollars into his war chest in an effort to unseat Feingold, the 95th wealthiest senator and a renowned champion of the middle

class. Disregard this fact, and disregard the effects of the stimulus, too: these are details, and Mr. Johnson doesn't think this election is about them.[113]

As this quote highlights, the media's characterization of the Tea Party as a populist movement allowed Tea Party candidates and members to claim a "folk" identity, regardless of their personal wealth or class status. A *Wall Street Journal* columnist concluded that the news coverage of the Tea Party as populist was more of a rhetorical performance than an accurate reflection of Tea Party values, asking: "What is populism? To judge by this coverage, populism is a trick that politicians perform—a clumsy disguise they adopt or a fake-folksy rhetorical line they try to put over."[114]

Undoubtedly, the racial logic of the Tea Party's working-class identity helped rationalize its anti-poor populist discourse. A *USA Today* author quoted a Tea Party attendee describing tea partiers as "people who are working hard for their families and they don't want their money taken away from them to be given to people who aren't working hard."[115] This tea partier suggested that tea partiers were hard-working white people, while those not working hard were non-whites. Edsall and Edsall emphasized the strategic use of similar rhetoric to cultivate conservative populism in the Reagan era, which used "the new Republican agenda of race and taxes to portray the Reagan administration as protecting the working man against 'big government.'" [116]

Calling the Tea Party "populist" had the additional effect of legitimizing Tea Party fury. Like "Tea Party," the term "populism" placed conservative activism in the context of American history, heritage, and citizenship. Through it, journalists painted the Tea Party's "paranoid...pathological hatred of the president"[117] as rooted in civic duty and democratic participation instead of in resentment, racism, or other negative systemic causes. If the tea partiers were hateful or acrimonious, it was because their citizen rights were being violated.

Class Branding Across News Outlets

How different news outlets represented class as part of the Tea Party's brand varied. Among the online news sites, there were clear ideological divisions. Prior to the release of an April 2010 *New York Times* poll that showed that Tea Party supporters were wealthier and more educated than the average American, *The Huffington Post* largely described tea partiers as "low and middle-income taxpayers" who were being controlled by the wealthy.[118] After the poll's publication, *The Huffington Post* rarely used working-class signifiers to depict the Tea Party. *Newsmax*, however, did not mention Tea Party class identity until after *The New York Times* poll was released. *Newsmax* cited the poll and focused on the Tea Party as a movement made of upper-middle-class people to dispel stereotypes of the Tea Party as a group of angry and resentful poor whites (i.e., domestic terrorists, militants, uneducated and ignorant people, racists, etc.). *Politico* largely refrained from giving the Tea Party a specific class label. Generally, class was invoked as a characteristic of the Tea Party identity, shaping its political brand through news narratives dependent upon offering up an interpretation of the Tea Party's value and meaning.

The use of class as part of the Tea Party branding in news narratives varied depending upon the extent to which editorial and opinion content played a role in reporting. In television news, CNN and ABC scarcely mentioned Tea Party class identity. Their few mentions specified a working-class or middle-class identity (i.e., "very middle class" on ABC; "working men and women" on CNN. After *The New York Times* released its survey data, MSNBC's descriptions changed substantially, from the Tea Party as "middle-class voters" to the Tea Party as a wealthy and powerful group. Fox News, by far, was the broadcast news outlet that most frequently and explicitly attributed working- and middle-class labels to the Tea Party, beginning early in its news coverage. Following *The New York Times* poll, however, Fox News largely ceased referring to the Tea Party's class identity.[119]

In the newspapers, where editorial content helped produce much of the initial Tea Party reporting, Tea Party descriptions varied and depended on the partisan leanings of the writers. *USA Today* did not report on Tea Party class identity; *The New York Times* and *Wall Street Journal* frequently used columnists to describe the Tea Party's class demographics, largely portraying tea partiers as either working-class or middle-class people. Almost all descriptions about class in *The Wall Street Journal*'s coverage occurred before *The New York Times* poll was released.

The mention of class in Tea Party news narratives also fell along ideological and partisanship lines. Politically "neutral" news outlets like *ABC News*, *Politico*, *USA Today*, and CNN avoided discussion of Tea Party class status. In partisan newspapers, cable shows, and blogs, conservatives used class identity to legitimize the Tea Party. For some conservative journalists and news commentators, such as those on Fox News, an "authentic" working-class identity helped the Tea Party refute allegations of Astroturfing and racism. Other conservative reporters, such as those at *Newsmax*, depicted the Tea Party as upper-middle class to make it more relatable, respectable, and legitimate and to distinguish conservatives from the highly visible Tea Party "fringe." Progressive columnists and outlets largely described tea partiers as working-class people being used by the rich. Like Fox News reporters, *Huffington Post* writers used the Tea Party's working- and middle-class identity to argue that it was an authentic movement voicing legitimate concerns about the government's failure to protect and serve average citizens. For *The Huffington Post*, tea partiers were suffering because of failed conservative policies, while at Fox, they were outraged and weighted down by a biased progressive agenda. Reporters, pundits, and spokespeople drew on different class-based stereotypes to explain the Tea Party's goals and significance.

Across these portrayals, the news media used the Tea Party to justify preexisting notions about the political and social world. Tea Party class identity was used to justify larger narratives about classism, racism, liberalism, elitism, and oppression, depending on the partisan ideology of the news outlet or its writers. The Tea Party's class identity, then, functioned more as a rhetorical device than an assessment of the Tea Party itself. The news media used the Tea Party to discuss the recession, to criticize the government, to analyze the state of the Republican Party, and to evaluate the overall divide between the "haves" and the "have-nots," be they divided by political power or by wealth. Journalists used ambiguous and flexible language to brand Tea Party class identity, mobilizing class resentment around certain political issues while eliding specificity about social inequality and categorization.

SECTION 2—ON RACE

Post-Race and Post-isms

Journalists and reporters used race and racism, too, to help brand and make meaning of the Tea Party. On April 15, 2009, MSNBC anchor Keith Olbermann introduced "actor and activist" Janeane Garofalo as a guest commentator on his nightly cable newscast. The evening's discussion topic was the Tax Day Tea Party protests. As scenes of Tea Party protestors rolled across the screen, Garofalo dismissed the idea that the Tea Party reenactments were merely harmless patriotic displays:

> Let's be very honest about what this is about. This is not about bashing Democrats. This is not about taxes, they have no idea what the Boston Tea Party was about. They don't know their history at all. This is about hating a Black man in the White House. This is racism straight up. That is nothing but a bunch of teabagging rednecks.[120]

This comment serves as just one example of the rhetoric that frequently circulated within the news public sphere about the Tea Party's racial politics. From the moment the controversial Tea Party demonstrations began, news pundits and reporters questioned whether racism, and not policy, motivated the new movement. As journalists described the Tea Party through its explicit anti-tax discourse, they implicitly produced it as a brand that symbolized ethnocentrism and racial resentment toward the "undeserving poor."[121] By debating the centrality of race and racism in Tea Party rhetoric and ideology, reporters helped fuel its news coverage. Further, covering race and racism spurred at least three early surges in Tea Party news coverage. As scholars like Robin Means Coleman argue, blackness and (I would add) whiteness are mass media and cultural products. As a result, the branding of the Tea Party through news shows how the media produced and articulated contemporary ideas and beliefs about race in American society.[122]

As a discursive construct and brand attribute, race allows visual phenotype markers to signify identity, social location, ability, and performance. Glenn Loury explains that the idea of race is based on visual markers that are difficult to alter, giving them a misleading sense of veracity. "Race," Loury notes, "is all about embodied social significations. In this sense, it is a social truth that race is quite real, despite what may be the biologic-taxonomic truth of the claim that there are no races."[123] Racialization affects our daily interactions, produces material realities, and perpetuates intergroup status disparities. In this way, while racial difference is not real in any scientific (biological or genetic) sense, it is real experientially.

In branding, racial identity is seen as an extension of market choice and neutral difference. Marketers view race as a commodity rather than a bodily signifier of group discrimination and oppression. Herman Gray explains:

> As it concerns group-based social inequities and disadvantage like race, this instantiation of difference moves public discourse from race to diversity to multiculturalism, sharpening a conception and practice of difference resonant and aligned with individual self-reliance, obligation, and consumer sovereignty....Race is visible, but emptied, made an exception, not to matter.[124]

In a brand culture, race signals a means through which people market and express themselves, but not through which they challenge neoliberalism, nationalism, structural violence, racial discrimination, or capitalist exploitation. Using race, the media perform affective brand labor: they deploy sentiments and generate belonging, attachment, and resentment (to paraphrase Gray). This focus on racial identity as an expression of group difference and diversity "prevents recognizing internal group differences and historical alignments of specific conditions of social subordination." "Journalistic practice," Gray notes, upholds multiculturalism and difference in its depictions of race, and equates media visibility of people of color with equality, rather than disparity or marginalization. In this way, the discursive production of race in American social life and media promotes, disseminates, and buttresses white male hegemony.[125]

Garofalo's accusation of Tea Party racism gestures to a long history of race and racism in American political discourse. Stuart Hall links the discourse that creates race and the experience of race when he writes "discursive 'knowledge' is the product not of the transparent representation of the 'real' in language but of the articulation of language on real relations and conditions."[126] As Samuel Sommers and Michael Norton found, "When laypeople think about White racism, they tend to focus on overt old-fashioned forms: participants' psychological impressions of racists consisted of 'fearful of change' and 'old-fashioned,' and demographic descriptions included 'Southern' and 'old.'"[127] As Tea Party protestors were described as predominantly white, older, and mostly concentrated in the South, they easily fit this stereotype, as shown in Garofalo's "redneck" reference.[128] Beyond a simple stereotype, which is a rigid, oversimplified, exaggerated belief about people that manages and categorizes traits, casting the Tea Party as racist made it a personal quality that evoked specific feelings and associations. Referring to the Tea Party as racist did not create a larger discussion about systemic racism. Rather, it became a question of maligning and attacking the Tea Party brand.

The 21st-century decline in explicitly racist discourse and attitudes in the United States compels people to look for signs and markers that signal the racist within.[129] In political communication, this means "implicit racism," or recognizing the ways that "people can speak about racially tinged issues without referring to race and still convey racial meaning implicitly."[130] Understanding the Tea Party's racial politics as key to its meaning was conveyed through both implicit and explicit news coverage that helped solidify the group's brand.

Both implicit and explicit race and racism have been fundamental to the history of branding in the United States. From the very first brands used to sell products such as tea, coffee, and cotton, race was used in marketing to demonstrate white goodness in intervening in the lives of people of color without explaining the political, economic, environmental, or structural reasons for their plight.[131] For example, an 1899 soap advertisement declared: "The first step towards LIGHTENING THE WHITE

MAN'S BURDEN is through teaching the virtues of cleanliness. PEARS SOAP is a potent factor in brightening the dark corners of the earth as civilization advances."[132]

One of the oldest and most notorious characters in American advertising history is Aunt Jemima, an invented Black woman who has been pictured on self-rising pancake mix (and later, at least forty other products) since 1893. Strikingly, the original inventor of self-rising flour failed miserably, selling his patent to a successor who became wildly successful after capitalizing on its name, based on a fictional minstrel character, Aunt Jemima, and hiring a Black former slave actress to play the character at fairs to attract crowds and generate sales.[133] Maurice Manring points out that highly racialized images such as Aunt Jemima played to a nostalgia for southern and white supremacy. As he explains, Aunt Jemima was an "image that traded heavily on her slave origins and ways" and "understanding the way the mammy was merchandised, and the way she is still bought and sold today, might teach us a great deal about our past and our present."[134] Aunt Jemima became one of the most successful brands in American history.

Other Black stock brand characters like Uncle Ben, Famous Amos, Old Grand-Dad, and Dr. Brown helped create not only a "corporate personality"[135] for new products but also emotionally meaningful stories that could be easily filtered through the lenses of race and class. Later, with products such as Black Barbie and Cabbage Patch dolls, race also functioned as an aesthetical difference that could meet the market's demand for both novelty and standardization.[136] That is, in branding, race became a marker of difference without distinction, providing no context, history, or reflection on the stigmatization, marginalization, and privilege assigned to global racial hierarchies, while simultaneously assuaging existing systems of racial power. This pattern of highlighting while also downplaying patterns of race and representation, and nodding to racial nostalgia and symbolism, continued in the news media's coverage of the Tea Party and the production of its brand.

Through implicit racism, journalists and reporters used race as a branding mechanism in Tea Party news stories from early on. Journalists described the Tea Party as a movement of angry, older, working-class, white, racist Americans. As mentioned earlier, Santelli's call to "reward people that could carry the water instead of drink the water" carried loaded racial cues. In a similar vein, one Fox News anchor explained that the Tea Party represented "the battle between Americans who want government entitlements and those who don't and object to paying for them."[137] Studies of government entitlement programs show that the public relies on racial prejudices in their opposition to or support for these efforts. In looking specifically at whites' attitudes toward welfare policy and spending, Martin Gilens found that whites' attitudes toward welfare policy and spending are significantly guided by perceptions that Blacks are lazy. That is, "the belief that black Americans lack commitment to the work ethic is central to whites' opposition to welfare."[138]

In describing the Tea Party as opposed to taxes and government spending on "undeserving" people, journalists made an implicit racial appeal to whites regarding Black (un)worthiness. Tali Mendelberg shares an anecdote from President Nixon's presidential campaign to show how conservatives use this racialized yet "color-blind" rhetoric:

> During the campaign, Nixon offered "freedom of choice" in opposition to school busing....What one former Alabama senator said of [George] Wallace now applied to Nixon too: "He can use all the other issues—law and order, running your own schools, protecting property rights—and never mention race. But people will know he's telling them 'A nigger's trying to get your job, trying to move into your neighborhood.'"[139]

In news stories, the Tea Party was described as a movement that opposed taxes, spending, big government, and the first Black president. Simultaneously, this description also carried coded racial messages that could cohere white racial prejudices among news audiences.

In other words, journalists used race and racism as qualities of character in their reporting on the Tea Party, rather than provide a larger examination of the context and structure of race and racism in relation to Tea Party formation. As an individual characteristic or moral failing, racism was reduced to personal rather than systemic exchange. This is a problem endemic to political branding in media and news—stories that convey an image for a political brand often convey these figures or entities through emotionally charged framing that relies on sentiment rather than fact, context, or history. Journalists, as a result, repeat the narratives about a brand without providing the details and information that can contribute to journalism's role in informing citizens and helping them better participate in democracy and social change.

Reporters' discussions of race and racism in the Tea Party also focused on spectacular moments—explicit displays that sparked news coverage and debates. Reporters for *The New York Times*, *Huffington Post*, MSNBC, and CNN regularly questioned whether the Tea Party was fueled by hostility toward people of color and reported on specific incidents of racism at Tea Party events. CNN and MSNBC also described Tea Party racism as potentially threatening and violent. MSNBC argued that the Republican Party was deliberately using Tea Party "race-baiting" to attract white voters—and, likewise, Fox News accused Democrats of using "race-baiting" to sabotage the Tea Party.[140] *New York Times* articles, columns, and polls also largely painted the Tea Party as an anti-Black group that attracted and accommodated racists. *Politico* and ABC primarily described how the Tea Party defended itself from racism accusations, but did not draw any conclusions about how race shaped the Tea Party's development. *USA Today* described the Tea Party as a white movement and reported on a few sensational shows of racial prejudice among its leaders, but otherwise did not discuss the Tea Party in the context of race and racism.

The conservative outlets, however, had a largely uniform approach to discussing race and the Tea Party. Fox News, *Newsmax*, and *The Wall Street Journal* all ran stories that depicted accusations of Tea Party racism as slander and political mudslinging, denied racism's existence in American society, and attributed any explicit shows of racism at Tea Party rallies to an isolated and insignificant few. The news media used rally signs to decode and identify racist Tea Party ideology. Additionally, there were three significant stories connected to surges in early Tea Party news coverage that involved racism accusations. Through reporting on and analyzing these incidents, journalists revealed different dimensions of Obama-era racial discourse and how embedded race was in the Tea Party brand.

Signs of Racism

For some reporters, protest signs (and their carriers) revealed the Tea Party's racism. As a *Huffington Post* blogger explained, the racist Tea Party "placards" made it "catnip to the news media."[141] Signs gained significant attention in news reports—journalists actively examined, discussed, and highlighted them as evidence of Tea Party racism. For instance, a CNN panel segment focused on deconstructing Tea Party signs with guests:

RICK SANCHEZ, CNN ANCHOR: You went to a rally recently, right?

JOHN AVLON, *DAILY BEAST* COLUMNIST: I went to the D.C. tea party rally on September 12.

SANCHEZ: And you took some pictures.

AVLON: That's right.

SANCHEZ: Let's go through these pictures. You ready? This is one is a picture. Let me do—describe this first one for us, if you would, John. Apparently, it's the president with Hitler and Lenin?

AVLON: Yes.

SANCHEZ: Is it? OK. Let me just ask the question, you at home watching right now. Is this racist? Roland, is this racist?

ROLAND MARTIN, CNN CONTRIBUTOR: Well, I think you're associating the president with two dictators.

SANCHEZ: ... makes people angry.

AVLON: That's the hate trifecta...

[crosstalk]

SANCHEZ: Tim, is this hateful or racist?

TIM WISE, AUTHOR AND GUEST: Well, I think it's pretty hateful. The only way it might be racial is, you think of Hitler. Hitler wasn't just a fascist. He was a racial fascist. So, if you say the Black guy running the country is a racial fascist, it might set off psychologically these notions of, oh, who's he going to come for? And then white folks get nervous because of that. It's possible.[142]

In interpreting the use of a Black president drawn as Hitler on a Tea Party sign, the panelist makes explicit the symbolic use of racial fascism and racism in attracting white supporters and constructing Obama as an oppressor. This notion of Obama as an oppressor of white Americans is a key part of the Tea Party brand, but is also made explicit in this news discussion. On MSNBC, an anchor also argued that Tea Party protest signs were racist:

The kind of poster that showed up in various town hall meetings, with the 9/12 protests serving as a road rage convention. The most blatant examples were there, along with the heavily coded ones. The president as the devil, the president as the blood-sucking alien, the president as undocumented worker, the president as Hitler.

And if you think that allusions to violence are not racially motivated, you may soon reconsider.[143]

Journalists also described Tea Party signs in relation to racial violence, drawing connections between American disenfranchisement of Black Americans and white mob violence. For example, a *Huffington Post* blogger wrote:

But even to see 50,000 people with signs like, "We come unarmed THIS time" and "The tree of liberty must be refreshed with the blood of tyrants" was chilling. I saw one placard that read, "I'm not a racist, I'm a patriot" standing right next to someone in blackface and I saw groups of them mock and shout down a group of immigrant rights activists. To witness those signs alongside ugly caricatures of Obama with a bone through his nose was to see an open declaration of the attempted hate crimes to come.[144]

Referring to those who held signs as "militant folks," Fox News also lent subtle credence to the idea that Tea Party signs that "compared the president to Hitler, to the mafia, to Muslim Marxists" were symbols of violence.[145]

Reporters cited some of the symbols and rhetoric of Tea Party signs as evidence of Tea Party racism; additionally, they interpreted and decoded signs that did not use explicitly racist references to make the racial references clear. An ABC correspondent said, "We've all seen the signs. There have been signs that compare Barack Obama to a monkey. There have been signs that have had the 'N-word' on them."[146] As mentioned in chapter 2, a *Huffington Post* story titled "10 Most Offensive Tea Party Signs," showed photos of Tea Party signs with "Obama's Plan White Slavery," "The American Taxpayers are the Jews for Obama's Ovens," "Obama—What you Talkin about Willis! Spend My Money?" and a photo of a Black man holding a knife to Uncle Sam's throat.[147]

Reporters generally drew on Tea Party signs as irrefutable evidence of Tea Party racism, particularly citing them when racism accusations surfaced from high-profile politicians, such as former president Jimmy Carter or members of the Congressional Black Caucus. For instance, one *Politico* blogger reported on a document about Tea Party racism released by the NAACP: "At its annual convention last week, the NAACP passed a resolution condemning bigoted elements of the tea party. Members have carried signs comparing President Barack Obama to Adolf Hitler and telling him to 'Go back to Kenya.'"[148]

As the media used signs to explain the motivations, goals, and feelings of Tea Party activists, supporters grew sensitive to how racially specific signs threatened to delegitimize the Tea Party. Consequently, Tea Party event organizers began policing signs, which caused some tea partiers to be publicly disavowed by fellow activists. In one example, *USA Today* reported that the owner of teaparty.org was "repudiated by the Houston Tea Party Society after being photographed holding up a sign with a racial epithet."[149]

Deciphering the Tea Party and the Meaning of Race in Modern News

In mid-March 2010, two weeks before the third key surge of Tea Party news coverage, four members of Congress reported that they were verbally and physically assaulted as they entered the Capitol for a controversial vote on health care policy. While white Representative Barney Frank was called a "homophobic slur," much of the subsequent news coverage focused on the incidents involving three Black congressmen, referred to as "members of the Congressional Black Caucus."[150] Noted civil rights activists and representatives James Clyburn and John Lewis claimed that several tea partiers directed racial epithets toward them. Capitol police also arrested another Tea Party protestor for spitting on Representative Emanuel Cleaver.[151] Yet, the news coverage of this and other incidents of Tea Party racial bias treated Tea Party racism as always in doubt and impossible to prove. Conservative reporters across media outlets most vehemently defended the Tea Party against accusations of racism, while other reporters and journalists maintained the rationale that it was never proven. While the overall news media theme of incredulity in relation to Tea Party racism was key to maintaining the integrity of the Tea Party brand, it also highlighted how journalists and reporters discuss race and racism in the contemporary moment.

Two weeks after the verbal and physical attacks on Black congress members, *The New York Times* described a speaker at a major Tea Party Express rally denying these claims:

> One speaker doubted Representative John Lewis's account that he had been spat on by a protester at a Tea Party rally on the Capitol, challenging him to a $10,000 bet to produce proof or take a lie detector test.[152]

A *Wall Street Journal* guest columnist raised similar doubts:

> Rep. John Lewis (D., Ga.) claimed that when he and other members of the Congressional Black Caucus walked through a tea party protest last week in Washington, they heard the N-word hurled at them 15 times. No video or audio recording—in an age when such recorders are ubiquitous—has surfaced to back up the claim. No one was arrested.[153]

In this way, journalists integrated the lack of witnesses and evidence into the official reports about the attacks, eventually shifting from reporting the incident as fact to describing it as "alleged" (an "alleged phony incident").[154] For example, an *ABC News* correspondent reported that "the NAACP points to the racial epithets *allegedly* hurled at black members of Congress by tea party members during the health care debate."[155] A *Newsmax* blogger wrote that the "NAACP and its leftist allies" offered no proof of "these oft-repeated accusations...[about] the allegedly racist tea party movement."[156] On MSNBC, an anchor wondered if tea partiers knew whether these acts were even racist.[157] Not only were the assaults reported unverified, they were *unverifiable*.

Unlike other "alleged" crimes on which journalists report, these reports suggested that there was no way to validate Tea Party racism, even with evidence of explicitly racist rhetoric. For example, Fox News anchor Bill O'Reilly and his show guest Al Sharpton discussed whether there was adequate evidence of the incident at the Capitol:

SHARPTON: People standing outside of Congress using the "n" word.

O'REILLY: How do you know they did that?

SHARPTON: I have seen the tape.

O'REILLY: There is no tape. There is no tape with the "n" word on it. There's no way. Let's be clear. There is no tape.
[crosstalk]

SHARPTON: So, everyone hallucinated the "n" word use?

O'REILLY: I don't know what happened and you haven't seen the tape.

SHARPTON: Against Barney Frank?

O'REILLY: You haven't seen the tape.

SHARPTON: There were all kinds of reporters that were there, Bill.

O'REILLY: No. No reporter said this one said the "n" word. The police who were there didn't hear any "n" word. I'm not saying it didn't happen. I know John Lewis. And I think Lewis is an honorable man. If he says it happened to him, if Lewis says it happened to him, I will believe Lewis....Absolutely. However, let's assume it did happen.

SHARPTON: OK.

O'REILLY: Let's assume it did happen. You can't hold the Tea Party accountable for that.[158]

This exchange shows O'Reilly refuting claims about racial attack from Tea Party protestors. Moreover, the validity of racism accusations rested upon the character of the aggrieved (i.e., the "honor" of the representatives). This could not substantiate their claims either. O'Reilly suggests that Black people have a vested interest in perpetuating, and not ending, racism. Moreover, this exchange shows that O'Reilly aims to protect the Tea Party's image from these "attacks" alleging racism, refuting these acts of racism as merely an attack on the Tea Party brand (as opposed to an issue of real societal concern).

Many contended that the incident never happened. In an interview with a *Huffington Post* blogger, a National Tea Party Federation leader said:

LEADER: We actually did some investigation, along with BigGovernment.com. And Andrew Breitbart's organization produced a number of videos, which refute not only the allegations but call into question the veracity of the charges being made. Not by Congressman Lewis per se, although I think he was sort of used, in particular. We subsequently sent a letter to the Congressional Black Caucus calling for any evidentiary documents and or videos.

INTERVIEWER: I saw that letter.

LEADER: And what we got was, as the *Christian Science Monitor* reported and actually called the Congressional Black Caucus. What they found is not only were they [the Caucus] angered by the letter and their inability to produce any documentation but also they [the *Monitor*] began to question some of the videos....And so it was clear that it simply did not happen.[159]

In fact, Jonsson's *Christian Science Monitor* article did not question the "veracity of the videos," but only noted that the racial epithets were not recorded.[160] The Tea Party leader's implication is clear—racism requires proof, but even proof of racist tea partiers could not show that the Tea Party itself was racist. Like gender and class, race was an intangible quality of the Tea Party brand. Alternatively, *Huffington Post* also reported that a "popular argument among tea partiers" was the idea that any people screaming slurs were planted "to make the movement look bad."[161] Through the coverage of this Tea Party incident, racism emerged as a conspiracy theory or paranoid delusion made up by Black Americans. Additionally, reporters' language racism echoes that of a criminal violation—"charges" of racism, "alleged" incidents, and "accountability." While racist rhetoric alone is not a crime, the news language used to describe racism treats it as such.

The news coverage of another major incident involving race and the Tea Party provides further insight into the ways that racism (systemic and structural bias based on racial hierarchies) and racialism (drawing attention to race) are constructed in public debates as synonymous—that is, reporters covering the Tea Party make no distinction between *criticizing* racism and *perpetuating* racism. In early July, the NAACP approved a resolution for "people of good will to repudiate the racism of the Tea Parties," citing various reports of racism at Tea Party. In response, Tea Party supporters said that the NAACP itself was racist because of its resolution. For example, in a *Politico* blog post, two Tea Party leaders argued that the NAACP was responsible for racism's prevalence:

The NAACP has a long history of liberalism and racism.

If you are a conservative—including a conservative African-American—there is no room for you at the NAACP. If you have opinions that differ from the NAACP and the liberal establishment, and if you are African-American, you are an "Uncle Tom," a "negro," "not black enough" and "against our people."

In other words, the NAACP fancies itself the thought police for millions of black Americans.[162]

Another *Politico* piece referred to the NAACP as "a bunch of old fossils." As these quotes show, the sound bites and narratives provided about the Tea Party made virtually no attempt to distinguish between those voicing concerns about racism and those professing racist ideologies and beliefs. According to such narratives, "The tea party is a truly post-racial movement...[and] is uninterested and uninvolved in the politics of race."[163] Through this argument, the Tea Party imagines itself as post-race. This rhetorical move is important in that it both nullifies the historical significance of Obama's election (as the first Black president) and dismisses racism as a motivating factor in the Tea Party's formation.

Some journalists called the NAACP racist in their treatment of the Tea Party—in this case, racism was described as a way that *Blacks* unfairly judged *whites* based on racial prejudice. As O'Reilly explained on Fox News:

> For people to now use these terms like racist, racist is a lazy, lazy way to describe someone. It's like you don't like your boyfriend, you call him a racist. I think that we've got to stop with this hateful rhetoric.
>
> And the more they use it, the more a legitimate mainstream organization like the NAACP uses these sloppy, lazy kind of broad-based stereotypes, the more they destroy their own credibility.[164]

In using the words *lazy* and *sloppy* to describe the NAACP, O'Reilly drew on the racially embedded use of these terms to historically describe Black people and justify their low status and mobility (and, even, enslavement) in American society. Again, there was an invocation of race and racism without an exploration of what it entails beyond the personal and individual level. This quote is fascinating in its description of "racism" as a charge, a matter of personal disagreement between people of different racial identities. Later on in the same discussion, O'Reilly argued that the NAACP resolution was actually a publicity stunt and part of the Democratic Party's overall election strategy:

> O'REILLY: Now last night, Karl Rove and Dick Morris basically said that [President of the NAACP Ben] Jealous is taking his marching orders from the Democratic party, that the Democratic party wants the controversies about the Tea Party to drive their constituents to the polls next November, because they fear that minority voters will not go [to the polls to vote] in an off year election. This is what Rove and Morris believe is behind this.

RIVERA: Well, I don't know what evidence they have, because to me to make a charge that incendiary, you better back it up. Here's a memo. Here's an email. Here's some kind of evidence—

O'REILLY: You know, it's logical.

RIVERA: Logic and evidence is different.

O'REILLY: I got it, I got it. We can't—it's speculation.

RIVERA: Right.

O'REILLY: But it was an interesting speculation.[165]

Not only was the "charge" of racism an empty signifier, O'Reilly argued that it was deployed strategically. Jonsson's *Christian Science Monitor* article explained that the refusal of some conservatives to denounce racist acts was part of a larger effort "to move into a 'post-shame' age in which the politics of race are dialed back to allow America to move forward."[166] Importantly, the central issue here for the news media is *not* racism—rather, reporters convey that tea partiers oppose the process of *calling* someone racist. In this way, being *called* a racist can be unfair, strategic, and destructive to a person or group's reputation. This argument suggests that it is, in fact, racist to accuse someone of being racist since the process requires referencing race and racial hierarchy (i.e., differentiating between the racist and the racially oppressed). The logic of victimization through racism is reversed and white supremacy is rendered irrelevant in these types of Tea Party news stories.

Many reporters even dismissed explicit Tea Party racism as anachronistic and unimportant. Within the Tea Party news stories, reporters downplayed rhetoric that appeared old or reflected an antiquated version of America. Explicit racism was cast as "fringe," "crazy," a "threat," "unstable," "unintelligent," or lacking in "civility." In some cases, the connections between old *people* and discarded *values* were made explicit, as in one *New York Times* article that spoke directly about the disproportionate elderly segment of Tea Party activists and their outdated ideas. In the piece, a *New York Times* guest columnist uses the example of racism to show how the old-versus-new political divide is based not on morality but, rather, the passage of time:

The Tea Party and the N.A.A.C.P. represent disproportionately older memberships. And herein lies a problem with so much of our discussion about race and politics in the Obama era: we tend not to recognize the generational divide that underlies it.

The question of racism in the amorphous Tea Party movement is, of course, a serious one, since so much of the Republican Party seems to be in the thrall of its activists. There have been scattered reports around the country of racially charged rhetoric within the movement.

But such incidents—or, maybe more accurately in some cases, an utter indifference toward racial sensitivities—shouldn't really surprise anyone. That's not necessarily because a subset of these antigovernment ideologues are racist, per se, but in part because they are just plain old.

...In other words, we are living at an unusual moment when the rate of progress has been dizzying from one generation to the next, such that Americans older than 60, say, are rooted in a radically different sense of society from those younger than 40. And this generational tension—perhaps even more than race or wealth or demography—tends to fracture our politics.[167]

Notably, this writer is not arguing that racism is evil, reprehensible, immoral, or rooted in a brutal, exploitative, white supremacist economic system. Rather, he describes racism as a generational trait, one that the younger or "newer" generation has escaped. In this framing, older people are not necessarily racist, just insensitive to appropriate racial discourse. Again, this type of news framing protects the Tea Party brand from any explicitly racist signs or rhetoric that may be documented, pinning any hateful messaging on the brand's consumers and loyalists rather than the brand itself.

Reporters used "old" as a gauge of political relevance not only with regard to the Tea Party but also with regard to its perceived adversaries and their brand identities. One *Huffington Post* piece quoted a Tea Party leader calling the NAACP a "bunch of old fossils looking to make a buck off skin color."[168] Similarly, *The New York Times* wrote that the "NAACP scratched an old wound...when it called on the tea party to expel racists."[169] In this framework, anyone accusing the Tea Party of racism was also outdated and irrelevant to a brand constructed as more modern and "energetic" than previous iterations of conservatism.

Another race-related surge in Tea Party news was linked to the resignation of prominent Tea Party rally speaker, Tea Party Express chairman, and conservative radio host Mark Williams. National news reporters frequently interviewed Williams as a Tea Party Express spokesman and often asked him about Tea Party racism. Early in the Tea Party's coverage, Williams was accused of using "racial imagery" in "call[ing] the president of the United States an Indonesian Muslim and a welfare thug" and "racist in chief."[170] Despite his racist language, reporters continued to interview Williams as an authority on racism. This was a prime example of raising the volume in allowing a conservative media personality to pass on his own messaging around the Tea Party in a way that both promoted his own brand and that of the Tea Party. Through these opinion spaces, non-conservative outlets also functioned as key platforms for Tea Party promotion and brand management, particularly in relation to gender.

In one CNN segment in September 2009, Williams disclaimed any racism in the "movement," telling CNN that he observed "very little racism or anger, and those [he saw] were on the fringes and were marginalized." When CNN showed Williams videotaped footage of Tea Party protest signs depicting President Obama as a witch doctor, he dismissed the significance of those representations and said they were carried by outliers of the group. Ironically, Williams himself would soon become one of those "outliers."

In July 2010, Williams posted what he called a satirical commentary on his blog. In a piece titled "The Lincoln Letter," Williams posed as NAACP president and chief executive officer Ben Jealous—or, in his words, "Precious Ben Jealous, Tom's Nephew NAACP Head Colored Person."[171] Williams wrote:

Dear Mr. Lincoln,
We Coloreds have taken a vote and decided that we don't cotton to that whole emancipation thing. Freedom means having to work for real, think for ourselves, and take consequences along with the rewards. That is just far too much to ask of us Colored People and we demand that it stop!
    ...Mr. Lincoln, you were the greatest racist ever. We had a great gig. Three squares, room and board, all our decisions made by the massa in the house. Please repeal the 13th and 14th Amendments and let us get back to where we belong.[172]

Williams's call to revoke the amendments abolishing legal slavery and extending legal citizenship to African Americans triggered an immediate response. After his letter was posted, Williams's words spread quickly throughout the blogosphere and reignited debates about the Tea Party's racism. The letter ultimately prompted the Tea Party Federation, an umbrella group for numerous Tea Party groups throughout the country (including the Tea Party Express), to disavow Williams's views. Within a week of publishing the blog post, Mark Williams resigned as chairman and spokesman of his Tea Party group. As Fox News put it, "The Tea Party ha[d] to fire one of its members for racial insensitivity."[173] Not only had explicit racism eliminated Williams's credibility, but it had been perceived to damage the Tea Party's brand in the process by providing a concrete non-"fringe" example of white supremacist beliefs and values at the Tea Party core.

In retaliation for the NAACP's resolution about Tea Party racism and Mark Williams's subsequent downfall, conservative blogger Andrew Breitbart released what became known as "the Sherrod video," which was titled "Video Proof: The NAACP Awards Racism."[174] Through intentionally deceptive edits, the video appeared to show a Black, high-level Obama administration agriculture official, Shirley Sherrod, admitting that she refused to help white farmers because of their racism. The grainy scene seemed to be spectacular proof of Fox News assertions that Black people, and the NAACP in particular, were the true "movement for racists" who used race to undermine white progress (as Williams had claimed).[175]

After watching the clip, one political analyst on an MSNBC morning show drew an immediate comparison to Mark Williams, saying, "How about if Shirley and Mark Williams, the Tea Party guy, are locked in a room together as their punishment?...It's every bit as hateful. I mean, look at that woman. I mean, aren't you ashamed?"[176] In other words, this pundit put Sherrod's alleged discrimination in refusing to assist a white farmer in the same category as a Tea Party leader who had advocated for the legalized return of African Americans to chattel slavery and non-personhood. (It's worth noting here that the Black woman government official in this statement is informally referenced by her first name while the white man framed as her counterpart is referenced by his full name. This, again, shows the way racism and sexism manifest subtly in journalistic narratives without substantive engagement.) Importantly, this type of comment reflects how news reports and commentators equated Black responses to racism with white racism and subjugation of Black people, drawing parallels between two groups situated drastically different in relation to power. In the days following the video's release, the full-length NAACP video and testimonies from the white farmers referenced in the video showed that Sherrod had, in fact, provided the necessary aid. She was cleared, but too late—she had already been fired from her post.

After Sherrod's vindication, Breitbart explained that he intentionally posted the deliberately misleading video on his popular website, Breitbart.com, as a tactical response to the NAACP's accusations about Tea Party racism:

This was not about Shirley Sherrod. This was about the NAACP attacking the "Tea Party" and this [video] is showing racism at an NAACP event. I did not ask for Shirley Sherrod to be fired. I did not ask for any repercussions for Shirley Sherrod....Racism is used by the left and the Democratic Party to shut up opposition. And [by releasing the Sherrod video] I am showing you that people who live in glass houses should not be throwing stones.[177]

CNN described Sherrod as having "changed her outlook and [realized that] people should move beyond race."[178] Thus, journalists vindicated Sherrod through showing that she had transcended race through helping whites, instead of validating her personal experience of racism (including the lynching of her father). A Fox News guest connected the Sherrod controversy to President Obama, arguing that it had "forced him to have to come from behind that curtain and address the issue" of race.[179] According to one *ABC World News* reporter, the Sherrod incident ultimately provided a "teachable moment" on "race, media, and the Obama administration."[180]

The Sherrod case proved to be a particularly revelatory opportunity for Fox News reporters to explain how they conceived of the media in racialized terms, producing a set of personal narratives around race that both raised the volume in relation to Tea Party reporting and minimized racism as a critical brand quality. According to O'Reilly, the Sherrod story resulted in a lot of finger-pointing at Fox News for "race-baiting." O'Reilly felt that his peers in other media outlets were accusing Fox News of "gin[ning] up the story to make blacks look bad."[181] According to paid Fox News contributor Bernie Goldberg, a guest on the O'Reilly show, the only way that the mainstream media understood race was through the lens of Black victimhood:

> If it doesn't fit their storyline on race, they're not interested. And the only storyline, Bill, the only storyline they care about is that white conservatives and FOX News are the racists in this story, in this picture. And they're out to get a poor, innocent, black woman. That is the only way the mainstream media today understands race. And it's pathetic.[182]

O'Reilly then declared that covering race on his show was fruitless:

> I don't want to have [the discussion of race] anymore. Every time I have it with somebody like you, with Al Sharpton or whatever, my words get taken out of context, I'm branded a racist. It doesn't do me any good personally.[183]

Thus, O'Reilly made a clear argument for understanding "racism" as a brand characteristic, something that impacts one's image, rather than a reference to one's own actions, ideology, or behavior. Racism here is constructed as a personal quality, much as it was used generally in Tea Party reporting in establishing and evaluating its value, importance, and meaning. Fellow Fox News host Glenn Beck echoed a similar sentiment. "You are supposed to tow [*sic*] a certain line in the media; if you don't, they will target you.

They will watch every word you say. And if it's [a liberal media advocacy group], they will tape everything you say and they won't stop until they drive you off the air. That's the goal here."[184] For O'Reilly, the apparent conflict around the media portrayal and coverage of race raised just one question: "What about the post racial America? What happened to that?"[185]

Post-Racial, Post-Racism, Post-Race, and the Tea Party Brand

These racialized Tea Party incidents, as described by media, exemplify how race functions in the post-racism branding era in which criticisms of racial performance in media regularly aim at moving targets. As Imani Perry argues, while "the media are often a convenient straw horse for racial images...they probably reflect racial ideology far more than they guide it."[186] The term "post-race" signals an era in which recognizing or referencing racial discrimination is often equated with racism—in other words, we are in a period in which the public is focused on transcending race rather than eliminating racism. As Darrel Enck-Wanzer points out, this means that President Obama is "operating within a racially neoliberal discursive field that binds him to antiracial (as opposed to antiracist) responses to subtly (and not so subtly) racist discourses."[187] The Shirley Sherrod fallout shows that limiting racial advocacy and activism to individual success applies to other Blacks in power (and shows the material consequences of perceived violations). In a contemporary brand culture, this neoliberal emphasis on personal, rather than structural, change is highlighted and advanced in Tea Party news coverage.

Neoliberal branding frameworks emphasize the individual's role in his or her own success or failure. In doing so, neoliberal discourse mirrors what Eduardo Bonilla-Silva calls "colorblind racism," in which whites use a "loosely organized set of ideas, phrases, and stories" to justify contemporary racial inequality.[188] Enck-Wanzer explains that in this context, "racism is 'shorn of the charge' and the structural irrelevance of race is underscored through the neoliberal fantasy of personal responsibility."[189] In other words, pundits, politicians, and scholars alike have frequently blamed racial disparities that disproportionately disadvantage African Americans on blackness and Black people's pathology rather than on systematic racism, discrimination, and disenfranchisement. An ideology of post-race reaffirms this idea by emphasizing personal and individual fulfillment as more important than group belonging or identification.

While other scholars refer to this as a "post-race" or "post-racial" era, I instead offer the term "post-racism" to reference the popularized idea that race is no longer important because systematic discrimination against people based on race has ceased. Through post-racism ideology, racism is cast as irrelevant and resolved, largely by pointing to incremental and exceptional achievement among racialized minorities. The media, unlike the Tea Party, cannot strictly adhere to a post-racial ideology—in heralding Obama's election as the birth of a "new age" in America, the media relied on a narrative that inherently embraced and acknowledged his racial identity. That makes racism key to the dominant narrative portraying Obama's victory as a racial triumph, because his success in spite of racial obstacles is what makes his election so remarkable. Still, this narrative suggests that racism was defeated in order for his victory to be significant, that his presidency signaled the end of racism itself. So Obama-era media discourse requires that the media draw on race as a trope while simultaneously denying the power of racism—in other words, deploying post-racism ideology.

As the news media used race in the branding of the Tea Party, they simultaneously gave insight into the ideologies of race and racism in the contemporary media and political environment. The Tea Party news narratives reveal five key dimensions in Obama-era discourse in relation to race and branding. First, the move to allow tea partiers to stand in for "America" depicts the embeddedness of racism in news discourse. The whiteness of tea partiers allowed news reporters to construct them and their concerns as representative of all Americans. This, too, means that Tea Party media coverage revealed a hyper-vigilance that amplified racial retaliation from minorities while downplaying explicit racism among whites.

The second key dimension of the media's racial branding of the Tea Party is the narrative impossibility of racism. That does not simply mean the denial of racism in specific incidents, as Bonilla-Silva and Jane Hill discuss,[190] but the impossibility of proving racism, no matter how explicit. The Tea Party reporting on accusations of racism often remained perpetually doubted, unverified, and unverifiable. So, even while Mark Williams called for Black people to be enslaved again under the law, Fox News referred to it as "sophomoric" and a "mistake," but not racism.[191] Similarly, even though there were frequent examples of explicit racism among Tea Party rallies and conventions, reporters and pundits regularly referred to these spectacles as "fringe," minimizing their presence in and influence on the Tea Party. Debates over the Tea Party's racism reflect a larger societal inability to precisely or definitely identify racist acts, ideas, or people, leaving the Tea Party to symbolize racism's "imaginary" social force.

Third, the equivalency of racism was also a rhetorical component of Tea Party news branding. In equating white dominance and prejudice with

Black responses to such discrimination, the news media drew on race and racism as only superficial distinctions. In describing the Tea Party, the news media suggested that racism was not about the material conditions of power and privilege according to race. Instead, racism became the process of simply differentiating between and evaluating people's behavior based on race. In this notion of racism, actual discrimination and withholding of resources as a longstanding institutional and historical practice were less important than name-calling and accusations. In this way, white bodies demanding power and a Black body obtaining power become ahistorically juxtaposed. Through news texts that drew on and amplified civil rights movement imagery and references in regard to the Tea Party, the group stood in for the oppression of white conservatives at the hands of a rising Black power. In branding the Tea Party in a news op-ed, Sarah Palin argued that the Tea Party was driven by the same "spark of patriotic indignation" as the one that fueled "those who marched for civil rights."[192] Similarly, a *Huffington Post* blogger referred to the Tea Party as "a new group of the dispossessed"[193] and news reporters covered the Tea Party leaders' "March on Washington" without discussing the lack of historical or social relevance to the original event. Using race to brand the Tea Party as a racially marginalized and disaffected group challenging a Black president required that news reporters also engage the active decontextualization and remaking of these historical symbols. While decontextualizing race and history happens frequently in news coverage, this practice in relation to the Tea Party allowed it to continue its function as a brand and signifier.

Fourth, in this vein, the news branding of the Tea Party also relied on depicting racism as a strategy rather than a dominant structure and way of life. In the news reports about the Tea Party, racism was described as a strategy of silencing whites and as a political rhetoric that controlled Black people. Conservative news outlets often described calling someone a racist as a way that Blacks unfairly judge whites based on Blacks' racial prejudice. Similarly, racism was described as a rhetorical tool and myth by which the Black elite kept other Blacks in line politically. For example, O'Reilly argued that the NAACP colluded with the Democratic Party to make its resolution denouncing the Tea Party's racism, all in an effort to "drive their constituents to the polls."[194] Importantly, what's at issue here is *not* racism. Rather it is the process of calling someone a racist that is discussed as a problem in contemporary political branding culture. In this way, referring to someone a racist is depicted as an attack on their brand, an unfair and strategic attempt to destroy another entity's reputation. The *accusation* of racism itself becomes racist.

As a result, the Tea Party's key leadership could be explicitly and frequently racist, and yet news organizations did not conclude it was a racist group—in other words, the Tea Party brand as represented by the news media was able to explicitly allude to race and elude accusations of racism at the same time, bolstering its appeal to certain demographic groups while protecting its image from others. This maneuvering is, in fact, indicative of the "post-shame" mantra attached to American racial attitudes, particularly in a brand culture fixated on individualist symbolism and personal meaning rather than structural context and consequences. Through this line of post-shame racial argument, one can conclude that without explicitly acknowledging the existence of racial hierarchies in regard to power, there is no racism—and without racism, there is no racial inequality. It is, as with all branding, a way of marking race as a difference without differentiation.

Finally, the news media's branding of the Tea Party through race signified that systemic white supremacy and racism were irrelevant to contemporary politics and society. For less conservative and more liberal news networks, reporting on Tea Party racism provided the disproportionately white news media and its audience with an opportunity for internal validation—that is, identifying the "racist out there" allowed some whites to both dismiss the personal relevance of racism and to alleviate any feelings of personal liability in perpetuating or benefiting from a system predicated upon racial inequality and white privilege. According to Linda Williams, the American news media use racial dramas to represent signs of racial virtue and villainy. In this way, melodrama manifests itself in racial conflicts that play out using the hyper-expressive body of the Black man, white woman, or white man.[195]

This particular point buttresses bell hooks's argument that expanding the media representation of marginalized people is generally about white audiences "eating the other"—consuming and appropriating race for their own consumption and ego, *not* about humanizing marginalized people.[196] Along similar lines, Herman Gray writes:

> The object of recognition is the self-crafting entrepreneurial subject whose racial difference is the source of brand value celebrated and marketed as diversity; a subject whose very visibility and recognition at the level of representation affirms a freedom realized by applying a market calculus to social relations.
>
> ...With increased attention to visibility and recognition, the emphasis on identity shifts from antiracist struggle to antiracial ones or...a moment where race and gender signal lifestyle politics. Rather than struggle to rearticulate and restructure the social, economic, and cultural basis of a collective disadvantage.[197]

In this way, the individualist and market-centric logics of a brand culture shaped the news media's coverage of race and racism in the Tea Party in a way that bolstered, protected, and even attracted supporters for the Tea Party brand while denying and ignoring larger structural and historical contexts. The news media portrayed race and racism as qualities of personal meaning and divergent significance, as a mode of consumption and appropriation, rather than a means by which issues of inequality and disadvantage could be addressed.

Additionally, while many scholars have noted the way that Black Americans have historically struggled with adhering to notions of "Black respectability," whiteness rarely, if ever, undergoes such examination. As a racialized melodrama, the Tea Party provided a space to air concerns about white respectability in the Obama era and permitted a larger discussion about the (in)appropriate performance of a politicized whiteness in a "post-race" environment. The news media depiction of the Tea Party as racist also allowed them to contain racism safely in a familiar frame. Moreover, these discussions around race, racism, and respectability provided more fodder by which the news media could produce content about the Tea Party, attract audiences, and engage in cross-media and interactive storytelling. In other words, they used race to raise the volume in coverage on the Tea Party and its brand.

Ultimately, journalists used the Tea Party as a racial bogeyman, a figure that represents modern racism in an era that denies its existence, providing the hyper-expressive bodies needed for the ongoing melodrama of race. That is, debates over the Tea Party's racism represent larger arguments about our inability to precisely or definitively identify racist acts, ideas, or even people, leaving the Tea Party to symbolize racism's "imaginary" social force. Moreover, the Tea Party used race to maintain a consistent spotlight on a narrow political stage. Within a "post-racial" political landscape, the question of racism fueled the Tea Party's growth and development.

SECTION 3—ON GENDER

Her Cup of Tea: Representations of Tea Party Women

In addition to hearkening the 1773 Boston Harbor event, the term "tea party" carries a distinctly feminine political and historical connotation in Anglophone societies. Victorian women used tea parties to navigate their exclusion from the sociopolitical spaces of men's coffee houses and to reinforce their gendered roles and duties in the home.[198] In the United States today, the word *tea* still evokes the image of a domestic and traditionally feminine role—as Hillary Clinton discovered during her husband's 1992 presidential campaign, when she made waves by commenting that she could have "stayed home and baked cookies and had tea."[199] As Kathleen Hall Jamieson explains, in this context "tea" symbolized domestication, motherhood, and homemaking, and a repudiation of a career outside the home.[200] Given this history, the contemporary Tea Party brand invoked gender and femininity in its very name.

Journalists covering the twenty-first-century Tea Party were fascinated by its female participants.[201] Women figured prominently in narratives explaining the Tea Party's political, cultural, and social significance. Moreover, the stories journalists told about female tea partiers reconceptualized gender, politics, and performance in a contemporary landscape. Ultimately, media reports on Tea Party women described the birth of a new brand of conservative political women and imbued the Tea Party's archetypal populism with modernism and progress, even as they reproduced problematic and regressive gender ideologies. This approach to reporting on Tea Party women expanded upon the already established pattern in political reporting that covers women politicians as a novelty.[202]

Tea Party women activists and candidates were particularly effective in attracting Tea Party news coverage. According to Daniel Reed, Christine O'Donnell's primary victory "started a media frenzy, as her nomination sparked renewed attention on the midterm elections on the cable news networks and the Internet."[203] Journalists identified Tea Party women activists and candidates based on their appearances at Tea Party events, leadership in local Tea Party groups, and endorsements from high-profile Tea Party leaders (Sarah Palin, in particular). In *Politico* and *Newsmax* articles, all of the potential speakers highlighted for the first Tea Party convention were women—former Alaska governor Sarah Palin, Minnesota congresswoman Michele Bachmann, and Tennessee congresswoman Marsha Blackburn.[204] Palin's speeches at various Tea Party Express rallies emphasized her importance as a Tea Party leader and bolstered perceptions of her centrality in midterm election organizing. Michele Bachmann also received press coverage for her appearances at Tea Party Express events and for creating the first Tea Party caucus in Congress. An MSNBC anchor referred to her as the "face of the Tea Party."[205]

Compared to their coverage of Tea Party men, journalists more frequently highlighted the funds that Tea Party women were able to raise (and, hence, spend) to describe and explain their political power, significance, and performance. *Politico* called Bachmann a "fundraising juggernaut."[206] Sharron Angle was noted for "rais[ing] a stunning $14 million from July through September...[while her opponent Harry] Reid raised about $2 million during that time."[207] According to *The Wall Street Journal*, Palin's "influence" lay in her "fund-raising abilities" and capacity to pump money into the campaigns she endorsed.[208] While these women were seen as unprepared for political office, the money they were able to raise and spend guaranteed their perceived power and coverage in the press. Male Tea Party candidates such as Senators Rand Paul and Scott Brown, on the other hand, were often described in the context of their surprising success, candidacies, and political prowess, and there was less emphasis on the money their campaigns raised. As Anthony DiMaggio puts it, "Ultimately, money speaks louder politically than do words"[209] especially for Tea Party women, who stood in as political commodities to both raise and wield funds, reinforcing the consumerist image of political women in media.

When one news poll suggested that female Tea Party supporters slightly outnumbered males, the media's feminization of the Tea Party became even more firmly entrenched. In April 2010, Quinnipiac University released a poll that said the Tea Party movement was "a group that has more women than men,"[210] after which press coverage changed substantially. *Politico* produced a full-feature story with a headline that announced "The Face of the Tea Party Is Female."[211] Drawing on the poll, the reporter asserted that "many of the tea party's most influential grass-roots and national leaders are women" and that "women might make up a majority of the movement as well." However, a "relatively consistent finding in national surveys of Tea Party supporters is that men outweigh women overall. Most surveys peg males as numbering 55% to 60% of Tea Partiers."[212] While portraying women in Tea Party leadership and as grass-roots supporters helped bolster the brand, this image was not rooted in reality.

Other news stories began to portray women as the most influential Tea Party leaders on both the national and local levels, helping extend the Tea Party brand as embracing and shaped by women. One *USA Today* author began an article about a competitive Colorado race with the following:

> Meet Lesley Hollywood, stay-at-home mom turned kingmaker.
>
> Thirty years old and new to politics, she has in short order become director of the Northern Colorado Tea Party and state coordinator of the national Tea Party Patriots, leading some of the had-it-up-to-here conservatives who have flipped the Senate race in this swing state upside down.[213]

Since the Tea Party was considered "leaderless," these women were recognized as Tea Party leaders through more informal, often feminized, references, like Hollywood's "kingmaker." Michele Bachmann was referred to as the "beloved of the tea party." Sarah Palin was a "king-maker, media personality, best-selling author," and "tea party personality." Sharron Angle, a Nevada Senate candidate, was the "tea party darling."[214] While the Quinnipiac survey was actually an outlier among most public opinion data on the Tea Party, new outlets continued to highlight feminine power and influence as a major component of the Tea Party narrative.

Sarah Palin, by far, received the bulk of the news coverage of Tea Party women. In part, Palin's news coverage followed from her high profile in the 2008 presidential campaign. Bill O'Reilly said that Sarah Palin "is a news magnet...there's just constantly news about this woman."[215] Early in the Tea Party coverage, MSNBC called her the "rock star in the Republican Party."[216] Eventually, reporters adopted this "rock star" description to describe her involvement with Tea Party events, particularly after she resigned from office and took on Tea Party–related engagements full-time. An *ABC News* correspondent said Palin received a "rock star-like welcome" at one Tea Party event.[217] *The New York Times* wrote that Palin represented a "new breed of unelected public figure operating in an environment in which politics, news media and celebrity are fused as never before."[218] Palin was a brand herself, what Peter Bjelskou calls "person-as-corporation," one of several "branded individuals populating the public sphere, especially its discursive epicenter, television...a new breed of agents who promote and embody their own product lines."[219] *Politico* described Palin as a "celebrity" who "has positioned herself as a tea party champion."[220] MSNBC called her a "tea party icon" and described her supporters as "fans."[221] On CNN, Palin was described as "rallying the Tea Party troops."[222] O'Reilly declared that "Palin comes closest" to being the Tea Party's leader.[223]

The media obsession with Sarah Palin helped bolster the Tea Party brand. After Dana Milbank asked his journalist colleagues to declare a moratorium on what he thought was an excessive media fixation on Sarah Palin, numerous reporters and writers discussed the profitability of Tea Party reporting.[224] On CNN's website, a conservative blogger wrote, "So why does Palin rate such a press gaggle?...Palin generates ratings and page views; she sells advertising."[225] Similarly, on *Huffington Post*, writers Alex Brant-Zawadzki and Dawn Teo argued that "right-leaning political commentators promote the Tea Parties, generating more anger and passion among their listeners, which in turn generates more fans and listeners, boosting ratings."[226] At the *Hollywood Reporter*, Paul Bond noted that "Sarah Palin and the Tea Party" had grabbed headlines because of "profitability, especially for cable news. They just can't quit her. She drives ratings."[227]

In the news coverage, Sarah Palin's political celebrity and political brand relied heavily on what Laurie Ouellette calls her "affective economy...that trades the 'private' performance of self and personal relations for the affective consumer connections that sell commercial television programs, websites, DVDs, and books."[228] She was a Tea Party emblem and reporters noted Palin's particular "brand"; she was "every mother, every daughter... every wife...every young businesswoman...[and a] Christian lady."[229]

Further, Palin represented both the "traditional values" and fiscal conservatism components of the Tea Party brand.[230] Palin's brand foregrounded authenticity—as one tea partier explained, she "walks the walk, talks the talk."[231] Or, in the words of another Tea Party female candidate interviewed on CNN, "even a lot of Democrats and independents admire her spunk and her willingness to stand up for what she believes and say what's on her mind."[232] Through the portrayal of these race, gender, and class characteristics, Palin was able to embody white working-class toughness and relatability alongside middle-class femininity. She was, as Laurie Ouellette and Alison Hearn describes of branded activists, a "branded sel[f]...normalizing the monetization of being, whereby an individual's specific 'personality' is processed and standardized by television editors, producers, and networks in order to be rendered functional, transferable, and ultimately profitable."[233]

Later, Palin would market this brand to obtain a book deal, reality show, and host position on Fox News, earning $100,000 for her speeches at Tea Party rallies and $12 million total in the year following her resignation as governor of Alaska in 2009.[234] According to Ouellette, Sarah Palin's "political celebrity has no economic value in the formal political system; only in the broader domain of media and consumer culture can its profit-making capacities be realized."[235] As the news media positioned Palin as a Tea Party leader, they lent her brand power by promoting it as a conservative movement and locus for successful political women.

In some cases, Tea Party women gained national attention following Palin's endorsement.[236] For instance, *Newsmax* described South Carolina Representative Nikki Haley's rise as a congressional candidate as a by-product of Palin's public support:

> In South Carolina's Republican gubernatorial primary, state Rep. Nikki Haley trailed a congressman, the lieutenant governor and attorney general for months. But a tea party surge and Sarah Palin's endorsement propelled her to an easy first-place finish. She faces Rep. Gresham Barrett in a June 22 runoff.[237]

The New York Times also highlighted Karen Handel, a Georgia gubernatorial candidate, as "at least the 50th candidate to win the Palin seal of approval."[238]

The Wall Street Journal said that "Ms. Palin's backing was seen as important to both [Nikki Haley's and Carly Fiorina's] victories."[239]

News reports also described the Tea Party women as protection against aggressive political attacks on the Tea Party brand. According to Politico, the "political elite" don't know "how to deal" with Tea Party women, and "it makes it harder to vilify a movement when its public face is a female one."[240] Mark Skoda, the founder of the National Tea Party Federation, expanded on this idea later in an interview:

> And if you want to have an antagonistic approach, you cannot have it against women, right? It's the idea you don't hit a woman. And the reality is that the Tea Party movement is so overwhelmingly led by women, and so positioned as a majority by women that if they recognized that, then all these antagonistic and derogatory comments are essentially focused on those women. And it will in fact diminish their own credibility.[241]

Skoda's quote shows that branding the Tea Party as a women-led movement presented an image that could avoid deflect criticism or attacks. According to Kathleen Hall Jamieson, attacking female candidates has consistently presented this type of political convention: "Playground rules set for boys are clear. Don't beat up smaller kids and don't hit girls. In politics the result plays out as a double bind for the male candidate confronting a female opponent."[242] Along these lines, Kim L. Fridkin et al. found that political attack ads harm men more than women, concluding that the perception of male aggression leads to more unfavorable attitudes toward their criticism of women opponents than vice versa.[243] In The New York Times, one Republican primary candidate sensitive to this perception was quoted as telling his female opponent to "stop hiding behind the skirt of Sarah Palin."[244]

Of course, this shield of womanhood was largely premised on white femininity. As Carla Peterson explains, historically white femininity relied on the notion that white women were pale, delicate, modest, pure, and dedicated to the manners and cultivation of the domestic sphere through traditional gender roles.[245] On the other hand, Black femininity has been popularly constructed as vulgar, hypersexual, dominating, publicly exposed, poor, criminal, emasculating, and neglectful of domestic and maternal duties.[246] In this way, Black women in politics, such as Michelle Obama or Shirley Sherrod, are less likely to receive such protection based on a presumed fragility or respectability.[247] Moreover, through the cult of white womanhood, white women have been able to escape or downplay acts of racism and bigotry. Historian Thavolia Glymph explains that even during slavery, "the very notion of a private sphere...functioned to conceal from scrutiny the day-to-day struggles between enslaved women and their mistresses, subsumed within a logic of patriarchy."[248] It is important to note that Tea Partiers used white women to defend the party from criticism regarding racism, maintaining this larger narrative of white femininity as somehow less violent, pervasive, or capable of oppressing people than any other form of whiteness, and more deserving of protection and gentility than male counterparts.

In Tea Party news stories, women activists and candidates regularly functioned as narrative interventions that simultaneously modernized the Tea Party and helped to shield it from criticism. Drawing on the misleading Quinnipiac poll, a *Politico* reporter explained the deeper significance of the Tea Party's female "face":

> When the tea party movement burst onto the scene last year to oppose President Barack Obama, the Democratic Congress, and the health care legislation they wanted to enact, some liberal critics were quick to label its activists as angry white men.
>
> As the populist conservative movement has gained a foothold over the past year, it's become increasingly clear that the dismissive characterization was at least half wrong.[249]

As the *Politico* story shows, Tea Party women disrupted the notion of the Tea Party as "angry white men." Tea Party women's media coverage, in fact, remade the Tea Party into a place where "conservative women have found their voices."[250] Conservative radio host Michael Graham's book title succinctly captured this rhetorical move: *That's No Angry Mob, That's My Mom.*[251] *Newsmax* ran an abbreviated version of *Politico*'s column and echoed this same sentiment, writing that "those who say the tea party movement consists mostly of angry white men will have to recast their stereotyping in at least one regard."[252] The feminization of the Tea Party in the press even helped nullify reports that the Tea Party represented a strain of white militancy and posed a domestic terror threat, even as some tea partiers, including sitting legislators, called for the creation of their own armies.[253]

Presenting the Tea Party as woman-led and dominated could help soften the perception of its brand. A brand dependent upon the expression of rage and anger could also be interpreted as dangerous, and descriptions of Tea Party anger ranged from moral outrage to something potentially violent and threatening. *USA Today* described a Democratic advertisement that called a Tea Party candidate a "crazy" person with views "so extreme they're dangerous."[254] Stories about Tea Party "armed militias," "secession," and "revolution" connoted terrorism and impending civil war drove Tea Party coverage. While the Tea Party brand could be useful in gaining support, news stories showed that it also had to be managed carefully, both within and outside of the news narratives that brought it into being.

As news media coverage positioned women as key to the Tea Party movement, they helped displace this image of the Tea Party as a form of violent masculinity and rebranded it with femininity. When *The Huffington Post* later interviewed Mark Skoda about a *New York Times* poll, he responded:

> It's interesting—when you look at the Tea Party demographics 55% are women, and as we know there is a great deal of wealth in the female population of America. I think that the sort of cartoonish association of Tea Partiers as being old white males, Southern, illiterate...I think it's again, the narrative doesn't fit the reality. Right?[255]

In contrast with these claims that the Tea Party was run and supported by women, a *New York Times* poll published only three weeks after the Quinnipiac poll showed that "the 18 percent of Americans who identify themselves as Tea Party supporters tend to be Republican, white, male, married and older than 45."[256] Specifically, the poll showed that Tea Party supporters were 59 percent male and 41 percent female. It also found that "Tea Party supporters are more likely to classify themselves as 'angry.'"[257] The idea of the Tea Party as angry white *women* became a new political spectacle, adding a sense of change and rejuvenation to post-Reagan conservative populism. Moreover, shaping the Tea Party brand of women around traditional hetero-patriarchal norms related to white femininity nullified typically negative stereotypes of angry, progressive women (such as references to feminists as lesbians or anti-men).

Both subtly and overtly, reporters also drew attention to Tea Party women in ways that defied the stereotype of old, outdated (i.e., racist), angry white men that persisted in Tea Party descriptions. According to a female Tea Party leader interviewed by *Politico*, women's influence explained the Tea Party's leaderless quality:

> Walker said it is women in particular who have pushed back against efforts to build a more centralized leadership structure for the tea party movement, which some organizers suggest could help the movement translate its energy into electoral success.
>
> "Most of the women do not want a large, top-down movement," Walker said. "We like the local flavor and independence of the tea parties. We don't need anyone to tell us what to do from DC or a large organization to lead us. We're capable of handling most of it on our own."[258]

The use of new media was also mentioned in reporting about Tea Party women, namely coverage of Sarah Palin. Palin was frequently noted for distributing her messages via digital technology, and this was often the only way her perspective was integrated into news reports. In an article about her political influence, *The Wall Street Journal* wrote:

> Through Facebook, Twitter and YouTube, former Alaska Gov. Sarah Palin has burst back into the political spotlight this month, while her family life has once again become part of the broader American conversation.
>
> ...Last week, SarahPAC posted a "Mama Grizzlies" video online aimed at reaching out to women voters....Political experts said the video—with its high production values and campaign-like blue hues—was impressive.[259]

MSNBC featured a story about a controversy involving Palin's use of Twitter, while *The New York Times* wrote that Palin had brought a political primary "alive" "through a breezy 194 words posted on Ms. Palin's Facebook page."[260] This notion of Tea Party conservatism as not only feminine but also tech-savvy and adept at new media helped to modernize the Tea Party brand and mark it as relevant to a new generation.

The Political Woman and the Tea Party Brand

Journalists' focus on Tea Party women candidates also reflected a major shift in women's performance on the political stage. Under the bright spotlight of American news coverage, political women have always had to negotiate gender norms carefully. In a 1935 news interview, Eleanor Roosevelt famously talked about her exceptional political work as a First Lady outside of the typical household and ceremonial duties associated with the role: "When people say a woman's place is in the home, I say, with enthusiasm, it certainly is, but if she cares about her home, that caring will take her far and wide."[261] As an extremely politically active First Lady and this quote reflects Roosevelt's deliberate use of rhetoric to blur the boundaries separating private and public spheres and the gender roles assigned to each—a move that was crucial in the rise of Tea Party women. The twenty-first-century rise of viable female candidates and activists has been cultivated through a reconfiguration of American values that simultaneously embrace and defy patriarchy (and the suffragist legacy), forcing women involved in American politics to adopt a very tricky public persona that Jamieson calls "the binds that tie."[262]

Women politicians have always had to carefully walk the line of pushing for women's equality while adhering to race, class, and gender norms to appeal to voters, colleagues, and the media that tells their stories. Research has shown that the media has tended to frame women politicians "through a feminine lens...focus[ing] more on [their] clothing, hair style, family, and other 'soft' matters," though some contemporary studies suggest that this is no longer the case in most modern elections.[263] Women historically have also received less press coverage than men and studies have shown that there is a major political disadvantage for female candidates who present stereotypically feminine characteristics or focus on perceived "men's issues" like crime or foreign policy.[264] Moreover, scholars have previously observed that the media often fail to mention the contributions of women candidates outside of "women's issues," negatively portray their viability as candidates, and mark their gender as especially pertinent to their candidacies.[265]

More recent research suggests that the press coverage of most non-presidential elections has become more equitable in terms of gender and that political stereotypes about women candidates do not always harm them.[266] These studies also suggest that those who run can win at the same rate as equally qualified men. The influence of gender varies and depends on the office a candidate seeks and their political party affiliation, especially for Republican women candidates who tend to be viewed negatively by members of both major parties.[267]

Still, while possibly waning in importance, gender remains a factor in elections and campaigns. There continues to be a significant disparity in the number of women who compete for office. When they do run, voters tend to assess them based on how well they conform to traditional feminine norms like compassion and likability. If the campaigns of women candidates are explicitly gendered through their special attention to issues affecting women or claiming their identities as women politicians, gender can negatively impact election outcomes.[268] Women politicians are also much more vulnerable to negative attacks based on gender stereotypes than male counterparts and are evaluated based on different issues.[269] They benefit from pushing back against gender stereotypes and claiming traits typically associated with men.

Though current research is not clear on the impact of gender, conventional wisdom in political campaigns dictates that it matters to voters and shapes the presentation of women candidates. In these ways, marketing women's political brands requires an emphasis on both addressing and assuaging gender hierarchies while men's political brands do not.[270]

In various ways, the news media described Tea Party women through stereotypically feminine attributes and traits. Tea Party women's roles as mothers or grandmothers were often used to explain their value as candidates or activists and account for their political involvement. On Fox News, O'Reilly forsook the title "Governor" and repeatedly referred to Palin as "Mrs. Palin."[271] CNN reported that Palin said she "would consider running for president in 2012 if she thought it was right for the country and for her family."[272] Being a grandmother and mother was particularly highlighted in depictions of Nevada Senate candidate Sharron Angle. The *Wall Street Journal* reported that Angle's "first foray into activism was when her son was held back in kindergarten" and she decided to start a school for him.[273] *Politico*'s article about Tea Party women repeatedly referred to female interviewees as mothers, grandmothers, or stepmothers. According to *Politico*, the Tea Party attracted conservative women because it was community organizing and seen as bypassing traditional politics and more akin to the organizing work that "revolves around family rituals."[274] In this way, domesticity maps onto the "domestic" of domestic policy, allowing health care and national debt to be framed as issues that require the skills of an attentive mother. As Amy Kaplan argues, "If domesticity plays a key role in imagining the nation as home, then women, positioned at the center of home, play a major role in defining the contours of the nation."[275]

Reporters' insistence that any qualified female candidate *must be a mother* was not exclusive to Tea Party or Republican candidates, however. A *New York Times* columnist wrote of Republican/Tea Partier Sarah Palin, Republican/Tea Partier Michele Bachmann, and Democrat Nancy Pelosi:

> What does it say about this country at this moment that, of the small handful of women who have achieved highly visible political roles, three are matriarchs of such very large families? Could it be that the skills of managing sprawling households translate well into holding office? Or that such a remarkable glut of mom cred makes a woman's bid for external power more palatable to voters?
>
> ...Whatever forces may be at play, taking a look at present dynamics, any American woman with long-range political ambitions might do well to also look to her nursery.[276]

In large part, the motherhood emphasis in Tea Party news coverage can be attributed to the descriptions provided by female candidates themselves (as opposed to their male counterparts), as shown in this *ABC News* clip:

SHARRON ANGLE (REP) (SENATORIAL CANDIDATE): I'm a mother and a grandmother.

RAND PAUL (REP) (US SENATE CANDIDATE): I'm a physician.

RON JOHNSON (REP) (US SENATE CANDIDATE): Full-time business person.[277]

As shown here, Tea Party news reports eroded the binary of what Angela High-Pippert calls "mom discourse" versus "policy discourse." According to Pippert, "'mom discourse' frames political participation in terms of women's status as mothers, rather than their expertise on policy issues," while "'policy discourse' is more rational and technical than mom discourse and more closely resembles the speech of officeholders than constituents."[278] Though women activists and candidates are able to garner attention using "mom discourse," it also leads to their portrayal as "emotional (rather than rational) and unreasonable...[and] the perception that they are less suited for politics than (rational) men."[279] In other words, journalists' and candidates' use of maternalist politics backfired.

Stories about Tea Party women in relation to motherhood reflected recent changes in the journalistic treatment of political women candidates. In earlier decades, the press typically focused on female candidates' clothing, marital status, and children. For example, Jamieson cites the following examples of female senators described in the *New York Times* in 1992:

> 59-year-old Ms. [Dianne] Feinstein...faces another race in 1994...no doubt she will rely, as she has in the past, on the assets of her husband, Richard C. Blum, an investment banker.

> The 42-year-old Ms. [Patty] Murray lives in the Seattle suburb of Shoreline, where in addition to her two children, ages 12 and 15, she cares for her aging parents.

> Ms. [Carol Moseley] Braun, who is divorced and the mother of a 15-year-old son.[280]

But, as described earlier, scholars have found that male and female candidates of equal standing are treated similarly by the press. According to this research, a woman candidate's gender is only discussed if seen as relevant to the issues and causes proclaimed in their campaign, such as women's rights or reproductive health. Although "mothering" was important in explaining some Tea Party female candidates, activists, or leaders' entrance into politics, their children and husbands were almost never further mentioned or discussed in detail in subsequent stories about them and the Tea Party. When descriptions of Tea Party women's physical appearances did occur, they were typically isolated to stories about their initial emergence into the political spotlight.

That is, being a mother functioned largely symbolically in the stories about some Tea Party women politicians that focus on the Tea Party, functioning as key to their brand identities. There was little substantive discussion or focus on how parenting responsibilities impacted their campaigns, political positions, or their everyday lives. Parenting was a signifier that enhanced their conservative brand. This was most clear in the cases of Tea Party women politicians who had no children and yet still received the label of "Mama Grizzly" (as discussed later).

Journalists characterized Tea Party women with other gendered tropes that dismissed, demeaned, or trivialized them as political candidates. A *New York Times* columnist marked the rise of Tea Party women as the "era of Republican Mean Girls."[281] On CNN, an anchor and his comedian guest joked about the appearance and age of female tea partiers:

ELIOT SPITZER (HOST): I heard you say before you're really frustrated by the Tea Party and the fact that the Tea Party seems to be driving the politics of the moment. What's the best response to it? How do you respond to them?

D. L. HUGHLEY (GUEST): Well, I think it's asinine to call them all racist. I don't think they are. I do find that their fascination with middle aged semi-attractive white women who shop at Lenscrafters is amazing to me.
[laughter]

Reporters consistently feminized Sarah Palin—she was a "cheerleader" and "Tea Party princess" in *The New York Times*, "Medusa," the "Queen of the Tea Party," the Tea Party's "informal godmother," and "Sister Sarah" on MSNBC.[282] The terms "cheerleader," "queen," and "princess" are particularly poignant, as these roles denote highly visible, public women lacking in actual power or influence—cheerleaders literally perform on the sidelines, and in the modern day, royal titles generally denote people whose power comes from inheritance rather than skills or talent.

At a joint campaign appearance, Bachmann and Palin were called "sorority" sisters who wore "coordinating outfits."[283] During her campaign, Senate candidate Christine O'Donnell had to refute allegations that she was a "witch."[284] In *The Wall Street Journal*, Sharron Angle was "petite, [and] has Irish red hair with and [sic] a pretty round face."[285] In *The New York Times*, Angle was the "Red Queen of the Mad Hatter tea party" who wore "girlish bangs," a "casino red suit and lipstick," and "had the slightly threatening air of the inebriated lady in a country club bar." While women leaders lent the Tea Party brand an important boost in terms of novelty and progress, they themselves were branded with gendered tropes that threatened their own images and political success.

As seen in coverage of other women politicians, the press typically described Tea Party women as unstable stars rather than viable political candidates. Constructing female candidates as unfit for political office is a common feature in the coverage of women politicians. As Lori Montalbano-Phelps explains, while all candidates must deal with issues of credibility, women in particular face a steeper challenge. "Due to historically limited participation of women in national politics, questions of credentials, and consequently legitimacy or participation in national politics, become major campaign obstacles."[286] A *USA Today* article on the Nevada Senate race asked whether Angle was "damaging vs. dangerous."[287]

In other places, Tea Party women were depicted as stupid and unprepared for office. In one highly publicized incident, O'Donnell questioned whether "the separation of church and state" was written in the Constitution. In fact, the exact phrase "separation of Church and State" is not in the Constitution and is an oft-debated interpretation of the First Amendment. But the media seized on the story as reflecting O'Donnell's ineptitude. *The Huffington Post* reported on O'Donnell's "apparent lack of awareness that separation of church and state is enshrined in the First Amendment," while an MSNBC anchor spoke directly to O'Donnell: "You're so dumb—how do you find the door every day?"[288] On ABC, Meghan McCain called O'Donnell a "nut job" who was "making a mockery of running for public office."[289] Frequently, journalists critiqued the women's direct messaging tactics through their own social media networks and reported that they avoided mainstream media, implying that the women feared hard questions rather than unfair or biased press treatment.

Sarah Palin, as the most featured Tea Party woman, received a significant amount of coverage dismissing her political career prospects. A CNN segment about Palin writing speech notes on her hand featured an interviewee saying, "If you can't answer the question 'What are your priorities?' without reading the palm of your hands, maybe you're not the best leader to be leading people."[290] A *Newsmax* blogger said he was "searching for Mr. Conservative" and complained that Palin was "polarizing" and not an "electable candidate."[291] Note that there was an implicit assumption that an "electable candidate" would be male. *Politico* argued that "Palin hasn't done so well on her own, with as many endorsements exposing weakness as showing strength... and others showing comical disorganization."[292] An article in *The New York Times* quoted a Palin fan who opposed Palin's political office run:

Judy Pruitt, a 70-year-old retiree in Lawrenceville, said she came to see Ms. Handel partly because of the Palin endorsement. But she had a swift answer when asked if she would welcome a 2012 Palin campaign.

"I'm not sure she's ready for the presidency," she said. "I do like listening to her, and I respect her views on things. But I think she can have more of an impact if she's not running. I really do."[293]

An exchange between two CNN anchors suggested that Tea Party women had also taken on the general tropes of Tea Party news coverage (and vice versa).

> KATHLEEN PARKER: The Republican Party is very, very disciplined and they will incorporate the Tea Party.
> ...
> ELIOT SPITZER: The Republican Party of George Bush, Sr., and even George W. Bush had the perception of discipline, but who's taken over the party? John McCain is an afterthought. John McCain is begging Sarah Palin, at least back when he was in the middle of a primary to come, hey, help me out Sarah. He almost threw her off the ticket. This has been a complete role reversal. You know, it's kind of staggering to those of us who don't feel comfortable with it, of course, you know, we still have Christine O'Donnell.
> [laughter][294]

According to this narrative, the female-led Tea Party was undisciplined, rowdy, emotional, and a site of buffoonery, but could be ultimately be refined through its assimilation into the "disciplined," male-led Republican Party. As these quotes reflect, Palin and other Tea Party women represented a political brand that generated "buzz" and influenced public discourse, but they were not political candidates prepared or qualified for office—in short, they were fit to be kingmakers, but never king.

Tea Party Feminism and the Mama Grizzly Brand

In some important ways, however, the news coverage of Tea Party women also defied typical portrayals of conservative women politicians by identifying them as feminists, often based on their own claims. In a piece titled "No Mystique about Feminism," a *New York Times* columnist noted that Sarah Palin "repeatedly laid claim to the 'feminist mantle,'" and argued the increase in Republican women winning political office marked an "emerging, conservative, feminist identity."[295] *Newsmax* sold a special issue of their magazine on "The New*er* Feminism," proclaiming that "Sarah Palin [had become] an icon of the new feminism" and heralding women in business and politics who were "smart, independent, successful, and [shaping] feminism today—even if it means being a mom and raising kids!"[296] In a piece on Christine O'Donnell in *Talking Points Memo*, she was quoted as claiming to be an "authentic feminist[...]" and "as a feminist, I celebrate my femininity."[297] Sharron Angle's name filled headlines when she was given an award from the Susan B. Anthony List, which referred to her as a "frontier feminist."[298] According to Angle, she "learned from the example" of her mother of what it mean to be a "true feminist," a feminist who "celebrat[ed the] differences [between men and women]...and how these differences were and created to work together and are truly complementary."

Historically, American feminism has undergone several phases that are, in part, reflected in the Tea Party claim to feminism. Early suffragists advocating for women's right to vote in the first wave of feminism beginning in the late nineteenth century often structured their demands around political equality to men, though a few used their roles as mothers and wives to demand access to the ballot. For example, wealthy socialite and suffragette Katherine Mackay argued that "the mothers of this country" were in the best position to vote on laws that would affect the lives and outcomes of their children.[299] During the women's liberation movement in the 1970s, generally described as the second wave of feminism, women argued for equal rights and access to employment, schools, and other community institutions, such as banks and libraries. Key to this second wave of feminism was reproductive health, both in terms of support for working mothers and securing the legal right to terminate pregnancies. But these demands for women's equality, as earlier ones, targeted structural impediments and advocated for changes in policy that would ensure support for women workers.

The rise of Black feminism in the 1970s criticized previous women's movements for centering white women and neglecting to address the role of white supremacy, class, nativism, hetero-patriarchy, imperialism, inequality, and racial exploitation in women's experiences of the world. Conservative feminism mirrors this approach to feminism, described by some as "white feminism," in both rhetorically and aesthetically prioritizing particular notions of white womanhood. In the 1990s, feminism's third wave, as Astrid Henry puts it, "celebrated a woman's right to pleasure" and challenged notions of sexual freedom, patriarchy, choice, and gender exploitation as framed by earlier feminist activists.[300]

With its focus on individualism, anti-choice positioning, deeply mater-nalist politics and lack of structural organizing around a policy agenda, Tea Party feminism deviates substantially from the progressive goals, discourse, interventions, and ideas connected to movements for women's equality. In their study on "Mama Grizzly" rhetoric and conservative claims to femi-nism, Katie Gibson and Amy Heyse argue that the Tea Party women drew on a form of "pseudo-feminism" that actually undermines women's rights by diverting attention away from systemic discrimination and oppression.[301] Still, the Tea Party's conservative "feminism" appropriates the rhetoric and symbolism of all these previous movements by arguing for women's equal access to and standing within American political and economic institutions, heralding women's voting and democratic power, excluding class or racial analysis, and centering traditional femininity as part of their brand. Mary Douglas Vavrus notes that many women in the "post-feminist" period have typically eschewed feminism as an unrealistic, unnatural, objectionable, victimizing ideology and aesthetic.[302] By claiming a feminist mantle at a time in which some notable progressive women shy away from that word, conservative feminists helped engage in a conservative rebranding of the term that gave them the symbolic allure of modernity.[303]

The news coverage of Tea Party feminism countered the typical framing of feminism in the press, reflecting its alignment with status quo beliefs. Angela McRobbie finds that "feminism is routinely disparaged" in media representations of women.[304] Susan Douglas writes that the "F-word" has been "stereotyped as man-hating, child-loathing, hairy, shrill, humorless, deliberately unattractive Ninjas from Hades" and Jenny Coleman agrees that "the last two decades have been marked by...an increasing rejection of the label 'feminist.'"[305] Typically, the news media have negatively de-picted feminist groups and favorably framed conservative women's orga-nizations. Journalists generally construct conservative women's organi-zations as representing conservative issues, while feminists are constructed as advocates for women's interests.[306] By claiming feminism, Palin chal-lenged this binary, suggesting that women's issues were conservative issues and conservative issues were women's issues.

Notably, journalists portrayed Tea Party women as a potent combina-tion of femininity and masculinity. While political women generally have had to be careful of appearing too weak or too assertive, Tea Party women were written as brazen and tough. Tea Party mothers drew on motherhood as a way to defend political engagement (as did Roosevelt before them), while still using masculinist imagery to project confidence and competence. *The New York Times* said that Palin was "hardened" by attacks on her.[307] In *The Wall Street Journal*, Sharron Angle was a "60-year-old grandmother of

10" who drove a "Harley Davidson Road King bike."[308] The primary example of this maternal aggression rhetoric was the "Mama Grizzly" label frequently claimed or assigned to Tea Party women. Expanding beyond Palin's "hockey mom" label during the 2008 campaign, women used the "Mama Grizzly" label to defend their perceived aggression as a function of their committed motherhood. For example, Angle explained her entry into politics: "I was just a mother, and the government had gotten between me and my child, and that's like getting between a mother bear and her cubs."[309] In *Politico*, a female tea partier also said of her activism that "Mama comes out fighting...when legislation messes with mama's kids."[310]

In this way, the Tea Party women explained aggression as a *feminine* quality—contrary to the typical rhetoric about female political candidates. While Jamieson argues that women politicians typically fail because they are judged against a masculine standard, she also concludes: "Women are judged against a masculine standard, and by that standard they lose, whether they claim difference or similarity. The bind is broken by positing a form of equality not solely based on a male norm."[311] By drawing on "Mama Grizzly" rhetoric, the Tea Party women sought to be judged in relation to a *female* norm. It proved to become its own political brand, fusing conservatism, toughness, and femininity.

Media coverage of "Mama Grizzlies" was markedly different than previous political labels for women voters and candidates, particularly 1990s "soccer moms." When journalists and campaign strategists emphasized the "soccer mom" voting bloc, they focused on women who were white, middle-class, consumerist, suburban, perceived as non-threatening, and largely confined to domestic concerns. Additionally, "soccer mom" news coverage focused on married women, excluding single mothers.[312] In contrast, the term "Mama Grizzly" makes the identity of mother a descriptor, not the noun—these women are more grizzly than mom. Grizzly bears dwell in the woods, survive off the land, are dangerously tough, and instinctively and murderously protect their offspring. Bears do not live in cities, which are considered Democratic strongholds and generally known as the domain of left-leaning, "latte-drinking" liberals, yuppies, hipsters, and people of color—all key characteristics of the Democrat brand. The term "Mama Grizzlies" dismisses the soccer mom's consumerism, eschews suburban and urban landscapes, and embraces the tough life of the wilderness.. Moreover, the "Mama Grizzlies" moniker seems to address Douglas's concern that

in the news, there remained a deep, unyielding contradiction between and discomfort with "female" and "power."..."Female" is still equated with being nice, supportive, nurturing, accommodating, and domestic—not compatible with anything that might involve leadership. "Power" is equated with domination, superiority, being tough, even ruthless. These two categories simply are not supposed to go together.[313]

Instead, "Mama Grizzlies" merge the traditionally masculine tropes of fierceness, toughness, and violence with feminine tropes—particularly the attentive and self-sacrificing mother. In short, journalists' portrayal of Tea Party women redefined what a (political) mother looked like and what she was able to do. Moreover, Palin's "Mama Grizzly" endorsement of candidates Carly Fiorina and Christine O'Donnell—neither of whom are mothers—reflects that the label was primarily rhetorical in its intent and use. As a brand, "Mama Grizzly" imbued those self-identifying politicos together under a collective expression of Tea Party anger, motherly care, domesticity, political novice, and career womanhood that attracted both funders and potential supporters, a brand extension of Sarah Palin herself.

Another unique feature in Tea Party news coverage was the attention given to women's regular attacks on their opponents' masculinity. ABC reported that Tea Party women's use of "man up" made it the "catch-phrase of the [2010 midterm election] campaign."[314]

JONATHAN KARL (ABC NEWS): [Voiceover] The concept, if not the exact phrase, began with none other than Christine O'Donnell, who had this to say about her primary opponent Mike Castle, back in early September.

CHRISTINE O'DONNELL: These are the type of cheap, underhanded, unmanly tactics that we've come to expect. This is not a bakeoff. Get your man pants on.

MSNBC deemed it the "phrase of the year."[315] *The New York Times* quoted Sharron Angle directing the term at her Senate opponent:

"Man up, Harry Reid," Sharron Angle taunted [Harry Reid] at their Las Vegas debate here Thursday night. That's not an idle insult, coming from a woman who campaigns at times with a .44 Magnum revolver in her 1989 GMC pickup.[316]

In this way, reporters branded female Tea Party leaders as "extraordinary conservative women" who were needed to deal with the perceived failure of conservative male congressional leaders.[317] These women drew on hyper-masculinity as part of their political brand.

Conservative women were not the only ones with a history of performing masculinity in electoral campaigns. Throughout the 2008 Democratic primaries, "the press consistently portrayed Hillary Clinton as a mythical man [and] attribute[d] to her those characteristics of hegemonic masculinity: tough, self-sufficient, stoic."[318] In 1988, a female presidential primary candidate asked whether America was "man enough to back a woman." Like "man enough," the Tea Party phrase "man up" emphasized "man" as a political ideal. As Montalbano-Phelps argues, "More than a clever play on words, [the expression 'man enough'] borrowed from outmoded ideas that man equals strength, man equals power. Such phraseology does little more than perpetuate negative stereotypes." [319]

Yet there were some important differences in the way Tea Party women used masculinity as a point of vulnerability for their opponents. Tea Party women did not simply perform masculinity. Rather, media accounts cast them as arbiters of masculinity and allowed them to reclaim masculinist tropes *as* feminine.

Of course, certain networks and outlets emphasized some of these narratives more than others. All of the outlets portrayed Sarah Palin as an influential and controversial Tea Party character. With the exception of *ABC News* and *Politico*, they all used feminizing descriptors to frame Tea Party women (i.e., cheerleader, queen, princess, mother, grandmother, etc.).[320] Fox News invoked sexism when it described the political Left as afraid of Palin and referred to her as "Mrs. Palin" instead of "Governor Palin," but rarely discussed women as a Tea Party topic.[321] Only *Newsmax*, *Politico*, *The Wall Street Journal*, and *The New York Times* explicitly analyzed the social significance of the rise of conservative Tea Party women. MSNBC, *USA Today*, *The Huffington Post*, and CNN all reported errors made by high-profile Tea Party women to show them as unqualified or unprepared, but MSNBC regularly emphasized this narrative in its coverage. *Newsmax* was the only outlet to explicitly argue that Sarah Palin symbolically represented a Tea Party constituency that favored social and traditional values; mentions of domesticity and motherhood in coverage from all of the news outlets further buttressed this point. While the Tea Party women helped fortify the Tea Party brand in news coverage, it was not so clear whether they had done the same for their own brands.

Tea Party Women and the Tea Party Brand

Ultimately, the Tea Party women were incredibly important to the Tea Party's rise in the press. They gave it celebrity, helped it defy stereotype and convention, and challenged notions of femininity and masculinity, while also receiving the same "outsider" treatment that the media typically give women politicians. This paradox is captured succinctly in a quote from Fox News: "There is no Tea Party leader [but] Sarah Palin comes closest."[322] In this way, Tea Party women also reflected a new conservative embrace of feminism. By providing the media with another narrative about revitalized conservatism among women, women branded the Tea Party as new while leaving power structures largely intact.

While Tea Party women embraced "traditional values," they also further complicated Douglas's notion that these Tea Party women "turned feminism inside out" when it came to substantive political issues. Indeed, the news stories about female activists and leaders in the Tea Party exemplified Karlyn Kohrs Campbell's argument that "culturally available subject-positions are, simultaneously, obstacles and opportunities."[323] Being a political woman in American society demands a delicate balance, often requiring that female politicians reify patriarchy by performing femininity. Tea Party women continue this legacy of women's tenuous political performance, conforming to patriarchy while unsettling its constitutive notions and practice. The rise of the Tea Party and its female leaders forced conservative media makers to explicitly embrace working mothers and repudiate sexism, rebranding conservatism as anti-sexist and supportive of women working outside the home. Moreover, the Tea Party woman's brand effectively demonstrated the presence and right of women to engage as both political leaders and activists, even if they are not ultimately perceived as viable. Simply dismissing Tea Party women as "post-feminist" or "enlightened sexists" appears inadequate.[324] It seems that that the Tea Party news coverage shows conservative female leaders in the process of rebranding (and selling) feminism itself.

Intersections and Overlap: Race, Gender and Class

The news stories that highlighted Tea Party beliefs and characteristics relied heavily upon race, gender, and class. Reports about Tea Party profiteering, identity development, branding challenges, and emotion frequently centered upon race, class, and gender, or more specifically, white working-class identity and racial resentment. These key social identities drove the Tea Party narrative, gave it salience as a national news story, explained the Tea Party's function as a cultural sign, and provided symbolic meaning and value to the Tea Party brand.

News narratives about the Tea Party attached race, gender, and class identities to "populism"; helped brand the Tea Party brand as white middle-class/working-class resistance; and provided the Tea Party brand with emotional meaning and symbolic value. While allegations of racism were seen by conservative reporters as a way of attacking the Tea Party brand, Tea Party women leaders were cited as brand ambassadors that embodied progress and modernity. As such, race, gender, and class collectively enhanced and bolstered the Tea Party brand as a new model for conservative political engagement.

Though this chapter has at times treated race, gender, and class politics in Tea Party news stories separately, the intersections between these categories were key in propelling the Tea Party brand. Intersectionality, a concept first coined by Kimberlé Crenshaw describes how systems of domination can produce compounding and specific manifestations of oppression for members of particular groups. Nicholas Winter provides a valuable summary of how intersectionality construct beliefs and functions in media and politics:

> Many powerful political symbols exist at the intersection of race and gender (and other) categories, either explicitly or implicitly. Thus, for example, the "soccer mom" is defined explicitly by her gender but, equally important, she is also defined by her race (white) and class (suburban middle); the paradigmatic "violent black criminal" is not just racial but also has a specific gender (male) and age (young); the "welfare queen" is black, female, and poor. These sorts of images, and related rhetorical issue frames, need not draw only on racial schemas or gender schemas individually, but rather can draw on both simultaneously or on some more-specific schemas for the intersectional categories. When they do so, race and gender interact such that the impact of both is something more complex than the sum of the separate dimensions.[325]

In Tea Party news stories, intersectional identities were particularly valuable to its brand image.

Familiar tropes of racism, classism, and sexism imbued the Tea Party with brand fluidity. This intersectional (dis)empowerment[326] produces rhetorical resonance and what Karen Johnson-Cartee calls *condensational symbols*:

> Condensational symbols are a shorthand means by which large numbers of beliefs, feelings, values, and perhaps world views are telegraphed to others sharing a similar culture. The example of "family values" is just such a condensation symbol. Conservatives using the phrase "family values" *evoke* a wealth of positive cognitions, attitudes, and past behaviors among those similar to themselves. Consequently it is perhaps more appropriate to say that condensational

symbols evoke stored meanings already residing within the minds of individuals sharing a given political culture.[327]

The Tea Party's race, class, and gender narratives overlapped and complicated one another, which helped propel the Tea Party as a news topic and allowed it to avoid simple constructions.

Tea Party women were important to the way reporters helped brand the Tea Party because they defied the "working-class, white male" stereotype. Their femininity diffused the notion of "angry white men" and the associations (racism, violence, etc.) that came with it. But the gender of Tea Party women leaders also allowed them to embody tropes associated with old-fashioned Republicans—uneducated, ignorant, rural, white, and masculine—while being hailed as new political figures. That is, the women's femininity helped retrofit a new Tea Party identity, as they embodied traditional notions of conservative male whiteness. In many ways, the Tea Party women's modernizing of an old political institution was similar to the newness that Barack Obama's blackness brought to right-leaning Democratic politics and that whiteness and class identity brought to the news framing of the Tea Party as a social movement for the oppressed. The reporting on Tea Party women provided the Tea Party brand with a narrative of progressive values and interests, distinguishing it from the established Republican brand while still maintaining conservative economic, political, and social ideas.

Attributing the term "populist" to tea partiers spoke to an imagined understanding of "the people" and reified a fallacious race- and class-based inference. If the tea partiers had been initially widely reported as predominantly African American, or female, or Jewish, and so forth, it would have likely been represented as a women's or a civil rights movement. Rather, the arrival on scene of a group of protesting white middle- or working-class men was referred to as "populism." As Edsall and Edsall explain, "At the core of Republican-populist strategy was a commitment to resist the forcing of racial, cultural, and social liberalism on recalcitrant white, working, and middle-class constituencies."[328]

Even explicitly classed phrases like "middle American" signify race. According to Herbert Gans:

> The term [Middle American] originally appeared as a synonym for the Silent Majority, Richard Nixon's label for his intended new conservative constituency. It gained further currency in stories about the white urban backlash against the ghetto uprisings and the War on Poverty. As a result, it became a quasi-political term to describe white ethnics who opposed racial-integration policies.[329]

"Middle America" is a hybrid term that combines class (middle-class), race (white), and national identity (American); understanding tea partiers as part of "middle America" affirmed the racial and gendered meanings inscribed in each. As a Fox News anchor explained to his colleague, Bill O'Reilly,

> Now the fact of the matter is, Bill, that the United States of America is, you know, overwhelmingly white, overwhelmingly middle class and so on. But you know, if you could attract people from the minority community, Hispanics, African-Americans and the rest, obviously you would like to do that. But you know...these are the people that happen to turn out. They still constitute, broadly speaking, an American majority.[330]

Indeed, about 77% of Americans identify as white—but a small predominantly white group does not then represent all of America.[331] Rather, journalists' argument that tea partiers represented "America" relied on their constructions as a raced and classed group, and masked the truth that the Tea Party had relatively little political support on a national scale. In one poll, 74% of Americans held unfavorable or undecided views of tea partiers; only 18% identified as members themselves.[332] Through their news narratives about the Tea Party, reporters produced it as a coherent brand that relied on specific ideas and traits of race (and racism), class, and gender.

As a result, Tea Party news stories provided novel spaces for journalists to raise questions about identity, authenticity, and belonging. Terms such as "real working men and women," "real doctors," and "real Americans" produced binaries that set the parameters of "real America" around white working- and middle-class bodies. Tea Party events and handmade signs were used as authentic evidence of the Tea Party's demographic makeup and political beliefs, and to minimize and sensationalize the pervasive presence of American racism. Moreover, these journalistic discussions that reified the Tea Party brand only served to buttress hegemonic ideologies about gender, race (and racism), class, and success. As news narratives depicted white working- and middle-class Americans as "real," they also implied there must be an "unreal" America full of "unreal" working men and women whose voices, values, and concerns were not as authentically American.

The Tea Party texts then help to elucidate the significance of post-racism and post-feminism in popular culture. As Ralina Joseph notes, post-feminism bolsters gender essentialism and heterosexism through hyper-expressive claims to femininity and maternity, while post-racism seeks to eliminate race as a category of identity through denying systemic racial oppression.[333]

Post-feminism reifies gender, while post-racism seeks to eradicate race in the ways in which it implicates racism.

The Tea Party narratives show that media coverage embodies post-racism ideology and hegemony, letting whites off the hook for their continued oppression of others. By describing Tea Party racism as "fringe," the media marginalized American racism as exceptional or abnormal. It also showed how the election of a Black president, and the defeat of his white competitors, provided new ways for whiteness to signal both American authenticity *and* oppression. As Joseph puts it, "Inclusion of white [people] as a racially aggrieved group can be seen as an ultimate post-racial move."[334]

Tea Party news stories also show a similar effort to minimize the importance of class in American society and de-center sexism, while drawing on both as key signifiers. Heralding the power of Tea Party women while denying their viability as political leaders affirmed sexism. Women like Sarah Palin were presented as empowering women and defying gender constraints while adhering to gender conventions. In this way, while Tea Party women do not easily integrate into academic understandings of post-feminist or anti-feminist politics, they reveal the nature of gender branding and commodification. Journalists' coverage of Tea Party women confirms the idea that feminism has been integrated into the very hegemonic politics that it sought to oppose.[335] Similarly, appealing to class groups while avoiding discussions or critiques of class inequality reifies capitalist ideology (e.g., meritocracy).

As discussed throughout this chapter, much of the literature on race, gender, and class in news examines implicit bias (e.g., visual representations, coded language), rather than explicit meaning-making.[336] This chapter shows that the news outlets substantially cover and analyze the impact of race/racism, gender/sexism, and class/social inequality in Obama-era politics, partly due to the expanded contributions of external media creators and citizen journalists. Although political candidates have always represented social ideals and norms, Tea Party news stories suggest that they have grown more willing to regularly acknowledge, and debate, the role of race, gender, and class in their portrayals. It is true that the election of government leaders belonging to historically underrepresented groups (and the rise of identity-based social movements) has previously heightened media attention to and coverage of systematic discrimination and exclusion in American politics and society. But, I am also proposing that the media's Tea Party coverage indicates that race, gender, and class are now standard analytical lenses in political news coverage for *all* candidates—not just those with marginalized identities. While President Obama's blackness was hypervisible in the news coverage, so, too, was the whiteness of the Tea Party. More than that, its whiteness became key to the news coverage of the Tea Party and, through those news media narratives, a prevailing attribute of the Tea Party brand.

Tea Party news reports showed the inversions in twenty-first-century politics: political activists as credible government candidates, feminists as anti-choice, white people as oppressed, and old people as the fiery radicals. Journalists were drawn to certain Tea Party stories because they helped to make sense of a new political era borne out of the 2008 presidential election. But they also reported on these identities as part of a political landscape increasingly affected by celebrity, marketing, and consumer culture—their coverage reflects the way that the "traditional voter-politician relationship [has been translated] into the logic of fandom and branding."[337] The focus on these identities in Tea Party news stories not only elucidates their salience in mediating and proliferating the Tea Party brand but also reveals how race, gender, and class politics are debated, constructed, and understood in an Obama-era, political branding age.

CHAPTER 4

Reading the Tea Leaves—the News about the News

Whether it was a "media war" on Fox News, a reporter's rant at CNBC, or a defamatory online video triggering the dismissal of a high-ranking Obama appointee, one thing was clear: Tea Party news narratives told a story about modern journalism. From the moment the Tea Party emerged into the national spotlight, reporters used it to debate and critique the role of the news media in a polysemous, technological, and partisan-driven journalistic age. Covering the coverage of the Tea Party, as well as its relationship to the media, was central to the Tea Party's brand and fueled its publicity and growth. This chapter tracks what that coverage looked like in the first two years of the Tea Party's development.

In an age in which the media is so clearly implicated in political branding, news journalists and pundits discussed, debated, and analyzed their role in promoting, identifying with, and even participating in the Tea Party. The news media described their work as guided by professional norms, but advanced by the bottom line—professionals across news outlets openly viewed themselves in competition with one another and engaged and criticized one another's conduct. The tension between media actors and Tea Party leaders and activists on the ground depended on the extent to which each promoted, or undermined, the Tea Party brand. In examining the relationship and interaction between the media and the Tea Party that helped its brand, this chapter uncovers the way that editorializing, meta-journalism, technology, cross-media interaction, and market-oriented coverage shapes the way the news media function in a brand culture.

Several early surges in Tea Party news coverage were devoted to debating the reporting itself. In part, these concerns came from within the Tea

Party itself, whose activists and spokespersons frequently disputed unfavorable coverage. As news professionals reported on the Tea Party, they also found themselves integrated into its story, resulting in frequent discussions about the role and meaning of journalism in the current political moment. Within the complexity of both *being* and *covering* the story, news coverage of the Tea Party captures a period in newsmaking marked by heightened media self-coverage, activism, and (self-)criticism; reporters raising the volume. Traditional divisions between news reporters and political elites blurred as paid pundits and anchors provided daily news content in the form of debate, expertise, and commentary.

"Raising the volume" refers to how the news media was more than just the medium through which information about the Tea Party traveled to American audiences; the media was also a topic in Tea Party stories and an actor that explicitly facilitated the Tea Party brand. In covering their function as a medium, topic, and political actor, journalists and reporters tracked the contemporary flows of an interconnective media environment and journalism in a digital age, what I refer to as "headphone culture."[1] In the first part of this chapter, I describe how journalism and the news media function in our current moment. In the subsequent sections, I highlight how the "media" functioned as a topic, political actor, and medium in Tea Party news coverage. I conclude with a reflection about the significance of political news in a "meta-journalistic" era, a moment in which the news media understand themselves as political actors alongside the figures and events about which they report.

A HISTORY OF NEWS AND RISE OF BRANDING

Over the last four centuries, American journalism has gone through several major structural, occupational, and professional shifts.[2] It was not until well into the eighteenth century that the first "free press" began to develop. Newspapers at the start of this "party-press era" functioned primarily as vehicles through which political parties and elites distributed news and commentary that reinforced their values, beliefs, perspectives, and reputations. Even in this revolutionary period, many editors were brought up on sedition charges for running papers criticizing the federal government.

Though the First Amendment decreed in 1791 that "Congress shall make no law . . . abridging the freedom of speech, or of the press"[3] and protected the right for Americans to express their opinions, its true vision did not flourish until the nineteenth century. While the party-press newspaper rivalries continued, journalism was again changed by the wide availability of a financially profitable tabloid press. This new "penny press" used reporters to collect and write up both fact-based and sensational information with mass appeal. This "popular press" introduced the modern concept of news and the common usage of the term "journalism." News commercialization continued to grow with the development of the telegraph, which allowed news to reach an expanding audience.

As communications technology expanded at the dawn of the twentieth century, the growth of news chains and media conglomerates standardized news practices, styles, values, and topics.[4] To distinguish themselves from advertising and public relations specialists, and increase their appeal to diverse audiences, magazine, newspaper, and radio reporters and publishers adopted journalistic codes upholding truthfulness, accuracy, and impartiality. The objectivity norm, the "separation of facts and values," was crucial to redefining American journalism.[5] In being objective, journalists aimed to create impartial and accurate news coverage and confine "overt persuasion" to editorial spaces.[6] Michael Schudson explains:

> According to the objectivity norm, the journalist's job consists of reporting something called "news" without commenting on it, slanting it, or shaping its formulation in any way. The value of objectivity is upheld specifically against partisan journalism in which newspapers are the declared allies or agents of political parties and their reporting of news is an element of partisan struggle.[7]

According to this definition, "good" journalism is assessed by whether reporting is based on facts, not emotions or opinions, and "makes a good faith attempt to portray social phenomena *as they really are*."[8] Objective journalists are "politically detached" and "remain autonomous *from* politics—to develop a position outside or beyond the rough-and-tumble of partisan politics."[9]

Even as political columnists began to thrive in the 1930s, they understood their roles as primarily interpretive and nonpartisan. According to Barbie Zelizer, journalists function as interpretive communities that circulate knowledge and legitimate their practices through journalistic authority, and through the "ability of journalists to promote themselves as authoritative and credible spokespersons of 'real-life' events."[10] The growth of watchdog journalism and investigative reporting (i.e., muckraking) also concretized the role of the press as a "fourth estate," a public service institution that would increase the transparency, accessibility, and accountability of the three government branches. Mark Deuze argues that that the role of a journalist is more ideological (defined by a set of shared beliefs and values) than occupational (reducible to a particular set of duties).[11]

Despite these idealized notions of journalism, the American news media has often upheld the status quo, served as mouthpieces for government and official authorities, and produced business-friendly, sensational, and entertaining content that appeals to both advertisers and consumers. Many decisions regarding appropriate and ethical journalistic behavior are left to news executives, not journalists themselves (or even their audience).[12] This has created a news landscape in which, according to one Breitbart News editor, "journalistic integrity is dead," leaving only the "weaponization of information" as a key approach in news reporting and audience-seeking.[13]

In large part, changes to federal regulation have produced these transformations in the forms and norms of American news. When the FCC was first established in the Communications Act of 1934 (originally as the Federal Radio Commission), it was required by Congress to enforce public access to national media (at the time, the radio) and to ensure that media also served the public interest. In the 1970s and 1980s, the Federal Communications Commission underwent an ideological change. Instead of believing the media to be a public resource that required close monitoring, the FCC became an institution that felt the media were best left to market forces. In addition to lax federal regulation and oversight, the Supreme Court struck down the fairness doctrine in 1987, which had required that all programming that focused on important public issues provide "ample play for the free and fair competition of opposing views."[14] Such a requirement, the Supreme Court explained, intruded on the broadcasters' First Amendment rights.

Even more federal media deregulation occurred in the following decade with the passage of the Telecommunications Act of 1996, which allowed for increased conglomeration, horizontal integration, and ownership, and less stringent rules regarding independent media and barring media monopolies. Notably, Rupert Murdoch and Roger Ailes launched Fox News in 1996, only a few months after the passage of the Telecommunications Act. Similarly, the 1980s saw conservative talk radio programs rise in the wake of the eradication of the fairness doctrine.[15]

Additionally, lax federal oversight of cable and online media content coupled with shifts in technology also contributed to a decrease in public service-oriented journalism. The transition from analog to digital broadband television transmission in 2009 pushed more Americans to obtain cable television and digital streaming services.[16] This move to platforms with even more channels and options increased the steep competition for viewers and audiences. In 2016, the FCC also led an auction for broadcast stations to sell off their desirable low-band spectrum to private mobile and wireless companies, resulting in some audiences (particularly in rural areas) losing access to key public affairs and public interest programming.[17] As cable and online content are less monitored and regulated than broadcast television, this move loosened regulatory reins even further. The overall step back of the federal government in monitoring public interest in media, especially the news, opened the door for the unfettered governing of media primarily by profits and value added.[18]

At the beginning of the twenty-first century, the pressures from commercial media interests and rapidly changing technological innovation have expanded the influence of branding and marketing in media and news.[19] A majority of US news outlets are now owned by global corporations that have vested interest in sectors outside of news, generating concern about a journalistic conflict of interest in covering these businesses and anything pertaining to their economic interests.[20] As professional news organizations have undergone a decline in audiences and advertising revenue, and an increase in the constraining forces of business and political interests, resources for investigative journalism and a commitment to public service values have also dwindled. Marketing and business approaches to journalism push news outlets to differentiate themselves from rivals through branding and marketing, diversifying their distribution platforms and embracing partisan news delivery and story selection. In many ways, branding practices have become even more important than breaking news in journalism today. As David Tewksbury and Jason Rittenberg put it, "The very meaning of news is shifting."[21]

Political branding's rise has been a key part of this shift. In his book *Packaging Politics*, Bob Franklin explains that political branding practices have transformed the news media into a promotional conduit for voter outreach and messaging instead of a space of critical, investigative inquiry and debate.[22] As a result, political reporters' emphasis on image and brand has led to a heavy reliance on press releases, briefings, and official bulletins rather than original reporting or interviews; and a tendency for the news to be manipulated through pre-packaged stories promoting a politician's brand or policy. As politicians today are better able to connect directly with supporters, voters, and donors through social media, their reliance on the news media for this function has decreased. Reporters and journalists rely more heavily on political communications experts and media management to get information.[23] The growth of communications staff and handlers limits reporters' ability to meaningfully interact with political candidates, which increases "conversational journalism," or journalists talking to other journalists, as a means of producing substantive news content.[24]

In light of these changes, the news media is even more pressed to produce innovative, relevant, and appealing political content that will reach audiences and fans, even as websites and social media require more and more content.[25] The mass availability of user-generated and professional news on the Internet and social media—and the resulting erosion of spatial and temporal boundaries that come with asynchronous and instantaneous communication—have transformed journalism's roles, boundaries, and functions.

Furthermore, news organizations have adopted marketing and branding practices in similar ways to politicians, using segmentation to reach niche audiences, changing their news layout and presentations, and creating content that is advertiser-friendly and foregrounds lifestyle trends and consumption.[26] Since the 1970s, political reporting has relied more heavily on marketing devices, such as news polls and on-air focus group discussions, staged "pseudoevents," and dramatic storytelling that "minimize underlying facts and evidence."[27] Journalists today depend even more heavily on online LISTSERVs to gather up-to-date public relations material for publication on blogs, social networks, and news websites, radically altering the production of news in a branding culture.[28]

ON BACKGROUND: JOURNALISM AND/OR/VERSUS/WITHIN THE NEWS MEDIA

In looking at the stories that the news media told about the Tea Party, one can also assess the function and routines of modern journalism—the practice of collecting, interpreting, and distributing information about current events to the public. "Journalism" and "news media" are distinct, but overlapping terms. The "news media" as I use it throughout this book refers to the converging ideological tendencies of the topics, routines, discourses, and rhetoric used across many platforms, outlets, and companies. The distinction here is between journalists as professionals who organize, summarize, and report on information and "journalism" as the process, norms, and values by which that collation happens. The "news media" refers to the practice and ideas that stand out among and across all news organizations, and the spaces and institutions in which they manifest. In a *Newsmax* article, a quote from an NBC interview with President Obama gestured to the generalized nature of the term:

He called it an environment fostered to some extent by the modern news media. "Frankly, it gets spun up in part because of how the media covers politics, in the 24/7 news cycle, cable chatter, and talk radio, and the Internet, and the blogs."[29]

Academics often use the phrase "news media" to refer to both an influential social and cultural institution and a corporate conglomerate fueled by financial competition and profit margins. According to one writer, the "media have become a way to colonize not only other nations but also one's own nation."[30] Communications scholar Timothy E. Cook referred to the news media as a "heady brew of 'mass media, middle media, and micromedia'" that tend toward homogeneity.[31]

A crucial rhetorical distinction revealed in the Tea Party news coverage was that a *journalist's* audience was often constructed as *citizens*, while the *news media* aimed their messages at *consumers*. As Margaret Scammell notes, "Typically, 'citizen' and 'consumer' are considered opposite categories, the first outward-looking, embracing public interest, the second, self-interested, inward-looking and private."[32] Reaching citizens requires an ethical and democratic approach to news production and distribution. But serving consumers demands a different "bottom line," one focused on circulation, profit-making, and attracting customers. Elihu Katz argues that the impact of branding on the news and political public sphere has led to a major transformation in the "political and economic establishment that has armed itself with image makers and spin doctors."[33] While citizens can mobilize and exert control on the ruling structure through the knowledge gained from journalism, they can also become easily manipulated consumers of a "representative publicity" as conveyed via the news media[34] (as opposed to informed citizens in a representative democracy).

"Journalism" is a term deeply imbued with civic and aspirational values that guide news workers in truthfully identifying, investigating, and summarizing current events—especially political events. Zelizer variously describes journalism as a profession, an institution, a text, a group of people, and a set of practices.[35] According to Schudson and Tifft, "The normative commitment of this occupational group [is to write] political news in order to inform the citizens of a democracy."[36] In this way, journalists have been long understood as critical to maintaining a non-tyrannical, people-led, and accountable government.[37] Though reporters on the ground may dismiss these sentiments as "just so much sanctimonious bullshit," American journalism scholars frequently discuss the profession reverentially.[38] Numerous academics describe its sacred role as promoting and enabling freedom and democracy; providing reliable, factual, and non-sensational information; ensuring transparency and accuracy; and enabling public service.[39] According to Thorbjorn Broddason, the "sacredness" quality is what, in fact, contributes to the notion of journalism as a profession, despite its lack of required formal training and codes of conduct.[40] Still, journalist associations have formalized journalistic conventions through handbooks and guides, and legal rulings have reified these guidelines as occupational norms.[41]

At the moment of the Tea Party's 2009 rise, the news media and journalism were undergoing massive systemic and conceptual transformations that were redefining political reporting.[42] Zelizer explains: "As journalism has flourished in form and in content, it now seems to be no clear place in the public imagination."[43] Anxieties regarding the declining newspaper industry (overblown, according to some) drove news workers to diversify their skills, platforms, and styles to compete with the massive growth of online content. Politicians harnessed technological advances to communicate their message directly to supporters through social media and evade journalistic gatekeeping, analysis, and access. User-driven spaces in news sites generated feedback, boosted audience interaction, and provided new metrics for evaluating stories (i.e., "most emailed," "most commented"). On a societal level, a declining faith in the media, the rise of "infotainment" news, journalists' embrace of post-9/11 national security ideology, media conglomeration, and shrinking news outlets nationwide shifted the context and demands of news production during the Tea Party's emergence. In the words of Bruce Williams and Michael Delli Carpini, "The technological changes occurring over the past two decades along with broader and quite profound political, cultural, and economic changes have destabilized the media regime of the mid-twentieth century."[44]

The growth of electronic technology and user-generated media has also pushed scholars and news workers alike to reevaluate distinctions between "real" journalists and other media information producers—also known as cyberjournalists, citizen journalists, bloggers, vloggers, online journalists, participatory journalists, and accidental journalists.[45] Some researchers and news professionals have heralded the Internet's transparency and democratizing potential "as a corrective to culturally biased and overly reductive journalistic work."[46] Other news critics and professionals have expressed concern about online content creators' lack of accountability and standards.[47] In a 2012 news broadcast, Fox News pundit Juan Williams declared, "I'm a real reporter, not a blogger out in the blogosphere somewhere."[48] Such delineations primarily rely on differences in employment status and compensation, rather than actual labor. But the resulting consternation regarding the value of user-generated news has evoked debates about journalism's definition in a new media age. These muddled lines,

Jane Singer argues, only increase the public's need for "the trustworthy analyst, the interpreter, the sense-maker—the journalist."[49]

Still, determining who does and doesn't count as a journalist is much more than strictly a rhetorical exercise, particularly in a brand culture. Those identified as professional journalists are granted a number of legal privileges.[50] Some of these press liberties include the right to provide unfettered media coverage of a political candidate, facile access to public records, special protection from defamation and libel charges, and the "fair use" of copyrighted material.[51] While the Federal Election Commission closely monitors and regulates the work of political lobbyists and activists, journalists are free from such oversight. Additional benefits for recognized journalists include credentials that grant access to public events (and officials) and offer protection from arrest, membership in journalist organizations, and professional recognition and awards for journalistic labor. Within the Tea Party narratives, there is a clear tension related to laypeople identifying as journalists and accessing press privileges while also refusing to conform to traditional press values and roles.

In certain ways, journalists' depictions of the Tea Party conspicuously paralleled the self-described state of the news media. Descriptions of Tea Party rallies were similar to depictions of the digital news environment— they were both explained as advanced, progressive, superior, fragmented, and a threat to preexisting media forms. The Tea Party's use of new technology to organize its rallies and publicize its message imbued it with a sense of modernity, and like online news, it challenged existing structures of power, politics, and authority in journalism. Like the Tea Party, journalism defies easy classification. Is it a profession? An occupation? A form of creative expression? Similar to their difficulty in defining contemporary journalism, reporters struggled to define the Tea Party, locate its parameters, and identify its members and spokespersons. And similar to how they described the Tea Party, the media also described itself as a brand and commodity in news narratives. New media technology decentralized the Tea Party and established new rules for interactivity, publicity, and self-promotion, just as it did for journalists.

As the Tea Party became a prominent news story, the impact and flows of Internet-based information spaces also exposed inextricable connections to the mainstream press and a massive convergence of discursive style, news features, and story selection. In the face of these complexities, defining media dichotomies blurred, including dichotomies of old versus new, big versus small, mainstream versus alternative, journalists versus bloggers, and hard news versus soft news. It was in this multilayered, multimodal, multimedia context that the Tea Party emerged and prospered.

Further, through Tea Party news stories, another narrative emerged about the news media's function as a topic, a political actor, and a system of interdependent but distinct mediums.

META-JOURNALISM

On a 2012 Sunday morning news show, a gay *Newsweek* columnist fought back tears as he discussed President Obama's recent announcement supporting gay marriage:

> I never understood the power of a president's words until that day...suddenly this man saying, "I'm with you, I get it...we are equal human beings and I want to treat you the way you treat me." That—that was overwhelming. That's all I can say. I was at a loss for words.[52]

This quote captures what many scholars have called "meta-journalism" or "journalism about journalism," also known as "meta-media" and "meta-coverage."[53] Meta-journalism is variously described as interpretive journalism with journalists as experts about news, "social news" that involves disseminating and redistributing other news, or the coverage of the news media functioning as "political agents who participate, and shape, in political events."[54]

Tea Party news stories are an example of meta-journalism. They drew attention to how the branding environment has caused journalists to talk about themselves and their own interiority as part of their coverage of media and politics. When journalists engage in meta-journalism they do not only evaluate others' media reporting and performance but they also perform their own emotional and personal connections to political brands. By subjectively presenting Tea Party news, reporters exemplified how the "contemporary shift to political brand cultures...[has been] authorized by an advanced capitalist market and the concurrent focus on individual consumer choices rather than a historically informed form of collective action."[55] Rather than emphasizing the Tea Party's importance as a movement, journalists drew on it as a cultural signifier. In their stories, fact and opinion were equally subjective and partisan.

The news media described the Tea Party as important because it *felt* important, because reporters cultivated emotional connections with it and their constructed audience, because it indexed political and social attributes by which one could attach or define oneself—because it was a brand. Journalists openly expressed how their positionality and beliefs impacted their reporting of the news, and other reporters covered and featured these expressions and outbursts as news itself.[56] Much of the Tea Party media coverage was a form of "meta-meta-journalism": journalism about journalists' feelings and beliefs about the news and events that they covered. Many journalists saw themselves in the Tea Party coverage. In examining the Tea Party news narratives, reporters' role in the production and story of the Tea Party brand becomes clear.

NEWS MEDIA SELF-COVERAGE

If the media were indeed branding the Tea Party through storytelling, how did it describe itself in the process? One particular incident in July 2010 provides insight into how the media discusses and conceives of journalism in a new media age. This can be seen in the way Fox News and various other news outlets reproduced Andrew Breitbart's highly edited video of Shirley Sherrod and "reverse racism" accusation, as I discussed in the previous chapter.[57]

The "Sherrod incident" quickly became a story about the state of journalism, the importance of journalistic standards, and the impact of digital content in a brand culture that thrives on commerce, identity construction, politics, and viral consumption. *The Wall Street Journal* said that the case showed "how a toxic political atmosphere and a rapid-fire media can quickly turn a minor event into a media conflagration."[58] An *ABC News* story included a sound bite from President Obama lamenting that "we now live in this media culture where something goes up on YouTube or a blog and everybody scrambles."[59] According to *The Huffington Post*, "The most outrageous aspects of the story are fairly typical of everyone involved: Breitbart, the so-called 'liberal' news media, Democrats, Fox News Channel and all points in between."[60] On *Politico*, staff reporters wrote that the Shirley Sherrod story "will remind journalists and politicians alike that personal reputations and professional credibility are at stake, and a bit more restraint and responsibility are in order."[61]

Some news outlets used the Sherrod case to define blogs and other online information as inherently untrustworthy. According to *The New York Times*, the Sherrod case was "humiliating" to the national news media and demonstrated the unethical inclinations of a media cycle driven by Internet news sources:

The controversy illustrates the influence of right-wing Web sites like the one run by Andrew Breitbart, the blogger who initially posted the misleading and highly edited video, which he later said had been sent to him already edited. (Similarly,

Mr. Breitbart used edited videos to go after ACORN, the community organizing group.) Politically charged stories often take root online before being shared with a much wider audience on Fox. The television coverage, in turn, puts pressure on other news media outlets to follow up.[62]

On CNN, an anchor scolded the NAACP for taking "information solely from these conservative bloggers" and concluded that the "lesson" of the Sherrod case is that "not everything you see on the Internet is true."[63] For one *Wall Street Journal* columnist, the Sherrod case was a "teachable moment," showing that "we are not skeptical enough of what new media can cook up in its little devil's den. Anyone can be the victim of a high-tech lynching, and... because of this we have to be careful, slow down, look deeper."[64] The *USA Today* editorial board wrote:

> It would be naive to think that blatantly partisan bloggers or cable TV hosts will favor truth over distortion. Whipping up anger is their stock in trade.... More objective outlets, meanwhile, received another lesson in the need to check the facts before rushing to give Internet posts legitimacy.[65]

In the *Huffington Post*, writers also pointed fingers at the traditional news media (and politicians) for advancing a story from the unreliable echo chamber of the "conservative blogosphere".[66] The two specific instances in which coverage included news reports from non-professional journalists ("citizen journalists" on *Huffington Post* and an "I-reporter" on CNN), these reports were only used as primary sources that supplemented professional journalists' larger framing or reporting about the Tea Party. This language regarding online content reflected the general treatment of user-generated journalism in Tea Party news stories.

Online news outlets instead shifted the blame for the Sherrod fallout onto factors outside the digital environment, particularly the conservative media echo chamber. All three political news sites argued that the Sherrod case showed that Democrats, and particularly the Obama administration, had acted too quickly because they were afraid of Fox News and the rest of the conservative media. Moreover, *Huffington Post* writers said that Sherrod's treatment showed how easily liberals were intimidated and controlled by the right. *Newsmax* posts defended Breitbart and criticized Sherrod's views on race. *Politico*'s coverage highlighted the faults of a 24/7 media culture fueled by sensationalism, enamored with the ratings success of partisan news stories, and changed by the viral tendencies of social media and "Web aggregators" like the *Drudge Report*. *Huffington Post* also mentioned sensationalism as a key driver in overall Tea Party news coverage, arguing that the contemporary media was attracted to "political freakshows."[67]

Fox News, in particular, was criticized for its initial reporting of the Sherrod story. Though a *USA Today* article suggested that partisanship was endemic to the work of all "cable TV hosts," other news outlets refused to give Fox News a pass for publicizing the Breitbart video and instead accused the cable news channel of failing to abide by journalistic norms. A *Huffington Post* writer referred to Fox News reporters as "miserable excuses for journalists [who] relentlessly plugged the entirely false story before and after Sherrod was fired" and "propagandists posing as 'journalists.'"[68] A CNN anchor said that the Sherrod incident reflected Fox's lack of "journalistic diligence" and that its regular intermingling of scheduled news and opinion programming signaled that "it operates by different journalistic standards, depending... on what time it is."[69] He continued, concluding that CNN was the better news organization because it had refused to run the story:

> Now, it's important to note that FOX News pounced on Breitbart's Shirley Sherrod scoop hours after he posted it Monday. By the way—and this is part of the story, too—at CNN, we knew as soon as FOX did that the Shirley Sherrod video was out there. We watched and we decided not to run it because there were just too many unanswered questions at the time.
>
> After FOX aired it, we did our due journalistic diligence and we're the ones, frankly, who fairly quickly debunked the FOX Breitbart story and undid the damage to an innocent woman's reputation.
>
> ... [I] learned in journalism school that there's a difference between reporting and distorting.

Fox News also discussed the role it had played in the Breitbart/Sherrod story in the context of journalism. Anchor Bill O'Reilly said that it showed that "journalism in America is on the verge of collapse."[70] O'Reilly claimed he had reported the Sherrod story because the "establishment press" regularly ignored "important stories" and kept accurate information from Americans. The "liberal media," he went on, were constitutionally bound to "serve the folks," but instead spent their time strategizing and cohering anti-conservative narratives in secretive online discussion groups like Journolist. Furthermore, O'Reilly said that "dishonest personal attacks [from the liberal news media were]... a major violation of journalistic ethics."[71]

Fox News also argued that it adhered to journalistic norms in general by correcting "liberal" media bias and providing coverage pertinent to conservative Americans, who it deemed a neglected and maligned constituency.

In this way, Fox News argued that it was engaged in journalistic public service, not political advocacy. O' Reilly also claimed that the network was the agenda-setter for the national news media, contending that Fox News was now the "dominant media force in America" and "set the daily discussion" for the rest of media.[72] These reports show the push to establish clearer boundaries around Fox News's role and reveal that the network felt responsible for adhering to its own specific notions of journalistic ethics.

Tea Party news texts reflected that "journalism" still carries ethical, sacred connotations in contemporary news culture, specifically invoking the label when describing perceived violations of journalistic norms. Moreover, this notion of journalism as sacred stood out as particularly important in a celebrity-, circulation-, and consumer-driven brand culture. In one instance, Fox's support and publicity of tea parties organized nationwide on Tax Day (the date of the annual federal tax deadline) drew concerns that it was "blurring lines between advocacy and journalism."[73] In an interview with *Politico*, Arianna Huffington, founder and namesake of *Huffington Post*, claimed that the citizen journalists she sent to cover the Tea Party would be "purely journalistic" and not "activists,"[74] drawing a clear line between political championing and the work of journalism. Bill O'Reilly discussed the importance of journalistic integrity when discussing a congressman's report about tea partiers that used racial epithets: "I'm a journalist. And journalists aren't supposed to believe what politicians tell them simply because they're politicians."[75] In another example, Fox News commentator and former NPR reporter Juan Williams said, "I have always thought of journalism in a way as a priesthood, you know, that you honor it, that you protect it."[76] Repeating these sentimental notions about journalism, an MSNBC anchor decried Fox's "illusion of journalistic credibility."[77]

Beyond the Sherrod case, the media was a general topic discussed within each outlet and platform in Tea Party news coverage. Reporters described "the media" as inextricably tied to political ideology and partisanship.

liberal media	conservative media
populist media	mainstream media
new media	right-wing media
lamestream media	state-run media
national media	left-leaning media
willing media	rapid-fire media
populist media	progressive media
traditional media	liberal establishment media
politically correct media	infidel media
corporate media	public media

Terms used to describe the media across news outlets, both by news reporters and Tea Party insiders, include:

Other language describing the Tea Party drew on juxtaposition, a pattern of grouping "media" with other words or groups that conveyed a significant relationship or association. For instance, news reports linked "white conservatives and Fox News" to suggest a relationship between the two. Other similar examples include:

- Liberal Media and the NAACP condemn Tea Party as racist[78]
- Left-Wingers in the media and Democrats[79]
- Media and elite universities[80]
- Media and our domestic enemies[81]

These descriptors connote a widespread belief that all media outlets and workers have inherent ideological biases that affect their content.

Perhaps most significant was O'Reilly's frequent argument that the Tea Party had exposed a "media war . . . between Fox News and talk radio on one side and *The New York Times* and the liberal networks on the other side."[82] Other media entities specifically named as players in the "media war" included NBC, MSNBC, the media watchdog group Media Matters, and Jon Stewart of the satirical news program *The Daily Show*. These media "enemies" allegedly wanted to "destroy" Fox News and "attack" the Tea Party. In this metaphorical media battle, the Sherrod case was just another "hand grenade" used to "weaken Fox."[83] Still, the Sherrod incident revealed the significant influence that Fox News held over both the Obama administration and the national news cycle, despite stated concerns about its veracity or objectivity, and the role the Tea Party revealed that the media played.

NEWS MEDIA AS A POLITICAL ACTOR

The story of Rick Santelli's rant against President Obama triggering the Tea Party reveals how contemporary journalists now participate in political branding. In news stories, there was very little explicit criticism of Santelli's lack of objectivity and overt activism in his call to mobilize a Tea Party protest, despite his professional position as a reporter. On the contrary, journalists who commented on Santelli's speech framed it as a success story. The *Chicago Tribune* argued that the "self-described rant" had raised Santelli's profile, increased his value to CNBC, and opened up possibilities for book contracts and talk shows.[84] In other words, journalism and journalists became part of a market paradigm that sees branding and monetary potential—rather than actual news quality or journalistic objectivity—as key indicators of success.

A *New York Times* article argued that in the past Santelli's outburst would have been embarrassing for cable news stations, but now presented an opportunity to "maximize publicity and Web traffic."[85] In another *New York Times* piece, a columnist bemoaned the absence of criticism as symptomatic of a news media more concerned with branding and self-expression than with journalistic integrity:

> Nobody at his network seemed concerned that Mr. Santelli had exceeded the bounds of news reporting. Instead, he was propped up by constant replays on CNBC and rival networks as a populist hero. It's all too likely that he will be rewarded with his own show someday.[86]

Other news outlets, including Fox News and MSNBC, avoided the quagmire of evaluating Santelli's violation of journalistic norms by not using the word *reporter* to describe Santelli, instead mentioning his financial trader background to explain his motivation or describing him as a "pundit" or "commentator."

Santelli, for his part, defended his speech in an apologia posted on CNBC's website titled "I want to set the record straight."[87] The piece largely took aim at critics. Rather than explaining his violation of traditional journalistic norms, Santelli denied that his tirade was staged for publicity, claiming that it was his typical "aggressive and impassioned style" that targeted both Republicans and Democrats alike. Additionally, he wrote that he had no affiliation with any Tea Party websites or "political agenda." Nonetheless, the anti-Obama, pro-business, and pro-wealthy themes of his tirade, as well as his own raced and gendered signification, mapped these attributes onto the Tea Party brand.

The coverage of Santelli as a political actor shows the rising significance of opinion spaces in which "professional communicators like politicians, journalists, experts, and other high-status intellectuals use the media as a staging ground to gather and debate the issues of the day".[88] Journalists in this new environment function more like celebrities—they aim to diversify their content across platforms, outlets, and genres. Although journalists in the past have been fired by higher-ups for blogging or airing personal political views, they are now encouraged to use social media to diversify their brand and expand their audience.[89] As one *New York Times* reporter wrote, social media sites like Twitter have changed the journalistic landscape by facilitating "me-first journalism" and functioning as a "gateway drug to full-blown media narcissism."[90]

Fox News was also discussed as a major political actor in the Tea Party narratives; its active support of the Tea Party was an ongoing topic. Media outlets voiced concerns that Fox News's participation in and promotion of Tea Party events was more activism than journalism. An MSNBC anchor said that the Fox News coverage of the tea parties demonstrated an "unprecedented politicization of the news media."[91] In some instances, news stories showed Fox News employees personally attacking public figures who criticized their coverage.[92] After Fox News host Bill O'Reilly called for Sherrod's resignation, the Obama administration quickly fired her; this hasty response was cited as evidence of the network's power and influence.

In response, Fox News repeatedly defended its news coverage, arguing their anchors were making a journalistic intervention, correcting the "liberal," "corrupt," and "obscene" turn of a "left-wing media" that was "damaging the nation" and was "on the side of monarchy."[93] According to Fox News, the "left-wing" news media marginalized the Tea Party because they were "out of touch" with Americans.[94] Bill O'Reilly complained that other news organizations "demonize[d]" the Tea Party and were "branding protestors as kooks and racists."[95] Still, O'Reilly argued that the conservative media would prevail because his show was "the number one show that dominate[d] cable news" and "politically correct media operations [were] going south fast,"[96] specifically referring to MSNBC, CNN, and *The New York Times*. Through its peer relationship with other news outlets, Fox News held them accountable to its own journalistic norms and values—and, through its partisanship, it advanced a conservative cause.

Across outlets, other conservative pundits and news commentators also argued that their mainstream competitors were actively engaged in a campaign to defame and eradicate the Tea Party and the entire conservative media regime. A *Wall Street Journal* editorial claimed that "liberal Democrats and their friends in the media" want to "dismiss and discredit the tea-party movement."[97] O'Reilly also complained specifically about mainstream media depictions of the Tea Party that portrayed "white conservatives and FOX news [as] the racists."[98] Another *Wall Street Journal* columnist contended that tea partiers "imagine their movement as a great uprising of the common people against . . . the arrogant power of the media."[99] According to him, Tea Party supporters like Fox News host Sarah Palin used a narrative of "martyrdom" to deflect and undermine legitimate criticism within news coverage.[100] Fox News managing editor Bill Sammon argued that, "The mainstream media hates the tea party movement almost as much as it hates Sarah Palin. . . . And the reason is simple: that's because both are a threat."[101]

The portrayal of the non-conservative media as a political adversary of the Tea Party and its brand made it difficult for reporters to interact with tea partiers or gain access to their events. *Politico* described a major Tea Party event that initially denied entrance to "non-friendly" media outlets.[102] Another *Politico* story quoted a Tea Party organizer who claimed to ban tea partiers who had an "association with liberal media outlets and [were] conspiring with each other to 'Take TPN [Tea Party Nation] and this convention down.'"[103] Reports about Tea Party candidates' "reporter-dodging" were also common. An *ABC News* report from a Tea Party event showcased the hostility that conservative activists directed toward its reporters:

> JONATHAN KARL (ABC NEWS): [*Voiceover*] They came to Washington, angry about President Obama's policies, to be sure, but also angry at the way they've been portrayed.... Many of them blamed us, the news media.
>
> ATTENDEE (TEA PARTY RALLY): You know what, back off. Back off....
>
> ATTENDEE (TEA PARTY RALLY): Give us some space. We don't want to talk to you.
>
> ATTENDEE (TEA PARTY RALLY): We want honesty from you. We want fair time from you. We want you to—you the media, to represent all the people, not just a certain portion of the people.[104]

Other outlets similarly noted numerous instances in which Tea Party leaders or supporters expressed disdain and were "rude" to reporters on assignment.

Some Tea Party supporters and activists specifically expressed concern that certain media outlets would undermine and attack the Tea Party brand. In their book *Tea Party Patriots*, Tea Party leaders Mark Meckler and Jenny Beth Martin warned that "if all you know about the Tea Party is what you've heard from the mainstream media, you haven't gotten an accurate portrayal of who we are and what we're trying to do."[105] Two Tea Party organizers wrote a guest column in *Politico* in which they complained that their group had undergone "16 months of liberal media scrutiny and bombardment."[106]

On the other hand, conservative media professionals were used as sources and spokespersons to publicize the Tea Party brand. On cable news, show hosts frequently interviewed journalists both as sources and as political experts. These guests both reported on current political events and used them to explain the political and media landscape. Media experts, personalities, and reporters frequently contributed to political blogs. As described earlier, Andrew Breitbart's video was infamously used as a Fox News source. Mark Williams, a conservative radio host and Tea Party organizer, and Dana Loesch, a St. Louis radio host, were both interviewed as Tea Party leaders. In this way, the boundaries separating political analyst, political reporter, and journalist were regularly blurred.

Sarah Palin, in particular, best represented the fusion of the Tea Party brand, political activism, and news media celebrity. After she resigned as governor of Alaska in 2009, Palin began fully maximizing her new career as a media and political personality. Even while still governor, Palin had begun working for Fox News, first as a paid commentator and then as a host with a special series called "Real American Stories".[107] In a press release, Palin expressed her appreciation for joining a "place that so values fair and balanced news".[108] She had also landed a reality show on TLC that featured her hunting, fishing, and having other rugged adventures in the Alaskan wilderness; the first episode attracted five million viewers, breaking network records.[109] She went out onto the Tea Party rally and conservative speech circuit, receiving as much as $100,000 for speaking at one Tea Party convention in Nashville (deemed a for-profit event).[110] She earned at least $12 million in the nine months after leaving behind her role as governor and its $125,000 annual public salary.[111]

In less than a year, Palin had used her political brand of conservative womanhood, ruggedness, and aggression to transition profitably from formal politician to celebrity, news host, and Tea Party brand advocate and social movement leader. She would later create her own online TV network and sign on for a new TV show as a judge, while at least one of her children, Bristol, would branch out on the Palin brand and secure a reality show and TV gigs of her own.[112] More than anyone else, Palin was indicative of a new brand of political and media leaders, further conflating the lines between politics, entertainment, and news.

Facts and Politics in Tea Party Reporting

Broader critiques describing the entire news media as an increasingly politicized institution were also a frequent theme in Tea Party media coverage. A *Politico* writer complained that a conservative blog had demanded that he "be cast off the media beat because I don't agree that the MSM [mainstream media], as a whole, 'hates' the tea party movement".[113] A *New York Times* columnist referred to the ideological fragmentation of contemporary media as the "political-media complex".[114] Another *New York Times* piece claimed that the news media fell into two camps: the "populist news media" (which is conservative and supports the Tea Party) and the "progressive news media" (which is liberal and supports the Left).[115]

In a profession fundamentally guided by values such as objectivity, neutrality, and fact-based reporting as a way of providing vital public information to a democratic citizenry, these moves away from journalistic ideals further transformed the meaning, routines, and goals of news. While early twentieth-century efforts to professionalize journalism and shift it from being a mere vehicle for public relations and propaganda promoted the idea that journalists aim to serve the public interest, dissipation of these roles also reflect an erosion of the idea of journalism as public service. Without a fourth estate of news media covering important events and actors, and separating brand from substance, it is less likely that citizens can knowledgeably evaluate and hold the government accountable.

In response to journalists' increasing political activism and inaccuracies within widely circulated political and news information, news reporters often looked to online media fact-checking groups for neutral information. Watchdog groups like Factcheck.org aim to "monitor the factual accuracy of major US political players" and serve as "nonprofit 'consumer advocate[s]'" for voters—a democratic mission traditionally attributed to professional journalists.[116] The majority of fact-checking organizations are run by current or former journalists. Like traditional journalists, fact-checkers aim to collect, verify, interpret, and present facts (or lies) in a subjective process that often reveals truth's inherent ambiguity and objectivity's futility, rather than reifies a neutral version of reality.

Fact-checking organizations claim objectivity. However, open challenges to powerful political groups sometimes provoke hostilities that place them at the center of political conflict, instead of outside of it. Additionally, a number of fact-checking groups are partisan, though their mission statements are similar to those of the nonpartisan entities. One specific example mentioned in Tea Party news texts is Media Matters for America (MMA), a nonprofit research group "dedicated to comprehensively monitoring, analyzing, and correcting conservative misinformation."[117] The MMA director appeared on MSNBC to describe inaccuracies in Fox News reporting about the Tea Party. *The New York Times* has variously referred to MMA as a "left-wing group" and a "media watchdog."[118] According to Fox News anchors, the "vicious, dishonest Media Matters organization" was just another political actor claiming authority and twisting facts to serve its own agenda:

O'REILLY: Here is back up. The Media Matters group, which Soros gave a million to in addition to the 1.8 million and we will get to that with Rove in a moment. They called today from Mara Liasson who is our Fox News analyst to be fired from NPR as well...

GLENN BECK: And we also now have George Soros giving a million dollars to Media Matters to come and assault us. Assault us, take us down. It's never, ever been done before, Bill. This isn't normal.

... They will watch every word you say. And if it's Media Matters, they will tape everything you say and they won't stop until they drive you off the air. That's the goal here. I think it's the goal that they have toward you and pretty much everyone on Fox News.[119]

In another example, on the other side of the political spectrum, *Newsmax* cited statistics from a study produced by the Media Research Center (MRC), which it described as "a watchdog organization founded by conservative L. Brent Bozell III."[120] According to the MRC, the "three big television networks" "maligned" and "ignored" the Tea Party movement. Attacks on the neutrality of fact-checking entities and disputes regarding their objectivity and the factuality of their claims imply that these groups actually function as a new form of journalism, rather than its referees. Of course, this fact-checking work only affects a political brand that relies on veracity as a key quality. But its usefulness in taking up a critical function of the press is important in providing information that does not rely on branding, image, and sensationalism for a public keen to be informed.

CONVERGING SPACES: "SOFT NEWS" AND TEA PARTY BRANDING

The news media's branding of the Tea Party also revealed the modern importance of editorial news content. Within the print media, the Tea Party became a story in the "soft news" commentary and opinion sections, areas more conducive to branding practices. As Matthew Baum notes, soft news relies on dramatic themes and commentary from celebrities, and depends less on authoritative and knowledgeable sources.[121] This allows for the communication of sentimental, image-dependent, and less fact-based qualities required of a brand. Additionally, as elaborated below, the print news coverage of the Tea Party reveals a clear blending of editorial/soft news and hard news in both style and content, a blending that better facilitated Tea Party branding.

Most media and politics research has "privileged fact-based reporting over other forms of news and commentary," implicitly promoting the idea that objective, hard-news content is the most influential coverage in matters of politics and governance.[122] Soft news (or "*softer* news") covers humorous, novel, opinionated, and entertaining content and provides a space where writers are freer to editorialize.[123] A key dimension in distinguishing between hard and soft news depends on "whether journalists' subjective impressions or opinions are apparent in a report" and if it includes "verbal and/or visual emotion-arousing elements." Jacobs and Townsley argue that this "space of opinion" opens the journalistic field for government agencies,

Table 4.1. NEWS AND OPINION ARTICLES

Surge 1 (4/12/09–4/18/09)	USA Today	Wall Street Journal	New York Times
Number of articles	News: 1 Opinion: 1	News: 2 Opinion: 3	News: 1 Opinion: 3
Authors	Oren Dorrell* Editorial*	Karl Rove Thomas Frank* Glenn Harland Reynolds	Gail Collins* Paul Krugman* Ben Stein*

Surge 2 (9/13/09-9/19/09)	USA Today	Wall Street Journal	New York Times
Number of articles **Authors**	News: 0 Opinion: 1 DeWayne Wickham*	News: 0 Opinion: 1 Gerald F. Seib*	News: 0 Opinion: 3 Bob Herbert* David Brooks * Barbara Ehrenreich & Dedrick Muhammad

Surge 3 (1/31/10–2/6/10)	USA Today	Wall Street Journal	New York Times
Number of articles **Authors**	News: 2 Opinion: 3 Dick Armey Editorial* Sarah Palin	News: 1 Opinion: 2 Robert B. Reich Thomas Frank*	News: 5 Opinion: 4 Robert Zaretsky* Gail Collins* Richard W. Stevenson Frank Rich*

Surge 4 (3/28/10–4/3/10)	USA Today	Wall Street Journal	New York Times
Number of articles **Authors**	News: 0 Opinion: 1 Stephen Prothero	News: 1 Opinion: 8 Juan Williams John Steele Gordon Karl Rove Daniel Henninger John Steele Gordon Thomas Frank* Shelby Steele Norman Podhoretz	News: 3 Opinion: 6 Gail Collins* David Brooks* Benedict Carey Wen Stephenson Gail Collins* Frank Rich*

Surge 5 (4/11/10–4/17/10)	USA Today	Wall Street Journal	New York Times
Number of articles **Authors**	News: 2 Opinion: 1 Rich Benjamin	News: 2 Opinion: 1 Thomas Frank*	News: 7 Opinion: 4 Charles M. Blow* Clyde Haberman Gail Collins* Bob Herbert*

(Continued)

Table 4.1. *(Continued)*

Surge 6 (4/18/10–4/24/10)	USA Today	Wall Street Journal	New York Times
Number of articles	News: 0 Opinion: 0	News: 1 Opinion: 5	News: 4 Opinion: 10
Authors		Jerry Bowyer*	Brian Stelter*
		Thomas Frank*	David Brooks*
		Editorial*	Gail Collins*
		Andrew Kohut	Ross Douthat*
		T. H. Breen	John Harwood
			Tyler Cowen
			Kate Zernike*
			Thomas L. Friedman*
			Liesl Schillinger
			Frank Rich*

Surge 7 (6/13/10–6/19/10)	USA Today	Wall Street Journal	New York Times
Number of articles	News: 3 Opinion: 1	News: 1 Opinion: 2	News: 3 Opinion: 9
Authors	Jonathan Turley	Douglas E. Schoen and Patrick H. Caddell	Editorial
		Gerald F. Seib*	
			Michael Cooper
			Charles M. Blow*
			Matt Bai*
			Kirk Johnson
			Ross Douthat*
			Matt Bai*
			Jennifer Steinhauer
			Ramesh Ponnuru
			Pamela Paul

Surge 8 (7/11/10–7/17/10)	USA Today	Wall Street Journal	New York Times
Number of articles	News: 2 Opinion: 0	News: 0 Opinion: 5	News: 2 Opinion: 3
Authors		Gerald F. Seib*	Charles M. Blow*
		Stephen Moore*	Gail Collins*
		Eric Felten*	Henry Alford
		Editorial*	

Surge 9 (7/18/10–7/24/10)	USA Today	Wall Street Journal	New York Times
Number of articles	News: 4 Opinion: 3	News: 1 Opinion: 1	News: 10 Opinion: 4
Authors	Assorted Opinions	James Webb*	Gail Collins*
	DeWayne Wickham*		Ross Douthat*
	Susan Page*		Frank Rich *
	Editorial *		Matt Bai*
			Corey Kilgannon*

Table 4.1. (Continued)

Surge 10 (10/17/10–10/23/10)	USA Today	Wall Street Journal	New York Times
Number of articles	News: 7 Opinion: 4	News: 4 Opinion: 4	News: 22 Opinion: 20
Authors	Susan Page*		Helene Cooper
	Ross K. Baker		Bob Herbert*
	Richard Wolf*		Jim Rutenberg*
	Assorted Opinion		Editorial*
			Frank Rich *
			Clyde Haberman*
			Maureen Dowd *
			Jesse McKinley*
			Michael Barbaro*
			Peter Baker*
			Editorial*
			Monica Davey*
			Jennifer Steinhauer*
			Maureen Dowd *
			Tom Brokaw
			Adam Liptak*
			John Hartwood*
			Ross Douthat*
			William Yardley*
			Lawrence Downes*

officeholders, think tanks, lobbyists, and advocacy groups to address "serious matters of social concern."[124]

Notably, print reporters' discussion, circulation, and analysis of the Tea Party largely originated in soft-news spaces—editorials, op-eds, and guest columns (see Table 4.1).[125] Later, the non-editorial sections drew on the tone, framing, language, details, and sourcing supplied by the initial opinion and commentary articles. For example, themes of the Tea Party as "new," "energetic," "working-class," and "tech-savvy" originated in opinion and guest columns and were reproduced throughout the hard news coverage (in some instances, even when demographic data dispelled such assertions). Many of the soft-news writers included high-profile Tea Party brand strategists, organizers, supporters, and promoters, including Sarah Palin, Glenn Harland Reynolds, and Dick Armey.

Additionally, the fact-based presentation style of the hard news sections frequently mirrored the more accessible and persuasive language used in blogs, editorials, and other opinion spaces, highlighting the ways that "'serious,' 'entertaining,' 'fact-based,' and 'commentary-based' styles of journalism are...increasingly being combined in new ways."[126] Opinion columns included direct quotes from tea partiers and experts, cited hard data and statistics, and covered specific events, similar to hard-news coverage. Frequently in hard-news stories, reporters editorialized and used informal and colloquial phrasing. For example, a *Wall Street Journal* reporter covering the Tea Party and the midterm elections argued that "Republicans on the campaign trail are bashing the president and his agenda."[127] In another story, a *USA Today* reporter contended that in tackling the economic recession, "tax increases and major reductions in Medicare, Medicaid and Social Security" were "the only solutions capable of raising enough money [but] are politically dangerous for the president and Congress."[128] In *The New York Times*, the reporter covering the Breitbart/Sherrod story concluded that "pretty much everyone else had egg on his face"; and another opened a piece about Santelli with "once upon a time."[129]

Moreover, textual and stylistic similarities in the placement and labeling of opinion articles and hard-news reporting make it difficult to distinguish between editorial and fact-based news coverage (an issue already commonly recognized within cable news reporting).[130] For example, Gerald Seib's op-ed column (Figure 4.1) in *The Wall Street Journal* is listed under the label "News," but the word *Opinion* is the heading for another page of columns (Figure 4.2).[131] Andrew Kohut's article about polling data falls under "Opinion" in *The Wall Street Journal*, but Megan Thee-Brennan and Marina Stefan's article on a *New York Times*/CBS poll is considered "news" in *The New York Times*.[132]

It is challenging to assign a category to the "Caucus" article written by Michael Barbaro or John Harwood's piece about gubernatorial candidate Carl Paladino (Figures 4.3 and 4.4).[133] These examples show the blurring of fact and opinion that enabled the Tea Party brand—was it a social movement or a political party? Is it an op-ed or hard-news article topic? The fading differences between opinion and hard news emphasize image and perception over substance, and minimize the importance of facts and information within political knowledge, thus enhancing the storytelling power and influence of branding in news reporting.

Tea Party news coverage in print news suggests that the growth of digital media has not only affected newsgathering practices and routines but also altered the language that professional journalists use in their reporting—specifically, the language and stylistic influences that previously characterized each of the mediums. Popular and scholarly understandings of new media content show that the term "new media" is often associated with soft news. Online news was originally understood as an arena that

U.S. NEWS

CAPITAL JOURNAL | By Gerald F. Seib

Tea Party and the Path to Power

Republicans need to pick up 10 Senate seats now held by Democrats to win control of the chamber.

ONLINE TODAY: Jerry Seib discusses tea party wins and this year's election at WSJ.com/Campaign.

Investigation of Spy Ring Nets a 12th

Continued from Page One

U.S. officials on June 26 canceled his visa. A day later, FBI agents rounded up 10 of the 11 members of the spy ring.

This courtroom sketch shows the 10 Russian spies who pleaded guilty in federal court of conspiring to serve as unlawful foreign agents Thursday. An 11th was arrested and jumped bail in Cyprus. Federal officials now say they have detained a 12th person, a 23-year-old man, as a result of the investigation into the spy ring. Below, vans carrying the deported Russian agents drive out of the Moscow airport on Friday.

CORRECTIONS & AMPLIFICATIONS

Figure 4.1: Seib column listed under "News" in *The Wall Street Journal*, July 13, 2010.

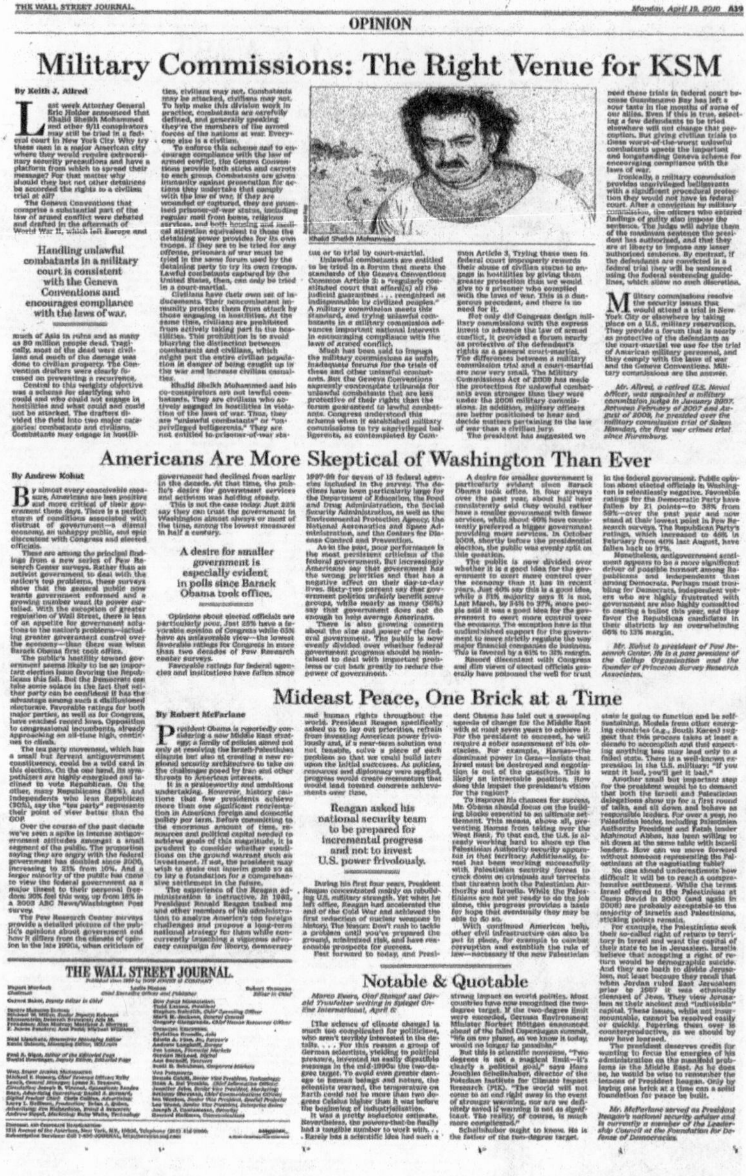
THE WALL STREET JOURNAL. Monday, April 19, 2010 A19

OPINION

Military Commissions: The Right Venue for KSM

By Keith J. Allred

Handling unlawful combatants in a military court is consistent with the Geneva Conventions and encourages compliance with the laws of war.

Americans Are More Skeptical of Washington Than Ever

By Andrew Kohut

A desire for smaller government is especially evident in polls since Barack Obama took office.

Mideast Peace, One Brick at a Time

By Robert McFarlane

Reagan asked his national security team to be prepared for incremental progress and not to invest U.S. power frivolously.

THE WALL STREET JOURNAL.

Notable & Quotable

Figure 4.2: Opinion section, *The Wall Street Journal*, April 19, 2010.

THE 2010 CAMPAIGN

The Caucus

DAYS TO ELECTION

15

Wielding Two-by-Fours Instead of Talking Points

By JOHN HARWOOD

SAN DIEGO — In Election 2010, there's no time for subtlety anymore.

Here in California and in much of the rest of the country, early voting has begun. Election Day itself arrives in 15 days.

That has President Obama and fellow Democrats racing this week and next, to outrun the Republican wave. And as they rip into Republican adversaries, they've not mincing words.

Take Senator Barbara Boxer, Democrat of California, who is battling Carly Fiorina, the former Hewlett-Packard chief executive, in her bid for a fourth term. Her television advertisements portray Ms. Fiorina as callously enriching herself while sending Hewlett-Packard jobs abroad; in an interview late last week, she excoriated her Republican rival as a failure.

"She doesn't tell people that

she got fired from that job," said Ms. Boxer, above. "She doesn't tell people that the stock price went down more than 50 percent when she was there.

"She doesn't tell people she got a $20 million severance pay when she was fired. It would take the ordinary Californian 100 years working full time to make that much."

Ms. Fiorina responded in kind. She accused Ms. Boxer of having "destroyed jobs in our state" while having "become a multimillionaire since she came to the U.S. Senate."

Senator John McCain, the 2008 Republican presidential candidate, came to Ms. Fiorina's aid over the weekend by calling Ms. Boxer "the most bitterly partisan, antidefense senator" and an "unpleasant" colleague to boot. Still, Ms. Boxer's feistiness and financial edge have given her a narrow lead.

Across the country, Democrats are scrambling to deflect voters' unhappiness with the party in power over the sputtering economy. In many cases, that is producing a counterattack of striking ferocity.

Democrats that ferocity takes the form of discrediting their rivals' backgrounds, as

in a release by the House Democratic Campaign Committee late last week titled "Breaking News: Allen West (FL-22) Tied to Criminal Organization." (The campaign of Mr. West, who is challenging Representative Ron Klein of Florida, the Democratic incumbent, said he had no ties to the organization in question, a motorcycle group.)

Other news it involves linking their opponents' policy agendas to objects of their constituents' fear (China's economic might) or loathing ("Wall Street executives"). In Michigan, an ad for Representative Mark Schauer, a Democrat, accuses his Republican opponent, Tim Walberg, of helping businesses outsource jobs to China during his earlier service in the House. Mr. Walberg called the ad "deceptive."

As President Obama continues his cross-country barnstorming to save Democratic candidates, he is warning of dire consequences from Republican rule for college students, clean energy projects, Head Start beneficiaries, AIDS patients and others. Republicans insist these are distortions.

The president himself rarely mentions by name the Republican opponents of Democrats he is stumping for. His efforts are largely geared toward framing a national message and churning Democratic turnout.

But a look at Mr. Obama's travel this week underscores the aggressiveness his party is displaying. He will appear with three veteran Democratic incumbents who are scrapping to extend their careers.

"Don't out by himself and not on our side," says an ad for Senator Patty Murray of Washington slamming her Republican opponent, Dino Rossi, for having "founded a bank with business lobbyists." Mr. Obama will appear with Ms. Murray on Thursday.

"Extreme and dangerous," so ad for the Senate majority leader, Harry Reid, says of his Republican opponent, the Tea Party favorite Sharron Angle. The president campaigns with Mr. Reid on Friday, after campaigning earlier that day with Ms. Boxer.

California would seem to be comparatively safe territory, since there, unlike in many other states, Mr. Obama retains a job approval rating above 50 percent. But virtually no Democrat can afford to let up in the final campaign sprint — and Ms. Boxer, one of the most outspoken feminists in Congress, isn't in her fight against Ms. Fiorina.

"She broke the glass ceiling when she got her job as C.E.O. of Hewlett-Packard," Ms. Boxer concluded. "But she got fired. She failed. So what she's bringing to the table is a failed record."

THE WEEK AHEAD

FUND-RAISERS President and Michelle Obama will be out in full force, with Mrs. Obama appearing at two events on Monday: one fund-raiser in Connecticut for Richard Blumenthal, the Democratic candidate for Senate and the state's attorney general, and another in New York at a Women's Leadership Forum dinner.

ON THE TRAIL Mr. Obama heads West for a rally on Wednesday in Portland, Ore. (for the Democratic candidate for governor, John Kitzhaber); an event in Seattle on Thursday (for Senator Patty Murray); to Los Angeles on Friday (for Senator Barbara Boxer); and "Moving America Forward" rallies in Los Angeles and Las Vegas (for Senator Harry Reid and Representative Dina Titus). He ends the week Saturday with events in Minneapolis, Vice President Joseph R. Biden Jr. and former President Bill Clinton also take to the trail, including on behalf of Senator Murray. On Monday, Sarah Palin stops in Reno, Nev., to help send off a Tea Party Express national bus tour before appearing in Florida on Saturday to headline a fund-raising rally.

DEBATES A series of debates begins on Monday when the West Virginia Senate candidates, Gov. Joe Manchin III, a Democrat, and the Republican John Raese and Jeff Becker of the Constitution Party, face off. On Tuesday, Alexi Giannoulias and Representative Mark Kirk will debate for the Illinois Senate seat once held by Mr. Obama, and on Wednesday in Pennsylvania, the Senate candidates Joe Sestak, the Democrat, will debate the Republican Pat Toomey. On Friday, Senator Rum Feingold and his Republican challenger, Ron Johnson, debate for the Wisconsin Senate seat, and a three-way debate is set for Sunday between Florida's Senate candidates: Gov. Charlie Crist, who is independent; Marco Rubio, the Republican candidate; and Democratic Representative Kendrick B. Meek. ASHLEY PARKER

The online version of The Caucus, a blog looking at the latest political news from around the country:
nytimes.com/politics

In Washington, a Senator Fights to Keep Her Seat

By WILLIAM YARDLEY

EVERETT, Wash. — Never mind Nevada. If you are among the party power brokers and political fortunetellers obsessed with America's most elusive elected position, Senate seat No. 51, head to Washington — the real one.

"It is the future of America that's at stake here," said Dino Rossi, the man who just might give the Republicans the Senate majority. "It is, as it's been dubbed, the 51st seat, potentially."

Or not.

"Can I just tell you," said Senator Patty Murray, a Democrat seeking her fourth term, "that's the same line I have heard in every election I've ever been in?"

In this one really different? Sure seems to be. Both parties, as well as independent groups, are pouring money into the race. Polls are close, with Ms. Murray most recently having the edge. Democrats are clearly worried; President Obama is about to make his second trip to the state to campaign for Ms. Murray. Michelle Obama is also on her way, as is Bill Clinton.

Washington State has a history of tossing out prominent senators, including Warren Magnuson and Slade Gorton. And Tom Foley, the onetime House speaker? Long gone.

But then there are the quirks. Can anyone even come close to predicting the outcome in a state where nearly everyone now votes by mail, often weeks before Election Day? Given that fact, does the so-called enthusiasm gap that is said to favor Republicans this year still play the same role?

Then again, just how said is the conventional wisdom that Washington State is steadily marching leftward? John McCain lost the state by 17 points in 2008, but Mr. Rossi lost the governor's race that same year to the incumbent, Christine Gregoire, by less than 7 points. Now he is riding a Republican wave.

"I've made this whole speech over and over again about how Washington is not a Democratic state, and people have literally laughed at me," said Chris Vance, a former chairman of the state Republican Party.

Compared with the relative hysteria elsewhere, the race can seem restrained. Mr. Rossi, known for balancing a tough budget in the legislature, is no Tea Party upstart, nor is he an outspoken social conservative. He is not a billionaire or a professional wrestler. He is also not a proven winner. His last two campaigns, both for governor, ended in defeat. Republicans recruited him once again this year, in part because he has what one supporter called "an honorable name."

Ms. Murray is the opposite of flash. After 18 years in office, she still reminds voters that she was a young mom in tennis shoes when she first took on lawmakers at the State Capitol in the 1980s. She is quick to say she is proud of President Obama and proud of bringing home millions of dollars in earmarks.

Without national scandals or wedge issues to work with, the candidates mostly argue about actual policy, principally fiscal, whether in person or in an endless stream of television commercials, some of which have been misleading.

Mr. Rossi says Ms. Murray is emblematic of a Congress that is bankrupting America by passing stimulus spending and the health care overhaul and by spending

millions on earmarks. He often accuses her of "playing class warfare" by suggesting that he wants to protect the wealthy. He says his message of low taxes and limited regulation is for the middle class.

"When people are broke and out of work, they're willing to lis-

President Obama went to Washington in August to help Senator Patty Murray's campaign.

Ms. Murray's Republican challenger, Dino Rossi, attending a rally in Everett last week.

Washington Senate

In a race that is more substance than style, Senator Patty Murray is seeking her fourth term in a state that heavily supported Barack Obama in 2008. Her opponent, Dino Rossi, is trying to ride a Republican wave into office.

2008 SENATE RESULTS
☑ Cantwell (D)   McGavick (R)

NEW YORK TIMES RACE RATING
Tossup

PREVIOUS SENATE RESULTS

	Dem.	Rep.
'04	[bar]	55
'98	[bar]	42
'00	[bar]	49

ten to other ideas," Mr. Rossi said in an interview here after rallying campaign supporters.

Mr. Murray says Mr. Rossi will bankrupt America by giving tax breaks to the wealthy, and she does not back down from her votes for the Democratic agenda. She says Mr. Rossi, who has vowed not to seek any earmarks, is misreading what voters want and what the state needs.

"They know I'm going to go 2,500 miles back to Washington, D.C., so that they've got the small investments they need to keep their businesses growing and get the infrastructure they need for their community," Ms. Murray said.

The candidates argue heatedly over things like the future of small businesses. Ms. Murray's supporters say she has helped make it easier for them to get loans. Mr. Rossi's say the requirements of the health care bill will hurt them, at will the end of the tax cuts enacted under President George W. Bush.

Don Root, a Seattle businessman, said that he had met with Ms. Murray at one point and that she had provided him she would try to prevent the estate tax from being reinstated. The tax is set to be restored next year.

"She always says she has some reason for not doing it at this time, but she had no problem at all voting for the bank bailout," said Mr. Root, whose company, GM Nameplate, manufactures a range of products and employs about 1,000 people, some overseas.

Mr. Root said he had twice vot-

ed for Ms. Murray, but this week at which the candidate signed a pledge to repeal the estate tax. Asked about Mr. Root's decision the next day, Ms. Murray said she had tried unsuccessfully to get Democrats to lower the estate tax but she expressed no regret.

"What I also have a responsibility to do, within a time when we have a very high debt and deficit," she said, "is to not push additional tax help to them the next 10 years and put us further in bankruptcy?"

Beyond policy, for many people the question is whether, even with the rising Republican tide, Mr. Rossi can win a statewide race.

Party leaders courted him for months before he finally entered the race in May. At one point he traveled to the other Washington to meet with Senator Mitch McConnell, the minority leader, and Senator John Cornyn, head of the National Republican Senatorial Committee. Mr. Rossi said he was seeking not their campaign support but confirmation that they were really committed to cutting federal spending.

"I don't need this job, and I didn't have enough confidence that they had enough guts to put the fiscal trains back on the track if they got the majority," Mr. Rossi said.

Their response, he said, alluded to Republican challengers across the country: "We have new people coming in, and it's going to be a whole new team. It has to be."

Groups Push the Legal Limits in Campaign Advertising

From Page A10

time for express advocacy ads, or more than 55 percent of its total. Tom Kise, a spokesman, challenged the completeness of the advertising figures but also said the organization had spent heavily on grassroots lobbying and other activities that balance out its political spending.

The group has also been filing with the I.R.S. based on a fiscal year, instead of the calendar year, so it may leave until July 2011 to get its ledgers in order.

American Future Fund, set up by a cadre of Republican political operatives, has devoted $9.3 million, or about 58 percent of its television advertising spending, to express advocacy.

Meanwhile, Crossroads GPS and Americans for Job Security have been more conservative, keeping their express advocacy spending on television to roughly 40 percent.

Several lawyers said that while the 50 percent limit is widely cited, the I.R.S. has never applied it and that 50 percent is the official limit for political spending. It could, in fact, be less.

Under the law, nonprofit 501(c)(4) "social welfare" organizations, 501(c)(5) labor unions and

501(c)(6) trade associations are supposed to be primarily focused on those tax-exempt purposes, as opposed to influencing elections. The crucial question is how a group's "primary purpose" is evaluated. Some tax lawyers advise their clients to keep their political spending to less than 40 percent of their budgets.

Another surprisingly murky issue is what, other than explicit appeals to voters about how they should cast their ballots, the I.R.S. actually considers political. Auditors weigh a host of factors, according to the agency, including whether an advertisement is

part of a continuing series by the group on the same issue. If it is, the group could make a stronger case that the ad is an example of an issue, not political, advocacy.

Most central observers, however, would probably consider many of the issue ads by these groups to be very much political. They attack or praise candidates, just like straight political advertisements, but they invariably add a tag line that urges voters to do something other than vote for or against candidates. A recent commercial by Crossroads GPS, criticizing Representative Joe Sestak, who is running for the

Senate in Pennsylvania, ends by urging viewers, "Tell Congressman Sestak, 'Stop the Medicare cuts,'" and displays his phone number.

Some pro-Republican groups, for legal or tactical reasons, have continued to script all of their commercials as issue ads, including the United States Chamber of Commerce and Americans for Prosperity, a group linked to the billionaire David Koch.

Problems with the I.R.S. could lead to tax penalties and revocation of tax-exempt status. But nonprofit groups engaging heavily in express advocacy could also run into issues with the Federal Election Commission. If the commission determines that a group's "major purpose" is political, the group is required to register as a political committee and disclose its donors.

The commission's three Republican members, however, are generally inclined to give these groups leeway, effectively deadlocking the commission because it is split along party lines, and a majority vote is required for it to act. But if most of a group's spending seems to be on express advocacy, the Republican commissioners would probably have to scrutinize the group, lawyers said.

A Profusion of 'Magic Words'

In legal parlance, they are called "magic words," and their use has exploded in this year's midterm races.

Television commercials that include them represent the most basic form of "express advocacy."

They are: "vote for," "elect," "support," "cast your ballot," "vote against," "defeat," "reject" and phrases like "Smith for Congress."

In 2010, outside interest groups have used magic words in one out of every 10 television advertisements as Senate races and one out of three in House races, according to an analysis by the Wesleyan Media Project.

In 2008, over the same time period, outside groups used them in just 3 percent of House race television ads and none in Senate ads.

New York

The New York Times

An Outsider, Or Merely Outlandish?

MOUNT KISCO, N.Y.

PETER
APPLEBOME

OUR
TOWNS

If any local race in New York was going to get really strange, it figured to be one involving Greg Ball, a state assemblyman running for the State Senate.

During his primary race, opponents said he was, essentially, unfit to hold office. "Assemblyman Greg Ball has a 'pattern of sexual misconduct towards women,'" went one statement. "The residents of Dutchess, Putnam and Westchester Counties are tired of the distractions, tired of the conspiracy theories and tired of all of the excuses. You can't take anything Greg Ball says seriously," went another.

And those were from his fellow Republicans, specifically the State Senate Republican Campaign Committee, which backed his opponent in the primary for the open seat in the 40th State Senate District. Mr. Ball won. Now, with perhaps control of the State Senate and redistricting in the balance, party leaders are backing Mr. Ball.

And then there are the Democrats.

"You don't find anyone in the Assembly minority sorry that the guy is leaving, and you won't find anyone in the Senate happy he could become a member," said Senator Diane J. Savino.

"There's not a lot that Democrats and Republicans agree on in Albany, but this is one where we totally agree: This guy doesn't deserve to be in public office."

Once, this might not have been a promising way to run for office. Now, who knows? In a year when the political lie is running wild, this may be one of those rare local races that's a window onto a lot more.

"You're talking to the most independent guy in the New York State Legislature, and that's why collectively, the insiders don't want me in Albany," said Mr. Ball, a former Air Force officer. "This is what happens when you take on the dysfunction and corruption they have all perfected."

Greg Ball is running for State Senate.

Mr. Ball, who won Tea Party before Tea Party was cool, is like a more toned-down version of Carl P. Paladino, smart, ambitious, attractive and a bent-seeking missile for controversy. He rose to prominence as the loudest local voice against illegal immigration and has been accused of using his pole charity, billed as a way to aid minority youth, to help finance his first campaign. Then there was the still-unexplained incident in which he reported a dead gun on his property, with a note around its neck alleging to a Hispanic gang not known to be in the area.

AND he has been dogged by personal issues involving women: a 2003 temporary protection order taken out by a former girlfriend who accused of sashing; a bar-room complaint in Albany by a server who said he had groped her; a sexual harassment allegation (previously dismissed) in the Legislature. He says the first was in the distant past, a mutual disagreement, and the other two complaints were politically motivated and without basis.

In a race viewed as almost deadlocked, gender issues have become the main line of attack by his Democratic opponent, Michael B. Kaplowitz. He ran an ad citing the former girlfriend's complaint. Female supporters of Mr. Kaplowitz held a news conference on Wednesday to criticize Mr. Ball's conduct; and his voting record on women's issues.

In response, Mr. Ball ran an ad of his own in which a woman identified as his former girlfriend defended him forcefully. It turns out she wasn't that former girlfriend, but Lauren Pistone, a Republican political consultant and Mr. Ball's finance director when he considered a run for Congress, the one defended Mr. Ball in July when similar issues arose.

She said Mr. Ball was being targeted because he was an outsider. "I call politics high school for adults," she said. "Greg broke into their clique and they didn't like it. I grew up in Putnam County. It's always been a very distinct quo area. He rocked the boat, and when you do that you get a visceral reaction."

Will people rally and see the ad as a defense by the woman he was accused of sashing? "I don't know," she said. "People take away what they want to take away."

You might think all this leaves Mr. Ball vulnerable, but Mr. Kaplowitz's vulnerability ties your mop many more; being part of the County Legislature in the county with the nation's highest property taxes. "People are interested in property taxes and foreclosures," Mr. Ball said, "not old issues dredged up two weeks before the election."

E-mail: zeos@nytimes.com

Paladino's Accidental Running Mate Is Also His Mop-Up Man

By MICHAEL BARBARO

Carl P. Paladino, the Republican candidate for governor, with Gregory J. Edwards, his running mate, and Michael R. Caputo, left, his campaign manager.

He was booed in Harlem once a crowd realized he was Carl P. Paladino's running mate. He has regularly reassured audiences that Mr. Paladino was speaking only metaphorically and would not really bring a baseball bat to Albany. And he has tried, with limited success, to make peace with gay leaders stung by Mr. Paladino's description of their parades as "disgusting."

As New Yorkers collectively cringe every few days at Mr. Paladino's boorish behavior and provocative pronouncements, Gregory J. Edwards, a mild-mannered former dairy farmer, has been thrust into the most thankless job in New York politics: translating, explaining and at times mopping up after him.

Mr. Edwards has embraced the role earnestly, if a bit warily. And it came to him largely by accident; he entered the race this summer as Rick A. Lazio's choice for lieutenant governor, and he had never heard of, never mind met, Mr. Paladino, a Buffalo businessman. In the topsy-turvy Republican primary that followed, Mr. Lazio lost, but Mr. Edwards won, so he agreed to a shotgun marriage with Mr. Paladino.

Now, the task of defending Mr. Paladino's curious, at times circuslike campaign has fallen on Mr. Edwards, 50, a square-jawed onetime Boy Scout prone to giving lectures about the American health care system and ending conversations with the word "seat." (As in: "How neat!" in a candy store owner who gave him a bar of chocolates.)

It is not an easy or especially joyous role. Even die-hard Republicans give him grief. A few nights ago, a middle-aged woman who described herself as a Fox News junkie walked up to Mr. Edwards at a local Republican Party cocktail party outside Rochester and, without an introduction, started to gripe about Mr. Paladino. "We just wish he were a bit more normal," she told him.

While Mr. Paladino's antics have made him a staple of local and even national television coverage, the vast majority of New Yorkers could not pick Mr. Edwards out of a lineup.

For the last four years, he has been the county executive of Chautauqua (sha-TAH-qua) in western New York, where he was born and raised, a farm-freckled, overwhelmingly white district of 139,000 — roughly the population of a neighborhood in Manhattan.

Politically, the pairing is less than ideal: filling the Republican ticket with two white men from the same corner of the state has raised questions about their ability to relate to a widely diverse state. But Mr. Edwards's appeal is broader than geography; as county executive, he demonstrated that Mr. Paladino's brand of Tea Party-infused politics, with its push for small government and low taxes, could be successfully turned into policy.

He distrusted these county agencies, merging them with existing offices. He reduced the public employment rolls, starting with his personal staff: he relies on a single full-time aide, compared with the four his predecessor had. And he cut property taxes four years in a row, making him a heroic figure within the state's Republican Party.

To his obvious chagrin, however, he was forced to raise next year's property taxes — a decision that he attributes to reckless financial management in Albany and that he credits with inspiring him to run for lieutenant governor. "My friend ways to do our job better," he said. "But the same foe offended their responsibilities onto county government."

Like most Republican leaders, Mr. Edwards originally expected Mr. Lazio to capture the party's nomination in September easily. Yet a few days after a lopsided primary, he found himself sitting across the table from Mr. Paladino at a diner in downtown Buffalo for what amounted to a job interview.

There was uneasiness on both sides. "Who was this guy behind the public presentation?" Mr. Edwards recalled wondering of Mr. Paladino. But over eggs and coffee, they bonded over a common contempt for Albany. Back at home, Mr. Edwards pored over a 43-page campaign manifesto that Mr. Paladino had written with his trademark flare and frankness. ("Are you kidding?" read one passage.)

Mr. Edwards, who practiced law until he became county executive, said he was quickly satisfied that behind the caricature of Mr. Paladino was a man with a serious plan for restructuring that state's bloated bureaucracy and raising its runaway spending. "I couldn't have run with a guy who was just angry," he said. Still, it's hard to overstate the differences between Mr. Paladino, who is impulsive, volcanic, simple-boiled and

Continued on Page A35

One Place Where Spitzer Isn't Forgiven: Harvard Club

By SEWELL CHAN and NICHOLAS CONFESSORE

In his emergence from political disgrace, Eliot Spitzer has played multiple roles: political commentator, financial columnist, college professor and, most recently, CNN host.

One role he will not be playing: a member of the Harvard Club of New York City.

This year, the club, in Midtown, turned down Mr. Spitzer's application for membership — a rare catch by the club — because officials there did not want to be associated with him and the prostitution scandal that forced him from the governorship of New York in 2008, according to a person told of the decision by Harvard officials.

Mr. Spitzer at first declined to discuss the rejection, but on Tuesday night, his spokeswoman, Lisa Linden, said in a statement, "The decision by the Harvard Club's admissions committee is disappointing."

Ms. Linden added: "Last year, Harvard asked Eliot to speak on ethics at the school. He supports the institution financially. It would seem that whoever made this decision at the club is out of step with the university itself."

Nicole M. Parent, the club's president, declined to comment on the decision.

"The proceedings of the admissions committee are confidential as per the bylaws of the club," she said.

Mr. Spitzer, a 1984 graduate of Harvard Law School, indeed gave a lecture at the Edmond J. Safra Center for Ethics at Harvard in November — though the topic was government regulation of the markets, not personal morality.

Other officials at the Harvard Club, which occupies an 1894 neo-Georgian structure on West 44th Street, also declined to discuss the decision to reject Mr. Spitzer, his application for membership.

The Harvard Club of New York City accepts nearly every eligible applicant, but one is turned down this year was Eliot Spitzer, a Harvard Law graduate.

ship was listed in the April edition of the club's bulletin. (Rejections are not similarly announced.)

By tradition, any two of the roughly 15 members of the club's admissions committee can block an applicant from becoming a member, according to two members familiar with the process. Membership is open to alumni, current or former faculty members and people who have certain other ties to Harvard. The club is independent of the university, though the two institutions collaborate on many activities.

Rejections are exceedingly rare, the two members said. The club, which has about 11,000 members, admits nearly everyone eligible who applies, and it offers steep discounts to lure young alumni and for a time suspended the requirement that applicants submit letters of recommendation. (An interview is still required.) Annual dues range from $99 to $1,992, depending on the member's age and place of residence; Harvard faculty members and officers also receive discounts.

This month, "Parker Spitzer," a weekday evening debate program hosted by Mr. Spitzer and Kathleen Parker, a conservative columnist, started its run on CNN. Reviews have been mixed.

Though he will not have access to the Harvard Club's dining rooms, squash courts, library or guest rooms, Mr. Spitzer, 51, has some options. He could rejoin the Princeton Club of New York, on West 43rd Street, one block to the south, where his membership has lapsed. Dues for alumni are slightly higher — ranging from $320 to $1,625 — and there are only two international-level squash courts, compared with four at the Harvard Club.

focused on opinion and analysis, rather than the transmission of factual information. People with virtually no professional or formal training (i.e., bloggers, vloggers, citizen journalists, and online activists) have historically been the primary producers of digital news and online journalism. In its early days, online news was best known for its partisan political commentary by laypeople unfamiliar with journalistic standards, ethics, practices, or accountability. As a result, scholars have framed online content as inherently flawed and likely to violate journalistic norms, ethics, standards, structure, style, and accuracy.[134] In other words, online journalism was considered less accurate, more opinionated, subjective (as opposed to objective), entertaining, and free of journalistic conventions typically attributed to hard news—that is, it corresponds directly to the soft news label.

Traditional media, such as television and print news, have been historically associated with hard news—they were seen as hierarchical bureaucracies managed by professionals who prioritized facts, objectivity, and neutrality in reporting. Print and television news coverage is confined by both time and space limits. The various levels of editorial bureaucracy at television and newspaper outlets and their focus on scheduled events have shaped hard-news newsgathering processes, which cover specific occurrences that can be explained quickly, simply, and concisely.[135] As mentioned earlier, these traditional mediums have been seen as unidirectional, authoritative, and bound by routine, even more so in the face of diverse and interactive online content. Television reporters with faces and descriptive graphics may seem even more authentic when compared to anonymous, detached (and possibly ghostwritten) digitized messaging. (Conversely, as Williams and Delli Carpini point out, the informal nature of digital content makes it also seem more authentic.[136]) New media, with its more rapid, open, varied, and engaging formats, has constructed and been constructed by traditional media, which is seen as more official, reliable, and accurate.

The two mediums have tended toward convergence: to be seen as legitimate, online political news sites have grown to be more like mainstream news outlets, while to compete with online audiences and promote an accessible and tech-savvy image, mainstream news outlets have grown to be more like new media outlets. The convergence of digital and traditional news mediums has led to an intra-outlet fragmentation—a reader who reads *The Wall Street Journal* online has access to substantially different content than one who reads the paper version. Online political news sites are expanding their readership with style and entertainment sections, and newspapers and other traditional media are now actively involved with blogging.[137] This shift is important. For example, while *The Wall Street Journal* published at least twenty pieces on the Shirley Sherrod incident, only three of them actually appeared in the newspaper's printed version; the others served as online commentary. The effect of new media on traditional media has changed news, allowing opinion to dominate the information that is produced and distributed by traditional outlets.

The Tea Party's emergence from opinion spaces also suggests that the use of opinion spaces increases when journalists do not have concrete facts about a political event or phenomenon. The absence of facts leaves open space in which guest columnists and contributors can spread misinformation, propaganda, and partisan political agendas. Journalists still feel pressured to be the first to report on or "break" a news story. Competing with the instantaneity of the Internet means providing news coverage on a topic immediately, even if it is primarily editorial. As seen in the Tea Party stories, themes constructed early in the life of a political story can permanently influence its media narrative, despite later corrections. Moreover, digital news aggregators like Google and Bing guarantee the perpetual online availability of inaccurate stories and facts.

Ultimately, the Tea Party coverage exposes convergences in the platform, style, and structure of online, broadcast, and print news mediums, which either undermine, set aside, refute, negate or do all of these to the utility of both the "hard versus soft news" and "old versus new media" dichotomies. The convergence of news and information transmitted by new and traditional mediums has several implications. First, the platform, style, and content of online and news information is becoming increasingly standardized. In some ways, this is a positive change. It is now easier to spot discrepancies or errors within stories on the Internet because there are more sources for the same story, even in alternative media. Moreover, as the presentation of news information becomes standardized, some segment of the news media may return to prioritizing the implementation of journalistic standards over staying ahead in technological innovation and content diversification. Scholars looking at the effects and influence of the news media on consumers' beliefs and civic participation must also take into account the different forms, functions, and platforms that traditional outlets assume in the current media environment and the orthodox turn of online content.

POLITICAL ACTORS, JOURNALISTS, AND THE BRAND

***There are various conclusions to draw from these examples of news reporters performing as political party spokespersons (and vice versa) and the "extra-journalistic" roles that created and promoted the Tea Party brand. Santelli's "rant" was an instance of a professional reporter organizing and laying claim to a political movement while on the clock. This "rant" found an audience and instant distribution among citizen journalist networks, increased his value to his news outlets, and emphasized citizenship as a rhetorical form in partisan news reporting. In the past, journalists who protested or participated in social movements, even on their own time, were censured or fired for compromising their "objectivity" and violating their news bureaus' nonpartisanship guidelines.[138] [139] Furthermore, the Federal Communications Commission (FCC) in the past had made clear that it would be willing to revoke a media license in light of "conduct which manifests a disregard of the goal of objectivity in news presentation."[140] In the contemporary news environment, media groups can expect to potentially benefit from their journalists' activism, and now do not police their conduct in the same way.

Moreover, in the Tea Party news texts, journalist behavior was measured by how well it upheld, or detracted, from their news outlet's brand. In certain ways, Fox News functions more like a political third party than the Tea Party ever did, bolstering its own political brand by cultivating the support of its audience, mobilizing viewers for protests around specific policy agendas, distributing focused political messages, and even nurturing its own political leaders through commentary, events, and rallies.

In covering the Tea Party, Fox News not only conveyed Republican messaging but also produced its own talking points and prepared its audience accordingly. Skocpol and Williamson also find that Fox News viewers and Tea Party participants are "heavily overlapping categories."[141] This suggests that Fox news workers are not just producing partisan media content, but are actually constructing a new American constituency—Fox News viewers as a type of citizen.

Because journalists and news media entities are operating as citizenship brands, news media outlets are even more influential than in the past, not in just providing information but also in cultivating allegiances, developing constituents, distributing messages, creating political platforms, and influencing other news organizations. The digital age emphasizes the content and language of journalistic reporting, rather than its source or outlet. Citizens choose news outlets based on how they conform to those citizens' values and partisan preferences, and reporters adapt their personas to fit the preferences of their citizen-consumers. Patriotism, nationalism, and citizenship are now integral to journalistic discourse, not only in its subject matter but in the way journalists see themselves and engage with the topics they cover. Fox News, specifically, seems to wield significant influence over not only politicians but other media outlets as well. As the Washington ad example suggests, Fox takes its performance as media watchdog and agenda-setter seriously, even if it means using other outlets and platforms to draw attention to a story that Fox is advancing.

In part, the coverage of the media as a political actor in Tea Party news stories suggests that the news media functioning in this capacity can be productive. News is no longer considered neutral, insulated, or the final authority on political events—and journalists are less likely to use the veneer of objectivity to pretend to be "above the fray." This is potentially good news, particularly when it comes to covering issues of race or gender. News topics, like business or crime, are more likely to be highlighted as political and bodies formerly marked as "neutral" through whiteness and maleness can be seen as just as implicitly biased and partisan as women or people of color covering the same beats. For example, in 2016, when journalists criticized presidential candidate Donald Trump explicitly for his racism and sexism, drawing attention to and addressing Trump's bias is an important way of serving a marginalized public. There may now be more space for journalists to own up to how their own viewpoints and perspectives impact the way they understand and interpret political events. This, too, may even elicit a similar response in journalism research; scholars focused on establishing metrics to evaluate and identify journalism can more adequately address how race or gender biases or prejudices affect what is considered a "good" story."

Furthermore, the growth of fact-checking spaces within existing news outlets, such as the Politifact.com project from the *Tampa Bay Times* and its nationwide affiliates, suggests that media monitoring is fast becoming a new category of news content. In addition to hard and soft news, there is now also a "factual" category evaluating accuracy in news and political information (rather than just reporting on political and news events). Ultimately, the rise of the political actor in news has produced, and been produced by, new venues for information and politics within the digital landscape.

However, there is a conservative bias in journalists' new role as political actors and activists. For example, in 2012 *Politico* suspended a Black reporter appearing on MSNBC for saying that Mitt Romney appeared on Fox News because he was more at ease with "white folks" like himself.[142] In 2017, when ESPN host Jemele Hill was suspended for two weeks for violating company guidelines after she used her personal Twitter account to say that Donald Trump was a white supremacist and call for NFL audiences who "feel strongly" to boycott advertisers of the Cowboys football team for perceived anti-Black comments from the team's owner.[143] Yet, Fox News host Bill O'Reilly repeatedly and explicitly accused the Democratic Party of orchestrating acts of Tea Party racism without any comparable fallout from Fox News or other news outlets. Similarly in support of the Tea Party, CNBC publicized Rick Santelli's antics calling for Tea Party rallies. And when Fox News host Jeanine Pirro said that Black NFL players protesting police violence were "full of crap" and praised President Donald Trump, there was no response from the network.[144] If journalist activism is only acceptable in the context of conservative news, then political expression by journalists advocating for the rights of people of color, women, queer people, or any other marginalized group—or journalists who are perceived as members of those groups—will be undermined and excluded from the public sphere.

The findings from analyzing the early work of journalists and reporters covering the Tea Party suggest that a lack of media regulation, expansive information feedback loops, media branding through journalists' revelations of interiority, and a heavy reliance on provocation, dependent sourcing, and platform maximization have opened up even more ways for branding and political branding mechanisms (such as race, gender, and class identities) to dominate news storytelling. Journalists and news reporters used drama, sensationalism, meta-journalism, and activism to *raise the volume* of Tea Party news coverage in reaching their audience, maintaining and dominating the news cycle, and serving the interests of their own brands while also promoting the Tea Party. They prolifically used branding mechanisms in covering Tea Party stories, including activism and advocacy, meta-journalism, and emotional performances. They explicitly challenged other media outlets to cover or respond to certain stories, and made cross-platform and intra-media contributions to cultivate themselves in ways similar to political parties and address their consumer-citizen audiences. They also provided messaging space to brand supporters, and relied heavily on polls for reporting.

If, as social theorist Jürgen Habermas[145] notes, news functions as a conduit that relays information between the ruling structure and larger public, and contributes to the construction of a "rational" society, then a political journalism that emphasizes branding produces an entirely different society. In a brand culture, where emotions, virality, and consumption take center stage, journalism is able to fixate more on image and the bottom-line than social change and progress. And, when that happens, it leaves a vacuum where serving the public interest used to be.

Conclusion

Boundaries Blurred

In 2017, Donald J. Trump became the president of the United States following a whirlwind presidential election. Trump, endorsed by Sarah Palin, had defeated two leading Hispanic Tea Party leaders during the Republican primary campaign. In Congress another Tea Partier, Paul Ryan, is the Speaker of the House and nearly two dozen members of Congress are part of the Tea Party Caucus today.[1] According to a recent study on the presidential election published by Harvard, only 11 percent of news media coverage during the campaign for the White House "focused on candidates' policy positions, leadership abilities or personal and professional histories."[2] The dominance of branding in politics and news continues to prevail.

The most discussed social movement today is Black Lives Matter, an activist network started by activists as a social media hashtag; its leaders are identified by their large Twitter following and known for its ties to celebrities like Beyoncé and JAY-Z. Though a different type of movement, born mostly by activists on social media and sustained through civil disobedience in the streets, Black Lives Matter continues the blending of celebrity, profiteering, branding, journalism, news, and media that the Tea Party debuted as key to modern social movement and political organizing in 2009. Unlike the Tea Party, the Movement for Black Lives has a clear anti-police brutality platform and activists have proposed numerous concrete solutions and policy ideas.

Bolstered by anti-police brutality demonstrations, uprisings, and actions around the country, movement figures such as Deray McKesson—with his now iconic blue vest—have become brands in themselves, using social media to develop, cultivate, and communicate with fans. Last fall, McKesson tweeted a link selling T-shirts bearing his often-tweeted slogan "I love my blackness—and yours," urging his followers to "get one."[3] Another fan tweeted that the store where he works is "sellin @deray's vest," which McKesson promptly retweeted.[4] Only one month into 2016, McKesson announced his decision to run for mayor of Baltimore, Maryland, drawing the financial support of social media executives from Twitter, YouTube, and Netflix.[5] A few months later, he received criticism when his photo appeared on a poster next to a Wells Fargo logo for a business luncheon sponsored by the bank known for predatory lending practices in minority communities.[6] On social media, one high-profile activist in the Movement for Black Lives, Nyle Fort, notes that "it's hard to tell the difference between the market and the movement nowadays, between community activists and corporate advertisements."[7]

Under the leadership of Trump advisor Stephen Bannon, Breitbart News has largely replaced the Tea Party as the new Republican anti-establishment political brand taking aim at Republican politicians in electoral contests. No Tea Party response to the State of the Union has aired on national television since CNN made history in 2011. In the year following Bachmann's rebuttal, with the spectacle of Tea Party rallies having largely subsided, its message became more centralized and institutionalized within established political organizations. And while in the 2016 Republican presidential primary competition former Tea Party candidates like Marco Rubio and Ted Cruz initially led the pack, the Tea Party brand is rarely, if ever, mentioned. Much has changed in the Tea Party's story, but its lasting influence on American politics, rhetoric, and media still remains.

As a case study, this book examined the Tea Party's emergence and portrayal in national online, cable, broadcast, and print news texts as a way of assessing the cultural, political, and media landscape at the beginning of the Obama era. This textual and discursive analysis of Tea Party news stories revealed a meta-narrative in which reporters portrayed, deployed, and debated a range of American identities, particularly those related to race, gender, journalism, and citizenship. Media reporters, pundits, and commentators branded the Tea Party as a populist protest of the Obama administration through their publicity, circulation, and shared emphasis on specific attributes. Conservative news outlets, hosts, and journalists bolstered this branding through their Tea Party promotion, organization, advocacy, and support.

Very little about the Tea Party as a protest, group, or event was new. After all, Tea Party–style demonstrations have occurred many times before in American history, white conservative, libertarian populism developed in the Reagan era, and national reports on Tea Party–inspired protests began during the end of President Bush's final term. Yet, the construction of the Tea Party *as news* highlights its significance at a specific sociopolitical moment. Gaye Tuchman once argued that the news shapes knowledge and provides a way for Americans to learn about themselves, others, and political institutions and leaders.[8] This book shows that the contemporary era is not just an age of race and new technology, but also an age of branding, performance, media inaccuracy, strategic spectacle, and market-oriented discourse and journalistic ethics.

The news media engages in branding as a discourse and a practice in helping brand the Tea Party in six particular ways: (1) describing it as a brand; (2) conveying shifting identities; (3) relaying brand attributes; (4) providing it with a platform; (5) serving as brand manager, activist, and promoter; and (6) producing meta-journalism. In describing the Tea Party as a brand, reporters and commentators explicitly referred to the Tea Party as such and tracked its rise as a money-making label. Journalists and pundits served as Tea Party brand managers by defending and promoting the brand. By conveying shifting identities of the Tea Party as a social movement and political party, the news media gave the Tea Party brand a narrative fungibility that allowed it to function as a multiple signifier: sometimes as a third political party and other times as a social movement that took up the tropes of historical civil rights struggles. In relaying brand attributes through a collective emphasis on particular attributes, newsmakers specifically highlighted race, gender, and class (among other qualities like militarism, religiosity, and anger) as primary Tea Party characteristics. The Tea Party was often portrayed as a white working-class movement, while Tea Party women were used to brand the Tea Party as a form of modern conservatism.

The news media provided the Tea Party with a platform by serving as a medium by which Tea Party strategists and organizers could communicate the Tea Party brand to target audiences. The media also provided a platform in another important way, allowing the Tea Party to become a story in the soft news spaces of online content, cable news punditry, and newspaper editorials. Some of the earliest newspaper reports published about the Tea Party came from articles written by people such as Karl Rove, Sarah Palin, and Dick Armey. This suggests that the need for more content and timely coverage, as well as a lack of staff and resources, means that more space is made available for political strategists to step in and provide frames for breaking news stories through which they can establish a political brand.

Finally, meta-journalism was a critical branding mechanism in establishing the Tea Party brand. The anxiety and discussion about the role of the media in constructing, publicizing, and disseminating Tea Party rhetoric and ideology helped to fuel its news coverage. Repeatedly and explicitly, the media kept coming up—both as a topic and as an actor—in the Tea Party news stories. The meta-media coverage of the Tea Party fits under branding because it shows how the news media is dealing discursively and transparently with its own role as a political actor in a branding culture—that is, by allowing reporters to function as political insiders and citizens with their own agendas, beliefs, and cross-media contributions. This type of emotional and sentimental reporting also displaces attention away from the policies and politicians journalists cover (the "substance"), and toward a disproportionate obsession with how they cover them (the "image").

Close examination clearly shows that professional news reporters and conservative media pundits initiated, facilitated, and organized national press coverage of the Tea Party as a brand. Activists and politicians across the political spectrum credit a business news reporter with starting the Tea Party movement, and the first twenty-first-century press coverage given to eighteenth-century-inspired tax protests appeared in *The Wall Street Journal*. Professional journalists mobilized and publicized Tea Party events, making appearances as headliners or publicly provoking coverage in other news spaces. Although there were nationwide protests of tax increases that drew on Boston Tea Party rhetoric occurring prior to Obama's presidency, they later became obfuscated in a narrative about an anti-Obama movement. Established Republican politicians and strategists overwhelmingly constructed the Tea Party's agenda, and the people most often featured by the press as Tea Party spokespersons also managed major political fundraising operations for Republican candidates and had key roles in conservative media outlets. Tea Party coverage was a frame focused on sentiment, brand qualities related to race, gender and class, branding, and financial and consumer success.

Years later, the 2016 presidential campaign also revealed a news media very explicitly preoccupied with profit over public interest. During the height of the political primaries, CBS CEO Leslie Moonves declared that Donald Trump's republican primary campaign "may not be good for America, but it's damn good for CBS."[9] He went on to comment:

> "Man, who would have expected the ride we're all having right now?...The money's rolling in and this is fun," he said.
>
> "I've never seen anything like this, and this going to be a very good year for us. Sorry. It's a terrible thing to say. But, bring it on, Donald. Keep going."

Former *Today* show anchor Ann Curry concurred with this idea, saying that "Trump is not just an instant ratings/circulation/clicks gold mine;

he's the motherlode."[10] In an HBO weekly news show, host John Oliver openly criticized Trump's political branding power and appealed to the media (and voters) to dig deeper:

> He has spent decades turning his own name into a brand synonymous with success and quality, and he's made himself the mascot for that brand, like Ronald McDonald or Chef Boyardee....But if he's going to actually be the Republican nominee, it's time to stop thinking of the mascot and start thinking of the man, because a candidate for president needs a coherent set of policies. Like the Tea Party, allegations of racism and xenophobia help fuel his media coverage and his public support. Trump is the fruition of the Tea Party.[11]

While the Tea Party brand may have faded from the news spotlight, the effects of a brand- and consumer-driven culture continue to drive politics today.

MOVING FORWARD

In examining the Tea Party's rise in news, this book tracks a number of trends in contemporary American media. The expansion of news coverage across multiple platforms has increased journalists' reliance on polling data and opinion spaces. At the same time, the growing competition has also diminished the already-scarce resources available for investigative journalism. In generating content on the Tea Party, news organizations reported on other media outlets, producing misinformation, cultivating brand allegiances, and issuing deliberate provocation. The Tea Party movement became a national story not only because of its constituencies and organizers on the ground that featured scheduled events, local meetings, and visual spectacles, but because it was produced by and within the news. The news media raised the volume of Tea Party news, creating the Tea Party as a brand through activism, promotion, and discourse that emphasized profit, emotional connections, social identities, and differentiation.

In the process, the Tea Party coverage revealed some of the ways brand culture impacts political news and journalism today, such as eliminating the distinction between fact and opinion, reducing activism, discursively disenfranchising citizens, rebranding citizenship, and orienting attention toward citizen-consumers. The Tea Party narratives reveal that not only are the boundaries between politicians, activists, celebrities, and journalists becoming increasingly blurry for those who work in the media, but that this dissolution is changing the material way traditional media is presented and further eroding the import and distinction between familiar journalistic categories such as hard or soft news, or fact-based versus opinion-based journalism. Newspaper reporting on the Tea Party emphasized celebrity figures over electoral candidates, rarely discussed concrete policy proposals, was preoccupied with scandal and sensationalism, and drew little (or no) distinction between opinion and fact-based reporting. This collapsing of differences manifested itself in the hazy separation of fact and opinion news spaces in which the Tea Party brand was launched. Political branding's influence has not only changed politics and campaigns, but has altered the very language, nature, and goals of news.

Instead of adhering to objectivity and functioning as "the fourth estate" in American democracy, media workers leveraged their national spotlight and reputation in other ways. Journalists' efforts to raise the volume and draw attention within a crowded media environment has produced a context in which it is increasingly routine (and even lauded) for news media and individual journalists to become characters, political players, and even publicists in their own stories. In Tea Party news stories, the regular discussion and critique of cross-platform news outlets suggests that their agenda-setting and legitimizing functions continue to be highly valued, particularly in light of so many competing multimedia narratives. In print news, the material blending of fact and opinion news suggests a larger convergence of all journalism in both style and multi-platform production, rapidly dissolving the boundaries between the mediums and the content they produce.

In news stories, the tendency to simplify discussions of race, gender, and class identity bolstered notions of American meritocracy and progress. These discussions did little to address the continued oppression of women or people of color, but rather made the Tea Party a brand that, like other neoliberal political consumer campaigns, "obscures the incongruous paradoxes of poverty and wealth, individualism and collectivity, race and imperialism."[12] In journalists' descriptions of Tea Party class identities, explicit racism and xenophobia were marked as an expression of working-class ignorance and anger instead of systemic and widespread ideologies. In covering gender, reporters portrayed Tea Party women as symbolizing women's advancement and newfound conservative inclusiveness, even as the women were dismissed as viable candidates and women's reproductive rights were undermined in proposed policies. Reporters' discussions of race and racism actually bolstered white supremacist logics and obfuscated racial disparities—the problem of race, according to some reporters, was the discussion of and belief in structural discrimination itself. For other reporters, the Tea Party functioned as a way of identifying and defining racism through its spectacle. Locating the racist "out there" eliminated the possibility of the racist within.

Effectively, the news texts about the Tea Party *rebranded citizenship itself.* They ignored class inequality as a systemic issue, and instead framed citizens as shareholders disappointed with their return on investments and the government as a business in need of new management and executive leadership. Branding engages citizens as consumers. It constructs citizenship through consumption, producing rhetoric that focuses on affluence and choice instead of "hard" political issues like social policy and legislation (which were mentioned in news stories significantly less than the Tea Party brand's performance and viability was). This is a very different understanding of the government than as an extension of the people's own ideas, values, and beliefs or the news media as the fourth estate—popular democratic notions that prevailed in decades past. The press's tendency to use twenty-first-century economics to assess American well-being has not just shaped the media agenda, but has constructed Americans as consumers, not citizens; taxpayers, not contributors; voters, not actors. This means that now the news media engages in discursive disenfranchisement, equating the value of citizens with their economic prosperity and financial success as opposed to any inherent value they have as voters, Americans, or members of the republic.

These news stories about the Tea Party show the ways that reporters and news contributors are rebranding citizenship. If we reconsider Santelli's rant about loses and drinkers, we can see that he was arguing for the president to poll citizens to make decisions about how to invest in the whole of society. Santelli also referred to the presumably wealthy white male traders behind him as "America." The Tea Party news narratives poignantly reflect a major shift in how citizens today express their criticism toward government—through the language of investors and shareholders, rather than norms of society and community building. It also changes our notion of civic participation to emphasize monetary exchange. For example, consider the 2015–2016 Democratic primary campaign, when candidates Hillary Clinton and Martin O'Malley unleashed negative campaign ads attacking fellow candidate Senator Bernie Sanders. The Sanders campaign used the attacks to raise a whopping $1.2 million dollars in less than 48 hours.[13] "Put your money where your mouth is" seems to be the new "get out and vote."

Such emphasis on neoliberal citizenship and political engagement threatens to reduce and disparage activism. New technology has amplified people's ability to mimic and manufacture social movements, and dominate media coverage with well-funded initiatives. This is important when we consider the potentially transformative effects of social movements on society and their importance in mitigating social inequality. The Tea Party was branded and covered immediately as a social movement, in part through its mobilization by conservative media outlets and funding by private donors and wealthy PACs, while a few years later there was little national news coverage of the largest protest march to occur in the American South in almost fifty years—the 2014 Moral Monday March.[14] This raises valid concerns about how average citizens can engage and effect change.

In the digital landscape, a professional news reporter raising the volume also functions as a citizen-consumer, explicitly representing a particular brand of politics and, like all other citizen-consumers online, producing a message that can spread to others. Was Rick Santelli, the "father of the Tea Party," a pundit? An activist? A journalist? A politician? A celebrity? He was, most aptly, a citizen-consumer. His ideological function and audience access was much more important than his specific job title, and the same was true for others like Sarah Palin, Arianna Huffington, and CNN's Rick Sanchez. While raising the volume may increase the profile and perceived relevance of news outlets, and give journalists a marketable brand, does it serve the public? In a headphone culture, does raising the volume make people plug into democratic engagement or tune out of politics altogether?

Examining the Tea Party's rise in the news media provides at least two possible answers to such questions. On one hand, journalists are prized for their intimate knowledge of political elites—they have become commentators, celebrities, and sources in their own news stories. As a result, they have created a meta-journalistic moment in which they function as an extension of the political branding establishment rather than the watchdogs that hold it accountable. At the same time, the Tea Party stories also revealed a news media capable of acknowledging its own biases, journalists connecting personally to audiences, and new media offering average people the power to subvert traditional mass media marginalization, trivialization, and dependency.

At its core, the Tea Party news stories formed a narrative that interrogated authenticity, and indexed a period marked by skepticism and anxiety about both virtual and physical worlds. According to Sarah Banet-Weiser, thinking through branding in the media also forces a reflection on

> [the] cultural spaces that we like to think of as "authentic"—self-identity, creativity, politics, and religion—and the ways these spaces are increasingly formed as branded spaces, structured by brand logic and strategies, and understood and expressed through the language of branding. This transformation of

culture of everyday living into brand culture signals a broader shift, from "authentic" culture to the branding of authenticity.[15]

Reporters often mentioned tensions related to authenticity and identity. Authenticity was a constant theme: in debates over the Tea Party as a social movement, in the descriptions of tea partiers as "real Americans," in justification for political and media personalities' actions, in the use of the Tea Party as a political brand, and even in the way the news media struggled to define journalism in a digital news era. The increasingly staged nature of media and politics leaves little room for something truly unexpected or unplanned to unfold.

The question of whether or not the Tea Party was real (as opposed to "Astroturf") gestures to a larger concern about the anonymity of the Internet and the scriptedness of almost all media that purports to portray "reality." It speaks to a larger societal inability to distinguish between the fact and fiction that make up the interconnected and intertextual nature of our everyday lives. Was the Tea Party a real movement or a massive publicity stunt by a weakened Republican Party and corporations blamed for the global economic crisis? Was it an opportunistic effort in which Republican leaders and strategists organized a variety of grass-roots protests into a massive social movement? Was it the development and spontaneous growth of local citizens connecting with and mobilizing one another using new technology? Or was it all of these at the same time?

If the Tea Party was an Astroturf publicity campaign sponsored by conservative political and business leaders, then this book serves as a detailed account of how to strategically manufacture a coherent protest movement through national news publicity and new media technology. If the Tea Party was a "real" grass-roots movement, this book speaks to the power that digital media gives people to organize events, develop far-flung alliances, and draw the support of political and media elites. In short, regardless of the narrative one believes about the Tea Party, the activist tendencies of the news media's contemporary circulations and configurations are at this book's center.

This book ultimately shows that in the current media environment, the distinctions between the press, publicists, activists, politicians, celebrities, and businesses are more symbolic than concrete. As part of a political brand culture, the news branding of the Tea Party leaves no "clear demarcation between marketer and consumer, between seller and buyer."[16] Indeed, as I've discussed, a veteran news reporter kicked off the Tea Party and triggered its national mobilization. This demonstrates that the media can be the origin point and co-producer of contemporary social movements, not just their conduits. More significantly, the media's branding of a political phenomenon can be much more politically influential than its on-the-ground mobilization.

Significantly, the news media creation of the Tea Party does not just depict a return to a "party-press" era of American news. While numerous paid journalists, reporters, and pundits advocated, promoted, and made appearances for the Tea Party, they rarely declared themselves Tea Party members. They framed their work as fulfilling the public service requirements expected of a free press. Moreover, if the news media covering the Tea Party is indeed a reprisal of eighteenth-century journalism, it is one that caries the moral, political, and professional authority that US journalism has accrued since the nation's founding.

What does it mean that journalists and news bureaus can now imagine themselves as citizen-activists instead of the "fourth branch of government"? How does this new view of journalists as political leaders and news outlets as third parties change definitions of journalism? Questions remain about the media as a political actor, when it is no longer the "fourth estate."

These findings push us to think about journalistic convergence a bit differently, or at least emphasize the important discursive convergence of the news. "Old media" like print and radio, were not outdated or marginalized in the 2009 rise of the Tea Party—rather, their legitimizing function was essential to its development. The "newness" of media today is not just about technology, but about new ways of melding media, genre, branding, and individualistic discourses of citizenship.

Considering politics to be primarily a form of brand and media circulation likely changes the way journalists cover candidates in the contemporary environment. The media should be even more guarded against being used primarily for public relations machines in this era. The Tea Party showed that the advancement of conservative ideology and even misinformation was not just a function of a conservative echo chamber working in concert, but also the rest of their media counterparts picking up and distributing it. In the process, politicians on both sides of the aisle respond to these frequently (and sometimes intentionally) inaccurate media organizations, sometimes leaving targets like Shirley Sherrod as casualties at the wayside.

This conservative dominance of the media sphere happens because many news outlets today prioritize the bottom line over public service. There is a need for journalists themselves to resist the cycling of this information and provocation from conservative media. They should be careful when mainstreaming conservative political brands and anti-Black ideologies built into these signifiers, and screening the people who contribute to the opinion spaces in their outlets. They can find different ways to evaluate the "success" of a political brand or movement outside of economic goals or profitability—that is, service to others, health outcomes, employee well-being, or quality-of-life indicators. There is also a need for more regulation. National journalist and broadcast organizations concerned about these trends should advocate and lobby for tighter public service government regulations and oversight. They can also push to get employers and media companies in line behind supporting good public-interest journalism.

Reporters covering race and racism, and other movements related to marginalized and vulnerable groups, need to develop and maintain a keen eye for false equivalence. When white supremacy is treated as similar to *critiques* of white supremacy, or sexism is portrayed as equally problematic as demands for women's equality, the democratic potential of the public sphere for all Americans is perpetually undermined. Until tighter regulations are placed, space needs to be made for pundits and commentators on the left to be as explicitly political as their conservative counterparts to ensure a truly representative public sphere. Otherwise, the Tea Party shows us exactly what the consequence is for these trends and how easily reproducible these can be.

Reflecting on the rise of the Tea Party in news also provides some insight into how news audiences can better navigate the current media environment as engaged citizens. Consumers concerned about the dominance of conservative political branding in news can challenge the space granted for misreporting of facts on air and demand a more informed and capable journalism focused on accurate evidence, context, and history in relaying information. News readers and viewers can call out questionable sources of information. Imagine if, like President Trump, President Obama had used his bully pulpit to more frequently criticize outlets like Breitbart and Fox News for spreading false stories. For activists in particular, treating politicians and movements as brands can change the way they appeal to other voters and hold public officials accountable.

In a 2012 HBO docudrama about the national rise of Tea Party leader Sarah Palin, a chief campaign strategist delivers a portentous line: "News is no longer meant to be remembered."[17] The strategist is, of course, both right and wrong. In a rapid media environment, details about political gaffes and scandals are quickly forgotten. But, as the rise of the Tea Party brand in news shows, certain issues and narratives continue to stand out despite media heterogeneity and fragmentation. While the details may be lost, the multimedia framing of political institutions, leaders, and phenomena can persist. Some phenomena are, in fact, remembered. This book examines the Tea Party precisely because of its ability to get attention, develop, and gain momentum under the spotlight of an increasingly fractured national news media. In describing the Tea Party, perhaps "docudrama" provides a useful term—not just for films that splice real-life footage into dramatic political reenactments, but for the state of a news media that produces endless narratives splitting the difference between facts and fictions. Branding, as a process, morphs facts into fictions, and vice versa. In constructing the Tea Party as a national brand, the news media produced a narrative that depicts the complexity, performances, and, perhaps, the impossibility of modern American journalism.

APPENDIX
Sources and Methodology

Analyzing news across different platforms reveals changes in news and informational consumption. As Michael Delli Carpini explains, younger Americans get less of their information from traditional news sources such as newspapers, and get more of it from the Internet than other groups.[1] Cable news is now the primary source of political news for many citizens, and its audience increases every year.[2] Thus, a comprehensive approach has helped me track the origins and flows of various Tea Party frames in key political information and civic engagement sites. I also selected the sources to represent a range of political and ideological views.

Each political blog I analyzed has different origins and goals. Arianna Huffington and other media executives started *The Huffington Post* in May 2005; it was the first commercial and native digital news outlet to win a Pulitzer Prize for reporting. It is a generally left-leaning online news and commentary magazine, though its 2011 acquisition by AOL and then AOL's subsequent acquisition by Verizon indicates that it may soon target a broader, nonpartisan audience.[3] *Newsmax* and *Politico*, on the other hand, both began as online news sites that later added print components. Journalist Christopher Ruddy started *Newsmax*, a conservative news magazine, in 1998.[4] A *New York Times* reporter called it "the right-wing populist's *Time* or *Newsweek*." The only conservative site with a larger audience in 2011 was Foxnews.com.[5] Much of *Newsmax*'s business model relies on selling conservative merchandise and advertisements, particularly to political campaigns that use the *Newsmax* subscriber email lists to contact potential supporters. Two former *Washington Post* reporters founded *Politico* to cover the 2008 presidential campaign. After the election, it continued to create news specifically for Beltway insiders (in fact, the print edition was delivered to Capitol Hill staffers for free).[6] Rather than merely commenting on the news, *Politico* aimed to compete with *The New York Times* and *USA Today* as a paper focused solely on politics. Though *Politico* has been criticized by both the left and the right for partisan bias, it is the only political news blog that explicitly commits to "neutral" journalistic practice and norms.[7]

MSNBC, CNN, and Fox News are the three major cable news outlets I examined. They each have different political audiences, viewer numbers, and beginnings. CNN is the oldest of the bunch and it created the 24-hour news cycle. The "CNN effect" changed the speed, depth, and rigor of political news reporting.[8] MSNBC, a partnership between Microsoft and NBC, is a left-leaning cable network started in 1996. Originally, it was created as a vehicle for NBC to provide up-to-the-minute reporting that drew on its already-existing NBC journalist and news producer staff. Though its lineup of pundits and news commentators include several conservative shows, MSNBC's programs overall tend to advocate for progressive positions and policies.[9] Rupert Murdoch and former NBC executive Roger Ailes started Fox News. It was "developed with the goal of providing a 'fair and balanced' antidote to the 'liberal media'" and caters to a conservative audience.[10] The content on these news channels is a combination of news and opinion programming. Pinning down where the news begins and the punditry ends is virtually impossible because even programs labeled as "just news" include interviews and segments with politicians, strategists, and commentators, as well as repeat claims from editorial shows.[11] For this reason, and because of the availability of primetime scheduling information, I focused on specific prime-time programs at the same 8:00 P.M. time slot: *The O'Reilly Factor* on Fox, *Countdown with Keith Olbermann* on MSNBC, and *Campbell Brown* on CNN.[12]

USA Today, *The New York Times*, and *The Wall Street Journal* have the widest circulations of American newspapers. *USA Today* and *the Wall Street Journal* vie for top circulation, with roughly 1.8 million and 2 million copies, respectively, sold in 2012.[13] *USA Today* was started in 1982 and is based near Washington, DC. Though it started off as an easy-to-read "infotainment" newspaper, it gradually developed a hard-news focus.[14] *The Wall Street Journal* was founded in 1874. It originally reported primarily on financial institutions and the New York Stock Exchange, but expanded into coverage of current news, sports, entertainment, and other typical news sections, but with a distinctly pro-business bias. *The New York Times* is the oldest among these three newspapers, but has the lowest circulation. It is "widely regarded as the national paper of record" and is included in most media studies and news analyses.[15]

DATA COLLECTION AND ANALYSIS

The Pew Research Center's Project for Excellence in Journalism tracks lead news stories in broadcast and print news outlets.[16] In 2009, its team of analysts coded 68,717 news reports. The Pew data codes only front-page news stories in print media, but all lead stories in cable news, producing substantive divergences in cable and newspaper data on Tea Party news coverage. This made the print data less useful in isolating news peaks (see Graph A.1).[17] Consequently, I used Pew data on cable news to identify ten week-long surges in Tea Party news coverage and to locate any distinctions in coverage patterns.[18] As Pew did not began to code data on the Tea Party until after its first major surge in April 2009, and 2011 data was not available until after this study began, I looked at surges from April 1, 2009 to January 1, 2011. But I also reviewed coverage in the print press prior to this, just to more specifically identify the Tea Party's origin point in the press, which was in September 2008. Specifically, I tracked Tea Party news stories from September 2008 (its first mention in *The Wall Street Journal*) to April 2009 through the Factiva and LexisNexis news article and transcript archives to understand how the group developed into a major news story.

I collected the news articles and broadcast transcripts through a keyword search for "tea party" in headlines or text. I obtained the blog stories by searching the front page of each site for headlines with "tea" or "tea party." In total, in the surges I analyzed 547 news articles and show transcripts (see Table A.1) totaling 1,095,289 words (or 4,380 pages of text data), in addition to five news articles (three in *The Wall Street Journal* and two in *The New York Times*) collected prior to April 1, 2009.[19] This comprised 4,380 pages of text data in newspaper, web, and television samples.

Using LexisNexis and Factiva, I collected Tea Party news stories in *USA Today*, *The Wall Street Journal*, and *The New York Times*. Using LexisNexis transcripts, I looked at cable news stories and segments about the Tea Party—specifically focusing on the 8:00 p.m. news segment in cable news and the 6:30 P.M. national news program on ABC. I used Archive.org to retrieve the daily home pages of *The Huffington Post*, *Newsmax*, and *Politico* during the surges, and looked at all stories that had "tea party" in the headline.[20] I also include news stories either mentioned or featured in the press coverage during each surge.

I focused on surges in Tea Party coverage because they set parameters that yield relevant, substantive, and manageable amounts of data about Tea Party news coverage over time. Each surge of coverage consolidates an extensive amount of the Tea Party news coverage around a specific event

Table A.1. NUMBER OF TEA PARTY STORIES 2009–2010

Surges	1	2	3	4	5	6	7	8	9	10	TOTAL
CNN	3	4	2	2	4	1	1	3	3	6[1]	29
MSNBC	5	5	4	5	5	4	4	5	3	5	45
FOX[2]	8	4	4	9	8	6	2	10	8	6	67
ABC	1	0	5	1	4	0	0	1	0	4	16
											157
NYT	8	3	10	8	18	14	12	5	14	44	136
WSJ	4	1	4	10	3	6	4	5	7	18	62
USA	3	1	5	3	3	1	1	2	7	13	39
											227
HUFF	13	11	7	2	17	8	0	10	10	7	85
NEWSM	2	0	3	7	13	5	2	6	3	3	44
POLI	4	3	1	4	6	0	1	7	4	4	34
											163
											547

1. The CNN show at this hour became the *Parker Spitzer* program during this surge.
2. Fox News and ABC News transcripts are based on segments, which mean two or three transcripts listed for these news outlets may have happened during the same broadcast hour. MSNBC provides transcripts based on entire shows.

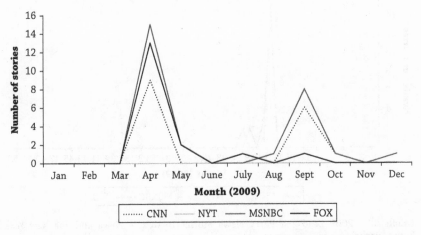

Graph A.1 2009 Lead Tea Party News Stories in Cable News and *The New York Times* (months).

or issue, making the contrasts, similarities, themes, and patterns in coverage much more apparent. In this way, I also show increases in the volume of Tea Party coverage and changes in its reporting over time.

Limiting my examination of the Tea Party to a specific number of surges significantly reduced the number of reports, which made the study more feasible and allowed close, in-depth analysis of the news coverage at the height of its density, consumption, and distribution. I selected surges based both on the number of stories and time (meaning proximity to previous surge in coverage) to avoid allowing the stories to cluster around one or two moments. Using surges provided an additional advantage. The surges I examined not only provide a systematic look at the Tea Party coverage in various outlets but also provide specific cases in which the same story was reported from multiple perspectives.

Graph A.1 shows that there were two significant Tea Party coverage surges in 2009: in the weeks surrounding April 15 (the date of the Tax Day Tea Party nationwide) and in September. Graph A.2 shows the specific weeks in which Tea Party coverage was at its highest within those months. The first two surges I examined were Surge 1 (Week 16): 4/12/09–4/18/09, and Surge 2 (Week 38): 9/13/09–9/19/09. Graphs A.3 and A.4 show the surges in the weeks and months of 2010 news coverage. I selected surges based on the number of stories and proximity to significant political events. Overall, the graphs suggest that MSNBC and Fox News gave relatively equal coverage to the Tea Party, and significantly exceeded CNN's reporting. Table A.2 lists the events that were most featured in these surges and their specific dates.

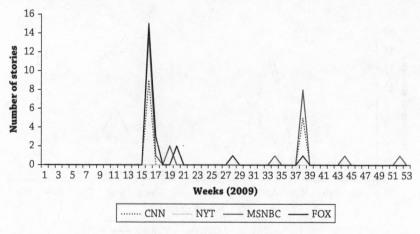

Graph A.2 2009 Lead Tea Party News Stories in 0Cable News and *The New York Times* (weeks).

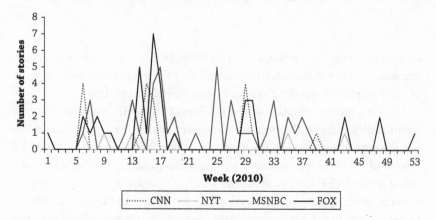

Graph A.3 2010 Lead Tea Party News Stories in Cable News and *The New York Times* (weeks).

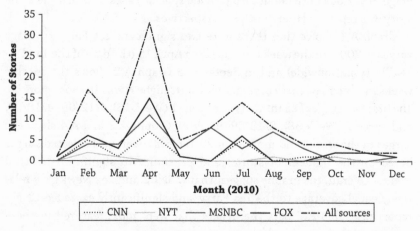

Graph A.4 2010 Lead Tea Party News Stories in Cable News and *The New York Times* (months).

Table A.2. DOMINANT NEWS TOPICS IN TEA PARTY SURGES

Surges	Dates	Key coverage topics
Surge 1	4/12/09–4/18/09	First tea parties/Tax Day protests
Surge 2	9/13/09–9/19/09	Rallies in DC
Surge 3	1/31/10–2/6/10	First Tea Party convention
Surge 4	3/28/10–4/3/10	Congress members report racial epithets at Tea Party rally, health care reform passed, Sarah Palin, Tea Party rally
Surge 5	4/11/10–4/17/10	Tax Day
Surge 6	4/18/10–4/24/10	Tax Day continued
Surge 7	6/13/10–6/19/10	Election
Surge 8	7/11/10–7/17/10	NAACP Tea Party resolution announced, Mark Williams letter to NAACP
Surge 9	7/18/10–7/24/10	Mark Williams resigns, Sherrod incident
Surge 10	10/17/10–10/23/10	Midterm election

As the Pew Research Center cautions, in news research "some of these shows are not news programs per se, but rather their content derives from the host's opinions and guests on any given day. Separating news and talk proves problematic because it is often difficult to distinguish between the two categories, and several programs offer both news and talk in the same hour."[21] As noted by the Pew Research Center's Annual Report on Journalism, opinion news reporting dominates news reporting on MSNBC and Fox, and comes close to breaking even at CNN (with 46 percent commentary/opinion versus 54 percent factual reporting).[22]

While commentary and opinion reporting has grown on these networks, the coverage of live events and reports dropped about 33 percent. With this concern in mind, I identified Tea Party editorial or opinion reports within the only platform in which they are most clearly delineated from "fact-based" pieces: newspapers. As mentioned in the previous section, within blogs, cable news, and even newspapers, these categories overlap; part of that ambiguity is emblematic of what I call "headphone culture."

I examined the stories produced during each surge for storytelling elements such as themes, frames, keywords, and other items outlined in Table A.3. First, I went through all of the transcripts, blogs, and articles, coding each according to the stated categories. Additionally, as certain topics frequently surfaced, I also coded them as analytical categories. For example, news representations of the media became an additional

Table A.3. ANALYTICAL STRUCTURE FOR EXAMINING TEA PARTY NEWS

Text/Discourse	Visuals	Sectors (Cable, Print, Blog)
Plot: Beginning, middle, end, heroes, anti-heroes, villain, characters. Representations: Race, gender, class, nation, citizenship, Tea Party, ethnicity. Goal: Entertain, inform—whom/about what? Action: What is it doing? Agents: Who is doing it? Ideology: Interpretations of what society has been and should be. Frames: (1) Persistent patterns of cognition, interpretation, presentation, selection, emphasis, and exclusion; (2) Organizing a storyline that provides meaning to a series of events (what are the events?) and connects them to each other. Reporting:Sourcing,background, explanation,evaluation,history, expectations, situation, main events, and conclusion,omission. Additional Considerations: Characterization, dialogue, sequencing, dramatization.	Images: Photos, graphics, people. Locations: Signs or symbols.	Similarities/differences: Opinions about the Tea Party, "Facts" about the Tea Party.

category. I went through these texts using keyword searches related to the most patterned items—race, gender, class, and media—to focus on these central themes. I then coded all of these notes and organized them by outlets and surge dates (and, for newspaper, opinion versus news reporting). Ultimately, this analysis of the media reports yielded useful insights on how news stories defined the Tea Party as a group, movement, brand, and political party, and what it represented as an American cultural sign.

Notes

HEADPHONE CULTURE: A PREFACE

1. Nicholas Kristof, "My Shared Shame: The Media Helped Make Trump," *New York Times*, March 26, 2016, https://www.nytimes.com/2016/03/27/opinion/sunday/my-shared-shame-the-media-helped-make-trump.html.

2. Victor Pickard, "When Commercialism Trumps Democracy," *Huffington Post* (blog), March 31, 2016, https://www.huffingtonpost.com/victor-pickard/when-commercialism-trumps-democracy_b_9582952.html.

3. James Poniewozik, "Battle of the Network Stars: Trump vs. Clinton," *New York Times*, July 13, 2016, https://www.nytimes.com/2016/07/17/arts/television/republican-democratic-conventions-trump-vs-clinton.html.

4. David Nakamura, "Obama on Trump: 'This Is Not Entertainment. This Is Not a Reality Show,'" *Washington Post*, May 6, 2016, https://www.washingtonpost.com/news/post-politics/wp/2016/05/06/obama-on-trump-this-is-not-entertainment-this-is-not-a-reality-show/?utm_term=.9e78b56a0a0f.

5. Khadijah White, "Why You Shouldn't Be Surprised by Donald Trump's Rise," *Role/Reboot* (blog), March 21, 2016, http://www.rolereboot.org/culture-and-politics/details/2016-03-shouldnt-surprised-donald-trumps-rise/.

6. Gideon Resnick, "David Duke Plans to Run for Congress," *Daily Beast*, July 12, 2016, https://www.thedailybeast.com/david-duke-plans-to-run-for-congress.

7. Nate Cohn and Toni Monkovic, "Is Donald Trump Winning? Among Whites and Men, for Sure," *New York Times*, July 13, 2016, http://www.nytimes.com/2016/07/14/upshot/is-donald-trump-winning-among-whites-and-men-for-sure.html?smid=tw-upshotnyt&smtyp=cur&_r=0.

8. "Ivanka Trump Tweets: 'Shop Ivanka Trump's Look from Her RNC Speech,'" CBS New York, July 22, 2016, http://newyork.cbslocal.com/2016/07/22/ivanka-trump-rnc-dress/.

9. Kelsey Snell, "White House Website Touts Melania Trump's Modeling and Jewelry Line," *Washington Post*, January 20, 2017, https://www.washingtonpost.com/news/powerpost/wp/2017/01/20/white-house-website-promotes-melania-trumps-modeling-and-jewelry-line/?utm_term=.2952058c2d5f.

10. Donald Trump (@realdonaldtrump), "Jackie Evancho's Album Sales Have Skyrocketed after Announcing Her Inauguration Performance. Some People Just Don't Understand the 'Movement,'" Twitter, January 4, 2017, https://twitter.com/realdonaldtrump/status/816718880731234304; Donald Trump (@realdonaldtrump), "Wow, the Ratings Are in and Arnold Schwarzenegger Got 'Swamped' (or Destroyed) by Comparison to the Ratings Machine, DJT. So Much

For...," Twitter, January 6, 2017, https://twitter.com/realDonaldTrump/status/817348644647108609.

11. John Calhoun Merrill and Ralph Lynn Lowenstein, *Viva Journalism! The Triumph of Print in the Media Revolution* (Bloomington, IN: AuthorHouse, 2010).

12. Kathleen Hall Jamieson and Joseph N Cappella, *Echo Chamber: Rush Limbaugh and the Conservative Media Establishment* (Oxford: Oxford University Press 2010).

CHAPTER 1

1. "Rick Santelli and the 'Rant of the Year,'" video, http://www.youtube.com/watch?v=bEZB4taSEoA.

2. Sheryl Gay Stolberg, "Critique of Housing Plan Draws Quick White House Offensive," *New York Times*, February 21, 2009.

3. Glenn Harlan Reynolds, "Tax Day Becomes Protest Day," *Wall Street Journal*, April 15, 2009, http://www.wsj.com/articles/SB123975867505519363.

4. I want to emphasize that the first time the "Tea Party" was invoked by Santelli it carried the connotation of *party* as a social gathering or rally. It was not yet considered a political party as discussed in the next chapter.

5. Brian Stelter, "CNBC Replays Its Reporter's Tirade," *New York Times*, February 23, 2009, sec. Business/Financial Desk, http://www.nytimes.com/2009/02/23/business/media/23cnbc.html.

6. Ibid.

7. Clarence Y. H. Lo, "Astrotruf versus Grassroots: Scenes from Early Tea Party Mobilization," in *Steep: The Precipitous Rise of the Tea Party*, ed. Lawrence Rosenthal and Christine Trost (Berkeley: University of California Press, 2012), 100.

8. Michael Calderone, "Fox Teas Up a Tempest," *Politico*, April 16, 2009, http://www.politico.com/news/stories/0409/21275.html.

9. Reynolds, "Tax Day Becomes Protest Day."

10. Liz Moor, *The Rise of Brands* (Oxford; New York: Berg, 2007).

11. Barbie Zelizer, "Journalists as Interpretive Communities," *Critical Studies in Media Communication* 10, no. 3 (1993): 219.

12. Jack Lule, "News as Myth: Daily News and Eternal Stories," *Media Anthropology*, ed. Eric W. Rothenbuhler and Mihai Corman (London: Sage Publications, 2005), 101–110.

13. Stephanie Greco Larson, *Media and Minorities: The Politics of Race in News and Entertainment*, Spectrum Series, Race and Ethnicity in National and Global Politics (Lanham, MD: Rowman & Littlefield, 2006); Timothy E. Cook, "The News Media as a Political Institution: Looking Backward and Looking Forward," *Political Communication* 23, no. 2 (July 2006): 159, https://doi.org/10.1080/10584600600629711.

14. Robert Busby and Sue Cronshaw, "Political Branding: The Tea Party and Its Use of Participation Branding," *Journal of Political Marketing* 14, nos. 1–2 (2015): 96–110; Matt Guardino and Dean Snyder, "The Tea Party and the Crisis of Neoliberalism: Mainstreaming New Right Populism in the Corporate News Media," *New Political Science* 34, no. 4 (2012): 527–548.

15. Margaret Scammell, "Political Brands and Consumer Citizens: The Rebranding of Tony Blair," *Annals of the American Academy of Political and Social Science* 611 (2007): 176–192; Kenneth M. Cosgrove, *Branded Conservatives: How the Brand*

Brought the Right from the Fringes to the Center of American Politics, Politics, Media, and Popular Culture, vol. 12 (New York: P. Lang, 2007); Sarah Banet-Weiser, *Authentic™: Politics and Ambivalence in a Brand Culture*, Critical Cultural Communication (New York: New York University Press, 2012).

16. Naomi Klein, *No Logo: No Space, No Choice, No Jobs*, 10th anniversary ed., 3rd ed. (New York: Picador, 2010), 7.

17. M. M. Manring, *Slave in a Box: The Strange Career of Aunt Jemima*, The American South Series (Charlottesville: University Press of Virginia, 1998), 5.

18. Cas Mudde and Cristóbal Rovira Kaltwasser, *Populism: A Very Short Introduction* (New York: Oxford University Press, 2017).

19. Christopher S. Parker and Matt A. Barreto, *Change They Can't Believe In: The Tea Party and Reactionary Politics in America* (Princeton: Princeton University Press, 2013); Guardino and Snyder, "The Tea Party and the Crisis of Neoliberalism," 527–548; Charles Postel, "The Tea Party in Historical Perspective: A Conservative Response to a Crisis of Political Economy," *Steep: The Precipitous Rise of the Tea Party*, ed. Lawrence Rosenthal and Christine Trost (Berkeley: University of California Press, 2012): 25–46.

20. Alan Brinkley, *Voices of Protest: Huey Long, Father Coughlin, and the Great Depression* (New York and Toronto: Vintage, 1983).

21. Jackie Smith, John D. McCarthy, Clark McPhail, and Boguslaw Augustyn. "From Protest to Agenda Building: Description Bias in Media Coverage of Protest Events in Washington, DC," *Social Forces* 79, no. 4 (2001): 1397–1423.

22. Banet-Weiser, *Authentic™*.

23. Klein, *No Logo*, xvii.

24. Alison Hearn, "Brand Me 'Activist,'" in *Commodity Activism: Cultural Resistance in Neoliberal Times*, ed. Roopali Mukherjee and Sarah Banet-Weiser, Critical Cultural Communication (New York: New York University Press, 2012), 29; Robert Waterman McChesney and John Nichols, *The Death and Life of American Journalism: The Media Revolution That Will Begin the World Again* (New York: Nation Books, 2011); Joseph E. Uscinski, *The People's News: Media, Politics, and the Demands of Capitalism*, 2014.

25. Kate Zernike, *Boiling Mad: Inside Tea Party America*, 1st ed. (New York: Times Books/Henry Holt, 2010).

26. "Reactions to the State of the Union," *Rachel Maddow Show*, aired January 25, 2011, on MSNBC.

27. Richard Meagher, "The 'Vast Right-Wing Conspiracy': Media and Conservative Networks," *New Political Science* 34, no. 4 (December 2012): 469–484, https://doi.org/10.1080/07393148.2012.729738.

28. Uscinski, *The People's News*, 2014.

29. Christopher R. Martin, "'Upscale' News Audiences and the Transformation of Labour News," *Journalism Studies* 9, no. 2 (2008): 178–194.

30. Celia Lury, *Consumer Culture*, 2nd ed. (Cambridge: Polity, 2011), 157.

31. Denzil Meyers, "Whose Brand Is It Anyway?" in *Beyond Branding: How the New Values of Transparency and Integrity Are Changing the World of Brands*, ed. Nicholas Ind (London: Kogan Page, n.d.), 23.

32. Lury, *Consumer Culture*, 159–160.

33. Ibid., 152.

34. Gaye Tuchman, *Making News: A Study in the Construction of Reality* (New York: Free Press, 1980).

35. Robert M. Entman, "Framing: Toward Clarification of a Fractured Paradigm," *Journal of Communication* 43, no. 4 (December 1993): 51–58, https://doi.org/10.1111/j.1460-2466.1993.tb01304.x.

36. Kirk Hallahan, "Seven Models of Framing: Implications for Public Relations," *Journal of Public Relations Research* 11, no. 3 (July 1999): 211–212, https://doi.org/10.1207/s1532754xjprr1103_02.

37. Ibid.

38. Cosgrove, *Branded Conservatives*, 25.

39. Melissa Aronczyk and Devon Powers, eds., *Blowing Up the Brand: Critical Perspectives on Promotional Culture*, Popular Culture and Everyday Life, vol. 21 (New York: P. Lang, 2010), 11.

40. Melissa Aronczyk, *Branding the Nation: The Global Business of National Identity* (Oxford; New York: Oxford University Press, 2013), 8.

41. Lury, *Consumer Culture*.

42. Ibid., 151; Adam Arvidsson, *Brands: Meaning and Value in Media Culture* (London; New York: Routledge, 2006), 77.

43. Banet-Weiser, *Authentic*™, 4.

44. Douglas B. Holt, *Brands and Branding* (Boston: Harvard Business School, 2003), 3.

45. Sylvia M. Chan-Olmsted and Jiyoung Cha, "Branding Television News in a Multichannel Environment: An Exploratory Study of Network News Brand Personality," *International Journal on Media Management* 9, no. 4 (November 13, 2007): 135–150, https://doi.org/10.1080/14241270701632688.

46. Arvidsson, *Brands*, 87.

47. Shalini Shankar, *Advertising Diversity: Ad Agencies and the Creation of Asian American Consumers* (Durham: Duke University Press, 2015). In studying Asian American branding, Shankar notes that in advertising, marketers "transform Asian Americans from "Model minorities" to "model consumers" and [use] consumerism to make claims of legitimacy and national belonging." In this way, Asian Americans are "brought into the fold of U.S. citizenry as model consumers" (22).

48. Lury, *Consumer Culture*, 155, emphasis in original.

49. Henry Jenkins, Sam Ford, and Joshua Green, *Spreadable Media: Creating Value and Meaning in a Networked Culture*, Postmillennial Pop (New York; London: New York University Press, 2013); Mark Deuze, Axel Bruns, and Christoph Neuberger, "Preparing for an Age of Participatory News," *Journalism Practice* 1, no. 3 (October 2007): 322–338, https://doi.org/10.1080/17512780701504864.

50. Andrew Chadwick, "Digital Network Repertoires and Organizational Hybridity," *Political Communication* 24, no. 3 (August 6, 2007): 283–301, https://doi.org/10.1080/10584600701471666; Andrew Chadwick, *The Hybrid Media System: Politics and Power*, Oxford Studies in Digital Politics (Oxford; New York: Oxford University Press, 2013); Chadwick, *The Hybrid Media System*, 5.

51. Chadwick, *The Hybrid Media System*, 95.

52. S. Elizabeth Bird, ed., *The Anthropology of News and Journalism: Global Perspectives* (Bloomington: Indiana University Press, 2010).

53. Robert D. Benford and David A. Snow, "Framing Processes and Social Movements: An Overview and Assessment," *Annual Review of Sociology* 26, no. 1 (August 2000): 611–639, https://doi.org/10.1146/annurev.soc.26.1.611.

54. Benjamin L. Carp, *Defiance of the Patriots: The Boston Tea Party and the Making of America* (New Haven: Yale University Press, 2011]).

55. Arlene P. Kleeb, *The Boston Tea Party, Catalyst for Revolution* (Ann Arbor: University of Michigan Press, 1973).

56. Josiah Quincy, *Memoir of the Life of Josiah Quincy, Jun. of Massachusetts* (Bedford, MA: Applewood Books, 2009), 451.

57. Cheryl L. Harris, "Whiteness as Property," in *Black on White: Black Writers on What It Means to Be White*, ed. and with an introduction by David Roediger (New York: Knopf, 2010), http://search.ebscohost.com/login.aspx?direct=true &scope=site&db=nlebk&db=nlabk&AN=724964.

58. Charles W. Mills, *The Racial Contract* (Ithaca: Cornell University Press, 1997).

59. Post Staff Report, "Palin, Tea Party Pledge to Bag Harry," *New York Post*, March 27, 2010, http://nypost.com/2010/03/27/palin-tea-party-pledge-to-bag-harry/.

60. Dana Milbank, *Tears of a Clown: Glenn Beck and the Tea Bagging of America*, 1st ed. (New York: Doubleday, 2010), 215.

61. "Countdown for April 15, 2009," *Countdown with Keith Olbermann*, aired April 15, 2009, on MSNBC.

62. Alex Altman, "Rand Paul's Tea Party Triumph in Kentucky," *Time*, May 19, 2010, http://content.time.com/time/nation/article/0,8599,1990183,00.html.

63. Jill Lepore, *The Whites of Their Eyes: The Tea Party's Revolution and the Battle over American History* (Princeton: Princeton University Press, 2010).

64. Ibid., 88.

65. Alfred F. Young, *The Shoemaker and the Tea Party: Memory and the American Revolution* (Boston: Beacon Press, 2000), xvii.

66. Lepore, *The Whites of Their Eyes*.

67. Desegregation/Richmond, Virginia, ABC Evening News, February 10, 1972, Vanderbilt News Archive, http://tvnews.vanderbilt.edu/program.pl?ID=19250.

68. Kathleen Hall Jamieson and Joseph N. Cappella, *Echo Chamber: Rush Limbaugh and the Conservative Media Establishment* (New York: Oxford University Press, 2008), xi.

69. "Boston Tax Party," editorial, *Wall Street Journal*, August 5, 2008, https://www. wsj.com/articles/SB121789224035011709?mod=googlenews_wsj; "God, Patriotism, and Taxes," editorial, *Wall Street Journal*, September 22, 2008, sec. Review and Outlook, https://www.wsj.com/articles/SB122204158558561239.
    The August article heralded an effort of "citizen activists" who were working to eliminate state income tax in Massachusetts: "The forces of the tax and spend status quo will descend on this initiative like British troops after the original Boston tea party, but somebody has to make an effort to stop the relentless growth of government." In the September editorial, the *Journal* again drew on the Boston Tea Party mythos to take aim at vice-presidential candidate Joe Biden for a campaign speech in which he argued that paying taxes was a patriotic duty.

70. According to the newspaper, activists nationwide were forming groups and organizing demonstrations against property tax increases. The *Journal* referred to one particular Massachusetts protest as a "tax revolt," writing that "about 100 Hampton residents formed a group called the Coalition for a Fair Assessment, and staged a protest at Hampton Harbor, waving tea bags in a mini re-enactment of the Boston Tea Party" (Jennifer Levitz, "Calls Grow to Cap Property Taxes," *Wall Street Journal*, January 5, 2009, http://online.wsj.com/article/ SB123111472983052521.html).

71. To pinpoint when the Tea Party movement emerged within national news, I used LexisNexis and the Vanderbilt University Television News Archive to locate

reports that included the search term "tea party." In my preliminary searches of television news coverage alone, I found mentions of various "tea party" tax-related protests in 1978, 1981, and 1983 that mobilized 1773 imagery and symbolism. While these twentieth-century "tea party" protests frequently focused on eliminating or reducing taxes, they also targeted undesirable tax spending (in other words, spending tax revenue on undesirable persons of color) ("Desegregation/Richmond, Virginia"). Interestingly, I found few mentions of a politically affiliated "tea party" or "tea party protests" between 2000 and 2008 in national news sources. While I found no "tea party" references to tax-focused political mobilization during this period, I did encounter stories about social functions, fairy tales, and museum events.

72. Theda Skocpol and Vanessa Williamson, *The Tea Party and the Remaking of Republican Conservatism* (New York: Oxford University Press, 2012).

73. Ronald P. Formisano, (*The Tea Party: A Brief History* [Baltimore: Johns Hopkins University Press, 2012]) explains that the term "Astroturf" came into use in the 1980s and is usually associated with corporate lobbying that creates campaigns that "are made to appear to be spontaneous mass activism but are actually front organizations with names that disguise their true purposes" (p. 7).

74. Skocpol and Williamson, *The Tea Party and the Remaking of Republican Conservatism*, 11–13.

75. Busby and Cronshaw, "Political Branding."

76. Anthony R. Dimaggio, *The Rise of the Tea Party: Political Discontent and Corporate Media in the Age of Obama* (New York: Monthly Review Press, 2011), 123.

77. Andrew Chadwick, *The Hybrid Media System: Politics and Power*, Oxford Studies in Digital Politics (Oxford; New York: Oxford University Press, 2013).

78. Ruud Koopmans, "Movements and Media: Selection Processes and Evolutionary Dynamics in the Public Sphere," *Theory and Society* 33, nos. 3–4 (2004): 367–391.

79. Melissa M. Deckman, *Tea Party Women: Mama Grizzlies, Grassroots Leaders, and the Changing Face of the American Right* (New York: New York University Press, 2016); Ronald P. Formisano, *The Tea Party: A Brief History* (Baltimore: Johns Hopkins University Press, 2012); Christopher S. Parker and Matt A. Barreto, *Change They Can't Believe In: The Tea Party and Reactionary Politics in America* (Princeton: Princeton University Press, 2013); Skocpol and Williamson, *The Tea Party and the Remaking of Republican Conservatism*.

80. William Bunch, *The Backlash: Right-Wing Radicals, Hi-Def Hucksters, and Paranoid Politics in the Age of Obama*, 1st ed. (New York: Harper, 2010), 210.

81. Guy Debord, *The Society of the Spectacle* (New York: Zone Books, 1994), 12.

82. Ibid., 14.

83. Barbie Zelizer, "When Facts, Truth, and Reality Are God-Terms: On Journalism's Uneasy Place in Cultural Studies," *Communication and Critical/Cultural Studies* 1, no. 1 (2004): 100–119.

84. Barbie Zelizer, "How Communication, Culture, and Critique Intersect in the Study of Journalism," *Communication Culture Critique* 1, no. 1 (2008): 86–91, esp. 90.

85. Todd Gitlin, *The Whole World Is Watching: Mass Media in the Making and Unmaking of the New Left* (Berkeley: University of California Press, 2003), xiv.

86. Kathleen Hall Jamieson and Paul Waldman, *The Press Effect: Politicians, Journalists, and the Stories That Shape the Political World* (New York: Oxford University Press, 2003).

87. Regula Hänggli and Hanspeter Kriesi, "Political Framing Strategies and Their Impact on Media Framing in a Swiss Direct-Democratic Campaign," *Political Communication* 27, no. 2 (May 14, 2010): 141–157, https://doi.org/10.1080/10584600903501484; Catherine Needham, "Brand Leaders: Clinton, Blair and the Limitations of the Permanent Campaign," *Political Studies* 53, no. 2 (June 2005): 343–361, http://onlinelibrary.wiley.com/doi/10.1111/j.1467-9248.2005.00532.x/abstract; Nicholas O'Shaughnessy, "The Marketing of Political Marketing," *European Journal of Marketing* 35, nos. 9–10 (October 2001): 1047–1057, https://doi.org/10.1108/03090560110401956; Margaret Scammell, "Political Marketing: Lessons for Political Science," *Political Studies* 47, no. 4 (September 1999): 718–739, https://doi.org/10.1111/1467-9248.00228.
88. Pippa Norris, "The Evolution of Election Campaigns: Eroding Political Engagement?" Political Communication in the Twenty-first Century (Dunedin: St. Margaret's College, University of Otago, New Zealand, 2004), 3.
89. David L. Swanson and Paolo Mancini, *Politics, Media, and Modern Democracy: An International Study of Innovations in Electoral Campaigning and Their Consequences* (Santa Barbara, CA: Praeger, 1996): 11.
90. Helmut Schneider, "Branding in Politics—Manifestations, Relevance and Identity-Oriented Management," *Journal of Political Marketing* 3, no. 3 (October 6, 2004): 43, https://doi.org/10.1300/J199v03n03_03.
91. Mary Douglas Vavrus, "Postfeminist News: Political Women in Media Culture," (Albany: State University of New York Press, 2002), 123.
92. Laurie Ouellette, "Branding the Right: The Affective Economy of Sarah Palin," *Cinema Journal* 51, no. 4 (2012): 190, https://doi.org/10.1353/cj.2012.0076.
93. Michael Schudson, *The Power of News* (Cambridge, MA: Harvard University Press, 1996), 30.
94. Elihu Katz, "Media Multiplication and Social Segmentation," *Ethical Perspectives* 7, nos. 2–3 (2000): 122.
95. Robert Waterman McChesney, *Rich Media, Poor Democracy: Communication Politics in Dubious Times*, The History of Communication (Urbana: University of Illinois Press, 1999), 6.
96. David Harvey, "Neo-liberalism as Creative Destruction," *Geografiska Annaler, Human Geography* 88, no. 2 (2006): 145.
97. Ibid., 47.
98. Robert Waterman McChesney and John Nichols, *The Death and Life of American Journalism: The Media Revolution that Will Begin the World Again* (New York: Nation Books, 2011), 174.
99. Uscinski, *The People's News*, 2014.
100. Manuel Castells, *The Rise of the Network Society*, The Information Age: Economy, Society, and Culture, vol. 1, 2nd ed., with a new preface (Chichester, West Sussex; Malden, MA: Wiley-Blackwell, 2010); Celia Lury, *Consumer Culture*, 2nd ed. (Cambridge: Polity, 2011).
101. Klein, *No Logo*.
102. Midwest News Index, "Midwest Local TV Newscasts Devote 2.5 Times as Much Air Time to Political Ads as Election Coverage, Study Finds," press release, 2006, https://midwestdemocracynet.files.wordpress.com/2013/12/mni_nov06_release.pdf.
103. Banet-Weiser, *Authentic™*, 149.

104. Libby Lester, "Lost in the Wilderness?: Celebrity, Protest and the News," *Journalism Studies* 7, no. 6 (December 2006): 907–921, https://doi.org/10.1080/14616700600980686; Verica Rupar, ed., *Journalism and Meaning-Making: Reading the Newspaper*, Hampton Press Communication Series, Mass Communication and Journalism (Cresskill, NJ: Hampton Press, 2010).

105. Simon Cottle, "Reporting Demonstrations: The Changing Media Politics of Dissent," *Media, Culture and Society* 30, no. 6 (November 2008): 853, https://doi.org/10.1177/0163443708096097.

106. Lawrence Rosenthal and Christine Trost, introduction to *Steep: The Precipitous Rise of the Tea Party* (Berkeley: University of California Press, 2012), 1–22, esp. 15.

107. Thomas Frank, "Here Comes the Plastic Pitchforks," *Wall Street Journal*, April 15, 2009, http://www.wsj.com/articles/SB123975925509119297; Olbermann, "Countdown for April 15, 2009."

108. Busby and Cronshaw, "Political Branding," 100.

109. Banet-Weiser, *Authentic*™, 4.

110. James A. Karrh, "Brand Placement: A Review," *Journal of Current Issues and Research in Advertising* 20, no. 2 (September 1998): 31, https://doi.org/10.1080/10641734.1998.10505081.

111. David Tewksbury, Jakob Jensen, and Kevin Coe, "Video News Releases and the Public: The Impact of Source Labeling on the Perceived Credibility of Television News," *Journal of Communication* 61, no. 2 (2011): 328–348.

112. Patrick Butler and Phil Harris, "Considerations on the Evolution of Political Marketing Theory," *Marketing Theory* 9, no. 2 (June 2009): 149–164, https://doi.org/10.1177/1470593109103022; Nigel Morgan, Annette Pritchard, and Roger Pride, eds., *Destination Branding: Creating the Unique Destination Proposition*, 2nd ed. (Amsterdam: Butterworth-Heinemann, 2008).

113. Manuel Adolphsen, "Branding in Election Campaigns: Just a Buzzword or a New Quality of Political Communication," in *Politische Kommunikation*, ed. K. Mok and M. Stahl (Berlin: Frank and Timme, 2009), 29–46; Butler and Harris, "Considerations on the Evolution of Political Marketing Theory"; Tim J. Groeling, *When Politicians Attack: Party Cohesion in the Media*, Communication, Society and Politics (Cambridge; New York: Cambridge University Press, 2010); Margaret Scammell, "Political Brands and Consumer Citizens: The Rebranding of Tony Blair," *Annals of the American Academy of Political and Social Science* 611 (2007): 176–192; Scammell, "Political Marketing"; Heather Savigny and Mick Temple, "Political Marketing Models: The Curious Incident of the Dog that Doesn't Bark," *Political Studies* 58, no. 5 (December 2010): 1049–1064, https://doi.org/10.1111/j.1467-9248.2010.00830.x.

114. Winston Tellis, "Information Technology in a University: A Case Study," *Campus-wide Information Systems* 14, no. 3 (1997): 78–91.

115. Alexander L. George and Andrew Bennett, *Case Studies and Theory Development in the Social Sciences*, BCSIA Studies in International Security (Cambridge: MIT Press, 2005), 5, 19.

116. Nelson Phillips and Cynthia Hardy, *Discourse Analysis: Investigating Processes of Social Construction* (Thousand Oaks, CA: Sage , 2002), 3.

117. Ibid., 3.

118. David Machin and Sarah Niblock, "Branding Newspapers: Visual Texts as Social Practice," *Journalism Studies* 9, no. 2 (April 2008): 246, https://doi.org/10.1080/14616700701848287.

119. Aurthur Asa Berger, *Media Analysis Techniques* (Thousand Oaks, CA: Sage Publications, 2005).

120. Teun A. Van Dijk, *News as Discourse* (Hillsdale, NJ: L. Erlbaum Associates, 1988), 55.

121. Noha Mellor, "'Why Do They Hate Us?': Seeking Answers in the Pan-Arab News Coverage of 9/11," in *Journalism after September* 11, ed. Barbie Zelizer and Stuart Allan (New York: Routledge, 2011), 149.

122. As in most scholarship on the subject, the use of "fake news" here refers to parody news programs that present real, current news in a comedic fashion. This is distinct from the rise of the term "fake news" to refer to deliberately deceptive or politically inexpedient information during the 2016 election and subsequent presidential administration under Donald Trump.

123. Noam Chomsky, "What Makes Mainstream Media Mainstream," *Z Magazine*, 1997; Kevin Wallsten, "Agenda Setting and the Blogosphere: An Analysis of the Relationship between Mainstream Media and Political Blogs," *Review of Policy Research* 24, no. 6 (2007): 567–587.

124. Geoffrey Baym, "The Daily Show: Discursive Integration and the Reinvention of Political Journalism," *Political Communication* 22, no. 3 (July 2005): 260, https://doi.org/10.1080/10584600591006492.

125. The rising demand for cross-platform broadcast media monitoring services, such as TV Eyes (http://www.tveyes.com), reflects this very different landscape.

126. Jamieson and Cappella, *Echo Chamber*, 4–5.

127. Ibid., 241.

128. As 2011 Pew data was not yet available when I was researching this book, the analysis of media coverage effectively ends in December 2010.

129. EBizMBA, "Top 15 Most Popular Political Websites," September 2010, archived at https://web.archive.org/web/20101001113656/http://www.ebizmba.com:80/articles/political-news-websites. While *Drudge Report* was a conservative site that had more unique monthly visitors than *Newsmax* in 2010, it was excluded from study because it was largely a news aggregation site rather than a primary source of conservative news.

130. Robert M. Entman, "Media and Democracy without Party Competition," in *Mass Media and Society*, ed. James Curran and Michael Gurevitch, 4th ed. (London; New York: Hodder Arnold; distributed in the US by Oxford University Press, 2005), 251–270; Adrienne Russell and S. Elizabeth Bird, "Salon.Com and New-Media Professional Journalism Culture," in *The Anthropology of News and Journalism: Global Perspectives*, ed. S. Elizabeth Bird (Bloomington: Indiana University Press, 2010); David Tewksbury and Jason Rittenberg, *News on the Internet: Information and Citizenship in the Twenty-first Century*, Oxford Studies in Digital Politics, 1st ed. (New York: Oxford University Press, 2012).

131. Media Education Foundation, "Race, the Floating Signifier, Featuring Stuart Hall; Transcript," 1997, http://www.mediaed.org/assets/products/407/transcript_407.pdf.

CHAPTER 2

1. Jack Mirkinson, "State of the Union 2011 Ratings: Fox News Dominates, CNN Second," *Huffington Post* (blog), January 26, 2011, http://www.huffingtonpost.com/2011/01/26/state-of-the-union-ratings-fox-news-cnn_n_814531.html.

2. Michael Falcone, "Michele Bachmann's Tea Party State of the Union Response Will Criticize 'Explosion of Government Spending,'" January 26, 2011, http://blogs.abcnews.com/thenote/2011/01/michele-bachmann-tea-party-state-of-the-union-response-preview.html; "Michele Bachmann State of the Union Response: Speech Attacks ObamaCare, Stimulus & More," *Huffington Post* (blog), January 25, 2011, http://www.huffingtonpost.com/2011/01/25/michele-bachmann-state-of-union-response_n_813972.html; Aliyah Shahid, "Michele Bachmann Tea Party Response to Obama's State of the Union: Urge Budget Cuts, Rips President," *New York Daily News*, January 25, 2011, http://articles.nydailynews.com/2011-01-26/news/27737928_1_health-care-reform-budget-cuts-gop-aides.

3. Bill Carter, "Tea Party Response to Air Live on CNN," *Media Decoder—New York Times*, January 25, 2011, http://mediadecoder.blogs.nytimes.com/2011/01/25/tea-party-response-to-air-live-on-cnn/.

4. "Tea Party HD." 2011 Archived at: https://web.archive.org/web/20110124014136/http://www.teapartyhd.com:80/aboutus.html.

5. Scott Rasmussen and Douglas E. Schoen, *Mad as Hell: How the Tea Party Movement Is Fundamentally Remaking Our Two-Party System* (New York: Harper, 2010).

6. "Reactions to the State of the Union," *Rachel Maddow Show*, aired January 25, 2011, on MSNBC.

7. Dana Milbank, "I'm Declaring February a Palin-Free Month. Join Me!" *Washington Post*, January 21, 2011, http://www.washingtonpost.com/wp-dyn/content/article/2011/01/20/AR2011012004349.html.

8. Ibid.

9. Joseph E. Uscinski, The People's News: Media, Politics, and the Demands of Capitalism, 2014.

10. "Countdown for April 14, 2009," *Countdown with Keith Olbermann*, aired April 14, 2009, on MSNBC.

11. Michael Calderone, "Fox Teas Up a Tempest," *Politico*, April 16, 2009, http://www.politico.com/news/stories/0409/21275.html.

12. A. J. Silk, "What Is Marketing?" (Boston: Harvard Business Press, 2006), 112.

13. Tim J. Groeling, *When Politicians Attack: Party Cohesion in the Media*, Communication, Society and Politics (Cambridge; New York: Cambridge University Press, 2010); James A. Karrh, "Brand Placement: A Review," *Journal of Current Issues and Research in Advertising* 20, no. 2 (September 1998): 31–49, https://doi.org/10.1080/10641734.1998.10505081.

14. Jooyoung Kim, Tae Hyun Baek, and Hugh J. Martin, "Dimensions of News Media Brand Personality," *Journalism and Mass Communication Quarterly* 87, no. 1 (March 2010): 119, https://doi.org/10.1177/107769901008700107.

15. D. Travis, "Emotional Branding: How Successful Brands Gain the Irrational Edge" (New York: Crown Business, 2000), 173; Sarah Banet-Weiser, *Authentic™: Politics and Ambivalence in a Brand Culture*, Critical Cultural Communication (New York: New York University Press, 2012); Walter S. McDowell, "Exploring a Free Association Methodology to Capture and Differentiate Abstract Media Brand

Associations: A Study of Three Cable News Networks," *Journal of Media Economics* 17, no. 4 (October 2004): 309–320, https://doi.org/10.1207/s15327736me1704_5.

16. Margaret Scammell, "Political Brands and Consumer Citizens: The Rebranding of Tony Blair," *Annals of the American Academy of Political and Social Science* 611 (2007): 176–192.

17. Darren G. Lilleker, *Key Concepts in Political Communication*, SAGE Key Concepts (London; Thousand Oaks, CA: Sage, 2006); Gareth Smith and Alan French, "The Political Brand: A Consumer Perspective," *Marketing Theory* 9, no. 2 (2009): 209–226.

18. Robert M. Entman, "Media and Democracy without Party Competition," in *Mass Media and Society*, ed. James Curran and Michael Gurevitch, 4th ed. (London; New York: Hodder Arnold ; distributed in the US by Oxford University Press, 2005), 251–270; Robert Waterman McChesney, *Rich Media, Poor Democracy: Communication Politics in Dubious Times*, The History of Communication (Urbana: University of Illinois Press, 1999).

19. Margaret Scammell, "Political Marketing: Lessons for Political Science," *Political Studies* 47, no. 4 (September 1999): 720–721, https://doi.org/10.1111/1467-9248.00228.

20. Pippa Norris, "The Evolution of Election Campaigns: Eroding Political Engagement?" Political Communication in the Twenty-first Century (Dunedin: St. Margaret's College, University of Otago, 2004); Scammell, "Political Marketing."

21. McChesney, *Rich Media, Poor Democracy*, 48.

22. Scammell, "Political Brands and Consumer Citizens," 189.

23. Catherine Needham, "Brand Leaders: Clinton, Blair and the Limitations of the Permanent Campaign," *Political Studies* 53, no. 2 (June 2005): 343–361, https://doi.org/10.1111/j.1467-9248.2005.00532.x.

24. Eleanora Pasotti, *Political Branding in Cities: The Decline of Machine Politics in Bogota, Naples, and Chicago* (Cambridge: Cambridge University Press, 2009).

25. Niall Caldwell and Joao R. Freire, "The Differences between Branding a Country, a Region and a City: Applying the Brand Box Model," *Journal of Brand Management* 12, no. 1 (September 2004): 51, https://doi.org/10.1057/palgrave.bm.2540201.

26. Naomi Klein, *No Logo: No Space, No Choice, No Jobs*, 10th anniversary ed., 3rd ed. (New York: Picador, 2010); Alejandra Marchevsky and Beth Baker, "Why Has President Obama Deported More Immigrants Than Any President in US History?" *The Nation*, March 31, 2014, https://www.thenation.com/article/why-has-president-obama-deported-more-immigrants-any-president-us-history/.

27. Fabrizio Macagno, "What We Hide in Words: Value-Based Reasoning and Emotive Language" (Windsor: OSSA Conference Archive, University of Windsor, 2013), 2.

28. Natalia Yannopoulou, Epaminondas Koronis, and Richard Elliott, "Media Amplification of a Brand Crisis and Its Affect on Brand Trust," *Journal of Marketing Management* 27, nos. 5–6 (2011): 541.

29. Sylvia M. Chan-Olmsted and Jiyoung Cha, "Branding Television News in a Multichannel Environment: An Exploratory Study of Network News Brand Personality," *International Journal on Media Management* 9, no. 4 (November 13, 2007): 135–150, https://doi.org/10.1080/14241270701632688.

30. Jamie Warner, "Political Culture Jamming: The Dissident Humor of *The Daily Show with Jon Stewart*," *Popular Communication* 5, no. 1 (2007): 17–36.

31. Banet-Weiser, *Authentic™*, 5.

32. Warner, "Political Culture Jamming," 20.

33. Pasotti, *Political Branding in Cities*.

34. Helmut Schneider, "Branding in Politics, Manifestations, Relevance and Identity-Oriented Management," *Journal of Political Marketing* 3, no. 3 (October 6, 2004): 41–67, https://doi.org/10.1300/J199v03n03_03.

35. Ibid., 52.

36. Markus Prior, *Post-Broadcast Democracy: How Media Choice Increases Inequality in Political Involvement and Polarizes Elections*, Cambridge Studies in Public Opinion and Political Psychology (New York: Cambridge University Press, 2007).

37. Alan French and Gareth Smith, "Measuring Political Brand Equity: A Consumer Oriented Approach," ed. Phil Harris, *European Journal of Marketing* 44, nos. 3–4 (April 6, 2010): 460–477, https://doi.org/10.1108/03090561011020534.

38. Yannopoulou, Koronis, and Elliott, "Media Amplification of a Brand Crisis and Its Affect on Brand Trust," 530–546.

39. Nicholas O'Shaughnessy, "The Marketing of Political Marketing," *European Journal of Marketing* 35, nos. 9–10 (October 2001): 1055, https://doi.org/10.1108/03090560110401956.

40. David Tewksbury and Jason Rittenberg, *News on the Internet: Information and Citizenship in the Twenty-first Century* (New York: Oxford University Press, 2012); James A. Karrh, "Brand Placement: A Review," *Journal of Current Issues and Research in Advertising* 20, no. 2 (September 1998): 31–49, https://doi.org/10.1080/10641734.1998.10505081; Catherine Needham, "Brand Leaders: Clinton, Blair and the Limitations of the Permanent Campaign," *Political Studies* 53, no. 2 (June 2005): 343–361, https://doi.org/10.1111/j.1467-9248.2005.00532.x; Yannopoulou, Koronis, and Elliott, "Media Amplification of a Brand Crisis and Its Affect on Brand Trust."

41. Mark D. Harmon and Candace White, "How Television News Programs Use Video News Releases," *Public Relations Review* 27, no. 2 (June 2001): 213–222, https://doi.org/10.1016/S0363-8111(01)00081-9.

42. Julie Moos, "The Atlantic Publishes Then Pulls Sponsored Content from Church of Scientology," *Poynter*, January 15, 2013, http://www.poynter.org/2013/the-atlantic-pulls-sponsored-content-from-church-of-scientology/200593/.

43. *Meet the Press*, aired February 7, 2016, on NBC.

44. David Machin and Sarah Niblock, "Branding Newspapers: Visual Texts as Social Practice," *Journalism Studies* 9, no. 2 (April 2008): 244–259, https://doi.org/10.1080/14616700701848287.

45. Ibid., 246.

46. Rasmussen and Schoen, *Mad as Hell*, 246.

47. Andy Bull, *Brand Journalism* (London: Routledge, Taylor & Francis Group, 2013).

48. James Santomier, "New Media, Branding and Global Sports Sponsorship," *International Journal of Sports Marketing and Sponsorship* 10, no. 1 (October 2008): 9–22, https://doi.org/10.1108/IJSMS-10-01-2008-B005.

49. Theda Skocpol and Vanessa Williamson, *The Tea Party and the Remaking of Republican Conservatism* (New York: Oxford University Press, 2012).

50. "Rick Santelli and the 'Rant of the Year,'" http://www.youtube.com/watch?v=bEZB4taSEoA.

51. Glenn Harlan Reynolds, "Tax Day Becomes Protest Day," *Wall Street Journal*, April 15, 2009, http://www.wsj.com/articles/SB123975867505519363; Sheryl Gay Stolberg, "Critique of Housing Plan Draws Quick White House Offensive," *New York Times*, February 21, 2009.
52. Elizabeth Price Foley, *The Tea Party: Three Principles* (New York: Cambridge University Press, 2012); Ronald P. Formisano, *The Tea Party: A Brief History* (Baltimore: Johns Hopkins University Press, 2012).
53. Rasmussen and Schoen, *Mad as Hell*, 225.
54. Michael Calderone, "Fox Teas Up a Tempest," *Politico*, April 16, 2009, http://www.politico.com/news/stories/0409/21275.html.
55. Karl Rove, "Republicans and the Tea Parties," *Wall Street Journal*, April 16, 2009, http://www.wsj.com/articles/SB123984928625323721.
56. Lawrence Rosenthal and Christine Trost, introduction to *Steep: The Precipitous Rise of the Tea Party* (Berkeley: University of California Press, 2012), 10.
57. Brian Stelter, "Jon Stewart's Punching Bag, Fox News," *New York Times*, April 24, 2010, http://www.nytimes.com/2010/04/24/arts/television/24stewart.html.
58. Calderone, "Fox Teas Up a Tempest."
59. Manu Raju, "Axelrod: Protests May Not Mean Much," *Politico*, September 13, 2009, http://www.politico.com/blogs/politicolive/0909/Axelrod_Protests_wont_mean_much.html?showall.
60. Rosenthal and Trost, *Steep*, 3.
61. Danny Shea, "Fox News Pulls Sean Hannity from Tea Party Rally," *Huffington Post* (blog), June 15, 2010; updated May 25, 2011, http://www.huffingtonpost.com/2010/04/15/fox-news-pulls-sean-hanni_n_539719.html; "Countdown for April 16, 2010," *Countdown with Keith Olbermann*, aired April 16, 2010.
62. Brian Stelter, "Fox Canceled Hannity's Attendance at Tea Party's Tax Day Rally in Cincinnati," *New York Times*, April 16, 2010, http://www.nytimes.com/2010/04/17/us/17fox.html?mcubz=0.
63. "Presidential Media Blitz; Who Is Yale Murder Suspect?" *Campbell Brown: No Bias, No Bull*, aired September 18, 2009, on CNN.
64. "Unresolved Problem," *The O'Reilly Factor*, aired April 20, 2010, on Fox News.
65. "The O'Reilly Factor," *The O'Reilly Factor*, aired July 15, 2010, on Fox News.
66. Antonella Maiello and Cecilia Pasquinelli, "Destruction or Construction? A (Counter) Branding Analysis of Sport Mega-Events in Rio de Janeiro," *Cities* 48 (November 2015): 118, https://doi.org/10.1016/j.cities.2015.06.011.
67. Jason Linkins, "Tea Party 'Crashers' Plan to Prank Conservative Activists," *Huffington Post* (blog), June 14, 2010, http://www.huffingtonpost.com/2010/04/14/tea-party-crashers-plan-t_n_537352.html.
68. Mayhill Fowler, "Mayhill Fowler: Tea Party Talk: Racism, Palin, and the Hostile Takeover of the Republican Party," *Huffington Post* (blog), July 19, 2010, http://www.huffingtonpost.com/mayhill-fowler/tea-party-talk-racism-pal_b_650795.html.
69. Matt Guardino and Dean Snyder, "The Tea Party and the Crisis of Neoliberalism: Mainstreaming New Right Populism in the Corporate News Media," *New Political Science* 34, no. 4 (December 2012): 527–548, https://doi.org/10.1080/07393148.2012.729741.
70. Ibid., 537.
71. Todd Gitlin, *The Whole World Is Watching: Mass Media in the Making and Unmaking of the New Left* (Berkeley: University of California Press, 2003).
72. Kenneth T. Andrews and Michael Biggs, "The Dynamics of Protest Diffusion: Movement Organizations, Social Networks, and News Media in the 1960

Sit-Ins," *American Sociological Review* 71, no. 5 (October 2006): 752–777, https://doi.org/10.1177/000312240607100503.

73. Reynolds, "Tax Day Becomes Protest Day."

74. See D. M. McLeod and J. K. Hertog, "The Manufacture of 'Public Opinion' by Reporters: Informal Cues for Public Perceptions of Protest Groups," *Discourse and Society* 3, no. 3 (1992): 259–275. And D. M. McLeod, "Communicating Deviance: The Effects of Television News Coverage of Social Protest," *Journal of Broadcasting and Electronic Media* 39, no. 1 (1995): 4–19.

75. Ruud Koopmans, "Movements and Media: Selection Processes and Evolutionary Dynamics in the Public Sphere," *Theory and Society* 33, nos. 3–4 (June 2004): 367–391, https://doi.org/10.1023/B:RYSO.0000038603.34963.de; Charlotte Ryan, *Prime Time Activism: Media Strategies for Grassroots Organizing* (Brooklyn: South End Press, 1991).

76. Simon Cottle, "Reporting Demonstrations: The Changing Media Politics of Dissent," *Media, Culture and Society* 30, no. 6 (November 2008): 853–872, https://doi.org/10.1177/0163443708096097.

77. Robert M. Entman, "Framing: Toward Clarification of a Fractured Paradigm," *Journal of Communication* 43, no. 4 (December 1993): 51–58, https://doi.org/10.1111/j.1460-2466.1993.tb01304.x.

78. Kate Zernike, "Convention Is Trying to Harness Tea Party Spirit," *New York Times*, February 6, 2010, http://www.nytimes.com/2010/02/06/us/politics/06teaparty.html.

79. "Media Coverage of Tea Party Unfair?" *The O'Reilly Factor*, aired March 29, 2010, on Fox News.

80. Michael Barbaro, "Paladino's Accidental Running Mate Is Also His Mop-up Man," *New York Times*, October 21, 2010, http://www.nytimes.com/2010/10/21/nyregion/21edwards.html.

81. Trey Ellis, "The Grave Danger of Conservative Blindness," October 21, 2010, http://www.huffingtonpost.com/trey-ellis/the-grave-danger-of-conse_b_771478.html; Brendan Nyhan, "How Much Are Tea Party Candidates Hurting the GOP?" October 21, 2010, http://www.huffingtonpost.com/brendan-nyhan/how-much-are-tea-party-ca_b_772072.html.

82. Jerry Bowyer, "Pennsylvania's Tea Party: Brewing for Years," *Wall Street Journal*, April 24, 2010, http://www.wsj.com/articles/SB10001424052702304198004575172383368596968.

83. "Countdown for April 14, 2010," *Countdown with Keith Olbermann*, aired April 14, 2010, on MSNBC.

84. Fredreka Schouten, "'Tea Party' Fundraising PACs Surge, but Cash Comes Slowly," *USA Today*, June 17, 2010.

85. Ibid.

86. Andy Barr, "Sarah Palin: GOP 'through' without Tea Party," *Politico*, October 18, 2010, http://www.politico.com/news/stories/1010/43794.html.

87. Kelly Kiely, "Squabbling Threatens to Ice 'Tea Party' Momentum," *USA Today*, February 5, 2010.

88. "Tempest in a Tea Party: Tea Party Anger," *World News with Diane Sawyer*, aired February 5, 2010, on ABC.

89. Arthur Delaney, "Tea Party Insanity: 'Burn the Books!' (VIDEO)," *Huffington Post* (blog), May 13, 2009, http://www.huffingtonpost.com/2009/04/12/tea-party-insanity-burn-a_n_185991.html.

90. Kenneth P. Vogel, "Tea Party's Growing Money Problem," *Politico*, August 9, 2010, http://www.politico.com/story/2010/08/tea-partys-growing-money-problem-040800.

91. "Punchlines; A Lighter Look at the News of the Week," *USA Today*, October 22, 2010.

92. Sarah Palin, "Why I'm Speaking at the Tea Party Convention," *USA Today*, March 3, 2010.

93. Kate Zernike, "Secretive Republican Donors Are Planning Ahead," *New York Times*, October 20, 2010, http://www.nytimes.com/2010/10/20/us/politics/20koch.html.

94. "Countdown for April 15, 2009," *Countdown with Keith Olbermann*, aired April 15, 2009, on MSNBC.

95. Cenk Uygur, "Where Are the Tea Party Protests about Wall Street?" *Huffington Post* (blog), April 23, 2010, http://www.huffingtonpost.com/cenk-uygur/where-are-the-tea-party-p_b_549067.html.

96. Jane Hamsher, "The Corporate Lobbyists behind the Tea Parties," *Huffington Post* (blog), April 13, 2009, http://www.huffingtonpost.com/jane-hamsher/the-corporate-lobbyists-b_b_186367.html.

97. Jim Rutenberg, "Democrats Back Third Parties to Siphon Votes from the G.O.P.," *New York Times*, October 23, 2010.

98. Warner, "Political Culture Jamming," 17–36.

99. Reynolds, "Tax Day Becomes Protest Day."

100. "Talking Points Memo and Top Story," *The O'Reilly Factor*, aired April 15, 2010, Fox News; Frank Rich, "The Rage Is Not about Health Care," *New York Times*, March 28, 2010, http://www.nytimes.com/2010/03/28/opinion/28rich.html.

101. Robert B. Reich, "The Necessity of Obamanomics," *Wall Street Journal*, February 5, 2010, http://www.wsj.com/articles/SB10001424052748704022804575041751435808716.

102. Liz Sidoti, "Sarah Palin Tea Party Convention Speech: Activists Can Hardly Wait," *Huffington Post* (blog), February 6, 2010, [http://www.huffingtonpost.com/2010/02/06/sarah-palin-tea-party-con_n_452153.html], archived at https://web.archive.org/web/20100212013223/http://www.huffingtonpost.com:80/2010/02/06/sarah-palin-tea-party-con_n_452153.html; Kathy Kiely, "'Tea Partiers' Flood Streets of Capital; Strategists on Hand to Help Organize Anti-Tax Activists," *USA Today*, April 16, 2010, sec. 9; Benedict Carey, "Mad as Hell. And...," *New York Times*, March 28, 2010.

103. Kate Zernike, "Tea Party Crowd Rallies in Nevada with a Challenge to a Homegrown Democrat," *New York Times*, March 28, 2010, sec A.

104. "Countdown for April 16, 2010."

105. Andy Ostroy, "Tea Parties: GOP Once Again Manipulating the Average Joe," *Huffington Post* (blog), April 16, 2009, http://www.huffingtonpost.com/andy-ostroy/tea-parties-gop-once-agai_b_187750.html.

106. "Ten Most Offensive Tea Party Signs and Extensive Photo Coverage from Tax Day Protests," *Huffington Post* (blog), December 28, 2009, http://www.huffingtonpost.com/2009/04/16/10-most-offensive-tea-par_n_187554.html.

107. Eric Felten, "Where Is the Outrage?" *Wall Street Journal*, July 16, 2010, sec. Weekend Journal, http://www.wsj.com/articles/SB10001424052748704682604575369123789386954.

108. Kenneth M. Cosgrove, *Branded Conservatives: How the Brand Brought the Right from the Fringes to the Center of American Politics*, Politics, Media, and Popular Culture, vol. 12 (New York: P. Lang, 2007), 72.

109. David A. Patten, "Shirley: Tea Party Now More Important than GOP," *Newsmax* 2011, March 29, 2010, https://www.newsmax.com/insidecover/sex-club-republican-expenses/2010/03/29/id/354165/.

110. Shelby Steele, "Barack the Good," *Wall Street Journal*, March 31, 2010, http://www.wsj.com/articles/SB10001424052702304370304575152023005805864.

111. "Interview with Jon Stewart," *The O'Reilly Factor*, aired February 3, 2010, on Fox News.

112. Reynolds, "Tax Day Becomes Protest Day."

113. Ryan Grim, "Cornyn: Teabaggers Forming Third Party a Danger to GOP," *Huffington Post* (blog), April 4, 2010, http://www.huffingtonpost.com/2010/02/02/cornyn-teabaggers-forming_n_446417.html.

114. Daniel Sinker, "When the Left Went Teabagging: As You Chuckle at the Right's Newfound Activism, Don't Forget That the Left Sucked Balls for Years," *Huffington Post* (blog), April 17, 2009, http://www.huffingtonpost.com/daniel-sinker/when-the-left-went-teabag_b_188329.html.

115. Oren Dorrell, "Tax Revolt a Recipe for Tea Parties; Nationwide Protests over Government Spending, Bailouts Planned for April 15," *USA Today*, April 13, 2009.

116. Liz Sidoti, "Sarah Palin Tea Party Convention Speech: Activists Can Hardly Wait," *Huffington Post* (blog), February 6, 2010, http://www.huffingtonpost.com/2010/02/06/sarah-palin-tea-party-con_n_452153.html.

117. Kathleen Parker et al., "Republican Ads; President Obama's Message; Politicians 'Man Up'; The Next Financial Meltdown; Women in Politics: Mean Girls or Politics as Usual; Presidential Mythbusters," *Parker Spitzer*, October 18, 2010.

118. Shayndi Raice, "Battle for GOP Ballot Slots," *Wall Street Journal*, June 18, 2010, http://www.wsj.com/articles/SB10001424052748703650604575312830738572058.

119. Liz Robbins, "Protesters Air Views on Government Spending at Tax Day Tea Parties across U.S.," *New York Times*, November 16, 2009, sec. A.

120. "Countdown for April 15, 2009."

121. Matt Guardino and Dean Snyder, "The Tea Party and the Crisis of Neoliberalism: Mainstreaming New Right Populism in the Corporate News Media," *New Political Science* 34, no. 4 (December 2012): 527–548, https://doi.org/10.1080/07393148.2012.729741; Richard Meagher, "The 'Vast Right-Wing Conspiracy': Media and Conservative Networks," *New Political Science* 34, no. 4 (December 2012): 469–484, https://doi.org/10.1080/07393148.2012.729738.

122. Ritchie Savage, "From McCarthyism to the Tea Party: Interpreting Anti-Leftist Forms of US Populism in Comparative Perspective," *New Political Science* 34, no. 4 (December 2012): 568, https://doi.org/10.1080/07393148.2012.729743.

123. Robert Busby and Sue Cronshaw, "Political Branding: The Tea Party and Its Use of Participation Branding," *Journal of Political Marketing* 14, nos. 1–2 (January 2, 2015): 98, https://doi.org/10.1080/15377857.2014.990850.

124. Brad O'Leary, "Brad O'Leary: Tea Party Endorsement Key in November Elections," *Newsmax*, April 13, 2010, http://www.newsmax.com/US/Leary-tea-November-elections/2010/04/13/id/355617.

125. Delaney, "Tea Party Insanity: 'Burn the Books!' (VIDEO)."

126. Jesse McKinley, "Battered Landscape for a California Democrat," *New York Times*, October 20, 2010, http://www.nytimes.com/2010/10/21/us/politics/21california.html; "Tea Party Convention," *The O'Reilly Factor*, aired February 5, 2010, on MSNBC.

127. Kenneth P. Vogel, "Tea Partiers Push Back after Bad Week," *Politico*, March 27, 2010, http://www.politico.com/news/stories/0310/35113.html.

128. W. Lance Bennett, "Beyond Pseudoevents: Election News as Reality TV," *American Behavioral Scientist* 49, no. 3 (2005): 364–378.

129. Mervi Katriina Pantti and Karin Wahl-Jorgensen. "'Not an Act of God': Anger and Citizenship in Press Coverage of British Man-Made Disasters." *Media, Culture and Society* 33, no. 1 (2011): 105–122; Karin Wahl-Jorgensen, "Emotion and Journalism," in *The SAGE Handbook of Digital Journalism* (Thousand Oaks, CA: Sage, 2016), 128–143.

130. Kevin Michael DeLuca and Jennifer Peeples, "From Public Sphere to Public Screen: Democracy, Activism, and the 'Violence' of Seattle," *Critical Studies in Media Communication* 19, no. 2 (June 2002): 125–151, https://doi.org/10.1080/07393180216559.

131. Arie S. Soesilo and Philo C. Wasburn, "Constructing a Political Spectacle: American and Indonesian Media Accounts of the "Crisis in the Gulf," *Sociological Quarterly* 35, no. 2 (1994): 367.

132. Matt Towery, "Tea Party Movement Confuses Both," *Newsmax*, April 15, 2010, http://www.newsmax.com/MattTowery/tea-party-John-McCain/2010/04/15/id/355810.

133. Zernike, "Convention Is Trying to Harness Tea Party Spirit"; Robbins, "Protesters Air Views on Government Spending at Tax Day Tea Parties across U.S."

134. Walter Benjamin, *Illuminations* (New York: Schocken Books, 1968).

135. Robbins, "Protesters Air Views on Government Spending at Tax Day Tea Parties across U.S."

136. Thomas Frank, "Here Comes the Plastic Pitchforks," *Wall Street Journal*, April 15, 2009, http://www.wsj.com/articles/SB123975925509119297.

137. Kiely, "'Tea Partiers' Flood Streets of Capital; Strategists on Hand to Help Organize Anti-Tax Activists."

138. Ostroy, "Tea Parties: GOP Once Again Manipulating the Average Joe."

139. "Patrick Swayze Dies; Who Killed Yale Student?" *Campbell Brown: No Bias, No Bull*, aired September 14, 2009, on CNN.

140. Valerie Bauman and Brian Bakst, "Tea Party Leaders Anxious about Extremists," *Newsmax*, April 15, 2010, http://www.newsmax.com/InsideCover/US-Tea-Party-Concerns/2010/04/15/id/355767.

141. Dan Weil, "Tea Partyers Split in Support of Palin, Paul," *Newsmax*, April 19, 2010, http://www.newsmax.com/InsideCover/palin-ron-paul-tea/2010/04/19/id/356202.

142. Helmut Schneider, "Branding in Politics—Manifestations, Relevance and Identity-Oriented Management," *Journal of Political Marketing* 3, no. 3 (October 6, 2004): 41–67, https://doi.org/10.1300/J199v03n03_03; Alvin. J. Silk, *What Is Marketing?* (Boston: Harvard Business School Press, 2006).

143. M. Adolphsen, "Branding in Election Campaigns: Just a Buzzword or a New Quality of Political Communication," in *Politische Kommunikation*, ed. K. Mok and M. Stahl (Berlin: Frank and Timme, 2009), 29–46; Eleanora Pasotti, *Political Branding in Cities: The Decline of Machine Politics in Bogota, Naples, and*

Chicago (Cambridge: Cambridge University Press, 2009); Schneider, "Branding in Politics—Manifestations, Relevance and Identity-Oriented Management."

144. Tim J. Groeling, *When Politicians Attack: Party Cohesion in the Media*, Communication, Society and Politics (Cambridge; New York: Cambridge University Press, 2010).

145. Gitlin argues that media coverage focuses on groups with a centralized structure and identifies charismatic leaders to represent their cause.

146. See L. Ashley, and B. Olson, "Constructing Reality: Print Media's Framing of the Women's Movement, 1966 to 1986," *Journalism and Mass Communication Quarterly* 75, 2 (1998): 263–277; McLeod and Hertog, "The Manufacture of 'Public Opinion,'" 259–275.

147. Robert D. Benford and David A. Snow, "Framing Processes and Social Movements: An Overview and Assessment," *Annual Review of Sociology* 26, no. 1 (August 2000): 613, https://doi.org/10.1146/annurev.soc.26.1.611.

148. Gitlin, *The Whole World Is Watching*, 11.

149. Jackie Smith et al., "From Protest to Agenda Building: Description Bias in Media Coverage of Protest Events in Washington, D.C.," *Social Forces* 79, no. 4 (June 1, 2001): 1400, https://doi.org/10.1353/sof.2001.0053.

150. S. Craig Watkins, "Framing Protest: News Media Frames of the Million Man March," *Critical Studies in Media Communication* 18, no. 1 (March 2001): 83–101, https://doi.org/10.1080/15295030109367125.

151. Smith et al., "From Protest to Agenda Building," 1397–1423, https://doi.org/10.1353/sof.2001.0053.

152. F. E. Dardis, "Marginalization Devices in US Press Coverage of Iraq War Protest: A Content Analysis," *Mass Communication and Society* 9, no. 2 (2006): 117–135.

153. J. M. Chan and C. C. Lee, "The Journalistic Paradigm on Civil Protests: A Case Study of Hong Kong," *The News Media in National and International Conflict* (Boulder: Westview Press: 1984),183–202; Douglas McCleod, "News Coverage and Social Protest: How the Media's Protect Paradigm Exacerbates Social Conflict," *Journal of Dispute Resolution* 2007, no. 1 (2007): http://scholarship.law.missouri.edu/jdr/vol2007/iss1/12.

154. Matt Guardino and Dean Snyder, "The Tea Party and the Crisis of Neoliberalism: Mainstreaming New Right Populism in the Corporate News Media," *New Political Science* 34, no. 4 (December 2012): 527–548, https://doi.org/10.1080/07393148.2012.729741.

155. David A. Weaver and Joshua M. Scacco, "Revisiting the Protest Paradigm: The Tea Party as Filtered through Prime-Time Cable News," *International Journal of Press/Politics* 18, no. 1 (2013): 61–84.

156. Michael P. Boyle, Michael R. McCluskey, Douglas M. McLeod, and Sue E. Stein, "Newspapers and Protest: An Examination of Protest Coverage from 1960 to 1999," *Journalism and Mass Communication Quarterly* 82, no. 3 (2005): 638–653.

157. See, for example, Carol Cratty, "Man Carries Assault Rifle to Obama Protest—and It's Legal," aired August 18, 29, on CNN, http://www.cnn.com/2009/POLITICS/08/17/obama.protest.rifle/.

158. Gitlin, *The Whole World Is Watching*, 3.

159. Gaye Tuchman, *Making News: A Study in the Construction of Reality*, First Free Press paperback edition (New York: Free Press, 1980), 134.

160. Jürgen Gerhards and Dieter Rucht, "Mesomobilization: Organizing and Framing in Two Protest Campaigns in West Germany," *American Journal of Sociology* 98, no. 3 (November 1992): 580, https://doi.org/10.1086/230049.

161. Charles Postel, "The Tea Party in Historical Perspective: A Conservative Response to a Crisis of Political Economy," in *Steep: The Precipitous Rise of the Tea Party*, ed. Lawrence Rosenthal and Christine Trost (Berkeley: University of California Press, 2012), 25–46.

162. Weaver and Scacco, "Revisiting the Protest Paradigm," 76.

163. Christopher S. Parker and Matt A. Barreto, *Change They Can't Believe In: The Tea Party and Reactionary Politics in America* (Princeton: Princeton University Press, 2013).

164. "Countdown for February 1, 2010," *Countdown with Keith Olbermann*, aired February 1, 2010, on MSNBC.

165. Weaver and Scacco, "Revisiting the Protest Paradigm," 76.

166. Jason Linkins, "Fox News Publishes Semi-Critical Article on Tea Party Participants," *Huffington Post* (blog), April 13, 2010, https://www.huffingtonpost.com/2010/04/13/fox-news-publishes-semi-c_n_535539.html.

167. Douglas B. Holt, *How Brands Become Icons: The Principles of Cultural Branding* (Boston: Harvard Business School Press, 2004), 3.

168. Celia Lury, *Consumer Culture*, 2nd ed. (Cambridge: Polity, 2011), 159.

169. Smith et al., "From Protest to Agenda Building," 1400, https://doi.org/10.1353/sof.2001.0053.

170. Rove, "Republicans and the Tea Parties," April 16, 2009.

171. Reynolds, "Tax Day Becomes Protest Day."

172. "Tax Day; Tax Protests," *World News with Charles Gibson*, aired April 15, 2009, on ABC.

173. Sinker, "When the Left Went Teabagging."

174. Skocpol and Williamson, *The Tea Party and the Remaking of Republican Conservatism*, 131.

175. Richard Hofstadter, *The Age of Reform: From Bryan to F.D.R.*, repr., Vintage Book History (New York: Vintage Books, 1990).

176. Cynthia Burack and R. Claire Snyder-Hall, "Introduction: Right-Wing Populism and the Media," *New Political Science* 34, no. 4 (December 2012): 439–454, https://doi.org/10.1080/07393148.2012.729736.

177. Postel, "The Tea Party in Historical Perspective."

178. Stuart Hall, Chas Critcher, Tony Jefferson, John Clarke, and Brian Roberts, *Policing the Crisis: Mugging, the State and Law and Order* (London: Macmillan, 1978).

179. Jonathan Gray, "Texts That Sell: The Culture in Promotional Culture," in *Blowing up the Brand: Critical Perspectives on Promotional Culture*, ed. Melissa Aronczyk and Devon Powers, Popular Culture and Everyday Life, vol. 21 (New York: Peter Lang, 2010), 311; Sinker, "When the Left Went Teabagging"; Palin, "Why I'm Speaking at the Tea Party Convention"; "Countdown for October 21, 2010," *Countdown with Keith Olbermann*, aired October 21, 2010.

180. Al Eisele, "Pondering Timothy McVeigh's Lethal Legacy," *Huffington Post* (blog), April 19, 2010, http://www.huffingtonpost.com/al-eisele/pondering-timothy-mcveigh_b_543807.html.

181. "Palin, Tea Party Activists Target Reid," *Newsmax*, March 26, 2010, https://www.newsmax.com/InsideCover/marine-general-James-Conway/2010/03/26/id/354001/.

182. Andie Coller and Daniel Libit, "Conservatives Use Liberal Playbook," *Politico*, September 18, 2009, http://www.politico.com/news/stories/0909/27285.html.

183. Reynolds, "Tax Day Becomes Protest Day."

184. Ibid.

185. "Policing the Net: Internet's Role in Tea Party Protests," *The O'Reilly Factor*, aired April 15, 2009, on Fox News.

186. Paul Krugman, "Tea Parties Forever," *New York Times*, April 13, 2009, sec. A, http://www.nytimes.com/2009/04/13/opinion/13krugman.html.

187. "Anger on Tax Day; President Obama Prepares to Visit Mexico," *Campbell Brown: No Bias, No Bull*, aired April 15, 2009, on CNN.

188. Frank, "Here Comes the Plastic Pitchforks"; "Countdown for April 15, 2009"; Skocpol and Williamson, *The Tea Party and the Remaking of Republican Conservatism*; Parker and Barreto, *Change They Can't Believe In*; Graham, "Sarah Palin Tea Party Convention Speech."

189. "Countdown for April 14, 2009."

190. Rove, "Republicans and the Tea Parties."

191. Palin, "Why I'm Speaking at the Tea Party Convention."

192. Reynolds, "Tax Day Becomes Protest Day."

193. Oren Dorrell, "Tax Revolt a Recipe for Tea Parties; Nationwide Protests over Government Spending," *USA Today*, April 13, 2009, sec. News.

194. Weaver and Scacco, "Revisiting the Protest Paradigm," 61–84.

195. Gitlin, *The Whole World Is Watching*, 284.

196. Kenneth T. Andrews and Neal Caren, "Making the News: Movement Organizations, Media Attention, and the Public Agenda," *American Sociological Review* 75, no. 6 (December 2010): 841–866, https://doi.org/10.1177/0003122410386689.

197. Sean J. Savage, "To Purge or Not to Purge: Hamlet Harry and the Dixiecrats, 1948–1952," *Presidential Studies Quarterly* 27, no. 4 (1997): 773–790.

198. Joseph A. Schlesinger, "The New American Political Party," *The American Political Science Review* 79, no. 4 (1985): 1152–1169.

199. Marty Cohen et al., *The Party Decides: Presidential Nominations before and after Reform*, Chicago Studies in American Politics (Chicago: University of Chicago Press, 2008).

200. J. David Gillespie, *Challengers to Duopoly: Why Third Parties Matter in American Two-Party Politics*, 1st ed, (Columbia: University of South Carolina Press, 2012); the nineteenth-century Anti-Masonic Party was the first American political party to create a system of quadrennial caucuses and a national convention to nominate a presidential candidate. Thereafter, the GOP and the Democratic Party followed suit. National conventions continue to function as major national media and publicity events for both parties.

201. J. David Gillespie, *Politics at the Periphery: Third Parties in Two-Party America* (Columbia: University of South Carolina Press, 1993), 24.

202. "Tempest in a Tea Party: Tea Party Anger."

203. Pauline Arrillaga, "Enraged to Engaged: Tea Party Backers Explain Why," *Newsmax*, June 19, 2010, http://www.newsmax.com/InsideCover/US-Tea-Party-Enduring/2010/06/19/id/362461.

204. "Obama Slams Tea Party 'Core' as Fringe Radicals, Birthers," *Newsmax*, March 30, 2010, https://www.newsmax.com/headline/deborchgrave-pakistan-kayani-taliban/2010/03/30/id/354233/.

205. "Tea Party Shaping Republican Party, Fall Faceoffs," *Newsmax*, June 12, 2010, http://www.newsmax.com/Newsfront/tea-party-fall-elections/2010/06/12/id/361804.

206. Kate Zernike, "With Tax Day as Theme, Tea Party Groups Demonstrate," *New York Times*, April 15, 2010, http://www.nytimes.com/2010/04/16/us/politics/16rallies.html.

207. Medea Benjamin, "Peace Activists Extend an Olive Branch to the Tea Party to Talk about War," *Huffington Post* (blog), April 13, 2010, https://www.huffingtonpost.com/medea-benjamin/peace-activists-extend-an_b_535772.html.

208. Kathy Kiely, "'Tea Party' Candidates Not Toning It Down; Some in GOP Getting Concerned," *USA Today*, July 12, 2010, http://usatoday30.usatoday.com/news/politics/2010-07-11-unvarnished_N.htm.

209. Robert B. Reich, "The Necessity of Obamanomics," *Wall Street Journal*, February 5, 2010, http://www.wsj.com/articles/SB10001424052748704022804575041751435808716.

210. Kyra Phillips, "Volcano Cancels Flights; Zero Tolerance Gone Too Far?; Job Outlook for New Grads," *CNN Newsroom*, aired April 16, 2010, on CNN.

211. Brad O'Leary, "Tea Party Endorsement Key in November Elections," *Newsmax*, April 13, 2010, https://www.newsmax.com/us/greece-greek-sovereigndebt-crisis/2010/04/13/id/355593/.

212. Kate Zernike and Megan Thee-Brenan, "Discontent's Demography: Who Backs the Tea Party," *New York Times*, April 15, 2010.

213. Reynolds, "Tax Day Becomes Protest Day."

214. Shayndi Raice, "Battle for GOP Ballot Slots," *Wall Street Journal*, June 18, 2010, http://www.wsj.com/articles/SB10001424052748703650604575312830738572058.

215. Ralph Hallow, "N. Dakota GOP Wants 'Tea Party' Energy," *Newsmax*, February 5, 2010, http://www.newsmax.com/Politics/N-Dakota-GOP-Wants-TeaParty/2010/02/05/id/349066/.

216. "Interview with Jon Stewart."

217. Grim, "Cornyn: Teabaggers Forming Third Party a Danger to GOP"; Jeff Zeleny, "G.O.P. Confidence Tested by Fears of Searing Divisions," *The New York Times on the Web*, April 13, 2010; Peter Katel, "Tea Party Movement," *CQ Researcher by CQ Press*, March 19, 2010, http://library.cqpress.com/cqresearcher/cqresrre2010031900.

218. Jordan M. Ragusa and Anthony Gaspar, "Where's the Tea Party? An Examination of the Tea Party's Voting Behavior in the House of Representatives," *Political Research Quarterly* 69, no. 2 (2016): 361–372.

219. Leon V. Sigal, "Sources Make the News," in *Reading the News*, ed. Robert Karl Manoff and Michael Schudson (New York: Pantheon Books, 1986), 33.

220. Gitlin, *The Whole World Is Watching*.

221. Ibid.

222. For example, see Simon Cottle, "Reporting Demonstrations: The Changing Media Politics of Dissent," *Media, Culture and Society* 30, no. 6 (November 2008): 853–872, https://doi.org/10.1177/0163443708096097.

223. Jürgen Gerhards and Dieter Rucht, "Mesomobilization: Organizing and Framing in Two Protest Campaigns in West Germany," *American Journal of Sociology* 98, no. 3 (November 1992): 582, https://doi.org/10.1086/230049.

224. Kate Zernike, "Convention Is Trying to Harness Tea Party Spirit," *New York Times*, February 6, 2010, http://www.nytimes.com/2010/02/06/us/politics/06teaparty.html.

225. Mark Leibovich, "Sarah Palin, Vocal and Ready...but for What?" *New York Times*, February 6, 2010, sec. A.

226. Margaret Scammell, "Political Brands and Consumer Citizens: The Rebranding of Tony Blair," *Annals of the American Academy of Political and Social Science* 611 (2007): 190.

227. "Countdown for April 15, 2009."

CHAPTER 3

1. Jonathan Weiler, "Why the Tea Party Is a Fraud," *Huffington Post* (blog), April 15, 2010, http://www.huffingtonpost.com/jonathan-weiler/why-the-tea-party-is-a-fr_b_539550.html.

2. Ben Stein, "When a Cure Fights Itself," *Wall Street Journal*, April 12, 2009.

3. Joel Richard Paul, "Which Tea Party?" *Huffington Post* (blog), July 16, 2010, http://www.huffingtonpost.com/joel-richard-paul/which-tea-party_b_648995.html.

4. Theda Skocpol and Vanessa Williamson, *The Tea Party and the Remaking of Republican Conservatism* (New York: Oxford University Press, 2012), 67.

5. Ibid.

6. Jill Lepore, *The Whites of Their Eyes: The Tea Party's Revolution and the Battle over American History* (Princeton: Princeton University Press, 2010), 7.

7. "Rick Santelli and the 'Rant of the Year,'" video, http://www.youtube.com/watch?v=bEZB4taSEoA.

8. Jacob S. Rugh and Douglass S. Massey, "Racial Segregation and the American Foreclosure Crisis," *American Sociological Review* 75, no. 5 (2010): 629. Rugh and Massey used the term "Hispanic" in their study, rather than "Latino" or nationality-specific categories.

9. Tea partiers regularly deployed "us vs. them" rhetoric. For example, one tea partier echoed the NRA slogan by stating, "They can have my country when they pry it from my cold, dead fingers" ("Patrick Swayze dies; Who killed Yale student?," *Campbell Brown: No Bias, No Bull*, aired September 14, 2009, on CNN.).

10. Naomi Klein, *No Logo: Taking Aim at the Brand Bullies*, (New York: Picador, 2000), xvii.

11. Brendan Nyhan, "How Much Are Tea Party Candidates Hurting the GOP?" *Huffington Post* (blog), October 21, 2010, http://www.huffingtonpost.com/brendan-nyhan/how-much-are-tea-party-ca_b_772072.html.

12. Martin Gilens, *Why Americans Hate Welfare: Race, Media, and the Politics of Antipoverty Policy* (Chicago: University of Chicago Press, 1999); Donald R. Kinder and Lynn M. Sanders, *Divided by Color: Racial Politics and Democratic Ideals*, American Politics and Political Economy (Chicago: University of Chicago Press, 1996).

13. Thomas B. Edsall and Mary D. Edsall, *Chain Reaction: The Impact of Race, Rights, and Taxes on American Politics* (New York: W.W. Norton & Company, 1992), 3.

14. Ibid., 19.

15. This number on welfare spending excludes healthcare funding, which comprises a significant portion of the federal budget. See Center for Budget and Policy Priorities (October 4, 2017), *Policy Basics: Where Do Our Federal Tax Dollars Go?* Retrieved from https://www.cbpp.org/research/federal-budget/policy-basics-where-do-our-federal-tax-dollars-go.

16. "*Why Americans Hate Welfare: Race, Media, and the Politics of Antipoverty Policy*."

17. Rick Perlstein, "Exclusive: Lee Atwater's Infamous 1981 Interview on the Southern Strategy," *The Nation*, November 13, 2012, https://www.thenation.com/article/exclusive-lee-atwaters-infamous-1981-interview-southern-strategy/.

18. Bob Cesca, "Southern Strategist Sarah Palin Denies the Southern Strategy," *Huffington Post* (blog), July 14, 2010, http://www.huffingtonpost.com/bob-cesca/southern-strategist-sarah_b_646554.html.

19. "Tax Day Tea Party Rallies; Volcano Disrupts Air Travel," *Campbell Brown*, April 15, 2010.

20. Katherine Bell, "'A Delicious Way to Help Save Lives': Race, Commodification, and Celebrity in Product (RED)," *Journal of International and Intercultural Communication* 4, no. 3 (August 2011): 163–180, https://doi.org/10.1080/17513057.2011.569972.

21. Michael A. Messner and Jeffrey Montez de Oca, "The Male Consumer as Loser: Beer and Liquor Ads in Mega Sports Media Events," *Signs: Journal of Women in Culture and Society* 30, no. 3 (March 2005): 1879–1909, https://doi.org/10.1086/427523; David Marsh and Paul Fawcett, "Branding, Politics and Democracy," *Policy Studies* 32, no. 5 (September 2011): 515–530, https://doi.org/10.1080/01442872.2011.586498.

22. Sylvia M. Chan-Olmsted and Jiyoung Cha, "Branding Television News in a Multichannel Environment: An Exploratory Study of Network News Brand Personality," *International Journal on Media Management* 9, no. 4 (November 13, 2007): 135–150, https://doi.org/10.1080/14241270701632688.

23. Hélène de Burgh-Woodman and Jan Brace-Govan, "We Do Not Live to Buy: Why Subcultures Are Different from Brand Communities and the Meaning for Marketing Discourse," *International Journal of Sociology and Social Policy* 27, nos. 5–6 (June 26, 2007): 193–207, https://doi.org/10.1108/01443330710757230.

24. Helmut Schneider, "Branding in Politics, Manifestations, Relevance and Identity-Oriented Management," *Journal of Political Marketing* 3, no. 3 (October 6, 2004): 41–67, https://doi.org/10.1300/J199v03n03_03.

25. Kathleen Kuehn, "Compassionate Consumption: Branding Africa through Product RED," *Democratic Communique* 23, no. 2 (2011): 23.

26. "Yes, We Can Change," January 26, 2008, http://www.cnn.com/2008/POLITICS/01/26/obama.transcript/index.html.

27. Stefanie Balogh, "Hillary Fights on for 'Sisters,'" *Hobart Mercury*, May 10, 2008.

28. Emily Friedman, "Can Clinton's Emotions Get the Best of Her?" ABC News, January 7, 2008, http://abcnews.go.com/Politics/Vote2008/story?id=4097786&page=1#.T2gW_Y7RBe8; Sara Stewart, "Notes from the Cracked Ceiling," *New York Post*, January 10, 2010, http://www.nypost.com/p/news/opinion/books/notes_from_the_cracked_ceiling_XwWlyyjvbstkzIM8IT8JHK.

29. Kate Phillips, "Clinton Touts White Support," *New York Times*, *The Caucus* (blog), May 8, 2008, https://thecaucus.blogs.nytimes.com/2008/05/08/clinton-touts-white-support/.

30. "Clinton Camp Says Obama Is Now 'The Black Candidate,'" *Huffington Post* (blog), January 27, 2008, http://www.huffingtonpost.com/2008/01/27/clinton-camp-says-obama-i_n_83451.html.

31. Drake Bennett, "Black Man vs. White Woman," *Boston Globe*, February 7, 2008, http://www.boston.com/bostonglobe/ideas/articles/2008/02/17/black_man_vs_white_woman/?page=full.

32. Anderson Cooper, "Fourth Democratic Debate," *New York Times*, July 24, 2007, http://www.nytimes.com/2007/07/24/us/politics/24transcript.html?_r=1&pagewanted=all.

33. Klein, *No Logo*; ibid., xxxi.

34. Ibid., xxiv.

35. Charlton D. McIlwain and Stephen M. Caliendo, *Race Appeal: How Candidates Invoke Race in U.S. Political Campaigns* (Philadelphia: Temple University Press, 2011), 121–122, emphasis in original.

36. Howard Kurtz, "For Clinton, a Matter of Fair Media," *Washington Post*, December 19, 2007, http://www.washingtonpost.com/wp-dyn/content/article/2007/12/18/AR2007121802184_pf.html.

37. Simon Jackman and Lynn Vavreck, "Primary Politics: Race, Gender, and Age in the 2008 Democratic Primary," *Journal of Elections, Public Opinion and Parties* 20, no. 2 (May 2010): 153–186, https://doi.org/10.1080/17457281003697156; ibid., 177.

38. Dick Morris and Eileen McGan, "The End of the Post-Racial Presidency," *DickMorris.Com* (blog), July 15, 2010, http://www.dickmorris.com/blog/the-end-of-the-post-racial-presidency/.

39. Ray Block Jr., "Backing Barack Because He's Black: Racially Motivated Voting in the 2008 Election: Racially Motivated Voting in 2008," *Social Science Quarterly* 92, no. 2 (June 2011): 424, https://doi.org/10.1111/j.1540-6237.2011.00776.x.

40. "McCain and Palin in Dayton, Ohio," *New York Times*, August 29, 2008, http://www.nytimes.com/2008/08/29/us/politics/29text-palin.html.

41. Khadijah White, "Michelle Obama: Becoming the (White) House-Wife," *Thirdspace: Journal of Feminist Theory and Culture* 10, no. 1 (2011), http://journals.sfu.ca/thirdspace/index.php/journal/article/view/white/434.

42. Laurie Ouellette, "Branding the Right: The Affective Economy of Sarah Palin," *Cinema Journal* 51, no. 4 (2012): 185, https://doi.org/10.1353/cj.2012.0076.

43. "McCain and Palin in Dayton, Ohio."

44. Toby Harnden, "John McCain 'Technology Illiterate' Doesn't Email or Use Internet," *The Telegraph*, July 13, 2008, http://www.telegraph.co.uk/news/newstopics/uselection2008/johnmccain/2403704/John-McCain-technology-illiterate-doesnt-email-or-use-internet.html.

45. "Barack Obama and John McCain Begin the Search for Running Mates," *Beltway Boys*, aired May 27, 2008, http://www.foxnews.com/story/0,2933,358785,00.html.

46. Ari Berman, "Smearing Obama," *The Nation*, March 13, 2008, http://www.thenation.com/article/smearing-obama/.

47. "Chris Matthews on Hillary Clinton and Rudy Giuliani," *Media Matters*, December 18, 2007, http://mediamatters.org/research/200712180005?f=s_search.

48. Dodai Stewart, "Chris Matthews Has a Sexist History with Hillary Clinton," *Jezebel* (blog), January 15, 2008, http://jezebel.com/345237/chris-matthews-has-a-sexist-history-with-hillary-clinton.

49. Michael Calderone, "Chris Matthews Sorry for 'Sexist' Comments," *Politico*, January 17, 2008, http://www.politico.com/story/2008/01/chris-matthews-sorry-for-sexist-comments-007961.

50. Ibid.

51. Imani Perry, *More Beautiful and More Terrible: The Embrace and Transcendence of Racial Inequality in the United States* (New York: New York University Press, 2011), 2.

52. Dave McKinney and Abdon Pallasch, "A Dream Fulfilled," *Chicago Sun-Times*, November 5, 2008.

53. Kevin Merida, "America's History Gives Way to Its Future," *Washington Post*, November 5, 2008, http://www.washingtonpost.com/wp-dyn/content/ article/2008/11/05/AR2008110500148.html.

54. "Washington Post's Nia-Malika Henderson, Huffington Post's Howard Fineman, CNN's Gloria Borger, Newsweek's Andrew Sullivan Speak about Gay Marriage, Romney's Bullying, Nixon," *The Chris Matthews Show*, aired May 13, 2012, on CNN.

55. Jonathan Freedland, "Magical Spell That Will Open a New American Era," *The Guardian*, January 19, 2009, https://www.theguardian.com/world/2009/jan/20/ barack-obama-inauguration.

56. Klein, *No Logo*, xxiv.

57. Glenn Harlan Reynolds, "Tax Day Becomes Protest Day," *Wall Street Journal*, April 15, 2009, http://www.wsj.com/articles/SB123975867505519363.

58. Ryan Grim, "Cornyn: Teabaggers Forming Third Party a Danger to GOP," *Huffington Post* (blog), April 4, 2010, http://www.huffingtonpost. com/2010/02/02/cornyn-teabaggers-forming_n_446417.html.

59. Daniel Sinker, "When the Left Went Teabagging: As You Chuckle at the Right's Newfound Activism, Don't Forget That the Left Sucked Balls for Years," *Huffington Post* (blog), April 17, 2009, http://www.huffingtonpost.com/daniel-sinker/when-the-left-went-teabag_b_188329.html.

60. Liz Sidoti, "Sarah Palin Tea Party Convention Speech: Activists Can Hardly Wait," *Huffington Post* (blog), February 6, 2010[http://www.huffingtonpost. com/2010/02/06/sarah-palin-tea-party-con_n_452153.html], Archived at https://web.archive.org/web/20100212013223/http://www.huffingtonpost. com:80/2010/02/06/sarah-palin-tea-party-con_n_452153.html;.

61. "Interview with Jon Stewart," *The O'Reilly Factor*, aired February 3, 2010, on Fox News.

62. Paul Krugman, "Tea Parties Forever," *New York Times*, sec. A, April 13, 2009, http://www.nytimes.com/2009/04/13/opinion/13krugman.html.

63. Pauline Arrillaga, "Enraged to Engaged: Tea Party Backers Explain Why," *Newsmax*, June 19, 2010, http://www.newsmax.com/InsideCover/US-Tea-Party-Enduring/2010/06/19/id/362461.

64. Naftali Bendavid, "Currents: They Don't Make Populism in the U.S. Like They Used To," *Wall Street Journal*, April 17, 2009, http://www.wsj.com/articles/ SB123992058646826949; Dan Weil, "Tea Parties Rally Around Nation on Tax Day, Vowing Independence From Major Parties," *Newsmax*, April 15, 2010, http://www.newsmax.com/Headline/tea-party-tax-day/2010/04/15/id/355828; Juan Williams, "Tea Party Anger Reflects Mainstream Concerns," *Wall Street Journal*, April 2, 2010; Kate Zernike and Megan Thee-Brenan, "Discontent's Demography: Who Backs the Tea Party," *New York Times*, April 15, 2010.

65. Gail Collins, "Celebrating the Joys of April 15," *New York Times*, April 15, 2010, sec. A.

66. Reynolds, "Tax Day Becomes Protest Day."

67. "Tea Party Convention," *The O'Reilly Factor*, aired February 5, 2010, on Fox News.

68. Francisco Panizza, *Populism and the Mirror of Democracy* (London: Verso, 2005), 11.

69. Kathleen Hall Jamieson and Joseph N. Cappella, *Echo Chamber: Rush Limbaugh and the Conservative Media Establishment* (New York: Oxford University Press, 2008).

70. John Gabriel, *Whitewash: Racialized Politics and the Media* (London; New York: Routledge, 1998); Tali Mendelberg, *The Race Card: Campaign Strategy, Implicit Messages, and the Norm of Equality* (Princeton: Princeton University Press, 2001); Michael Omi and Howard Winant, *Racial Formation in the United States: From the 1960s to the 1990s*, 2nd ed. (New York: Routledge, 1994).

71. Jennie Phillips, "Constructing a Televisual Class: Newsmagazines and Social Class," in *Class and News*, ed. Don Heider (Lanham, MD: Rowman & Littlefield, 2004), 146.

72. Martin Gilens, "Poor People in the News: Images from the Journalistic Subconscious," in *Class and News*, ed. Don Heider (Lanham, MD: Rowman & Littlefield, 2004), 44–60.

73. Herbert J. Gans, *Deciding What's News: A Study of CBS Evening News, NBC Nightly News, Newsweek, and Time*, 1st ed. (New York: Pantheon Books, 1979), 24.

74. Gans, *Deciding What's News*, 24.

75. Deepa Kumar, "Media, Class and Power: Debunking the Myth of a Classless Society," in *Class and News*, ed. Don Heider (Lanham, MD: Rowman & Littlefield, 2004), 6.

76. Ibid., 17.

77. J. H. Newton et al., "Picturing Class: Mining the Field of Front-Page Photographs for Keys to Accidental Communities of Memory," in *Class and News*, ed. Don Heider (Lanham, MD: Rowman & Littlefield, 2004), 61–84. Deepa Kumar ("Media, Class and Power") argues that while lifestyle, occupational status, or income can be indicators of class, American society is in fact divided into a "capitalist class" (people who own or control a means of production), a "middle class" (people who have some autonomy and control over their work, but depend on the capitalist class), and the "working class" (people who have little or no control over their work or its conditions).

78. Don Heider and Koji Fuse, "Class and Local TV News," in *Class and News*, ed. Don Heider (Lanham, MD: Rowman & Littlefield, 2004), 87–108.

79. De Burgh-Woodman and Brace-Govan, "We Do Not Live to Buy."

80. Messner and Montez de Oca, "The Male Consumer as Loser."

81. Josh Greenberg and Graham Knight, "Framing Sweatshops: Nike, Global Production, and the American News Media," *Communication and Critical/Cultural Studies* 1, no. 2 (June 2004): 151–175, https://doi.org/10.1080/147914204 10001685368.

82. Herbert Gans explains that the media historically used the term "Middle America" to refer to President Nixon's conservative working- and middle-class constituency. It later "became a quasi-political term to describe white ethnics who opposed racial-integration policies" (*Deciding What's News*, 24).

83. Norman Podhoretz, "In Defense of Sarah Palin," *Wall Street Journal*, March 29, 2010, http://www.wsj.com/articles/SB10001424052748703909804575 1237 73804984924.

84. "Anger on Tax Day; President Obama Prepares to Visit Mexico," *Campbell Brown: No Bias, No Bull*, aired April 15, 2009, on CNN, http://www.cnn.com/ TRANSCRIPTS/0904/15/ec.01.html.

85. "Talking Points Memo and Top Story," *The O'Reilly Factor*, aired April 15, 2009, on Fox News.

86. Sarah Palin, "Why I'm Speaking at the Tea Party Convention," *USA Today*, March 3, 2010.

87. "Talking Points Memo and Top Story," *The O'Reilly Factor*, aired September 14, 2009, Fox News; "Obama Administration Apologizes," *Campbell Brown*, aired July 21, 2010, CNN.

88. Kate Zernike, "Tea Party Supporters Doing Fine, but Angry Nonetheless," *New York Times*, April 17, 2010, http://www.nytimes.com/2010/04/18/weekinreview/18zernike.html?pagewanted=all; "Countdown for April 17, 2009," *Countdown with Keith Olbermann*, aired April 17, 2009, on MSNBC.

89. "Talking Points Memo and Top Story," aired April 15, 2009.

90. Andy Ostroy, "Tea Parties: GOP Once Again Manipulating the Average Joe," Huffington Post (blog), April 16, 2009, http://www.huffingtonpost.com/andy-ostroy/tea-parties-gop-once-agai_b_187750.html emphasis in original.

91. Paul, "Which Tea Party?"

92. "Talking Points Memo and Top Story," aired September 14, 2009.

93. Arrillaga, "Enraged to Engaged."

94. "Tempest in a Tea Party: Tea Party Anger," World News with Diane Sawyer, aired February 5, 2010, on ABC.

95. Williams, "Tea Party Anger Reflects Mainstream Concerns."

96. Kate Zernike and Megan Thee-Brenan, "Poll Finds Tea Party Backers Wealthier and More Educated," New York Times, April 14, 2010, http://www.nytimes.com/2010/04/15/us/politics/15poll.html?_r=2.

97. "Countdown for April 16, 2009," Countdown with Keith Olbermann, aired April 16, 2009, on MSNBC; "Countdown for April 17, 2009," Countdown with Keith Olbermann, aired April 17, 2009, on MSNBC; "Countdown for April 15, 2010," Countdown with Keith Olbermann, aired April 15, 2010, on MSNBC.

98. Arianna Huffington, "Tea and Empathy: The Connection between High Unemployment, Record Foreclosures, and Right Wing Rage," Huffington Post (blog), June 15, 2010, http://www.huffingtonpost.com/arianna-huffington/tea-and-empathy-the-conne_b_539445.html.

99. Jerry Bowyer, "Pennsylvania's Tea Party: Brewing for Years," *Wall Street Journal*, April 24, 2010, http://www.wsj.com/articles/SB1000142405270230419800457517238336859968.

100. Dan Weil, "Poll: Tea Partyers Wealthier, More Educated than Most," *Newsmax*, April 15, 2010, https://www.newsmax.com/InsideCover/barack-Obama-mocks-Tax/2010/04/15/id/355869/.

101. "Talking Points Memo and Top Story," *The O'Reilly Factor*, aired April 16, 2010, on Fox News.

102. "Talking Points Memo and Top Story," *The O'Reilly Factor*, aired October 20, 2010, on Fox News.

103. CNN and ABC were the only news outlets that did not refer to the Tea Party as "populist."

104. Panizza, *Populism and the Mirror of Democracy*, 3.

105. Michael Kazin, *The Populist Persuasion: An American History*, rev. ed (Ithaca: Cornell University Press, 1998), 2.

106. J. David Gillespie, *Challengers to Duopoly: Why Third Parties Matter in American Two-Party Politics*, 1st ed. (Columbia: University of South Carolina Press, 2012), 72; Carol A. Horton, *Race and the Making of American Liberalism* (Oxford; New York: Oxford University Press, 2005).

107. Elisabeth R. Gerber, *The Populist Paradox: Interest Group Influence and the Promise of Direct Legislation* (Princeton: Princeton University Press, 1999).

108. Bendavid, "Currents."

109. Ronald P. Formisano, *The Tea Party: A Brief History* (Baltimore: Johns Hopkins University Press, 2012), 18.

110. David Brooks, "No, It's Not about Race," *New York Times*, September 19, 2009, http://www.nytimes.com/2009/09/18/opinion/18brooks.html; "Is Tea Party Taking over GOP?; Aiming for a Clean Future; Hard Hitting Poli-Tics," *Parker Spitzer*, aired October 19, 2010, on CNN.

111. Rich Benjamin, "Yes, I Love Taxes; Call Me Old-Fashioned, but I Think It's Unpatriotic to Demonize the Funding of Our Government," *USA Today*, April 15, 2010, http://www.pressreader.com/usa/usa-today-us-edition/20100415/283815734820719.

112. Les Leopold, "The Tea Party: Economic Populists or Wall Street Toadies?" *Huffington Post* (blog), February 2, 2010, http://www.huffingtonpost.com/les-leopold/the-tea-party-economic-po_b_445603.html.

113. Daniel Cluchey, "The Price of Tea," *Huffington Post* (blog), October 20, 2010, http://www.huffingtonpost.com/daniel-cluchey/post_1085_b_767489.html.

114. Thomas Frank, "Here Comes the Plastic Pitchforks," *Wall Street Journal*, April 15, 2009, http://www.wsj.com/articles/SB123975925509119297.

115. Oren Dorrell, "Tax Revolt a Recipe for Tea Parties; Nationwide Protests over Government Spending," *USA Today*, April 13, 2009, sec. News.

116. Edsall and Edsall, *Chain Reaction*, 12.

117. "Patrick Swayze Dies; Who Killed Yale Student?" *Campbell Brown: No Bias, No Bull*, aired September 14, 2009, on CNN.

118. Ostroy, "Tea Parties."

119. Fox News made one mention of tea partiers as "average, middle-class American stakeholders and people like Sarah Palin" ("Biden weighs in on Palin's popularity," *The O'Reilly Factor*, aired April 23, 2010, on Fox News).

120. "Countdown for April 16, 2009," *Countdown with Keith Olbermann*, aired April 16, 2009, on MSNBC.

121. Kinder and Sanders, *Divided by Color*; Gilens, *Why Americans Hate Welfare*.

122. Robin R. Means Coleman, *African American Viewers and the Black Situation Comedy: Situating Racial Humor*, Garland Studies on African American History and Culture (New York: Garland Publishing, 2000).

123. Glenn C. Loury, *The Anatomy of Racial Inequality* (Cambridge, MA: Harvard University Press, 2002), 58.

124. Herman Gray, "Subject(Ed) to Recognition," *American Quarterly* 65, no. 4 (2013): 469–471, https://doi.org/10.1353/aq.2013.0058.

125. Ibid., 480, 475; Eduardo Bonilla-Silva, *Racism without Racists: Color-Blind Racism and the Persistence of Racial Inequality in the United States* (Lanham, MD: Rowman & Littlefield, 2006); Robert M. Entman and Andrew Rojecki, *The Black Image in the White Mind* (Chicago: University of Chicago Press, 2000); Oscar H. Gandy, *Communication and Race: A Structural Perspective*, Communication and Critique (London: Arnold; New York: Oxford University Press, 1998); Laura Mulvey, "Visual Pleasure and Narrative Cinema," *Screen* 16, no. 3 (1975): 6; Teun A. Van Dijk, "Power and the News Media," *Political Communication in Action* (1996): 9–36.

126. Stuart Hall, "Encoding/Decoding," in *Media and Cultural Studies: Keyworks*, ed. Meenakshi Gigi Durham and Douglas Kellner, rev. ed., Keyworks in Cultural Studies 2 (Malden, MA: Blackwell, 2006), 167.

127. Samuel R. Sommers and Michael I. Norton, "Lay Theories about White Racists: What Constitutes Racism (and What Doesn't)." *Group Processes and Intergroup Relations* 9, no. 1 (2006): 131.

128. Chris Cillizza, "Tea Partiers: Where Do They Live?" *Washington Post*, April 21, 2010, http://voices.washingtonpost.com/thefix/republican-party/tea-parties-where-they-live.html.

129. John L. Jackson, *Racial Paranoia: The Unintended Consequences of Political Correctness*, paperback ed. (New York: Basic Civitas Books, 2010).

130. Tali Mendelberg and John Oleske, "Race and Public Deliberation," *Political Communication* 17, no. 2 (April 2000): 173, https://doi.org/10.1080/105846000198468. In her historical study of explicit and implicit racial appeals in political messages, Tali Mendelberg, in *The Race Card*, found that "the enormous shift in public norms of racial discourse . . . created a near-universal tendency to self-censor. Some people censor themselves because they aspire to be egalitarian, others because they wish to conform to the social pressure of norms of discourse. Implicit appeals are more effective than explicit appeals because they avoid the conscious perception that they derogate African Americans and thus circumvent self-censorship" (26). Importantly, Mendelberg's study also showed that implicitly racial messages—which draw on rhetorical symbols and use the language of individualism and local control to appeal and cohere "racially resentful white voters" (26)—are less effective when they are explicitly and publicly challenged.

131. Celia Lury, *Consumer Culture*, 2nd ed. (Cambridge: Polity, 2011), 114.

132. Anne McClintock, "Soft-Soaping Empire: Commodity Racism and Imperial Advertising," in *Travellers' Tales: Narratives of Home and Displacement*, ed. Jon Bird et al. (London: Routledge, 1994), 128.

133. M. M. Manring, *Slave in a Box: The Strange Career of Aunt Jemima*, The American South Series (Charlottesville: University Press of Virginia, 1998).

134. Manring, *Slave in a Box*, 2, 16.

135. Klein, *No Logo*, 6.

136. Lury, *Consumer Culture*, 116.

137. "Pinheads and Patriots: Snoop Dogg, Henry Garrett," *The O'Reilly Factor*, aired April 16, 2009, on Fox News.

138. Gilens, *Why Americans Hate Welfare*, 3.

139. Mendelberg, *The Race Card*, 96–97.

140. "Countdown for September 16, 2009," *Countdown with Keith Olbermann*, aired September 16, 2009, on MSNBC; "Countdown for October 18, 2010," *Countdown with Keith Olbermann*, aired October 18, 2010, on MSNBC.

141. Trey Ellis, "The Grave Danger of Conservative Blindness," *Huffington Post* (blog), October 21, 2010, http://www.huffingtonpost.com/trey-ellis/the-grave-danger-of-conse_b_771478.html.

142. "Who Killed Yale Student?; Are Critics of President Obama Racists?" *Campbell Brown: No Bias, No Bull*, aired September 16, 2009, on CNN.

143. "Countdown for September 16, 2009,"

144. Dave Zirin, "Sports and the Uncivil Society," *Huffington Post* (blog), September 18, 2009, http://www.huffingtonpost.com/dave-zirin/sports-and-the-uncivil-so_b_291789.html.

145. "Talking Points Memo and Top Story," aired September 14, 2009.

146. "Tax Day; Tax Protests," *World News with Charles Gibson*, April 15, 2009, on ABC.

147. "10 Most Offensive Tea Party Signs and Extensive Photo Coverage from Tax Day Protests," *Huffington Post* (blog), December 28, 2009, http://www.huffingtonpost.com/2009/04/16/10-most-offensive-tea-par_n_187554.html.

148. Scott Wong, "McConnell Ducks Questions about Tea Party Racism," *Politico*, July 18, 2010, http://www.politico.com/blogs/politicolive/0710/McConnell_ducks_questions_about_tea_party_racism.html?showall.

149. Kathy Kiely, "Squabbling Threatens to Ice 'Tea Party' Momentum," *USA Today*, February 5, 2010.

150. Patrick O'Connor and James Hohmann, "Dems Say Protestors Used N-Word," *Politico*, March 20, 2010, http://www.politico.com/news/stories/0310/34747.html; John Steele Gordon, "As Peaceful as a Tea Party," *Wall Street Journal*, April 2, 2010.

151. O'Connor and Hohmann, "Dems Say Protestors Used N-Word."

152. Kate Zernike, "Tea Party Crowd Rallies in Nevada with a Challenge to a Homegrown Democ-Rat," *New York Times*, March 28, 2010, sec. A.

153. Gordon, "As Peaceful as a Tea Party."

154. David Limbaugh, "It's Wrong to Call Obama a Post-Racial President," *Newsmax*, July 16, 2010, http://www.newsmax.com/Limbaugh/Obama—post—racial—race—card—Eric—Holder—FCC—New—Black—Panther—Party/2010/07/16/id/364852; "Talking Points Memo and Top Story," October 20, 2010; Matt Towery, "Tea Party Movement Confuses Both," *Newsmax*, April 15, 2010, http://www.newsmax.com/MattTowery/tea-party-John-Mc-Cain/2010/04/15/id/355810.

155. "Racial Charge; Tea Party and Race," *World News with Diane Sawyer*, aired July 13, 2010, on ABC, emphasis mine.

156. Deroy Murdock, "Note to NAACP: Tea Party Is NOT Racist," *Newsmax*, July 16, 2010, http://www.newsmax.com/Murdock/naacp—tea—party—racists—david—webb-/2010/07/16/id/364871.

157. "Countdown for July 14, 2010," *Countdown with Keith Olbermann*, aired July 14, 2010, on MSNBC.

158. "Talking Points Memo and Top Story," aired September 14, 2009.

159. Mayhill Fowler, "Mayhill Fowler: Tea Party Talk: Racism, Palin, and the Hostile Takeover of the Republican Party," *Huffington Post* (blog), July 19, 2010, http://www.huffingtonpost.com/mayhill-fowler/tea-party-talk-racism-pal_b_650795.html.

160. Patrick Jonsson, "Why 'Tea Party' Defenders Won't Let N-Word Claims Rest," *Christian Science Monitor*, April 28, 2010, http://www.csmonitor.com/USA/2010/0428/Why-tea-party-defenders-won-t-let-N-word-claims-rest.

161. Kenneth P. Vogel, "Tea Partiers Push Back after Bad Week," *Politico*, March 27, 2010, http://www.politico.com/news/stories/0310/35113.html.

162. Mark Meckler and Jenny Beth Martin, "On Being Labeled as 'Racist,'" *Politico*, July 14, 2010, http://www.politico.com/news/stories/0710/39745.html.

163. Ibid.

164. "Fridays with Geraldo," *The O'Reilly Factor*, aired July 15, 2010, on Fox News.

165. "Fridays with Geraldo."

166. Jonsson, "Why 'Tea Party' Defenders Won't Let N-Word Claims Rest."

167. Matt Bai, "When It's about Race, It's Probably about Age, Too," *New York Times*, July 18, 2010.

168. "Mark Williams, Tea Party Express Spokesman: NAACP Is Racist (VIDEO) (TRANSCRIPT)," *Huffington Post* (blog), July 14, 2010, https://www.huffingtonpost.com/2010/07/14/mark-williams-tea-party-express-naacp-racist_n_646989.html.

169. Charles Blow, "Dog Days of Obama," *New York Times*, July 17, 2010, http://www.nytimes.com/2010/07/17/opinion/17blow.html.

170. "Patrick Swayze Dies; Who Killed Yale Student?"; Nicholas Graham, "'Tea Party' Leader Melts Down on CNN: Obama Is an 'Indonesian Muslim Turned Welfare Thug,'" *Huffington Post* (blog), September 15, 2009, http://www.huffingtonpost.com/2009/09/15/tea-party-leader-melts-do_n_286933.html.

171. Joy-Ann Reid, "'Tea Partier' Mark Williams Writes 'Letter to Abe Lincoln'...from the 'Coloreds' **UPDATED**," *The Reid Report* (blog), July 14, 2010[http://blog.reidreport.com/2010/07/tea-partier-mark-williams-writes-open-letter-to-lincoln-from-the-coloreds], archived at http://wayback.archive-it.org/all/20100823023856/http://blog.reidreport.com/2010/07/tea-partier-mark-williams-writes-open-letter-to-lincoln-from-the-coloreds/.

172. Matt Finkelstein, "Tea Party Leader Mocks NAACP 'Coloreds' in Online Screed," *Political Correction*, July 15, 2010, http://politicalcorrection.org/print/blog/201007150012.

173. "Tea Party Leader Expelled for Racial Comments," *The O'Reilly Factor*, aired July 21, 2010, on Fox News; Michael A. Memoli and Kathleen Hennessey, "Tea Party Express Spokesman Resigns after Racist Blog Post," *Los Angeles Times*, July 24, 2010, http://articles.latimes.com/2010/jul/24/nation/la-na-tea-party-20100724.

174. Michael J.W. Stickings, *Snookered: Right-Wing Propaganda and the Truth about Shirley Sherrod*, *Huffington Post* (blog), July 21, 2010; updated May 25, 2011, https://www.huffingtonpost.com/michael-jw-stickings/snookered-right-wing-prop_b_654232.html

175. "Mark Williams, Tea Party Express Spokesman." While this exchange on CNN was reported and shared in *The Huffington Post*, it originally occurred on *The Situation Room with Wolf Blitzer*.

176. Bob Cesca, "Fooled Again by Breitbart and the Wingnut Right," *Huffington Post* (blog), July 21, 2010, http://www.huffingtonpost.com/bob-cesca/fooled-again-by-breitbart_b_654594.html.

177. "This Was about the NAACP," *USA Today*, July 23, 2010.

178. Kristi Keck, "Sherrod Fallout Twists White House Message from Rah-Rah to Race," *CNN Politics* (blog), July 25, 2010, http://www.cnn.com/2010/POLITICS/07/23/obama.race.message/.

179. "Impact," *The O'Reilly Factor*, aired September 18, 2009, on Fox News.

180. "This Week," *This Week*, aired July 25, 2010, on ABC.

181. "Talking Points Memo and Top Story," *The O'Reilly Factor*, aired July 22, 2010, on Fox News.

182. "Talking Points Memo and Top Story," *The O'Reilly Factor*, aired March 29, 2010, on Fox News.

183. "Impact," *The O'Reilly Factor*, aired September 18, 2009.

184. "Juan Williams Fired from NPR," *The O'Reilly Factor*, aired October 21, 2010, on Fox News.

185. "Talking Points Memo and Top Story," *The O'Reilly Factor*, aired July 23, 2010, on Fox News.

186. Perry, *More Beautiful and More Terrible*, 48.

187. Darrel Enck-Wanzer, "Barack Obama, the Tea Party, and the Threat of Race: On Racial Neoliberalism and Born Again Racism," *Communication, Culture and Critique* 4, no. 1 (March 2011): 24, https://doi.org/10.1111/j.1753-9137.2010.01090.x.

188. Eduardo Bonilla-Silva, *Racism without Racists: Color-Blind Racism and the Persistence of Racial Inequality in America*, 5th ed. (Lanham, MD: Rowman & Littlefield, 2017).

189. Enck-Wanzer, "Barack Obama, the Tea Party, and the Threat of Race," 26.

190. Bonilla-Silva, *Racism without Racists*; Jane H. Hill, *The Everyday Language of White Racism*, Blackwell Studies in Discourse and Culture 3 (Chichester; Malden, MA: Wiley-Blackwell, 2008).

191. "Tea Party Leader Expelled for Racial Comments," aired July 21, 2010.

192. Palin, "Why I'm Speaking at the Tea Party Convention."

193. Sinker, "When the Left Went Teabagging."

194. "Interview with Jon Stewart," aired February 3, 2010.

195. Linda Williams, *Playing the Race Card: Melodramas of Black and White from Uncle Tom to OJ Simpson* (Princeton: Princeton University Press, 2001).

196. bell hooks, *Reel to Real: Race, Sex, and Class at the Movies* (New York: Routledge, 1996).

197. Gray, "Subject(Ed) to Recognition," 461–462.

198. Mary E. Heath, "A Woman's World: How Afternoon Tea Defined and Hindered Victorian Middle Class Women," *Constructing the Past* 13, no. 1 (2012): 1.

199. "Making Hillary an Issue," *Frontline*, aired March 26, 1992, on PBS, http://www.pbs.org/wgbh/pages/frontline/shows/clinton/etc/03261992.html.

200. Kathleen Hall Jamieson, *Beyond the Double Bind: Women and Leadership* (New York: Oxford University Press, 1995).

201. I confined my examination of Tea Party women to stories that specifically mention the Tea Party. I did not examine stories unrelated to the Tea Party (for instance, the many news stories about the unplanned pregnancy of Sarah Palin's teenage daughter).

202. Maria Braden, *Women Politicians and the Media* (Lexington: University Press of Kentucky, 1996).

203. Daniel C. Reed, "Christine O'Donnell and the Delaware Senate Race," in *Key States, High Stakes*, ed. Charles S. Bulllock (Lanham, MD: Rowman & Littlefield, 2012), 30.

204. Associated Press, "Palin, Tea Party Activists Target Reid," *Newsmax*, March 26, 2010, https://www.newsmax.com/InsideCover/marine-general-James-Conway/2010/03/26/id/354001/; Kenneth P. Vogel, "Tea Party Nation Leaders Lash Out," *Politico*, January 30, 2010, http://www.politico.com/news/stories/0110/32255.html.

205. "Countdown for July 22, 2010," *Countdown with Keith Olbermann*, aired July 22, 2010, on MSNBC.

206. Jake Sherman, "Bachmann Forms Tea Party Caucus," *Politico*, July 16, 2010, http://www.politico.com/news/stories/0710/39848.html.

207. Susan Page, "Showdown in Nevada Winner Takes All?; Senate Race Will Show the Potency of Angry Voters and Tea Party," *USA Today*, October 21, 2010.

208. Jonathan Weisman, "U.S. News: Palin's Ground Game Spurs Campaign Buzz," *Wall Street Journal*, July 17, 2010.

209. Joel Turner and Scott Lasley, "Randslide: Tea Party Success in the Establishment's Backyard," in *Key States, High Stakes: Sarah Palin, the Tea Party, and the 2010 Elections* ed. Charles S. Bullock (Lanham, MD: Rowman & Littlefield, 2011), 79–90.

210. Quinnipiac University, "March 24, 2010-Tea Party Could Hurt GOP In Congressional Races, Quinnipiac University National Poll Finds; Dems Trail 2-Way Races, But Win if Tea Party Runs," March 24, 2010, https://poll.qu.edu/national/release-detail?ReleaseID=1436.

211. Kenneth P. Vogel, "Face of the Tea Party Is Female," *Politico*, March 26, 2010, http://www.politico.com/news/stories/0310/35094.html.

212. Skocpol and Williamson, *The Tea Party and the Remaking of Republican Conservatism*, 42; Tom Rosenstiel discusses the way journalists increasingly rely on surveys to shape, interpret, and organize political news stories. Kathleen Frankovic and Lawrence R. Jacobs and Robert Y. Shapiro also write about the influence of partisan bias and ideology upon contemporary public-opinion polls, survey questions, and the ways that poll findings are reported (Kathleen Frankovic, "Reporting 'the Polls' in 2004," *Public Opinion Quarterly* 69, no. 5 (2005): 682–697; Lawrence R. Jacobs and Robert Y. Shapiro, "Polling Politics, Media, and Election Campaigns," *Public Opinion Quarterly* 69, no. 5 (2005): 635–641.

213. Susan Page, "In Colorado, Reflections of an Anxious Electorate; Tea Party Jolts GOP; a Fight among Dems," *USA Today*, July 19, 2010.

214. Thomas Frank, "Conservatives and the Cult of Victimhood," *Wall Street Journal*, March 31, 2010, sec. Opinion, http://www.wsj.com/articles/SB1000142405270 2304739104575154170119046794; Page, "In Colorado, Reflections of an Anxious Electorate; Tea Party Jolts GOP; a Fight among Dems"; "Talking Points Memo and Top Story," aired April 16, 2010; "Countdown for July 22, 2010."

215. O'Reilly, "Talking Points Memo and Top Story," July 23, 2010.

216. "Countdown for April 17, 2009."

217. "On the Money; Financial News," *World News with Diane Sawyer*, ABC, April 14, 2010.

218. Mark Leibovich, "Sarah Palin, Vocal and Ready . . . but for What?" *New York Times*, February 6, 2010, sec. A.

219. Peter Bjelskou, *Branded Women in U.S. Television: When People Become Corporations*, Critical Studies in Television (Lanham, MD: Lexington Books, 2015), 4.

220. Vogel, "Tea Partiers Push Back after Bad Week."

221. "Countdown for April 15, 2010."

222. "Too Big to Fail Again?; NASA: End of the Final Frontier; Faith & Facts," *Campbell Brown: No Bias, No Bul*, aired April 14, 2010, on CNN.

223. "Talking Points Memo and Stop Story," aired April 16, 2010.

224. Dana Milbank, "I'm Declaring February a Palin-Free Month. Join Me!" *Washington Post*, January 21, 2011, http://www.washingtonpost.com/wp-dyn/content/article/2011/01/20/AR2011012004349.html.

225. Edward Morrissey, "Media Chase Palin, and Her Sway Grows," aired June 3, 2011, on CNN, http://www.cnn.com/2011/OPINION/06/03/morrissey.palin.tour.

226. Alex Brant-Zawadzki and Dawn Teo, "Anatomy of the Tea Party Movement: The Media," *Huffington Post* (blog), March 18, 2010, http://www.huffingtonpost.com/alex-brantzawadzki/anatomy-of-the-tea-party_b_380691.html.

227. Paul Bond, "Cable News' Sarah Palin Sickness," *Hollywood Reporter*, January 25, 2011, http://www.hollywoodreporter.com/news/cable-news-sarah-palin-sickness-75720.

228. Ouellette, "Branding the Right," 189.

229. "Countdown for February 5, 2010," *Countdown with Keith Olbermann*, aired February 5, 2010, on MSNBC; "Another Toyota Recall; New Orleans Celebrates Super Bowl Victory," *Campbell Brown*, aired February 8, 2010, on CNN.

230. Dan Weil, "Tea Partyers Split in Support of Palin, Paul," *Newsmax*, April 19, 2010, http://www.newsmax.com/InsideCover/palin-ron-paul-tea/2010/04/19/id/356202.

231. "Another Toyota Recall; New Orleans Celebrates Super Bowl Victory."

232. Jeff Zeleny, "Palin Wades into Republican Midterm Primaries," *New York Times*, July 18, 2010, http://www.nytimes.com/2010/07/18/us/politics/18palin.html.

233. Laurie Ouellette and Alison Hearn, eds., "Producing 'Reality': Branded Content, Branded Selves, Precarious Futures," in *A Companion to Reality Television* (Chichester: Wiley Blackwell, 2014), 451.

234. William Bunch, *The Backlash: Right-Wing Radicals, Hi-Def Hucksters, and Paranoid Politics in the Age of Obama* (New York: Harper, 2011).

235. Ouellette, "Branding the Right," 189.

236. Vogel, "Tea Party Nation Leaders Lash Out."

237. Associated Press, "Palin, Tea Party Activists Target Reid."

238. Weisman, "U.S. News."

239. Zeleny, "Palin Wades into Republican Midterm Primaries."

240. Vogel, "Face of the Tea Party Is Female."

241. Fowler, "Mayhill Fowler: Tea Party Talk."

242. Jamieson, *Beyond the Double Bind*, 176.

243. Kim L. Fridkin, Patrick J. Kenney, and Gina Serignese Woodall, "Bad for Men, Better for Women: The Impact of Stereotypes during Negative Campaigns," *Political Behavior* 31, no. 1 (March 2009): 53–77, https://doi.org/10.1007/s11109-008-9065-x.

244. Zeleny, "Palin Wades into Republican Midterm Primaries."

245. Carla L. Peterson, *Doers of the Word: African-American Women Speakers and Writers in the North (1830–1880)* (New Brunswick, NJ: Rutgers University Press, 1998).

246. Patricia Hill Collins, *Black Feminist Thought: Knowledge, Consciousness, and the Politics of Empowerment*, rev. 10th anniversary ed. (New York: Routledge, 2000); Patricia Hill Collins, *Black Sexual Politics: African Americans, Gender, and the New Racism*, Sociology Race and Ethnicity (New York: Routledge, 2006); Marian Meyers, *African American Women in the News: Gender, Race, and Class in Journalism* (New York: Routledge, Taylor & Francis Group, 2013).

247. White, "Michelle Obama."

248. Thavolia Glymph, *Out of the House of Bondage: The Transformation of the Plantation Household* (Cambridge; New York: Cambridge University Press, 2008), 12.

249. Vogel, "Face of the Tea Party Is Female."

250. Vogel, "Face of the Tea Party Is Female."

251. Michael Graham, *That's No Angry Mob, That's My Mom: Team Obama's Assault on Tea-Party, Talk-Radio Americans* (Washington, DC; New York: Regnery Publishing, 2010; distributed to the trade by Perseus Distribution, 2010).

252. David A. Patten, "Poll: Women Make Up Majority of Tea Party Ranks," *Newsmax*, March 29, 2010, https://www.newsmax.com/insidecover/eu-britain-people-heather/2010/03/29/id/354118/.

253. Frank Rich, "Welcome to Confederate History Month," *New York Times*, April 18, 2010.

254. Page, "Showdown in Nevada Winner Takes All."

255. Fowler, "Mayhill Fowler."

256. "New York Times/CBS News Poll: National Survey of Tea Party Supporters" (*The New York Times* and CBS News, April 5, 2010), http://documents.nytimes.com/new-york-timescbs-news-poll-national-survey-of-tea-party-supporters?ref=politics; "New York Times/CBS News Poll: National Survey of Tea Party Supporters"; Kate Zernike, "Secretive Republican Donors Are Planning Ahead," *New York Times*, October 20, 2010, http://www.nytimes.com/2010/10/20/us/politics/20koch.html. Survey methodology likely explains some of the differences in the Tea Party polls. The Quinnipiac poll targeted registered voters and asked them whether they were "part of the Tea Party movement" or had a "favorable opinion" of the Tea Party. The New York Times poll surveyed two distinct and generalizable samples of all Americans generally and people who identified as Tea Party supporters.

257. "*New York Times*/CBS News Poll."

258. Vogel, "Face of the Tea Party Is Female."

259. Weisman, "U.S. News."

260. Zeleny, "Palin Wades into Republican Midterm Primaries"; "Countdown for July 19, 2010," *Countdown with Keith Olbermann*, aired July 19, 2010, on MSNBC.

261. S. J. Parry-Giles and D. M. Blair, "The Rise of the Rhetorical First Lady: Politics, Gender Ideology, and Women's Voice, 1789–2002," *Rhetoric and Public Affairs* 5, no. 4 (2002): 565–599.

262. Jamieson, *Beyond the Double Bind*, 165.

263. R. Watson, "Madam President: Progress, Problems, and Prospects for 2008," *Journal of International Women's Studies* 8, no. 1 (2006): 78; Minita Sanghvi and Nancy Hodges, "Marketing the Female Politician: An Exploration of Gender and Appearance," *Journal of Marketing Management* 31, nos. 15–16 (October 13, 2015): 1676–1694, https://doi.org/10.1080/0267257X.2015.1074093; Danny Hayes and Jennifer L. Lawless, *Women on the Run: Gender, Media, and Political Campaigns in a Polarized Era* (New York: Cambridge University Press, 2016).

264. Leonie Huddy and Theresa Capelos, "Gender Stereotyping and Candidate Evaluation," in *The Social Psychology of Politics*, edited by Victor C. Ottati et al. (New York: Kluwer Academic/Plenum Publishers, 2002), 29; Mendelberg, *The Race Card*; Jamieson, *Beyond the Double Bind*.

265. Erika Falk, *Women for President: Media Bias in Nine Campaigns*, 2nd ed. (Urbana: University of Illinois Press, 2010); Caroline Heldman, Susan J. Carroll, and Stephanie Olson, "'She Brought Only a Skirt': Print Media Coverage of Elizabeth Dole's Bid for the Republican Presidential Nomination," *Political Communication* 22, no. 3 (July 2005): 315–335, https://doi.org/10.1080/10584600591006564; Mendelberg, *The Race Card*.

266. Hayes and Lawless, *Women on the Run*.

267. Kathleen A. Dolan, *When Does Gender Matter? Women Candidates and Gender Stereotypes in American Elections* (Oxford; New York: Oxford University Press, 2014); Nichole M. Bauer, "The Effects of Counterstereotypic Gender Strategies on Candidate Evaluations," *Political Psychology* 38, no. 2 (April 2017): 279–295, https://doi.org/10.1111/pops.12351.

268. Julie Dolan, Melissa M. Deckman, and Michele L. Swers, *Women and Politics: Paths to Power and Political Influence*, 2nd ed. (Boston: Longman, 2011); Bauer, "The Effects of Counterstereotypic Gender Strategies on Candidate Evaluations."

269. Erin C. Cassese and Mirya R. Holman, "Party and Gender Stereotypes in Campaign Attacks," *Political Behavior*, July 24, 2017, https://doi.org/10.1007/

s11109-017-9423-7; Tessa M. Ditonto, Allison J. Hamilton, and David P. Redlawsk, "Gender Stereotypes, Information Search, and Voting Behavior in Political Campaigns," *Political Behavior* 36, no. 2 (June 2014): 335–358, https://doi.org/10.1007/s11109-013-9232-6.
270. Sanghvi and Hodges, "Marketing the Female Politician."
271. "Impact," aired September 18, 2009.
272. "Another Toyota Recall; New Orleans Celebrates Super Bowl Victory."
273. Stephen Moore, "The Weekend Interview with Sharron Angle: Angling for Harry Reid," *Wall Street Journal*, July 17, 2010, http://www.wsj.com/articles/SB10001424052748704682604575369093396496532.
274. Vogel, "Face of the Tea Party Is Female."
275. Amy Kaplan, "Manifest Domesticity," *American Literature* 70, no. 3 (September 1998): 582, https://doi.org/10.2307/2902710.
276. Liesl Schillinger, "A Sorority of Three, and Counting," *New York Times*, April 18, 2010, sec. ST.
277. "Dare; Catch Phrase," *World News with Diane Sawyer*, ABC, October 20, 2010.
278. Theresa Carilli and Jane Campbell, eds., *Women and the Media: Diverse Perspectives* (Lanham, MD: University Press of America, 2005), 201.
279. Ibid., 209.
280. Jamieson, *Beyond the Double Bind*, 1995, 170.
281. Maureen Dowd, "Playing All the Angles," *New York Times*, October 17, 2010, sec. WK.
282. Blow, "Dog Days of Obama"; Fowler, "Mayhill Fowler"; Michael D. Shear, "Tea Party Candidates Part Ways on Foreign Policy," *New York Times*, October 22, 2010, sec. A; "Talking Points Memo and Top Story," July 22, 2010.
283. Schillinger, "A Sorority of Three, and Counting."
284. "Countdown for October 21, 2010," *Countdown with Keith Olbermann*, aired October 21, 2010, on MSNBC.
285. Moore, "The Weekend Interview with Sharron Angle."
286. Lori Montalbano-Phelps, "Performing Politics: Media Aesthetics for Women in Political Campaigns," in *Women and the Media: Diverse Perspectives*, ed. Theresa Carilli and Jane Campbell (Lanham, MD: University Press of America, 2005), 192.
287. Page, "Showdown in Nevada Winner Takes All"
288. "Howard Fineman on What Christine O'Donnell's Constitutional Ignorance Says about the Tea Party (VIDEO)," *Huffington Post* (blog), October 19, 2010, http://www.huffingtonpost.com/huff-tv/howard-fineman-christine-odonnell-constitution_b_769044.html; "Countdown for September 16, 2009," Countdown with Keith Olbermann, aired September 16, 2009, on MSNBC.
289. "Vote 2010; Feeling Blue," *World News Sunday*, ABC, October 17, 2010.
290. "Another Toyota Recall; New Orleans Celebrates Super Bowl Victory."
291. John LeBoutillier, "Searching for Mr. Conservative," *Newsmax*, March 29, 2010, http://www.newsmax.com/JohnLeboutillier/Palin-Romney-Bush-Obama/2010/03/29/id/354112.
292. Ben Smith, "Sarah Palin: Will She Do It?" *Politico*, July 14, 2010, https://www.politico.com/story/2010/07/sarah-palin-will-she-do-it-039708.
293. Zeleny, "Palin Wades into Republican Midterm Primaries."
294. "Is Tea Party Taking over GOP?; Aiming for a Clean Future; Hard Hitting Poli-Tics."
295. Ross Douthat, "No Mystique about Feminism," *New York Times*, June 14, 2010, sec. A.

296. Newsmax, "Sarah Palin and the Newer Feminism," *Newsmax*, November 2009, https://shop.newsmax.com/Product.aspx?ProductCode=Z-28-588.

297. Ryan Reilly, "TPM's Top Ten Quotes from Christine O'Donnell, the Woman Who's against Everything," *Talking Points Memo* (blog), September 16, 2010, http://talkingpointsmemo.com/muckraker/tpm-s-top-ten-quotes-from-christine-o-donnell-the-woman-who-s-against-everythinghttp://talkingpointsmemo.com/muckraker/tpm-s-top-ten-quotes-from-christine-o-donnell-the-woman-who-s-against-everything.

298. Sarah Posner, "'Frontier Feminist' the Right's Favorite in Nevada," Religion Dispatches, June 10, 2010, http://religiondispatches.org/frontier-feminist-the-rights-favorite-in-nevada.

299. Joan Marie Johnson, *Funding Feminism: Monied Women, Philanthropy, and the Women's Movement, 1870–1967*, Gender and American Culture (Chapel Hill: University of North Carolina Press, 2017), 47.

300. Astrid Henry, *Not My Mother's Sister: Generational Conflict and Third-Wave Feminism* (Bloomington and Indianapolis: Indiana University Press, 2004), 14.

301. Katie L. Gibson and Amy L. Heyse, "Depoliticizing Feminism: Frontier Mythology and Sarah Palin's 'The Rise of The Mama Grizzlies,'" *Western Journal of Communication* 78, no. 1 (January 2014): 97–117, https://doi.org/10.1080/10570314.2013.812744.

302. Mary Douglas Vavrus, *Postfeminist News: Political Women in Media Culture* (Albany: State University of New York Press, 2002), 173–178.

303. For a more in-depth discussion of how conservative women have engaged feminism to bolster a right-wing agenda, see Ronnee Schreiber, *Righting Feminism* (New York: Oxford University Press, 2008).

304. Angela McRobbie, "Post-feminism and Popular Culture," *Feminist Media Studies* 4, no. 3 (November 2004): 258, https://doi.org/10.1080/1468077042000309937; Mary Douglas Vavrus, *Postfeminist News: Political Women in Media Culture* (Albany: State University of New York Press, 2002), 173–178.

305. Susan J. Douglas, *Enlightened Sexism: The Seductive Message That Feminism's Work Is Done*, 1st ed. (New York: Times Books, 2010), 11; Jennyty: las e check the URL in the note. I got a "page not found" error when I clicked it.t went to an article on an Eric Cancer Coleman, "An Introduction to Feminisms in a Postfeminist Age," *Women's Studies Journal* 23, no. 2 (2009): 4.

306. Ronnee Schreiber, "Who Speaks for Women? Print Media Portrayals of Feminist and Conservative Women's Advocacy," *Political Communication* 27, no. 4 (October 29, 2010): 432–452, https://doi.org/10.1080/10584609.2010.516800.

307. Leibovich, "Sarah Palin, Vocal and Ready . . . but for What?"

308. Moore, "The Weekend Interview with Sharron Angle."

309. Ibid.

310. Vogel, "Face of the Tea Party Is Female."

311. Jamieson and Cappella, *Echo Chamber*, 18.

312. Vavrus, *Postfeminist News*, 119.

313. Douglas, *Enlightened Sexism*, 272.

314. "Dare; Catch Phrase."

315. "Countdown for October 22, 2010," *Countdown with Keith Olbermann*, aired October 22, 2010, on MSNBC.

316. Dowd, "Playing All the Angles."

317. Fowler, "Mayhill Fowler."

318. Eileen T. Walsh, "Representations of Race and Gender in Mainstream Media Coverage of the 2008 Democratic Primary," *Journal of African American Studies* 13, no. 2 (2009): 121–130.
319. Montalbano-Phelps, "Performing Politics," 192.
320. ABC did report on the way Tea Party women deployed the term "man up" during the midterm elections.
321. In "Masculine Republicans and Feminine Democrats," Nicholas J.G. Winter explains that people generally map gender ideologies onto the Republican and Democratic parties (609). Republicans are generally seen as more masculine and Democrats are generally seen as more feminine. Also, Winter found that "a candidate's party affiliation might influence voters' perceptions of his or her enactment of masculinity and femininity" (609). See Nicholas J.G. Winter, "Masculine Republicans and Feminine Democrats: Gender and Americans' Explicit and Implicit Images of the Political Parties," *Political Behavior* 32, no. 4 (2010): 587–618.
322. "Talking Points Memo and Top Story," October 20, 2010.
323. Karlyn Kohrs Campbell, "Agency: Promiscuous and Protean," *Communication and Critical/Cultural Studies* 2, no. 1 (March 2005): 4, https://doi.org/10.1080/1479142042000332134.
324. Douglas, *Enlightened Sexism*, 271.
325. Nicholas Winter, *Dangerous Frames: How Ideas about Race and Gender Shape Public Opinion* (Chicago: University Press of Chicago, 2008), 159–160, emphasis in original.
326. Here I borrow from Kimberlé Crenshaw's concept of "intersectional disempowerment," used to analyze the Clarence Thomas/Anita Hill hearings (Kimberlé Crenshaw, "Whose Story Is It, Anyway?: Feminist and Antiracist Appropriations of Anita Hill," in *Race-ing Justice, En-gendering Power: Essays on Anita Hill, Clarence Thomas, and the Construction of Social Reality*, ed. Toni Morrison [New York: Pantheon, 1992], 406).
327. Karen S. Johnson-Cartee, *News Narratives and News Framing: Constructing Political Reality*, Communication, Media, and Politics (Lanham, MD: Rowman & Littlefield, 2005), 167, emphasis in original.
328. Edsall and Edsall, *Chain Reaction*, 12–13.
329. Gans, *Deciding What's News*, 24.
330. "Talking Points Memo and Top Story," aired September 14, 2009.
331. United States Census Bureau, "State and County Quick Facts: USA," Census.gov, 2017, https://www.census.gov/quickfacts/fact/table/US/PST045217#.
332. "The Tea Party movement February 5–10th, 2010," CBS News/New York Times poll (February 11th, 2010, 6:30 pm EST) press release.
333. Ralina L. Joseph, "'Tyra Banks Is Fat': Reading (*Post* -)Racism and (*Post* -)Feminism in the New Millennium," *Critical Studies in Media Communication* 26, no. 3 (August 2009): 237–254, https://doi.org/10.1080/15295030903015096.
334. Ibid., 243.
335. See, for example, Sarah Banet-Weiser, "Girls Rule!: Gender, Feminism, and Nickelodeon," *Critical Studies in Media Communication* 21, no. 2 (June 2004): 119–139, https://doi.org/10.1080/07393180410001688038.
336. Entman and Rojecki, *The Black Image in the White Mind*; Mendelberg, *The Race Card*; Winter, *Dangerous Frames*; Marian Meyers, "African American Women and Violence: Gender, Race, and Class in the News," *Critical Studies in Media*

Communication 21, no. 2 (June 2004): 95–118, https://doi.org/10.1080/073931
80410001688029.

337. Ouellette, "Branding the Right," 190.

CHAPTER 4

1. This medium/topic/political actor distinction is in some ways artificial, as each analytical category implicates the other. For example, Rick Santelli's widely circulated televised rant tells a story about the importance of different mediums, shows how a news segment became a national news story, and captures the moment Santelli became a Tea Party leader.

2. Géraldine Muhlmann, *A Political History of Journalism* (Cambridge; Malden, MA: Polity, 2008); Mary-Rose Papandrea, "Citizen Journalism and the Reporter's Privilege," *Minnesota Law Review* 91, no. 3 (2007): 515–591; George Henry Payne, *History of Journalism in the United States* (New York: D. Appleton and Company, 1920); Thomas E. Patterson, "Fourth Branch or Fourth Rate?: The Press's Failure to Live up to the Founders' Expectations," in *The Media, Journalism, and Democracy*, ed. Margaret Scammell and Holli A. Semetko (Burlington, VT: Ashgate, 2000), 3–12; Michael Schudson and Susan E. Tifft, "The Press," in *The Institutions of American Democracy*, ed. Geneva Overholser and Kathleen Hall Jamieson (Oxford: Oxford University Press, 2005); Linda Williams, *Playing the Race Card: Melodramas of Black and White from Uncle Tom to OJ Simpson* (Princeton: Princeton University Press, 2001).

3. Patterson, "Fourth Branch or Fourth Rate?" 3.

4. Wilson Lowrey and Peter J. Gade, eds., *Changing the News: The Forces Shaping Journalism in Uncertain Times* (New York: Routledge, 2011); George Henry Payne, *History of Journalism in the United States* (New York: D. Appleton and Company, 1920); Michael Schudson, *Discovering the News: A Social History of American Newspapers* (New York: Basic Books, 1978); Schudson, and Tifft, "The Press."

5. Louis Day, "The Journalist as Citizen Activist: The Ethical Limits of Free Speech," *Communication Law and Policy* 4, no. 1 (January 1999): 6, https://doi.org/10.1080/10811689909368667.

6. Allan Rachlin Day, *News as Hegemonic Reality: American Political Culture and the Framing of News Accounts* (New York: Praeger, 1988); Stephen Vaughn, *Encyclopedia of American Journalism* (New York: Routledge, 2008).

7. Michael Schudson, "The Objectivity Norm in American Journalism," *Journalism* 2, no. 2 (2001): 150.

8. Hsiang Iris Chyi, Seth C. Lewis, and Nan Zheng, "A Matter of Life and Death?: Examining How Newspapers Covered the Newspaper 'Crisis,'" *Journalism Studies* 13, no. 3 (June 2012): 307 emphasis in original, https://doi.org/10.1080/14616 70X.2011.629090.

9. Ronald N. Jacobs and Eleanor R. Townsley, *The Space of Opinion: Media Intellectuals and the Public Sphere* (New York: Oxford University Press, 2011), 241, emphasis in original.

10. Barbie Zelizer, *Covering the Body: The Kennedy Assassination, the Media, and the Shaping of Collective Memory* (Chicago: University of Chicago Press, 1992), 8.

11. Mark Deuze, "The Web and Its Journalisms: Considering the Consequences of Different Types of Newsmedia Online," *New Media and Society* 5, no. 2 (June 2003): 203–230, https://doi.org/10.1177/1461444803005002004.

12. Day, "The Journalist as Citizen Activist," 1–34; Wilson Lowrey, "Mapping the Journalism–Blogging Relationship," *Journalism: Theory, Practice and Criticism* 7, no. 4 (November 2006): 477–500, https://doi.org/10.1177/1464884906068363; Gaye Tuchman, *Making News: A Study in the Construction of Reality* (New York: The Free Press, 1978); Edson C. Tandoc and Ryan J. Thomas, "The Ethics of Web Analytics: Implications of Using Audience Metrics in News Construction," *Digital Journalism* 3, no. 2 (March 4, 2015): 243–258, https://doi.org/10.1080/2167081 1.2014.909122.

13. McKay Coppins, "What If the Right-Wing Media Wins?" *Columbia Journalism Review*, Fall 2017, https://www.cjr.org/special_report/right-wing-media-breitbart-fox-bannon-carlson-hannity-coulter-trump.php.

14. Robert B. Horwitz, "Communications Regulation in Protecting the Public Interest," in *The Press*, ed. Geneva Overholser and Kathleen Hall Jamieson (New York: Oxford University Press, 2005), 284–302, esp. 289.

15. Cynthia Burack and R. Claire Snyder-Hall, "Introduction: Right-Wing Populism and the Media," *New Political Science* 34, no. 4 (December 2012): 439–454, https://doi.org/10.1080/07393148.2012.729736.

16. Sam Sewall, "The Switch from Analog to Digital TV," Nielsen, November 2, 2009, http://www.nielsen.com/us/en/insights/news/2009/the-switch-from-analog-to-digital-tv.html; Pew Research Center Journalism and Media, "Cable News Fact Sheet," June 1, 2017, retrieved from http://www.journalism.org/fact-sheet/cable-news/; Charles Postel, "The Tea Party in Historical Perspective: A Conservative Response to a Crisis of Political Economy," in *Steep: The Precipitous Rise of the Tea Party*, ed. Lawrence Rosenthal and Christine Trost (Berkeley: University of California Press, 2012), 25–46. Postel notes that more than 90 percent of Americans had access to more than a hundred television channels by the end of 2010. Nielsen found that nearly 20 percent of homes "unready" for the digital conversion became cable subscribers. There has been a decline in cable subscribers "cutting the cord" overall because many have switched to pay-for-TV digital subscriptions (such as Hulu or YouTube TV), but according to Pew, average cable news audiences have increased overall since 2007 (with particularly high spikes during election years).

17. For example, the University of South Florida's sale of its public spectrum resulted in the shuttering of its public television station and the layoffs of "a number" of station employees. Howard University also submitted a bid to sell its station WHUT, the only Black-owned public television station in the country, but later withdrew because of the price offered. See Joseph Lichterman, "Howard University Decides It Won't Sell Its Public TV Station in the FCC Spectrum Auction," Nieman Lab, February 17, 2017, http://www.niemanlab.org/2017/02/howard-university-decides-it-wont-sell-its-public-tv-station-in-the-fcc-spectrum-auction; "Tampa Public TV Station Going Dark after Selling Spectrum," Broadcasting Cable, February 9, 2017, http://www.broadcastingcable.com/news/local-tv/tampa-public-tv-station-going-dark-after-selling-spectrum/163214; "Spectrum," Corporation for Public Broadcasting, October 31, 2013, https://www.cpb.org/spectrum.

18. Pew, "Cable News Fact Sheet." Pew notes that the total revenue for all three major cable news networks—MSNBC, Fox News, and CNN—have increased since 2006, particularly due to licensing fees.

19. Richard Butsch, "Ralph, Fred, Archie and Homer: Why Television Keeps Recreating the White Male Working-Class Buffoon," in *Gender, Race, and Class in Media: A*

Critical Reader, 3rd ed., ed. Gail Dines and Jean McMahon Humez (Thousand Oaks, CA: Sage, 2011), 101–109; Manuel Castells, *The Rise of the Network Society: The Information Age: Economy, Society, and Culture*, vol. 1 (Malden, MA: Wiley-Blackwell, 2010); Sylvia M. Chan-Olmsted and Jiyoung Cha, "Branding Television News in a Multichannel Environment: An Exploratory Study of Network News Brand Personality," *International Journal on Media Management* 9, no. 4 (November 13, 2007): 135–150, https://doi.org/10.1080/14241270701632688; Robert M. Entman and Andrew Rojecki, *The Black Image in the White Mind: Media and Race in America*. Studies in Communication, Media, and Public Opinion (Chicago: University of Chicago Press, 2000); George Gerbner, "The Stories We Tell and the Stories We Sell," *Journal of International Communication* 18, no. 2 (August 2012): 237–244, https://doi.org/10.1080/13216597.2012.709928; Jooyoung Kim, Tae Hyun Baek, and Hugh J. Martin, "Dimensions of News Media Brand Personality," *Journalism and Mass Communication Quarterly* 87, no. 1 (March 2010): 117–134, https://doi.org/10.1177/107769901008700107; Stephen Lacy and Ardyth Broadrick Sohn, "Market Journalism," in *Changing the News: The Forces Shaping Journalism in Uncertain Times*, ed. Wilson Lowrey and Peter J. Gade, 159–176 (New York: Routledge, 2011); Robert Waterman McChesney, *Rich Media, Poor Democracy: Communication Politics in Dubious Times* (Urbana: University of Illinois Press, 1999); Papandrea, "Citizen Journalism and the Reporter's Privilege"; David Tewksbury and Jason Rittenberg, *News on the Internet: Information and Citizenship in the Twenty-first Century* (New York: Oxford University Press, 2012).

20. Matt Guardino and Dean Snyder, "The Tea Party and the Crisis of Neoliberalism: Mainstreaming New Right Populism in the Corporate News Media," *New Political Science* 34, no. 4 (December 2012): 527–548, https://doi.org/10.1080/07393148.2012.729741.

21. Tewksbury and Rittenberg, *News on the Internet*, 1.

22. Bob Franklin, *Packaging Politics: Political Communications in Britain's Media Democracy*, 2nd ed. (New York: Bloomsbury Academic, 2004).

23. Frank Esser and Bernd Spanier, "News Management as News: How Media Politics Leads to Metacoverage," *Journal of Political Marketing* 4, no. 4 (December 30, 2005): 27–57, https://doi.org/10.1300/J199v04n04_02.

24. Ibid., 149.

25. Boczkowski, Pablo J., and Eugenia Mitchelstein. *The News Gap: When the Information Preferences of the Media and the Public Diverge*. (Cambridge: MIT Press, 2013).

26. David Machin and Sarah Niblock, "Branding Newspapers: Visual Texts as Social Practice," *Journalism Studies* 9, no. 2 (April 2008): 244–259, https://doi.org/10.1080/14616700701848287.

27. Charles K. Atkin and James Gaudino, "The Impact of Polling on the Mass Media," *The ANNALS of the American Academy of Political and Social Science* 472, no. 1 (March 1984): 119–128, https://doi.org/10.1177/0002716284472001011; W. Lance Bennett, "Beyond Pseudoevents: Election News as Reality TV," *American Behavioral Scientist* 49, no. 3 (November 2005): 364–378, https://doi.org/10.1177/0002764205280919; Daniel J. Boorstin, *The Image: A Guide to Pseudo-Events in America* (New York: Atheneum, 1971). The observation regarding the increased use of focus groups is based on a search of focus group usage in the Vanderbilt Television Archive in news programs since 1968. This analysis suggests that the use of focus groups in national news reporting has occurred exponentially much more frequently in the last two decades.

28. Richard D. Waters, Natalie T. J. Tindall, and Timothy S. Morton, "Media Catching and the Journalist–Public Relations Practitioner Relationship: How Social Media Are Changing the Practice of Media Relations," *Journal of Public Relations Research* 22, no. 3 (July 2, 2010): 241–264, https://doi.org/10.1080/10627261003799202.

29. "Obama Slams Tea Party 'Core' as Fringe Radicals, Birthers," *Newsmax*, March 30, 2010, https://www.newsmax.com/headline/deborchgrave-pakistan-kayani-taliban/2010/03/30/id/354233/.

30. Peter Weibel, "Public Images and Images of Power," *Ars Electronica* (1988), http://90.146.8.18/en/archives/festival_archive/festival_catalogs/festival_artikel.asp?iProjectID=9090.

31. Timothy E. Cook, "The News Media as a Political Institution: Looking Backward and Looking Forward," *Political Communication* 23, no. 2 (July 2006): 159–171, https://doi.org/10.1080/10584600600629711, 165.

32. Margaret Scammell, "Citizen Consumers: Towards a New Marketing of Politics?" *Media and the Restyling of Politics: Consumerism, Celebrity and Cynicism*, ed. John Corner and Dick Pels (London: Sage, 2003), 117–136, esp. 125.

33. Elihu Katz, "Media Multiplication and Social Segmentation," *Departmental Papers (ASC)* (2000): 122–132, esp. 122, http://repository.upenn.edu/asc_papers/161/.

34. Ibid..

35. Barbie Zelizer, *Taking Journalism Seriously: News and the Academy* (Thousand Oaks, CA: Sage, 2004).

36. Schudson and Tifft, "The Press," 18.

37. John C. Merrill, "Journalism and Democracy," in *Changing the News: The Forces Shaping Journalism in Uncertain Times*, ed. Wilson Lowrey and Peter J. Gade (New York: Routledge, 2011), 45–62.

38. Erik Ugland and Jennifer Henderson, "Who Is a Journalist and Why Does It Matter?: Disentangling the Legal and Ethical Arguments," *Journal of Mass Media Ethics* 22, no. 4 (2007): 241–261.

39. Sandra L. Borden and Chad Tew, "The Role of Journalist and the Performance of Journalism: Ethical Lessons from 'Fake' News (Seriously)," *Journal of Mass Media Ethics* 22, no. 4 (October 29, 2007): 300–314, https://doi.org/10.1080/08900520701583586; Mark Deuze, "What Is Journalism?: Professional Identity and Ideology of Journalists Reconsidered," *Journalism: Theory, Practice and Criticism* 6, no. 4 (November 2005): 442–464, https://doi.org/10.1177/1464884905056815; Arthur S. Hayes, Jane B. Singer, and Jerry Ceppos, "Shifting Roles, Enduring Values: The Credible Journalist in a Digital Age," *Journal of Mass Media Ethics* 22, no. 4 (October 29, 2007): 262–279, https://doi.org/10.1080/08900520701583545; Ivor Shapiro, "Evaluating Journalism," *Journalism Practice* 4, no. 2 (April 1, 2010): 143–162, https://doi.org/10.1080/17512780903306571.

40. Thorbjorn Broddason, "The Sacred Side of Professional Journalism," in *The Media, Journalism and Democracy*, ed. Margaret Scammell and Holli A. Semetko (Aldershot; Burlington, VT: Ashgate, 2000), 147–168.

41. Hayes et al., "Shifting Roles, Enduring Values"; Ugland and Henderson, "Who Is a Journalist and Why Does It Matter?"

42. Pertti Alasuutari, ed., *Rethinking the Media Audience: The New Agenda* (London; Thousand Oaks, CA: Sage, 1999); Geoffrey Baym, "The Daily Show: Discursive Integration and the Reinvention of Political Journalism," *Political Communication* 22, no. 3 (July 2005): 259–276, https://doi.org/10.1080/10584600591006492;

S. Elizabeth Bird, ed., *The Anthropology of News and Journalism: Global Perspectives* (Bloomington: Indiana University Press, 2010); John Calhoun Merrill and Ralph Lynn Lowenstein, *Viva Journalism! The Triumph of Print in the Media Revolution* (Bloomington, IN: AuthorHouse, 2010); Andrew Rojecki, "Modernism, State Sovereignty and Dissent: Media and the New Post-Cold War Movements," *Critical Studies in Media Communication* 19, no. 2 (June 1, 2002): 152–171, https://doi.org/10.1080/07393180216558; Tewksbury and Rittenberg, *News on the Internet*; Nikki Usher, "Professional Journalists!! Hands Off!! Citizen Journalism as Civic Responsibility," in *Will the Last Reporter Please Turn Out the Lights: The Collapse Of Journalism and What Can Be Done to Fix It*, ed. Robert W. McChesney and Victor Pickard (New York: New Press, 2011).

43. Zelizer, *Taking Journalism Seriously*, 7.

44. Bruce Alan Williams and Michael X. Delli Carpini, *After Broadcast News: Media Regimes, Democracy, and the New Information Environment*, Communication, Society and Politics (New York: Cambridge University Press, 2011).

45. Stuart Allan, *Online News: Journalism and the Internet* (Maidenhead: Open University Press, 2006); Jane B. Singer, "Journalism and Digital Technologies," in *Changing the News: The Forces Shaping Journalism in Uncertain Times*, ed. Wilson Lowrey and Peter J. Gade (New York: Routledge, 2011), 213–229.

46. Allan, *Online News*.

47. Louis Day, "The Journalist as Citizen Activist: The Ethical Limits of Free Speech," *Communication Law and Policy* 4, no. 1 (1999): 1–34 ; Hayes et al., "Shifting Roles, Enduring Values"; J. D. Lasica, "Blogs and Journalism Need Each Other," *Nieman Reports* 57, no. 3 (2003): 70–74; Laura McGann, "The Rise of the Right: Conservatives Are Wading into Investigative Reporting," in *Will the Last Reporter Please Turn Out the Lights*, 257–263.

48. Frances Martel, "Heated Juan Williams/Michelle Malkin Shoutfest Gets Personal with Eyerolls, 'Snotty' Accusations," *Mediaite*, June 13, 2012, http://www.mediaite.com/tv/heated-juan-williamsmichelle-malkin-shoutfest-gets-personal-with-eyerolls-snotty-accusations/.

49. Singer, "Journalism and Digital Technologies," 226.

50. Neil Pandey-Jorrin, "Is Everyone Now a Journalist?: How the FEC's Application of the Media Exemption to Bloggers Weakens FEC Regulation," *Administrative Law Review* 60, no. 2 (2008): 409–430.

51. Serena Carpenter, "How Online Citizen Journalism Publications and Online Newspapers Utilize the Objectivity Standard and Rely on External Sources," *Journalism and Mass Communication Quarterly* 85, no. 3 (September 2008): 531–548, https://doi.org/10.1177/107769900808500304; Doug McGill, Jeremy Iggers, and Andrew R. Cline, "Death in Gambella: What Many Heard, What One Blogger Saw, and Why the Professional News Media Ignored It," *Journal of Mass Media Ethics* 22, no. 4 (October 29, 2007): 280–299, https://doi.org/10.1080/08900520701583560.

52. "Sullivan on Obama Support of Gay Marriage: He's a 'Father Figure.'" *Real Clear Politics*, May 13, 2012, http://www.realclearpolitics.com/video/2012/05/13/sullivan_reacts_to_obama_support_of_gay_marriage_hes_a_father_figure.html.

53. Deuze, "The Web and Its Journalisms," 210; Esser and Spanier, "News Management as News."

54. Susana Salgado and Jesper Strömbäck, "Interpretive Journalism: A Review of Concepts, Operationalizations and Key Findings," *Journalism: Theory, Practice and Criticism* 13, no. 2 (February 2012): 144–161, https://doi.

org/10.1177/1464884911427797; Bolette Blaagaard, "Media and Multiplicity: The Journalistic Practices in Resurgence of Nationalism and Xenophobia in Europe," *Translocations: Migrations and Social Change* 6, no. 2 (2010); Esser and Spanier, "News Management as News," 30.

55. Sarah Banet-Weiser, *Authentic™: Politics and Ambivalence in a Brand Culture*, Critical Cultural Communication (New York: New York University Press, 2012), 151.

56. I borrow "positionality" from Frances A. Maher and Mary Kay Tetreault who in "Frames of Positionality: Constructing Meaningful Dialogues about Gender and Race" define this concept as the way that "gender, race, class, and other aspects of our identities are markers of relational *positions* rather than essential qualities" (Frances A. Maher and Mary Kay Tetreault, "Frames of Positionality: Constructing Meaningful Dialogues about Gender and Race," *Anthropological Quarterly* 66, no. 3 [1993]: 118–126, esp. 118, emphasis in original).

57. Adam J. Rose, "Shirley Sherrod Resigns USDA Job After Controversy (VIDEO) (UPDATED)," *Huffington Post* (blog), July 20, 2010, http://www.huffingtonpost.com/2010/07/20/shirley-sherrod-resigns-usda-naacp_n_652185.html; Keach Hagey and Kenneth P. Vogel, "Andrew Breitbart's Day of Vindication," *Politico*, June 6, 2011, http://www.politico.com/news/stories/0611/56382.html.

58. Jonathan Weisman, "U.S. News: Worker Fired in Video Flap Gets White House 'Sorry,'" *Wall Street Journal*, July 22, 2010, https://www.wsj.com/articles/SB10001424052748704684604575381383310864008.

59. "On Edge; Political Culture," *World News with Diane Sawyer*, ABC, July 22, 2010.

60. Bob Cesca, "Fooled Again by Breitbart and the Wingnut Right," *Huffington Post* (blog), July 21, 2010, http://www.huffingtonpost.com/bob-cesca/fooled-again-by-breitbart_b_654594.html.

61. John F. Harris and Jim Vandehei, "The Age of Rage," *Politico*, July 23, 2010, http://www.politico.com/news/stories/0710/40146.html.

62. Sheryl Gay Stolberg, Shaila Dewan, and Brian Stelter, "For Fired Agriculture Official, Flurry of Apologies and Job Offer," *New York Times*, June 22, 2010, sec. A.

63. "Anger on Tax Day; President Obama Prepares to Visit Mexico," *Campbell Brown: No Bias, No Bull*, aired April 15, 2009, on CNN.

64. Peggy Noonan, "Declarations: The Power of Redemption," *Wall Street Journal*, July 22, 2010, http://online.wsj.com/article/SB10001424052748703467304575383731552735178.html.

65. "Sherrod Case Mirrors USA's Elusive Racial Harmony," editorial, *USA Today*, July 23, 2010.

66. "Mark Williams, Tea Party Express Spokesman: NAACP Is Racist (VIDEO) (TRANSCRIPT)," *Huffington Post* (blog), July 14, 2010, https://www.huffingtonpost.com/2010/07/14/mark-williams-tea-party-express-naacp-racist_n_646989.html; Michael J. W. Stickings, "Snookered: Right-Wing Propaganda and the Truth About Shirley Sherrod," *The Huffington Post* (blog), July 21, 2010, http://www.huffingtonpost.com/michael-jw-stickings/snookered-right-wing-prop_b_654232.html.

67. Jason Linkins, "Tea Party 'Crashers' Plan to Prank Conservative Activists," *Huffington Post* (blog), June 14, 2010, http://www.huffingtonpost.com/2010/04/14/tea-party-crashers-plan-t_n_537352.html.

68. Mark Potok, "Shirley Sherrod and the Right: A Day That Will Live in Infamy," *Huffington Post* (blog), July 21, 2010, http://www.huffingtonpost.com/mark-potok/shirley-sherrod-and-the-r_b_654315.html.

69. "Journalism in America; Storm Threatens Gulf," *Rick's List*, aired July 22, 2010, on CNN.
70. "Talking Points Memo and Top Story," *The O'Reilly Factor*, aired July 22, 2010, on Fox News.
71. Ibid.
72. "Fridays with Geraldo," *The O'Reilly Factor*, aired July 15, 2010, on Fox News; "Talking Points Memo and Top Story," *The O'Reilly Factor*, aired July 23, 2010, on Fox News.
73. Michael Calderone, "Fox Teas up a Tempest," *Politico*, April 16, 2009, http://www.politico.com/news/stories/0409/21275.html.
74. Michael Calderone, "'Journalists Not Activists,'" *Politico*, April 15, 2009, http://www.politico.com/blogs/michaelcalderone/0409/Huffington_on_tea_party_coverage_Journalists_not_activists.html.
75. "Media Coverage of Tea Party Unfair?" *The O'Reilly Factor*, aired March 29, 2010, on Fox News.
76. "Juan Williams Fired from NPR," *The O'Reilly Factor*, aired October 21, 2010, on Fox News.
77. "Countdown for April 16, 2010," *Countdown with Keith Olbermann*, aired April 16, 2010, on MSNBC.
78. Heather Hollingsworth, "NAACP Condemns Tea Party Racism in Resolution," *Huffington Post* (blog), July 13, 2011, http://www.huffingtonpost.com/2010/07/13/naacp-tea-party-racism-re_n_644832.html.
79. "Tea Party Convention," *The O'Reilly Factor*, aired February 5, 2010, on Fox News.
80. Matt Bai, "When It's About Race, It's Probably About Age, Too," *New York Times*, July 18, 2010.
81. Nick Wing, "Tea Party Group's Chief Spokesman Mark Williams RESIGNS After NAACP Controversy," *Huffington Post* (blog), July 23, 2010, http://www.huffingtonpost.com/2010/07/23/tea-party-groups-chief-sp_n_657518.html.
82. "Impact," *The O'Reilly Factor*, aired September 18, 2009, on Fox News.
83. "Talking Points Memo and Top Story," aired July 22, 2010.
84. Phil Rosenthal, "Rant Raises Profile of CNBC On-Air Personality Rick Santelli," *Chicago Tribune*, February 23, 2009, http://articles.chicagotribune.com/2009-02-23/news/0902220319_1_rant-mr-santelli-jim-cramer.
85. Brian Stelter, "CNBC Replays Its Reporter's Tirade," *New York Times*, February 23, 2009, sec. Business/Financial Desk, http://www.nytimes.com/2009/02/23/business/media/23cnbc.html.
86. Alessandra Stanley, "What Are You Doing? Media Twitterers Can't Stop Typing," *New York Times*, February 28, 2009, sec. C.
87. Rick Santelli, "Rick Santelli: I Want to Set the Record Straight," CNBC, March 2, 2009, http://www.cnbc.com/id/29471026.
88. Jacobs and Townsley, *The Space of Opinion*, 10.
89. Stuart Allan, *Online News: Journalism and the Internet* (Maidenhead: Open University Press, 2006), 86.
90. Stanley, "What Are You Doing? Media Twitterers Can't Stop Typing."
91. "Countdown for April 16, 2010."
92. For instance, LL Cool J complained about a previous Fox News interview being used to advertise Sarah Palin's new Fox News show as if he was an upcoming guest. Also, Howard Dean called Fox's publicity of Breitbart's video racist. In response, Fox senior executives released official statements that suggested both men were professional failures (Alexander Mooney, "Dean Says Fox News Racist

for Sherrod Coverage," *CNN Politicalticker*, July 26, 2010, http://politicalticker. blogs.cnn.com/2010/07/26/dean-says-fox-news-racist-for-sherrod-coverage/; Alex Koppelman, "Fox News, Sarah Palin vs. LL Cool J," *Salon*, March 31, 2010, https://www.salon.com/2010/03/31/palin_ll/).

93. "Talking Points Memo and Top Story," *The O'Reilly Factor*, aired April 15, 2009, on Fox News.

94. "Personal Story," *The O'Reilly Factor*, aired April 16, 2009, on Fox News.

95. "Talking Points Memo and Top Story," *The O'Reilly Factor*, aired September 14, 2009, on Fox News.

96. antiwylinout, *Stephen Colbert on The O'Reilly Factor* (YouTube, n.d.), http://www.youtube.com/watch?v=QquTUR9nbC4; "Talking Points Memo and Top Story 10/20," *O'Reilly Factor* (New York, NY, October 20, 2010), LexisNexis.

97. "Boston Tax Party," editorial, *Wall Street Journal*, August 5, 2008, https://www.wsj.com/articles/SB121789224035011709?mod=googlenews_wsj.

98. "Talking Points Memo and Top Story," July 23, 2010, 23.

99. Thomas Frank, "Conservatives and the Cult of Victimhood," *Wall Street Journal*, March 31, 2010, sec. Opinion, http://www.wsj.com/articles/SB1000142405270 23047391045751541701190467 94.

100. Ibid.

101. Calderone, "Fox's Sammon Bashes MSM; Todd Calls It 'Absurd Attack' UPDATE."

102. Kenneth P. Vogel, "Nashville Storyline: MSM at Tea Party," *Politico*, February 6, 2010, http://www.politico.com/news/stories/0210/32624.html.

103. Kenneth P. Vogel, "Tea Party Nation Leaders Lash Out," *Politico*, January 30, 2010, http://www.politico.com/news/stories/0110/32255.html.

104. "Tax Time; Tea Party," *World News with Diane Sawyer*, ABC, April 15, 2010.

105. Mark Meckler and Jenny Beth Martin, *Tea Party Patriots: The Second American Revolution*, 1st ed. (New York: Henry Holt and Co, 2012), 11.

106. Mark Meckler and Jenny Beth Martin, "On Being Labeled as 'Racist,'" *Politico*, July 14, 2010, http://www.politico.com/news/stories/0710/39745.html.

107. Daily News Staff, "Palin's 'Real American Stories' to Premiere on April Fools' Day," *New York Daily News*, March 31, 2010, http://www.nydailynews.com/en-tertainment/tv-movies/sarah-palin-real-american-stories-fox-news-debuts-april-fools-day-article-1.168150; Dave Cook, "Sarah Palin Signs with Fox after Being Attacked on '60 Minutes,'" *Christian Science Monitor*, January 11, 2010, https://www.csmonitor.com/USA/Politics/The-Vote/2010/0111/Sarah-Palin-signs-with-Fox-after-being-attacked-on-60-Minutes.

108. Fox News, "Palin to Join Fox News as Contributor," Fox News, January 11, 2010, http://www.foxnews.com/politics/2010/01/11/palin-join-fox-news-contributor.html.

109. Jack Mirkinson, "'Sarah Palin's Alaska' Ratings Break TLC Records," *Huffingtonpost.com*, November 15, 2010, http://www.huffingtonpost.com/2010/11/15/sarah-palins-alaska-ratings-tlc_n_783740.html; Alessandra Stanley, "How's That Outdoorsy Stuff Working for Ya?" *New York Times*, November 11, 2010, http://www.nytimes.com/2010/11/12/arts/television/12palin.html.

110. William Bunch, *The Backlash: Right-Wing Radicals, Hi-Def Hucksters, and Paranoid Politics in the Age of Obama* (New York: Harper, 2011).

111. Brian Montpoli Bunch, "Sarah Palin's Earnings over 9 Months Estimated at $12 Million," *CBS News*, April 13, 2010, http://www.cbsnews.com/news/sarah-palins-earnings-over-9-months-estimated-at-12-million/.

112. Linda Feldman, "Why Sarah Palin Launched Her Own Online TV Network," *Christian Science Monitor*, July 28, 2014, https://www.csmonitor.com/USA/Politics/Decoder/2014/0728/Why-Sarah-Palin-launched-her-own-online-TV-network; Daniella Diaz, "Sarah Palin to Host Reality Show as TV Judge," CNN Politics, March 22, 2016, http://www.cnn.com/2016/03/22/politics/sarah-palin-court-show-judge-judy/.

113. Michael Calderone, "Fox's Sammon Bashes MSM; Todd Calls It 'Absurd Attack' Politico," *Politico*, February 7, 2010, http://www.politico.com/blogs/michaelcalderone/0210/Foxs_Sammon_bashes_MSM_Todd_calls_it_absurd_attack.html.

114. Richard W. Stevenson, "The Muddled Selling of the President," *New York Times*, January 31, 2010.

115. David Brooks, "No, It's Not about Race," *New York Times*, September 19, 2009, http://www.nytimes.com/2009/09/18/opinion/18brooks.html.

116. Factcheck.org, "About Us," 2012, http://factcheck.org/about/.

117. "About Us," Media Matters for America, 2012, http://mediamatters.org/about.

118. Brian Stelter, "Jon Stewart's Punching Bag, Fox News," *New York Times*, April 24, 2010, http://www.nytimes.com/2010/04/24/arts/television/24stewart.html.

119. *The O'Reilly Factor*, "Juan Williams Fired from NPR," aired October 21, 2010.

120. Joseph Curl, "Study: Networks Snub, Malign Tea Party Movement," *Newsmax*, April 14, 2010, https://www.newsmax.com/insidecover/us-small-business-pessimism/2010/04/13/id/355634/.

121. Matthew A. Baum, "Circling the Wagons: Soft News and Isolationism in American Public Opinion," *International Studies Quarterly* 48, no. 2 (June 2004): 313–338, https://doi.org/10.1111/j.0020-8833.2004.00303.x.

122. Jacobs and Townsley, *The Space of Opinion*, 10; Kathleen Hall Jamieson and Karlyn Kohrs Campbell, *The Interplay of Influence: News, Advertising, Politics, and the Mass Media*, 5th ed. (Belmont, CA: Wadsworth, 2000).

123. Baum, "Circling the Wagons," emphasis added; Carsten Reinemann et al., "Hard and Soft News: A Review of Concepts, Operationalizations and Key Findings," *Journalism: Theory, Practice and Criticism* 13, no. 2 (February 2012): 221–239, https://doi.org/10.1177/1464884911427803; Todd M. Schaefer and Thomas A. Birkland, "Encyclopedia of Media and Politics," in *Encyclopedia of Media and Politics* (Washington, DC: CQ Press, 2007), 106–107.

124. Jacobs and Townsley, *The Space of Opinion*, 13.

125. This chart is based on articles in which the Tea Party is mentioned either more than once outside of interview quotes, in the top graph, or is a central topic in the article, or all of these. The asterisks indicate professional staff writers of the respective news outlets.

126. Jacobs and Townsley, *The Space of Opinion*, 10.

127. Naftali Bendavid, "GOP House Leaders Seek to Avoid Past Mistakes," *Wall Street Journal*, October 19, 2010, sec. US, http://www.wsj.com/articles/SB10001424052702303496104575560361114358350.

128. Richard Wolff, "A Soaring Debt, and Painful Choices; Erasing the USA's Red Ink Won't Be Easy—or Popular," *USA Today*, April 13, 2010.

129. Stelter, "CNBC Replays Its Reporter's Tirade"; Stolberg, Dewan, and Stelter, "For Fired Agriculture Official, Flurry of Apologies and Job Offer."
130. See, for example, Michael Barbaro, "Paladino's Accidental Running Mate Is also His Mop-up Man," *New York Times*, October 20, 2010, http://www.nytimes.com/2010/10/21/nyregion/21edwards.html; John Harwood, "The Caucus; Days to Election 15: Wielding Two-by-fours Instead of Talking Points," *New York Times*, October 18, 2010, http://query.nytimes.com/gst/fullpage.html?res=9C00E5DB1130F93BA25753C1A9669D8B63; Gerald F. Seib, "Tea Party and the Path to Power," *Wall Street Journal*, July 13, 2010, http://www.wsj.com/articles/SB10001424052748703283004575362950960543866.
131. Andrew Kohut, "Americans Are More Skeptical of Washington Than Ever," *Wall Street Journal*, April 19, 2010; Seib, "Tea Party and the Path to Power."
132. Kohut, "Americans Are More Skeptical of Washington Than Ever"; Megan Thee-Brenan and Marina Stefan, "'The Sytem Is Broken': More from a Poll of Tea Party Backers," *New York Times*, April 18, 2010, sec. A.
133. Michael Barbaro, "Paladino's Accidental Running Mate Is Also His Mop-up Man," *New York Times*, October 21, 2010, http://www.nytimes.com/2010/10/21/nyregion/21edwards.html; John Harwood, "DAYS TO ELECTION 15: Wielding Two-by-Fours Instead of Talking Points," *New York Times*, October 18, 2010, sec. A.
134. Serena Carpenter, "How Online Citizen Journalism Publications and Online Newspapers Utilize the Objectivity Standard and Rely on External Sources," *Journalism and Mass Communication Quarterly* 85, no. 3 (September 2008): 531–548, https://doi.org/10.1177/107769900808500304; Nikki Usher, "Professional Journalists!! Hands Off!! Citizen Journalism as Civic Responsibility," in *Will the Last Reporter Please Turn Out the Lights*.
135. Jamieson and Campbell, *The Interplay of Influence*.
136. Bruce Alan Williams and Michael X. Delli Carpini, *After Broadcast News: Media Regimes, Democracy, and the New Information Environment*, Communication, Society and Politics (New York: Cambridge University Press, 2011).
137. Rachel Sklar, "Sexy Beasts, Sexy Branding: The Daily Beast and Politico Unveil New Style Sections," *Mediaite*, September 10, 2009, http://www.mediaite.com/online/sexy-beast-sexy-branding-the-daily-beast-unveils-new-style-section/.
138. Day, "The Journalist as Citizen Activist."
139. Though the Supreme Court has expressed support for news bureaus' right to restrict their employees' activism, only the hiring organization can enforce such codes; these decisions are often based on perceptions of potential financial losses or gains.
140. Lili Levi, "Reporting the Official Truth: The Revival of the FCC's News Distortion Policy," *Washington University Law Quarterly* 78, no. 4 (2000): 1016.
141. T. Skocpol and V. Williamson, *The Tea Party and the Remaking of Republican Conservatism* (New York: Oxford University Press, 2012), 137.
142. Jeremy Peters, "Politico Suspends Reporter over Romney Comments," *New York Times*, June 22, 2012, http://thecaucus.blogs.nytimes.com/2012/06/22/politico-suspends-reporter-over-romney-comments/.
143. Specifically, NFL Dallas Cowboys owner Jerry Jones threatened to punish and bench players who protested police brutality against African Americans by kneeling during the national anthem. This followed comments from President Donald Trump calling for NFL owners to stop the protest by firing players and to "get that son of a bitch off the field." For more see Daniel Politi, "ESPN

Suspends Jemele Hill after She Suggested NFL Advertising Boycott on Twitter," *Slate*, October 9, 2017, http://www.slate.com/blogs/the_slatest/2017/10/09/espn_suspends_jemele_hill_after_she_called_for_nfl_advertising_boycott_on.html.

144. Jeanine Pirro, "Judge Jeanine Pirro: Players Taking a Knee, Commissioner Roger Goodell, Shame On All of You," *Fox News*, September 24, 2017, http://www.foxnews.com/opinion/2017/09/24/judge-jeanine-pirro-nfl-players-taking-knee-commissioner-roger-goodell-shame-on-all.html.

145. Jürgen Habermas, "The Public Sphere: An Encyclopedia Article," in *Media and Cultural Studies: Keyworks*, rev. ed., ed. Meenakshi Gigi Durham and Douglas Kellner, Keyworks in Cultural Studies 2 (Malden, MA: Blackwell, 2006), 73–78.

CONCLUSION

1. Khadijah White, "Why You Shouldn't Be Surprised by Donald Trump's Rise." *Role/Reboot*, March 21, 2016, http://www.rolereboot.org/culture-and-politics/details/2016-03-shouldnt-surprised-donald-trumps-rise/.

2. Thomas E. Patterson, "News Coverage of the 2016 Presidential Primaries: Horse Race Reporting Has Consequences," *Shorenstein Center*, July 11, 2016, http://shorensteincenter.org/news-coverage-2016-presidential-primaries/.

3. Deray McKesson (@deray), "The 'I Love My Blackness. And Yours.' Tee Shirt, Tank, or Hoodie. Get One," Twitter post, September 4, 2015, https://twitter.com/deray/status/639933790983426048.

4. Keith Forestt [@Rahdney], "We Sellin' @deray's Vest at My Job [Tweet]," *Twitter* post, September 8, 2015.

5. Michael Grothaus, "Twitter and Netflix Execs Back BLM's DeRay Mckesson in Mayoral Run," *Fast Company*, March 23, 2016, http://www.fastcompany.com/3058181/fast-feed/twitter-and-netflix-execs-back-blms-deray-mckesson-in-mayoral-run.

6. Naomi LaChance, "Wells Fargo Sponsorship of Black Lives Matter Panel Draws Scorn," *The Intercept*, May 27, 2016, https://theintercept.com/2016/05/27/wells-fargo-sponsorship-of-black-lives-matter-panel-draws-scorn/.

7. Nyle Fort, "It's Hard to Tell the Difference between the Market and the Movement Nowadays, between Community Activists and Corporate Advertisements," Facebook status update, March 5, 2016.

8. Gaye Tuchman, *Making News: A Study in the Construction of Reality* (New York: Free Press, 1978).

9. Paul Bond, "Leslie Moonves on Donald Trump: 'It May Not Be Good for America, but It's Damn Good for CBS,'" *Hollywood Reporter*, February 29, 2016, http://www.hollywoodreporter.com/news/leslie-moonves-donald-trump-may-871464.

10. Nicholas Kristof, "My Shared Shame: The Media Helped Make Trump," *New York Times*, March 26, 2016, https://www.nytimes.com/2016/03/27/opinion/sunday/my-shared-shame-the-media-helped-make-trump.html.

11. "Donald Trump: Last Week with John Oliver," *Last Week Tonight with John Oliver*, aired February 28, 2016, on Comedy Central, https://www.youtube.com/watch?v=DnpO_RTSNmQ.

12. Katherine Bell, "'A Delicious Way to Help Save Lives': Race, Commodification, and Celebrity in Product (RED)," *Journal of International and Intercultural*

Communication 4, no. 3 (August 2011): 164, https://doi.org/10.1080/17513057.2011.569972.

13. Dylan Stableford, "Hillary Clinton on Benghazi Committee: "If I Were President . . . I Would Have Done Everything to Shut It Down," *Yahoo News*, October 5, 2015, https://www.yahoo.com/news/hillary-clinton-on-benghazi-committee-if-i-were-152549533.html.

14. The Moral March was part of the Moral Monday Movement and took place in Raleigh, North Carolina, on February 8, 2014. Led by religious and faith leaders, the movement focuses on engaging in civil disobedience to protest discriminatory laws that aim to promote "conservative governance."

15. Sarah Banet-Weiser, *Authentic™: Politics and Ambivalence in a Brand Culture* (New York: New York University Press, 2012), 5.

16. Ibid., 7.

17. *Game Change*, directed by Jay Roach, written by Danny Strong, aired 2012, on HBO.

APPENDIX

1. Michael X. Delli Carpini, "Gen.Com: Youth, Civic Engagement, and the New Information Environment," *Political Communication* 17, no. 4 (October 2000): 341–349, https://doi.org/10.1080/10584600050178942.

2. Kevin Coe et al., "Hostile News: Partisan Use and Perceptions of Cable News Programming," *Journal of Communication* 58, no. 2 (June 2008): 201–219, https://doi.org/10.1111/j.1460-2466.2008.00381.x.

3. Mike Shields, "Huffington Post Shrinks Its Name to HuffPost, in a Step Back from Founder," *Wall Street Journal*, April 25, 2017, https://www.wsj.com/articles/the-huffington-post-shrinks-its-name-to-huffpost-1493110800. In 2017, new CEOs of HuffPost expressed "interest in reaching Trump voters"; see Michael Calderone, "The Huffington Post Is Now HuffPost," *Huffington Post* (blog), April 25, 2017.

4. Farhad Manjoo, "Newsmax Knows Its Audience," *Wired*, August 12, 2000, http://www.wired.com/culture/lifestyle/news/2000/12/40375.

5. Jeremy Peters, "A Compass for Conservative Politics," *New York Times*, July 10, 2011, http://www.nytimes.com/2011/07/11/business/media/newsmax-a-compass-for-conservative-politics.html

6. Harry Jaffe, "Politico Hopes to Rock Washington Media," *Washingtonian*, January 22, 2007, http://www.washingtonian.com/articles/people/politico-hopes-to-rock-washington-media/.

7. Ibid.

8. Steven Livingston, "Clarifying the CNN Effect: An Examination of Media Effects according to Type of Military Intervention," *Harvard University John F. Kennedy School of Go+vernment*, 1997.

9. Jacques Steinberg, "Cable Channel Nods to Ratings and Leans Left," *New York Times*, November 6, 2007, http://www.nytimes.com/2007/11/06/business/media/06msnb.html.

10. Coe et al., "Hostile News," 205.

11. Eric Hananoki, "Fox's News Programs Echo Its 'Opinion' Shows: Smears, Doctored Videos, GOP Talking Points," Media Matters for America, October 13, 2009, http://mediamatters.org/research/2009/10/13/foxs-news-programs-echo-its-opinion-shows-smear/155660.

12. *Campbell Brown* was later cancelled and replaced with *Rick's List* and *Parker Spitzer* during that time slot in the summer and fall of 2010, which includes Surge 9 and Surge 10 data.

13. "Access ABC: ECirc for US Newspapers," 2012, http://abcas3.accessabc.com/ecirc/newstitlesearchus.asp, archived at http://archive.is/20120526062542/http://abcas3.accessabc.com/ecirc/newstitlesearchus.asp.

14. James McCartney, "USA Today Grows Up," *American Journalism Review*, September 1997, http://ajr.org/article.asp?id=878; Lisa Nehus-Saxon, "National Paper Makes Debut," *The Spokesman Review*, January 31, 1990, https://news.google.com/newspapers?nid=1314&dat=19900130&id=SnUzAAAAIBAJ&sjid=ZfADAAAAIBAJ&pg=6922,6933974&hl=en.

15. Ronald N. Jacobs and Eleanor R. Townsley, *The Space of Opinion: Media Intellectuals and the Public Sphere* (New York: Oxford University Press, 2011).

16. I did not examine the online publications from the television and print news organizations (i.e., cnn.com or *The Wall Street Journal* blog).

17. More details on Pew's coding protocol can be found at http://www.journalism.org/about_news_index/methodology.

18. I focused on the five weekdays for TV coverage, since the cable news channels work on these schedules. This means that the Sunday opinion news spaces on ABC were not examined, though they undoubtedly would have impacted my overall reporting from the station.

19. Based on the total number of words divided by the average words per page in a standard document (300).

20. Archive.org does have missing content, but it is currently the most reliable source of website content over time.

21. Pew Research Center, "News Coverage Index Methodology," PEJ News Coverage Index (Pew Research Center: Journalism and Media, August 25, 2011), http://www.journalism.org/about_news_index/methodology.

22. Mark Jurkowitz et al., "The State of the News Media 2013: An Annual Report on American Journalism" (Pew Research Center's Project for Excellence in Journalism, n.d.), http://www.stateofthemedia.org/2013/special-reports-landing-page/the-changing-tv-news-landscape/.

INDEX

Kaplan, Amy, 132
Karl, Jonathan, 140, 165
Karrh, James
Katz, Elihu, 23, 154
Kazin, Michael, 97
Kentucky, 16
Kilgannon, Corey, **170**
King, Martin Luther, Jr., 65
Klein, Naomi, 6, 78, 83, 87
Koch brothers (Charles and David),
    61, 67
Kohut, Andrew, **170**, 172–**173**
Koronis, Epaminondas, 38
Kristof, Nicholas, vii
Krugman, Paul, 67, 89, **169**
Ku Klux Klan, 6, 61

Larson, Greco, 3
Lenin, Vladimir, 106
Lepore, Jill, 16, 77
Lewis, John, 109–111
LexisNexis, 197, 207n71
Liasson, Mara, 167
libel, 156
libertarianism, 58, 62, 183
Lincoln, Abraham, 115
Liptak, Adam, **171**
LL Cool J, 247n91
Lo, Clarence, 2
Loesch, Dana, 46, 165
Loury, Glenn, 102
Lule, Jack, 3
Lury, Celia, 9–12, 62

Machin, David, 27, 40
Mackay, Katherine, 137
Maddow, Rachel, 8, 34
magazines, 62, 83, 137, 150, 195
Maher, Frances A., 246n55
"mainstream media," 28, 54, 63, 117,
    135, 161, 164–166
Manring, Maurice, 6, 104
marketing, ix–xi, 40, 58,
    152–153, 190
  class and, 80, 92
  gender and, 80, 131
  niche, 9, 23, 40, 153
  political, 8, 22, 24, 26, 35–38,
    48–50, 83, 147
  race and, 80, 87, 102, 206n47

relationship to branding, 10, 12, 25,
    35–36, 38
  See also branding; public relations
Martin, Jenny Beth, 165
Martin, Roland, 107
Marxism, 108
Maryland, 183
masculinity, 129, 138–142, 240n321
Massachusetts, 71
Massey, Douglass, 78
mass media, 14, 20, 22, 28–29, 40, 68,
    102, 154, 189
Matthews, Chris, 86–87
McCain, John, 85–87, 90, 136
McCain, Meghan, 135
McCarthyism, 61
McChesney, Robert W., 23–24, 37
McIlwain, Charlton, 83
McKesson, Deray, 182–183
McKinley, Jesse, **171**
McKinney, Dave, 87
McRobbie, Angela, 138
McVeigh, Timothy, 96
Meckler, Mark, 165
media anthropology, 14
media consolidation, ix, 24
  media deregulation, 8, 23, 151
  See also Telecommunications Act
    of 1996
media effects research, 14
Media Matters for America (MMA),
    162, 167–168
Media Research Center (MRC), 168
media watchdogs, vii, 150, 162,
    167–168, 180, 189
Medicaid, 172
Medicare, 172
Meet the Press, 40
Meetup, 66
Mellor, Noha, 27
Mendelberg, Tali, 105
meta-journalism, 8, 148, 157–162,
    181, 184
methodology, of book, 3, 12–14, 26–30,
    195–202
  See also discourse analysis;
    multiplatform narrative analysis;
    semiotics
Meyers, Denzil, 9
micro-media, 154

prairie, 6–7
Tea Party's, 6, 17, 21, 46, 51–54, 63–64,
  67–68, 90, 95, 97–99, 123, 128–129,
  143–144, 163, 166, 183, 229n103
white, 6, 17, 51, 64, 90, 95, 97, 99,
  128–129, 144
Postel, Charles, 61, 64
post-racial discourse, 34, 101–106, 112,
  118–122, 145–146
post-shame discourse, 113, 121
Powers, Devon, 10
preservatism, 61
  See also nativism
privatization, 13, 23, 75
protest paradigm, 60
Prothero, Stephen, **169**
Pruitt, Judy, 136
public relations, 22, 24–25, 39, 150,
  153, 167, 191
  press releases, 40, 152, 166
  See also video news reports (VNRs)
public sphere, ix–x, 17, 23, 28, 81,
  85–86, 102, 125, 154, 181, 192

Quick, Becky, 41
Quinnipiac University, 124–125,
  128–129, 237n256

race, 17, 66, 159, 208n71, 231n130,
  246n55
  citizenship and, 11
  news coverage and, xi, 4–5, 7, 12–13,
    22, 31, 34, 59, 103, 180–185, 187,
    191–192, **202**
  populism and, 64
  Tea Party's use of, vii, 2, 4, 5, 16, 32,
    45–46, 51–52, 57, 62, 64–65,
    69, 78–139, 142–146, 142–147,
    161–162, 164, 181, 186–188, **201**
  See also blackness; post-racial
    discourse; whiteness
racism, 17, 34, 66, 83, 180–181, 192,
  207n71
  Donald Trump's, vii, 180, 186
  "overcoming" rhetoric, 84, 87
  post-racism, 119, 145–146
  "reverse racism" rhetoric, 158
  Tea Party's, vii, 2, 4, 45–46, 51–52, 57,
    62, 64–65, 69, 78–139, 142–146,
    161–162, 164, 181, 186–188, **201**

white womanhood and, 127–128
  See also angry white men; anti-
    Semitism; nativism; Nazis;
    preservatism; slavery; Southern
    Strategy; white supremacy;
    xenophobia
raising the volume, ix–xi, 13, 36, 73, 76,
  80–81, 97, 115, 117, 122, 149,
  181, 186–187, 189
rallies, 1, 4, 8, 16, 20, 32, 34, 43, 53,
  55–56, 61–68, 80, 88–92, 94, 109,
  119, 123, 126, 156, 165–166, 179,
  181–183, **201**
  signs, 28, 48, 51–52, 54, 56–57, 60,
    93, 106–108, 114–115, 145, **202**
Rasmussen, Scott, 34, 40
Reagan, Ronald, x, 49, 56, 79, 99, 129, 183
  "Reagan revolution," 52, 90
reality journalism, 55
reality TV, vii, 55, 85
Reed, Daniel, 123
Reich, Robert B., **169**
Reid, Harry, 124
religion, vii, 5, 18, 83, 184, 189, 252n14
  See also anti-Semitism; Christian
    Right; evangelicals; Jewish
    communities; Muslims
Republican Party (GOP), vii, 33, 37, 42,
  66, 68, 99, 134, 163, 222n200,
  240n321
  2016 Republican National
    Convention, viii
  candidates, 16, 35, 40, 57–58, 71,
    81–82, 126–127, 131–132, 172,
    182, 186
  PACs, 49
  Tea Party's relationship to, 4, 32,
    48–49, 51–53, 59, 67, 69–73, 79,
    89–90, 92–93, 95, 101, 105–106,
    114, 125, 129, 136, 144, 179,
    185, 190
  See also Southern Strategy
Reynolds, Glenn Harland, 68, **169**, 171
Rich, Frank, **169–171**
Rick's List, 253n12
Rittenberg, Jason, 152
Romney, Mitt, 180
Roosevelt, Eleanor, 130, 138
Rosenstiel, Tom, 235n212
Rosenthal, Lawrence, 43